FURTHER OFFSHORE

BY THE SAME AUTHOR

Ready to Sail: a step-by-step guide to boat seaworthiness

FURTHER OFFSHORE

A Practical Guide for Sailors

Ed Mapes

First published 2008 by
Sheridan House Inc.
145 Palisade Street
Dobbs Ferry, NY 10522
www.sheridanhouse.com

Library of Congress Cataloging-in-Publication Data

Mapes, Ed
    Further offshore : a practical guide for sailors / Ed Mapes.
        p. cm.
    ISBN 978-1-57409-253-0 (hardcover : alk. paper)
        1. Seamanship—Handbooks, manuals, etc.
    2. Sailing—Handbooks, manuals, etc.
    3. Ocean travel—Handbooks, manuals, etc. I. Title.

    VK543.M258 2008
    623.88—dc22   2007048307

ISBN 978 1 57409 253 0

Edited by Jeremy McGeary, Janine Simon
Designed by Keata Brewer

Printed in China

To Kim, my steadfast companion and supporter,
and to Eddie, my little sailor

VOYAGER Mediterranean moored in Bermuda

CONTENTS

Contents

PART 1

THE BIG PICTURE

CHAPTER 1

THE VOYAGE PROJECT

A time comes in many sailors' lives when they realize they want to expand their horizons and begin sailing offshore, with a view to taking extended cruises or visiting foreign lands. The decision to fulfill this dream engages them in a process at the end of which they, and their chosen boat, will be fully prepared for the new adventure.

That process can be intimidating. Selecting a boat and equipping it for the rigors of offshore sailing and cruising present major stumbling blocks for many would-be voyagers. The preparations encompass so many aspects and details that many become stymied by the prospect of getting everything done, and their progress gets short-circuited. Bogged down with a ponderous equipment list, for example, some sailors succumb to "harbor paralysis." They never manage to break away because the boat just never seems ready.

The way to avoid such pitfalls is to organize the process, reduce it into components, prioritize real needs, and realize that we may never achieve everything exactly as we'd envisioned it. I've developed a method by which I break this process down into specific phases,

allowing me to accomplish the task more smoothly, in a timelier manner, and with fewer omissions. I call this the Voyage Project.

Over the years I've had the opportunity to provide planning assistance to other people, helping them navigate their way through their own Voyage Projects.

Here's how it works.

Phase 1: To Go or Not to Go?

Begin by asking yourself if you are serious about the project. On close examination, you may discover that extended offshore voyaging is really a fantasy and actually fulfilling it means taking on more than you care to. If your honest conclusion is that you want to go ahead, your first task is to select a boat that suits your style of sailing and your cruising objectives.

Examine objectively your sailing style and the type of cruising you plan to do, as these will be major determinants in the decisions you make. How you plan to sail affects every aspect of your planning, from the boat you select, its gear, sail inventory, and tankage capacities, to routing, selection and training of your crew, and your final preparations for departure.

The best way to gain these insights is to get experience before committing to the task of preparing for such an endeavor. Take opportunities to charter boats, preferably in the waters you intend to visit, to learn more about the boats and the areas. I advise anyone whose plans include ocean passages to take an educational offshore-sailing passage as a way to accumulate valuable experience at sea under expert tutelage. The confidence gained usually fosters sailing dreams, but sometimes people discover that sailing offshore is not what they expected. If you come to this realization early on, you can abandon an eventually ill-fated project before spending thousands of dollars and devoting years to it.

Phase 2: Acquire the Appropriate Boat

Obviously, the success of voyaging and cruising depends to a great extent on the seaworthiness of the boat you sail in and how well it is suited to the voyaging and cruising you have in mind.

You may be considering outfitting the boat you currently own or you may be thinking of replacing it with one that will better meet your goals. Chapter 4, *The Proper Ocean Sailing Vessel*, provides information to help guide your decision.

Phase 3: Equip Your Boat.

Using the parameters you've set yourself in Phase 1 as a basis, concentrate first on the essential gear, as outlined in Chapter 5, *Offshore Essentials: Gear and Instruments*. Once this important stage in the outfitting is taken care of, you can be satisfied that your boat is basically equipped to go. Adding lower priority items will add to the cost, take more time, and may not be worth the investment in either.

Phase 4: Perform a Thorough Inspection

Perform an honest, thorough inspection of the boat, including all systems, fixtures, and fittings. Most breakdowns and failures occur because equipment is inadequate or inferior and boat systems have been poorly maintained. A comfortable familiarity sets in the longer we own a boat and problems arise when it's suddenly put into rough conditions.

This was the reason I wrote *Ready to Sail*, and I refer you to that book for an in-depth discussion of this systematic approach for ensuring your boat's seaworthiness. Encountering boats for delivery that I knew little about, I needed a systematic inspection process by which I could both assure myself of their seaworthiness and also become familiar with all their systems and gear. This methodology has proven itself over time, and has allowed me to detect defects that would have been easy to miss otherwise. The book also discusses procedures for effecting many commonly needed repairs.

In essence, the process begins with an overall, critical look at the vessel. I call this the First Impressions, and the first step is to ascertain her vital statistics:

Length Overall (LOA)
Waterline Length (LWL)
Beam
Draft
Displacement
Sail Plan
Underwater Configuration

This is also the time to gather together all the ship's papers, legal documents, owner's manuals, and so forth. After the preliminary steps, we proceed to examine, in great detail:

Hull and appendages (keel and
  rudder)
Mast, spars, rigging, sails, and canvas
Ground tackle and windlass
Steering system and self-steering
  mechanisms
Propulsion machinery
Electrical system
Piping and tankage
Shipboard amenities
Safety equipment

In *Ready to Sail* you'll find detailed information and descriptions of how to examine all aspects of each system. Checklists for each chapter that organize the inspections are reprinted in this book so you can use them to assist in your own inspections. Once you've completed the inspection process, and noted all defects discovered on the checklists, you can begin the next phase of your preparations.

Phase 5: Make Repairs

Go right down the checklists and rectify every defect. Make certain all repairs are done right, and be sure to re-examine any that were carried out by subcontractors. It's your welfare that's on the line out at sea, not theirs, and you need to protect it.

Remember that sailing offshore requires a high degree of self-sufficiency. The more closely you're involved with the inspection and subsequent repairs made to the boat, the more knowledgeable and independent you become.

Phase 6: Choose Your Crew

If you plan on sailing with crew, you should decide on the number, and even the specific individuals, quite early in your preparations, as these choices will affect other aspects such as outfitting berths, providing enough safety gear and water capacity, and ultimately, provisioning. You'll also need time to prepare the crew.

I learned how vital it is to prepare crew ahead of time when getting ready for regattas and long distance offshore passages. The more knowledgeable and capable each crewmember becomes, the better he or she can contribute to a team effort. It's best to assemble your crew, along with possible replacements, several months prior to your planned departure. This early notice gives them time to prepare, and for you to educate them about your boat's layout and systems.

In Chapter 17, *Preparing the Crew*, you'll find guidance on how to manage the selection process and crew education that are so important to a successful voyage. The chapter contains checklists of topics for crew discussions and of literature to send the crew in advance of the voyage to help them in their own preparations.

Phase 7: Voyage Planning

In this phase, you will be taking care of a variety of matters, the goal of which is freeing yourself so that you can take off to spend time on the water. Determining the route you'll take and gathering all pertinent charts, light lists, tide and current tables, and ancillary literature is covered in Chapter 16, *Voyage Routing.*

Matters of Health

You may want to begin by making sure that your health is up to the rigors to which offshore sailing or extended cruising will expose you. Explain your upcoming plans to your doctor and dentist so they can advise you on any treatment you might want to undergo before you leave home. Get all your vaccinations updated, and inquire into whether any inoculations are required or recommended for travel to your intended destination.

Require, too, that everyone who will sail with you have both a thorough physical examination and a dental check-up and have any medical or dental conditions that come to light treated prior to sailing. I can't describe the misery suffered on one delivery voyage by a crewmate who had an abscessed tooth when he joined the boat, but said nothing. Aspirin, Ibuprofen, and Tylenol provided no relief, and he paid a dear price throughout our six-day passage.

As the time for your departure draws close, consult with your doctor and dentist again, ask for extensions of any prescriptions that may expire en route, and

obtain emergency medical phone numbers you can reach when at sea.

Health insurance is not inexpensive, but it is available in several formats. Chapter 13 describes some of the alternatives.

Give due consideration to the medical aspects of your voyage not just prior to departure but as they may arise once you are on your way. If you or any member of your proposed crew have pre-existing medical conditions, weigh the risk of being caught offshore without medical help nearby.

Personal Matters

If you are leaving for a circumnavigation or an extended cruise, you will want to make decisions on what to do with your home and other real estate holdings. Selling your primary home may well be your best course of action. Anyone who has been involved with rental property understands the problems inherent in attempting to lease it out, and they can multiply in your absence. If you do choose to take that course, engage the services of a management company that you can trust. You may want to maintain a home base, which can be a condominium or townhouse where the maintenance is handled by the association.

You will need to make arrangements to ensure your bills are paid and that your mail will be forwarded. You can have friends or relatives help with this, but a professional service or accountant may be a more reliable solution. Chapter 8, *Communications,* offers suggestions and lists resources.

You must designate someone whom you trust, usually a relative, to act with Power of Attorney on your behalf in legal and financial matters. Power of Attorney documents can be drawn to be very specific in their purpose, or generalized. A General Power of Attorney form is included as Appendix 6. You can modify it to limit or specify the powers it conveys to your representative.

Insurance

Yacht insurance for offshore sailing comes with more stringent requirements on both boat and crew than for home-based cruising. Companies that offer it usually require a vessel to have been surveyed within less than one year, including an inspection of the rigging aloft. Regardless of insurance regulations, you can use a full survey report as a valuable tool to guide your repair and refit program. Along with the survey, make sure that a qualified rigger goes over all the standing rigging, and repair or replace any defective components. All rigging over seven years of age should be replaced, both for insurance purposes and prudence. Chapter 14 covers the topic of yacht insurance in more detail.

Part of the survey will require the boat be out of the water. Take the opportunity to service underwater components, and to apply bottom paint.

Ship's Documents

Begin to accumulate all the ship's papers you will need to satisfy the variety of requirements demanded as you go from country to country. These documents include:

Current USCG Documentation (most countries will not recognize a State registration)
Bill of Sale
Current Registration
Cruising Permits for those countries that require them (Bahamas and Canada, for example)
Complete crew list, with names, addresses, and passport numbers
Clearance Papers from the last port of call
Insurance Papers
Stores list
Ship's Logbook

Do not list crewmembers as paying passengers, because some countries levy high fees for them. The Ship's Logbook is a legal document that provides officials (for example a Coast Guard boarding party) with a chronological history of your voyages. It can be crucially important in their identification of your vessel as one of pleasure, not of smuggling.

Your Coast Guard Documentation certificate must be renewed yearly, so before leaving on an extended cruise out of the USA, notify the USCG Documentation Office informing them of your intention to be away. Provide a permanent address to which the Office can mail the form you fill in annually to renew the documentation. You are subject to a substantial fine if the form lapses.

Travel Documents

Obtaining passports can take months. Start the process at least six months prior to the sailing date and instruct all members of the crew to do the same.

Some countries you plan to visit may require that you obtain visas, and their procedures differ regarding when they are issued and for how long they are valid. If planning an extended layover, you may be asked to pay a bond in addition to receiving a visa to stay in the country. You may also be asked to purchase an open ticket home, or to institute a bond in that amount upon arrival in the country or when applying for a visa. This money is deposited into a fund, earning no interest, and will be refunded when you leave, less applicable charges of course.

Some countries demand proof that you and each member of the crew have funds available to at least purchase an airline ticket home. If you will be traveling to countries with such a requirement, plan on having for each person on board at least $1,500, which can be in the form of cash or travelers checks. If you sail with crew not related to you, they should demonstrate that these funds are available before you allow them to join the ship's company.

Information on visa and proof-of-funds requirements can be obtained from travel agents or from the State Department.

Most countries will demand an Entry and/or Exit fee of each crewmember. These fees range from $15 to $50 or more per person, so have the funds available when checking into customs. Foreign customs and immigration officers like the official look a vessel's own rubber stamp imparts to documents you fill out on entry and departure. Have one made up with the name of your boat, owner, and documentation number, and a little scrollwork for effect.

Navigation and Communications

Become very competent in all the skills of basic coastal navigation, including chartwork, log keeping, and dead reckoning. Practice conversions from true headings to magnetic and to compass headings, and deducing information from tide and current tables.

Even though GPS technology has seemingly made traditional navigation skills redundant, I encourage offshore sailors to consider learning the art of celestial navigation. Not only is it seamanlike to have such knowledge as a backup in case electrical failure takes out the GPS, practicing it can be very enjoyable. Making landfall having found your way solely by observing the heavenly bodies brings a sense of satisfaction beyond description.

When offshore, your long-distance communications system will keep you in touch with loved ones, the rest of the world, and the weather. Well in advance of your departure date, choose the method you will use, whether satellite phone or SSB radio, and have the gear installed. This will give you time both to ensure it works as designed and also to practice communicating with shore bases and downloading weather information from the sources you select. If you intend to use a weather routing service, this is the time to make arrangements with a company and make sure you can reliably download its products.

Self Preparation

Sailing at sea and cruising require as much independence as you can muster, in all regards. That demands competence in a variety of skills and disciplines. While these begin with the sailor's basics of navigation, weather interpretation and prediction, and sail repair, they extend further to include diesel engine maintenance and repair and first aid and other medical procedures.

You need to become familiar with your boat and in the operation and maintenance of all of its equipment. That includes sails for heavy weather and procedures for handling the boat in rough conditions. Make an effort to sail on windy days to practice reefing, setting and dousing storm sails, heaving-to, and using the sea anchor.

Practice man-overboard recovery techniques to learn how your boat handles during those maneuvers. They should become second nature so you can perform them without advance notice and in the dark.

To gain confidence and build up the abilities you'll need for ocean sailing, get offshore experience. You can do this by signing on for an offshore training passage designed to teach the necessary knowledge and skills. You can also volunteer as crew on other vessels, and take the

opportunity to glean as much knowledge as possible from the experiences.

If you intend to spend time in foreign countries, consider taking language courses before you leave. You will enjoy a richer and less stressful experience if you can converse with people in their native language.

Phase 8: Meal Planning and Provisioning

You can begin planning for meals at any time once you know who will be in your crew. I recommend you keep this aspect of the cruise as easy as possible and that you avoid having to prepare different dishes for each person on board. Your goal should be to provide healthy, nutritious meals that taste good, are easy to fix, create a minimum of waste, and are easy to eat with minimum clean-up. Meal preparation at sea is most efficient when one nutritious meal at a time is prepared for everyone.

Provisioning is only done when the time to departure is measured in hours, rather than days.

Chapter 18, *Meal Planning and Provisioning*, goes into these topics in detail.

Phase 9: Final Preparations before Departure

You're getting down to the nitty-gritty now, the crew has assembled, and excitement is building. Anyone who has progressed this far, and has attained this point of preparedness, knows the feeling of anticipation ahead of finally leaving port. This is not the time to get sloppy, though. To prevent omissions, I recommend a measured approach.

Please refer to Appendix 3, *Inspection Checklist for Voyage Preparations*.

"You can't control the weather once you're at sea, but you'd better control the weather you leave in."

One of the worst storms I've ever sailed through began barely two days out of New York Harbor, on my first ocean passage as a raw crewman. The cold front that rolled through, with its Force 8 northwesterlies, just as we sailed across the Gulf Stream was very predictable, if we'd only been monitoring the weather more closely. Had our departure been delayed a couple of days, though, I'd have missed the most memorable sail I've ever had!

Never leave on a passage without knowing what systems are controlling the current weather, and what systems will dictate the weather for the next 96 hours in the area toward which you'll be sailing.

To understand the general trends, begin monitoring the weather several weeks before your planned departure date, using all available means, including TV, the Internet, NOAA weather radio near the coasts, and nearby airports. This is also a good opportunity to practice operating any equipment you'll be using to download weather information at sea, and ensure that it will work satisfactorily.

Prepare a schematic view of the boat plainly indicating the locations of all seacocks and through-hull fittings. This can be copied from the Owner's Manual, or obtained from the manufacturer, and updated with any modifications you or others have made. There should be a wood bung tied to each fitting. Locations of all fire extinguishers should also be indicated on the boat schematic, so everyone can locate each one. A sample schematic appears as Appendix 10.

Your route planning should be finished by now. Great Circle Courses should be plotted, currents taken into account, and waypoints have been entered on the charts and into the GPS where they've been arranged in the order in which they'll be used.

Celestial navigators should have all publications and plotting equipment on hand, along with the timepiece and sextant. You've plotted the planets, the sun, and the moon on the Starfinder for the longitude where you expect to be two days after departure, and you've preplanned for taking sights. Doing this beforehand saves time and energy that can be at a premium on the first few days out, while you become acclimatized to being at sea.

With the crew list finalized, routing determined, and dates of landfall estimated, you can put together the Float Plan. This must be done very shortly before departure, and people at the home base notified, along with people at the first destination, if possible. A sample Float Plan is available in Appendix 5.

The watch system should by now be established and the schedule filled in and posted in a designated spot.

A sharpened emergency knife should be placed in a readily accessible location, such as by the rail along the companion-way steps.

Hold your crew orientation and instructional session before setting out. Chapter 17, *Preparing the Crew*, offers suggestions for this all-important "cockpit chat."

You've inspected the vessel and ascertained that all gear and systems are fit for sea, as outlined in Chapter 19, *Final Vessel Preparations for Sea*. Now just briefly go over the boat to ensure the last details are in place: The sails are ready, all lines are on hand, and winch handles, spare blocks, and other loose equipment are in place and set to go.

You are ready to leave on your voyage.

CHAPTER 2

PASSAGEMAKING WITH SHORTHANDED CREW

Many boats sailing the oceans on extended cruises have crews of only two people. Most often the crew consists of a man and woman, who must both possess an array of skills in order to maintain and steer the vessel successfully.

We are all familiar with the following scenario: a man who is gung ho to go cruising and his partner goes along so he can fulfill his dream. She knows little about sailing, and would be lost if he were injured or became ill. Such relationships seldom last, because ocean sailing places equal demands, physically and emotionally, on everyone, and both parties must share in the joy and tackle the hardships together.

As I emphasize throughout the book, putting into action a plan to go cruising is a big undertaking. Couples who believe it is what they want to do, before embarking on a project that will consume a great deal of time and money, have to ask themselves and each other how committed they are to taking up the sailing life. If they are both equally eager to do it, then they should, because the adventure and memories they can make together can be boundless. If either one is not, they should drop the project.

One of the first decisions any would-be cruisers have to make is about how big a boat they want. Whatever size they choose, whether that's influenced by their budget or their comfort level, the vessel must be equipped and rigged to be easily handled by a small crew. A bigger boat has advantages in performance, comfort, and storage space, but these must be weighed against the need to handle larger sails, bigger lines, and heavier ground tackle. Modern equipment such as electric winches can make the boat physically more manageable, but if the need arises, the crew should be able to perform any task on board manually, without the aid of such technology.

The best way to find the right size is to gain experience on boats of a variety of sizes. Two avenues commonly used are to charter or to sail on friends' boats. At every opportunity, use your time on board to test your ability to operate it. Maneuver under power to gain a feel for performance and handling characteristics. Hoist the sails by hand as far as possible, and then finish the job using the manual winch. Practice reducing sail by reefing the main and rolling in the genoa. An able sailor should be able to roll in the jib or genoa by hand once the sheet is released. If that's not possible, the sail, and therefore perhaps the boat, is probably too big.

Check out the ground tackle on each vessel and think about how you would hoist the anchor if the windlass failed for any reason. You want to be sure you could hoist the anchor using only human power. Cruising yachts commonly use a large primary anchor on an all-chain rode, a combination which is very heavy. To haul it back, you would need to tie a line to the chain and lead it back to a primary winch in the cockpit.

As a guide to selecting your boat, refer to Chapter 4, *The Proper Ocean Sailing Vessel*. Once you've decided on the boat, concentrate on making it as easy to sail as possible, and I don't mean in the sense of being comfortable and with all the conveniences of home. A generator, DC refrigeration, a microwave oven, and a television can make voyaging more like condominium living, but I'm more concerned with boat and sail handling. Equip the boat with gear that will help you avoid dangerous situations and will enable you to keep it under control, especially when the going gets rough.

I look at safety at sea as having two distinct components. The first is avoiding trouble and the second is dealing with trouble when it becomes unavoidable.

The best way to avoid bad weather is to choose the most propitious time for your departure to assure you of at least several days of favorable conditions. Given a 96-hour weather outlook, nothing beyond the first 48 hours is considered trustworthy; it's to be used as a guideline only. Therefore, if you're embarking on a 10-day passage, most of those days will be in conditions beyond anyone's ability to foresee at departure. Try, through observation and study, to get a feeling for the rhythm of weather systems as they pass through the area where you'll be sailing. Never leave with a low pressure system or cold front near your waters.

If you leave in good conditions, with nothing threatening on the horizon, your next duty is to monitor the weather carefully and be prepared for what might develop at sea. That brings about the second component of safety; being able to cope with rough conditions if they arise. Sooner or later, a vessel sailing offshore will encounter gale force winds and high seas. For the knowledgeable, experienced offshore crew, dealing with heavy weather becomes a matter of routine, and such situations are more of an inconvenience than dangerous.

Storm management begins with equipping the vessel properly, backed up by knowing how and when to take specific actions dictated by the wind and sea state. Very simply put, it's a matter of matching your sail plan and ship's orientation to those conditions. Every crew should have a clear idea of the procedures to be employed as heavy weather sets in, but it's even more important for shorthanded crews. I think of shortening sail or setting storm sails before heavy winds and seas make those maneuvers more difficult as being "ahead of the curve." Race crews may prefer to wait until the boat is overpowered, but they accept those risks and have many experienced hands on board to complete difficult sail changes. Short-handed crews don't have that luxury; they have to think ahead and perform the necessary tasks when it's relatively easy to do so.

Both people on board must be intimately familiar with the boat and its equipment. They should know the location of all lines on the mast, boom, and leading back to the cockpit. There should be no confusion when the time comes to take in a reef in the dark. In order to shorten sail quickly and effectively, each person has to know what steps to take, when they're taken, and what lines are involved. This comes from working together, and from practicing the steps involved in reefing, rolling in the jib, and deploying the trysail and the storm staysail or the storm jib.

I strongly recommend that, to avoid the risks of going forward to the mast in building wind and seas, the boat be rigged so that the mainsail can be reefed from the cockpit.

All of the principles and techniques of good seamanship I describe in this book apply equally aboard any vessel, whether fully crewed or shorthanded. Of the equipment I describe in Chapter 5, *Offshore Essentials: Gear and Instruments*, I consider two items indispensable on vessels with small crews: radar and an overboard alarm. I strongly recommend that these two devices be on board all short-crewed vessels because they enable couples to sail together more safely and with greater confidence.

There will be times when the risk of fatigue requires that both people rest. Radar makes this possible as it maintains a watch for other vessels. Modern sets do this in an energy-saving mode to boot. When the watchman function on a Furuno radar, for example, is engaged, the radar sweeps the horizon at programmed intervals of time (I use 15 or 20 minutes) and then returns to a standby, energy-saving mode. You select a range, in miles, and if a contact enters the circle within that radius, the alarm sounds. The contact shows up on the monitor, and you are aroused with ample time to assess any risk and take evasive action if necessary. Without the fear of running into something while I'm off watch, I've found it easier to get restful sleep.

The overboard alarm has changed my sailing world as much as any gear that has been introduced in the last 10 years. Now I can be confident that even if a crewmember breaks a rule and somehow falls overboard, the alarm sounding in the main saloon will let me know about it instantly. This peace of mind is invaluable to the worrywart skipper.

Another piece of equipment that becomes essential on a shorthanded boat is self steering, whether in the form of a vane system, an electronic autopilot, or both. With only two crew aboard, most of the time only one will be on watch. That person will not want to be steering by hand. Not only is it fatiguing, it makes performing other tasks on board almost impossible.

Safety at sea has many facets. Sail handling and storm management are only two of them. On boats with small crews, avoiding illness and injury becomes even more important. If one member of a couple is incapacitated, the other effectively becomes a single-hander. Staying fit and healthy has to be a state of mind. Just as we assume the responsibility for maintaining the boat while at sea, we must apply the same effort to looking after ourselves. Simple things like inboard jacklines, always using a boom preventer, and wearing harnesses are basic common sense, but the need to be safe has to govern every movement made, every task undertaken, and every tactic employed. When the boat is in constant motion, we have to use that motion to our advantage, and try never to be caught off balance by an unexpected wave. Falling down the companionway or being flung across the saloon is never good, and can inflict serious injuries. We must get into the "sea mode", which means that counteracting or using the boat's motion becomes second nature.

There's yet another element important for successful shorthanded passagemaking; that is the effort both people make to work together, help each other, share the load and avoid strife. For the most successful sailing duos, this actually takes no conscious effort; their relationship is such that it's natural for them. Compassion and caring for the other person are just as important to safe shipkeeping as sail management or storm tactics. Tough going and hardships are a normal part of offshore sailing; it's how we deal with them that determines what kind of mariners we are. When two people are willing to sail together, share the tasks at hand, com-

pensate when the other needs a break, and help each other without question, the difficult times pass as just another day at sea. Being awakened for watch with a kind word and gentle touch is so much better than hearing a yell from the cockpit. Finding some hot cocoa waiting in a mug sure beats trying to get dressed, gain your bearings, assess the boat's situation, and then heat up water yourself. These are just examples of how to make passagemaking easier for one another, and it's amazing how little things make a big difference.

One of the wackiest deliveries I ever sailed was also one of the most memorable. Three of us attempted to sail a boat from Tortola to Annapolis, Maryland. Ken had been offshore with me once before, but not for several years. Judy was taking her first offshore trip, but was an experienced sailor and eager for more. After over 350 miles, most of which we hand steered because the batteries failed to hold a charge, the engine shut down once and for all one evening at around 20:00. Without battery power, no engine, and the boat taking on water (we emptied the bilge every couple of hours) the decision was made to reciprocate our course back to Tortola.

It took four days punctuated by squalls, light winds, and calms to sail the 350 miles to port. In that time, everyone in the crew pitched in to assist with any and all tasks that arose. A crewmember would stand watch a couple hours extra to allow the shipmate some much needed rest. Meals prepared for one were readied for all. Rather than quibbling if someone was 10 minutes late for watch, this crew pulled together as a unit and made this passage, fraught with so much difficulty, a real pleasure to sail. We all had mixed feelings as we sailed in and the boat gently kissed the wall in Tortola. Yes, we were safe and off the perfidious ocean, but our adventure together was over.

When crews work together with that kind of spirit and cooperation, very little can deter them from making successful, fun, and memorable passages.

CHAPTER 3

VOYAGING AND CRUISING WITH CHILDREN

Cruising as a family can be a wonderful experience for children and adults alike, and taking on the challenge together can strengthen the bonds between them.

Initially, children may not greet with much enthusiasm the idea of leaving their familiar world of schools, friends, and routines to enter one of uncertainty. There are, though, plenty of measures you can take to help them feel more at home on the boat. The most important may be to let them participate in the decision-making processes so that they have opportunities to contribute and to make the plan include their ideas and needs.

Provide the children with their own private spaces on board, where they can study, play, and ponder their own thoughts. Make it a point to keep abreast of what they're thinking and feeling, sound out their opinions, fears, and expectations, and take steps to allay their concerns.

A key to getting them to feel that they are part of the program, and will benefit from it, is to assign them responsibilities. Show them what you expect them to do and follow up by making sure they take their duties seriously and express your appreciation and praise their efforts when they perform them capably.

Cruising in company with another boat with children of similar ages, even on a temporary basis, can be a big benefit. Both the children and the parents appreciate the occasional breaks from each other that such an arrangement provides.

Encourage your children to explore the new places you visit and to meet people from different countries. This keeps their active young minds occupied. One of the chief benefits from the whole cruising experience is that children experience a variety of cultures and people they'd never otherwise encounter.

If you have a computer aboard, allow the children access to it both for entertainment and for study. You might want to set them up with free e-mail accounts to use when on board or at Internet cafes as a way to keep in touch with friends and relatives at home. Many cruising families establish their own Websites, to which the children contribute.

Educating Children Offshore

Parents who take their children out of school are required by law to provide for their continued education. Most choose home schooling as the easiest and most effective way to do this. Over the years, numerous articles have appeared in magazines and other publications attesting to the positive impact cruising has on children, who benefit not only from the array of experiences they encounter, but also from higher scholastic achievement. Children returning from a cruise and whose parents have ensured their ongoing education have commonly outpaced their peers in school. These children have been home schooled.

At present, between 1.5 and 2 million children are home schooled in the USA each year, a number which has been increasing annually by 11 percent, and cruising families can take advantage of the growth in programs and resources which has followed.

States have different laws governing home schooling. Some states merely ask to be informed that your child is being home schooled, others mandate specific curriculum guidelines, and still others require home school students to take state standardized tests. Contact your home state's department of education well before your departure date so that you can make appropriate arrangements.

Once you've ascertained your state's requirements and you've taken steps to follow them, focus on how to manage the home schooling. Some parents create their own curriculum, following school guidelines. Others use commercial programs that include lesson plans, texts, activities, and testing. While your local public or charter schools can sometimes offer help, accessing it is usually impractical while cruising.

Many parents enlist the help of tutors and friends, or enroll their children in classes offered at museums, libraries, or junior colleges. Most people who decide to home school their children while cruising assume the entire task themselves. It's a big commitment, but with the right planning and dedication, many find that it can enhance the cruising experience for the whole family. Several home schooling, cruising families I've spoken to passed along the following tips:

- Make sure that you have all of the necessary books, study guides, and lesson plans in hand before you set off.
- Take along a supply of notebooks and pens and pencils. Bring calculators.
- Study aids you can take along include a computer, dictionaries, an encyclopedia, and a world atlas.
- Establish regular "school" hours when possible, both while at sea and when at anchor.
- Be prepared to spend the time administering lessons and explaining new concepts. It will require patience on your part.
- Encourage the children to take up hobbies or to pursue subjects in which they take a special interest.

Home Schooling Resources

Information on the concept and practical aspects of learning outside of school is available from a variety of resources:

- Family Unschoolers Network: Dept. W, 1688 Belhaven Woods Court, Pasadena, MD 21122-3727; tel: 410/360-7330, www.unschoolers.org
- Homeschool World: www.home-school.com

- Learn in Freedom: www.learninfreedom.org
- A to Z Home's Cool: http://homeschooling.gomilpitas.com

PART 2

THE BOAT AND FITTING OUT

CHAPTER 4

THE PROPER OCEAN SAILING VESSEL

Over the course of my career I've sailed the oceans in a wide variety of boats, and from that experience I've developed what I believe are well founded views regarding the seaworthiness of different vessels. I've been on passages that were uncomfortable, wet, or unsafe, or were long simply because the boat was painfully slow. I've also seen a variety of failures involving the boats and their gear. Consequently, I've come to some conclusions about the compromises needed to make a fine offshore sailing vessel.

Opinions abound regarding what makes the ideal boat, but all must of necessity share certain characteristics. When choosing a boat, individuals must take into consideration what their real intentions are and what kind of use it will see most of the time. Someone intending to sail and gunkhole near the coast will need a different kind of boat than a sailor making occasional short offshore passages between destinations, and the cruiser who will tackle extended passages of thousands of miles will again have other requirements.

Likewise, the accommodations needed by a retired couple will differ from those of a five-person crew involved in ocean voyaging and racing. It's important therefore that before selecting your boat, you examine your needs.

THE BOAT

Mono or Multi Hulls

A fundamental decision that has to be made early on is to determine the number of hulls. For some people, multihulls make more sense as cruising vessels than monohulls, while others will consider only a monohull.

Multihulls offer certain advantages that should not be dismissed out of hand. Especially off the wind, which is ideally how we sail when cruising, they are good to superior sailing vessels. Most modern multihulls will not sink if holed. They usually have shoal draft, and some are equipped with daggerboards that provide additional lateral resistance when it's needed. Catamarans also offer a relatively enormous amount of room belowdecks for accommodations and gear matched by abundant space on deck. Many owners appreciate not having to climb a companionway ladder to go from the saloon to the deck. Multi-hulls generally have a kinder motion, with built-in roll resistance. The two smaller diesel engines usually found in catamarans make a lot of sense, and provide redundancy in the event that one engine fails.

Among the disadvantages to consider are water slapping noisily between the hulls when underway and often a more severe pounding motion upwind. Sailing them to windward is often difficult and much less efficient than sailing off the wind.

Should a multihull capsize, its inverted stability makes righting it impossible without outside help. Because the wide beam of multihulls is more than many marinas can accommodate, especially in foreign ports, dockage can be quite limited and more expensive.

How Big is Big Enough?

In my experience, the most desirable ocean-sailing yacht is big, strong, and fast. Big is a relative term, and I should qualify it: I recommend you acquire the biggest boat that you can afford and that you can physically handle with your intended crew. Size is a factor in the accommodations and room on board, and in waterline length (LWL) which is so integral to hull speed. Hull speed is related to LWL by the equation:

$$\text{Hull Speed (knots)} = 1.34 \times \text{Square Root of LWL (feet)}$$

This simple formula says a lot: It tells us that to maximize our boat speed, we should sail the longest waterline we can manage.

The less time you spend at sea, the less you are exposed to the vagaries of weather and to the risk of breakdowns, injury, and illness. Speed through the water also steadies the boat's motion, making it less tiring for the crew and safer. Greater speed translates into regular, steady progress that is such an aid to crew morale, bolstering the spirits of all aboard as each waypoint is achieved and the track line progresses steadily across the chart.

Size also factors into a vessel's behavior in waves. Small, light boats are affected to a much greater degree by wave action than are larger boats of moderate to heavy displacement. Although they may have an advantage in their ability to plane readily, they are less manageable in a seaway, and following waves are more disruptive to the helm. Self-steering systems are forced to exert much greater effort to maintain their heading when the transom is easily pushed to leeward by a quartering sea.

Stability is a Function of Size

Studies of the behavior of various craft in large breaking seas have shown that any vessel will be capsized by a breaking wave higher than 60 percent of the boat's overall length. In other words, a 60-foot sailboat will be capsized if hit by a 36-foot breaking wave on its beam.

There are factors that make some boats more resistant to capsizing in all but these extreme wave conditions.

Full-keeled boats tend to capsize

more easily than boats of similar lengths that have fin keels. Tests demonstrate that the fuller keel tends to "trip" a boat more readily as the wave pushes it sideways. Lighter displacement boats are also more liable to capsize when hit beam-on by large breaking waves. In waves overtaking from astern, a situation encountered when running in storm conditions, the beamy, lighter boats are once again less stable.

A sailboat's stability is a measure of its ability to carry sail and of its ability to resist capsize. Its initial stability is determined to a great extent by the shape of the hull, but the farther a vessel heels, the greater is the effect of the position of its center of gravity on the resistance to heeling, or righting moment.

Figure 4-1 shows the relationship between Center of Buoyancy (CB), Center of Gravity (CG), and Righting Arm in an upright vessel. The Righting Arm is the horizontal distance between a line drawn vertically through the CB and a line drawn vertically through the CG; their relationship dictates direction of the force known as Righting Moment (RM). RM either recovers the boat from heeling or inverts during a capsize. The heeling force is normally the effect of wind pressure on the sails, usually depicted as working at the Center of Effort (CE) of the sail plan, but it can also be from wave action.

At small angles of heel, the CB moves away from the CG, more quickly in a shallow, beamy hull than in a deeper, narrow hull of the same displacement. The righting arm continues to increase as the CB moves outboard, until the boat reaches a point at which the CG begins to rotate back toward the CB. Depending on the hull type, this is usually between 50 and 70 degrees of heel. The righting arm remains positive, and the boat, once the heeling force is removed, will revert to upright until the point at which the CG is vertically above the CB, and the righting arm is zero. The angle of rotation

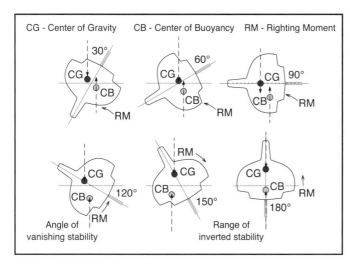

FIGURE 4-1

Heeling and Righting Forces on a Sailboat

at which this occurs is called the Angle of Vanishing Stability (AVS). In Figure 4-1, this occurs between heel angles of 120 and 150 degrees. After that point, RM is negative and the boat will continue to rotate until it reaches its next position of stability, which is when it is completely inverted.

At small angles of heel, the beamy hull will have greater stability, due to its form, than the narrow hull, but a low center of gravity coupled with narrow beam will produce a higher AVS than a high center of gravity coupled with a beamy hull. The higher the AVS, the less stable the vessel is in the inverted position, and the more likely it will be to right itself, usually as a consequence of wave action.

The disadvantages of a multihull in this situation are obvious. When the boat's roll continues and it capsizes, the wide beam that produced its initial resistance and stiffness becomes the factor that keeps it inverted. Some other external force will then be required to right the vessel, which would otherwise be content to remain inverted indefinitely.

Hull and Keel Configuration

The keel preferred for offshore work is a longer, modern fin type with external lead ballast attached with keel bolts arranged to distribute the weight over a wide area of the hull. The keel bolts should be accessible for inspection where they fasten through the bottom of the boat.

Deep, thin keels attached to the hull over a relatively small area are appropri-ate on ocean racers, where the crews are aware of and accept the risks. They are not suitable for cruising yachts. Keels with wings likewise, despite the advantages they offer in sailing performance, do not lend themselves well to cruising. In a grounding, wings can turn an inconvenience into a serious threat to the boat, because they tend to dig into the bottom much like a Bruce anchor would. Heeling the boat, instead of lifting the keel tip from the sea bed, causes it to dig deeper, and attempts to kedge or tow the boat off can subject the keel to damaging shear loads.

Interestingly, boats with a more traditional hull shape, one that's narrower and of somewhat heavier displacement, are the most stable all round. They are stiffer, have higher angles of vanishing stability, they are easier to control in following seas, and they are more resistant to capsize by waves.

In choosing a boat that will enable you to achieve your sailing goals in the manner that best suits you, you'll have to reach a compromise between a variety of design attributes. The ultra-light, wide-beam ocean racing boats are the epitome of speed, but they achieve that at some expense in terms of safety and comfort. Heavy-displacement cruising boats have the advantage of better ultimate stability, but at the cost of lower boat speed, cumbersome motion, and more sluggish handling characteristics.

Hydrodynamically, the stern of the double-ender makes sense as it's designed to handle waves overtaking from astern, but the narrow aft end limits the available space belowdecks and for deck lockers, making it unsuitable in the eyes of many boat owners. The double-ender also tends to squat at higher speeds because of the limited reserve buoyancy in the stern.

A wider stern, designed to add waterline length as the boat heels, and ending at a slightly reversed transom is the most suitable compromise. The transom should allow water to drain rapidly from the cockpit in the event of a pooping by a following sea. A built-in step to facilitate boarding from the swim ladder is also a useful feature on a cruising boat.

In the end, the vessel that makes the most sense for the majority of people is one of medium displacement and moderate beam, optimized LWL, a low center of gravity, and a modern keel. It should be strongly and soundly built and have a robust rig.

Gauging a Vessel's Intended Use

There are differences between boats built for ocean sailing and those more suited to day sailing between islands. Ask builders about their boats' intended use, specifically whether they are designed and built to withstand the rigors of long offshore passages.

By examining specific items on a boat, you can learn a lot about what it was designed for. Look closely at the spars and standing rigging, and compare their sizes against those on other boats. Is the gear substantial compared with other boats? Details such as toerails, pad eyes, cleats, and deck gear can help you gauge the designer's intent.

On deck, look closely at the stem fittings and anchor roller. How substantial are the stanchions, bow pulpit, stern pushpit, and mast pulpit? How securely are the boom bails fastened? In the cockpit, ensure that the drains are adequate, check the clearance between the cockpit floor and the companionway, and that lockers close securely.

Examine the bilge pumps, both manual and electric, to assess their capacity. Check the listed capacities of the water and fuel tanks. Boats built for making long passages usually have larger tanks.

Construction Materials

The vast majority of offshore vessels today are built of fiberglass. Builders favor it because it lends itself to series production of relatively inexpensive boats. Owners like it because as well as making boats more affordable it requires less maintenance than other materials.

Steel is prone to rust and corrosion, and their prevention requires constant vigilance, although modern paints can reduce the maintenance demands. Because of its weight, steel is best suited to boats of 40 feet and above. Below that, hulls become disproportionately heavy and require a great sail area to drive them through the water. Steel hulls designed with chines to simplify construction can be aesthetically unattractive to some people.

Fiberglass is lighter, and with its combination of strength and elasticity, it is a superior construction material. It must be handled carefully during construction, to ensure the finished laminate contains resin and its fiber reinforcements in their proper proportions.

27

Indeed a thick hull, improperly laid-up, is not nearly as strong as a thinner hull constructed with the correct techniques.

The deck-to-hull joint is another indicator of the strength and integrity of the vessel. Builders use a variety of methods to attach the deck to the hull of fiberglass boats, but my preference is for those that include fiberglass bonding on the interior of the joint. This creates a connection that's usually trouble free and better able to withstand the torque effects of ocean sailing without leaking.

Bulkheads are designed to provide internal stiffening and integrity, and should be securely fastened to the hull and deck in such a manner that they cannot loosen in a seaway. Loose bulkheads no longer support the hull as intended, which will cause it to flex excessively, in turn causing interior cabinetry to become loose.

Hulls should be strengthened by means of internal structural supports. Sometimes these take the form of a molded grid incorporating floors, frames, and longitudinals. In other boats stringers and transverse frames are laid in separately and tied into the bulkheads. When inspecting a boat that interests you, look beneath the floorboards to assess the system used to lend strength and integrity to the hull.

Rig

When narrowing your search for the most suitable yacht you'll have to decide on what rig you'll be most comfortable sailing. In years past, two-masted vessels, especially ketches, were popular because of the variety of sail combinations they permit. The boat could be fully canvassed in lighter airs while offering many options for shortening sail to suit different conditions. Not being as tall as those of modern sloops, in light breezes, these rigs fail to capture the stronger wind that's a bit higher up.

In recent decades, the development of stronger spars, better sail materials, and superior hull technology has led to the current predominance of single-mast vessels. The cutter rig, or a sloop with additional inner forestay, is now very popular.

The taller spar allows the sails to capture and utilize more wind aloft, and often a roller furled genoa will further improve sailing performance in lighter wind conditions. The inner forestay is perfect for deploying a storm staysail (preferably hanked-on) when the genoa is furled or removed in anticipation of severe conditions.

A removable inner forestay permits the greatest flexibility. It can be set up when needed and then detached from the deck and stowed at the mast when sailing conditions don't warrant the use of a staysail.

A valuable addition to the sail inventory, a storm trysail that sets on its own track on the mast, will enable a sturdy offshore yacht, when properly managed, to weather practically any storm.

Mast and Rigging

Most offshore sailors prefer the mast to be stepped on the keel because they feel that it is a more secure arrangement than when it's stepped on the deck. Because the mast step is then in the bilge area, it should be inspected routinely for corrosion. A deck-stepped mast can be very secure, but the step must be supported by a rigid structure designed to transmit the mast loading to the keel. The connection between mast base and deck support is also crucial.

The standing rigging is another indication of the boat's strength. Most non-racing ocean-going sailboats are rigged with 1x19 stainless-steel wire rope. Rod rigging is comparatively more expensive, it can fail without showing external signs of weakness, and it's very difficult to store spare material on board. For these reasons, it's found mostly on racing yachts. Check the tensile strength of all the standing rigging. Two shrouds should be able to support the weight of the loaded boat.

Stainless steels are alloys of iron that contain chromium in various proportions to impart corrosion resistance, among other properties. Stainless steels in the 300 series also contain nickel to further enhance corrosion resistance. The alloys most commonly found in sailboat applications are Type 304 and Type 316. The latter is a little less strong, but its better resistance to corrosion in a salt-water environment makes it the preferred material for marine use. Stainless steels in the 400 series for the most part contain less or no nickel, and are not well suited to marine applications. Try to identify the stainless steel used in the standing rigging of the boat by asking questions. Series 400 stainless steel, which you can identify by its attraction to a magnet, is to be avoided in any application on a boat, including fittings and hose clamps.

Poorly installed or deteriorating chainplates frequently are cited as a cause when a boat fails survey. Water penetrating the deck can cause serious degradation to chainplates and their attachment points. When these are concealed in the boat's joinerwork, a disastrous failure can occur with no forewarning. The chain plates should be fabricated of high-grade stainless steel and be regularly inspected for corrosion.

The chainplates, port and starboard and on the stem and transom, should be attached to solid structural members that distribute the rigging loads to the vessel's backbone without causing local distortions. Ideally, for strength and redundancy, each stay and shroud should have its own chainplate. Chainplates attached to the outside of the hull are more likely to cause leaks and, by forcing the jib's sheeting angle outboard, reduce upwind sailing efficiency.

Steering

Few systems are more important to the safety of a sailboat than the steering. The best insurance policy for a solid steering component is the name of the company who manufactures it. Edson is considered the industry leader in yacht steering systems, but even its name on the components is no guarantee against failure as the result of improper installation or poor maintenance. It's very important to have the steering system examined closely by a qualified marine surveyor. Beginning at the wheel and pedestal, all the connecting mechanisms and fittings including those on the rudderstock must be functional and accessible. The rudder is of course part of the system, and must likewise be examined to ensure it is securely attached to the stock and for signs of damage, delamination, or water ingress.

Interior Arrangement

Your boat's layout and accommodations are as important as any other feature. The interior must be suited to the intended use, provide the desired number of berths and heads, and be functional. You will need lots of storage space below. Try to envisage the quantities of provisions you'll need on passages, given the number of crew aboard and make sure the vessel you choose has the storage space to accommodate them.

Galley

Much of the food storage capacity should be in the galley or within easy reach of it so you won't have to search for stores in distant parts of the boat.

The galley stove should be large enough to handle the meals you expect to prepare. Traditionally on yachts, the stove was situated on the port side, but the reasons for that are long forgotten and so ignored in many modern designs. The stove is easiest to use when mounted on gimbals so that it remains level when the boat heels or rolls when under way. Make sure the stove can be locked in the gimbals so it can't fly out in the event of a knockdown. This is often not a standard feature, and you may have to create your own solution.

Ensure the galley has plenty of work-space for meal preparation, and security for the cook in the form of a stainless steel grab bar and/or a strap. Deep double sinks work best, and you can add valuable counter space by making a cover to fit over one or both of them. A pullout chopping board is another useful addition.

Provide the galley with ample ventilation including a fan, and place a fire extinguisher so that it's handy to the stove, but not over it.

Propane is the most popular choice of cooking fuel. It burns efficiently without smoke, it's easy to store, and it's cost effective. However, propane can form an explosive mixture with air. It's heavier than air and can collect in the bilge where it can remain undetected despite the odor added to it during manufacture. For that reason, very definite and strict standards promulgated by the American Boat & Yacht Council (ABYC) and the National Fire Prevention Association (NFPA) are followed in the design of propane installations in boats. If you have questions about a propane system, consult a surveyor or an ABYC-certified installer.

Navigation Station

On a cruising yacht, the nav station serves two important roles. At sea, it is the command station, where navigation information and weather data are analyzed and plotted. When the boat's in port, it becomes the office. A crucial feature is therefore a comfortable, secure seat from which the navigator can work without risk of being thrown across the boat. It must also have adequate, accessible stowage to accommodate all the navigation tools, books, and charts, as well as space to mount the instruments and, probably, a laptop computer.

Fuel Capacity

Even if a boat is fitted with what seems to be adequate fuel tankage, you may need to add more to achieve your desired range. A rule of thumb for fuel is that you should be able to carry enough to provide a 1,000-mile motoring range as a minimum.

To calculate fuel range, you'll need to know the boat's fuel capacity, the average speed achieved at cruising rpm, and the engine's average hourly fuel consumption at that speed. Be conservative in your estimates. When calculating for an ocean delivery or a passage on VOYAGER, I use a speed of 5.5 knots at cruising rpm. This is a conservative figure, and I usually surpass it, especially when motorsailing, but it has served as a useful basis for fuel range computations.

Most 40-foot sailboats will use an average of .75 gallons of diesel per hour, again, conservatively speaking. To obtain a more precise number, consult with the manufacturer, or actually measure your boat's consumption.

If a boat burns .75 gallons per hour at an average speed under power of 5.5 knots, we can calculate its consumption in miles per gallon as follows:

It takes 1 hour to burn .75 gallon
To burn 1 gallon will therefore take
   1/.75 hours

At 5.5 knots, in that time, the boat
   will travel 5.5 x 1/.75 miles
   (7.33 miles)
So, the fuel consumption rate is
   7.33 miles per gallon

If the boat has a fuel capacity of 100 gallons, supplemented by 40 gallons in jerry jugs, we can calculate the expected range under power as follows:

$$\begin{aligned}
\text{Fuel range in miles} &= \text{fuel in gallons} \\
&\quad \times \text{miles/gallon} \\
&= 140 \times 7.33 \\
&= 1026 \text{ miles}
\end{aligned}$$

When making this calculation for your boat, be conservative, and you may well exceed your estimated range. Just be certain you have a few gallons of fuel available to make landfall, and call the passage a success!

Water Capacity

The boat should carry enough water to allow each member of the crew a bare minimum of half a gallon per day while at sea. Many boats built for inland or near-coastal sailing, besides being inadequately rigged and constructed, lack the water capacity required of offshore vessels. On vessels taken on extended passages, a water maker is often installed to supplement the water supply.

Adequate holding tanks are a necessity on any sailboat with people living aboard. While they are superfluous at sea, their use is required in many ports throughout the world, and increasingly so as more societies take steps to protect their local environment.

Looks Are Important, Too

As you work your way through acquiring, fitting out, and ultimately voyaging in your boat, you'll be spending a lot of time both on board and looking at it, so it only makes sense to select a vessel that appeals to your eye. Once you've narrowed your list of possibilities based on the above criteria, you can let your sense of aesthetics guide you in your final selection.

Factor in Fitting Out

While doing research for your boat, keep in mind that you'll spend up to another 40 percent of the purchase price outfitting it with gear necessary for offshore sailing or cruising. The actual added cost will depend on what gear is already aboard or supplied by the manufacturer, and of course how "tricked out" you ultimately want her.

Don't allow the desire to overequip your boat paralyze you. Ocean sailing is not meant to be like staying in a 5-star hotel with all the conveniences of life on shore. The marine environment is hard on boats and gear, and breakdowns happen, so it makes perfect sense to keep the boat as simple and bulletproof as possible.

Numerous books and publications are available as references as you narrow down the list of possibilities in your search for a boat. (See Appendix 10 for some recommendations.) Don't hesitate to enlist the aid and advice of a competent marine surveyor and don't be afraid to consult with a boat's manufacturer to get your questions answered.

CHAPTER 5

OFFSHORE ESSENTIALS: GEAR AND INSTRUMENTATION

What equipment and instrumentation should be aboard the well prepared offshore sailing vessel?

Opinions vary widely and the answer largely comes down to individual tastes and preferences. I've sailed on vessels from across the spectrum, feeling vulnerable and at risk on some at one end and royally pampered on those at the other. Most sailors seek a middle ground, shipping aboard enough gear to provide for safe and comfortable passages while avoiding needless extras.

As they advance in their preparations for a cruise or an offshore passage, a number of sailors become obsessed with outfitting the boat with non-essential gear and eventually the expense involved and the delays incurred overwhelm their ability to proceed. Some never manage to leave port. A way to avoid this trap is to keep your boat and the fitting out as simple and efficient as possible.

A noticeable trend toward the use of gadgets, most of them dependent on electrical power, is under way in the sailing world. Many sailors, in my estimation, are becoming too dependent on

having the electronics do their thinking and planning for them. At the same time, they are not acquiring the necessary basic skills of navigation and seamanship. The term "screen sailor" has been coined to describe someone who sits at a console watching the boat's position move slowly across a computer screen.

Passagemaking is all about seamanship, independence, and self-reliance. I wonder if sailors today have enough basic navigation skills to be able to cope should an electrical failure shut down the new instrumentation. We all know Murphy's Law. Every piece of gear added brings with it the chance it will break down. Failures at sea can lead to uncertainty, confusion, and loss of confidence, so I recommend you limit the potential for breakdowns by keeping the equipment simple.

EPIRB

When activated, an Emergency Position Indicating Radio Beacon (EPIRB) transmits an internationally recognized distress signal to aircraft, satellites, land stations and rescue vessels. This device, in my mind, has revolutionized offshore sailing, and is absolutely essential on any oceangoing vessel today.

The EPIRB's transmissions are recognized by COSPAS/SARSAT weather and mapping satellites. On receiving a distress signal from an EPIRB, a satellite computes a fix and transmits the information to ground stations, called Local User Terminals (LUTs). Located worldwide, LUTs relay the data to Mission Control Centers (MCCs). The MCC tracks the signal, and identifies the transmitting vessel using the database of registered EPIRBs. The local Rescue Control Center (RCC) is then alerted, and can initiate Search and Rescue procedures.

New technology, the 406 MHz EPIRB, is replacing previous models. The 406 transmits on two emergency frequencies in the VHF band, 406.025 and 406.028 MHz. Older EPIRBs transmitted on 121.5 (civilian) and 243.0 (military) MHz. NOAA will cease monitoring these signals as of February 1, 2009.

A 406 MHz EPIRB is usually provided with a lithium battery with a 5-year storage life and models are available that contain a built-in GPS receiver or that can be connected to an onboard GPS. Some are also fitted with a strobe light. A 406 EPIRB must be registered with NOAA. This registration is key, because the MCC uses the information it contains to identify the vessel, call the emergency contacts listed to verify the distress, and provide vessel type and description and other information to the appropriate RCC.

In the event that you are sailing a vessel other than your own, when delivering another yacht, for example, and take your own EPIRB with you, you may contact NOAA and attach that vessel's characteristics to your registration information. Once that voyage is concluded, notify NOAA to return your registration information to your own boat. The people at NOAA are very accommodating. You can obtain registration information and assistance from NOAA by calling 1-888-212-SAVE or 1-301-457-5678.

Needless to say, an EPIRB is crucial equipment for the offshore voyager. It should have a battery well within the five-year renewal period, and be tested to make sure it functions. The whole crew, of course, should be instructed in its use.

Self-Steering System

A means of self steering, whether mechanical or electronic, is a necessity on long passages. This is especially so if the crew consists of three or fewer people, so they do not become fatigued from prolonged periods of steering by hand.

Windvane self steering is the older method. It utilizes a vane that reacts to changes in apparent wind as the boat's heading changes or the wind shifts. When the apparent wind changes, it causes the vane to deflect, and a control mechanism transmits that movement to a steering device which makes a course correction.

Vane systems commonly use one of two different control mechanisms. One employs a servopendulum, which is normally connected to the boat's main rudder. In the other, movements of the vane activate a trim tab attached to the trailing edge of a small, auxiliary rudder.

The obvious major advantage of windvanes is that they require no electrical power. The trim tab/auxiliary rudder is large enough to steer the boat even in the event the primary rudder is lost. In well-maintained systems, breakdowns are infrequent, and can usually be repaired at sea. In light following breezes or while motoring, vane systems can have difficulty holding course, and they can be overpowered when sailing in big following seas. They have metal components that are subject to the ravages of weather, corrosion, and physical damage, and their mechanisms need periodic cleaning to minimize friction. They also must be very securely mounted on the transom, a real consideration for the auxiliary rudder method because it is sizable and heavy.

The chief disadvantage of windvane steering is that the boat's heading must be monitored closely. Because the vane responds to changes in the apparent wind, a change in the true wind direction will cause the boat's heading to change with it.

Electronic autopilots steer to a constant magnetic heading, which you can set and adjust using the control panel. A change in wind direction will not cause the boat's heading to change, but the sails will no longer be trimmed appropriately and the boat will lose drive.

The control unit is electrically connected to a fluxgate compass and the Central Processing Unit (CPU). The compass provides heading information to the CPU, which compares it to the programmed course. When the boat strays off course, the CPU sends an electrical impulse to the drive unit. The drive unit, which may be an electric motor or an electro-hydraulic system, corrects the course via a linkage to the boat's steering mechanism.

Although electronic autopilots have become more efficient over time, their main downside is their consumption of energy. By trimming the sails to keep the boat balanced, you can reduce the helm load and thus help the autopilot work less hard. A breakdown in a component of the system usually calls for complete replacement, especially at sea, so it's advisable to carry a complete second unit to provide spares.

If the budget permits it, a combination of a windvane system and an electronic autopilot would provide the ultimate in self-steering capabilities.

I discuss self steering in more detail in Chapter 9.

Global Positioning System (GPS)

By vastly simplifying the tasks of finding a boat's position and calculating courses, this satellite-based navigation system has induced many people to leave behind their lakes and harbors to explore places to which they might otherwise not have ventured. The prices of GPS receivers have decreased to the point where almost anyone can afford one. Aboard a cruising boat, it's usual to have a primary system installed in the nav station and connected to the boat's electrical system backed up by at least one secondary, handheld unit in case of electrical failure.

While GPS is convenient and easy to use, celestial navigation is fascinating to study. Learning the traditional techniques and employing them on a passage provides a great sense of achievement, and serves as a crucial backup against electrical breakdown or GPS satellite failure.

Communications Equipment

Communications equipment is an important element in the outfitting of an offshore vessel. A variety of means are available, from VHF radios used for short-range voice communications to satellite systems for connecting to the Internet. All have their uses, but some I consider essential.

VHF Transmitter/Receiver

A VHF radio is still the basic, essential device that should be aboard every sailboat. It is indispensable for inland and coastal locations, and offshore the VHF permits ship-to-ship communications and is also useful for contacting the authorities ahead of landfall.

There should be a fixed unit on board in the navigation station, and a remote unit or a handheld in the cockpit for convenience when underway. The handheld would also be available for duty in the abandon ship bag, should that ever be called upon.

All offshore boats should be equipped with a short-wave radio receiver. These devices are inexpensive and provide access to time signals as well as to High Seas and Offshore weather broadcasts from NOAA.

Satellite Telephone

A short-wave receiver was my sole source of weather information for about 20 years, and I've kept it as a backup even since I began downloading weather via satellite telephone. These weather chart data downloads have helped me a great deal with offshore forecasting and the satellite phone is also valuable for long-distance communications with ground stations for a variety of purposes including obtaining emergency medical advice.

As prices of the equipment, software, and calling plans have declined, the satellite phone is becoming an affordable option for offshore communications. Satellite telephones also facilitate long distance communications, e-mail, and weather-data downloads. Software for accessing weather information and e-mail are simply loaded into a laptop computer. An external antenna is not absolutely necessary for the phone to function, but it improves connectivity and minimizes signal loss, and is a worthwhile investment for offshore use. You'll need a spare battery and both AC and DC charging adaptors.

I've opted for the satellite phone, but preferences vary between sailors as to whether a satellite phone or a single-sideband radio (SSB) is the best solution for long distance communications. One or the other should be on board any vessel sailing offshore.

A key advantage of the satellite phone is that, in the event of an abandon ship emergency, the phone can go along into the liferaft. Also, the antenna is far simpler to install than an SSB antenna and is not lost in a dismasting, which would cripple an SSB.

SingleSideband Radio (SSB)

With the addition of an SCS Pactor modem, an SSB radio can be used to send and receive e-mail transmissions and packets of information. It also provides access to the Ham frequencies (channels 13 and 38) and marine frequencies, but to transmit on Ham frequencies you need a Ham Operator's license. A license is not required to access weather information or to issue a distress call.

The SSB radio's antenna is critical to the high quality of reception needed when acquiring Internet downloads. The antenna itself is often integral with the backstay, from which it must be heavily insulated. Providing the antenna with an adequate ground plane usually involves connecting the radio and tuner units and all large metal objects on the boat with copper straps two to four inches wide. The installation should be done by a professional.

Laptop Computer

A laptop computer is needed if you want to download, decode, and display weather information. It is of course handy, too, for exchanging e-mails, checking the Internet, and running games for entertainment. The laptop must have a serial port.

I use UUPlus software to compact data and minimize download times for e-mails and weather charts. UUPlus is also able to take the encoded chart information, transform it, and display the chart in readable form. UUPlus actually has the NOAA charts on its server, www.uuplus.com. Ordering them is simple and you can receive them almost instantly.

Electrical System

Unless you are of that rare breed who hopes to go cruising and leave at home everything electrical, you will depend for almost everything on board, from communicating with home to showering, on electricity. Your boat's electrical system therefore needs to be up to the task.

Batteries

Deep-cycle batteries are available in three types, wet cell, gel cell, and Absorbed Glass Mat (AGM). Gel-cell, and more recently, AGM batteries have become popular for use in boats. They are sealed, so they can't spill corrosive electrolyte if upended, and they don't discharge gas when being charged. They require less monitoring than wet cells, are able to discharge and accept charging more readily (leading to shorter charging times), and provide an adequate number of discharge cycles.

Gel-cell batteries accept a 10- to 15-percent higher charge rate than do wet-cell batteries without overheating or damaging the plates. They also have a low self-discharge rate which means they can be left unattended for several months without going flat. The discharge rate is affected by temperature extremes, but a rate of 4% per month is a good rule of thumb.

The main caveat concerning gel cells is that they must not be overcharged. Overcharging at over 14.2 volts causes a phenomenon called gassing, the process by which electrolyte is lost, leading to battery destruction. Since gel-cell batteries are sealed, the electrolyte cannot be replenished, as it would be in wet-cell batteries.

If you will be leaving on an extended cruise, make sure the house batteries are not more than two or three years old. If you have more than one battery aboard, they should all be the same type and age. A boat being fitted out for extended cruising should have at least 400 amp hours of capacity in its house battery, whereas one used for intermittent offshore passages or coastal cruising may only need 200 amp hours. The required capacity can be determined by calculating the "average" electrical usage on a given "normal" day's operation. What constitutes "normal" will vary between skippers, depending on how frugal each is. Design your batteries' capacity to match your usage habits.

In Chapter 10, *Alternative Energy*, you will find a sample calculation for an average day's electrical usage.

High Output Alternator with External Regulator

In my seminars I don't categorize this as essential offshore equipment. I do recommend, though, that if you are outfitting for extended ocean passages or cruising, you take into consideration the decreased charging times, fuel savings, and extended battery life that a high-output alternator makes possible. However, installing one can become complicated. Consult with the engine manufacturer to determine the maximum power you can safely take off the front of the engine and how the alternator might be supported. You'll probably want an electrician to do the installation.

Belt tension is critical in getting the best use of a high-output alternator, and the alternator will require double drive belts. This may well necessitate fabrication of a mounting bracket and additional pulley for the front of the engine. It's best if separate belts drive the alternator and the water pump.

To protect the batteries, you'll need an external regulator suited to the type of batteries you have. This is crucial to prevent gassing, loss of battery electrolyte, and damage to the batteries that can be caused by overcharging.

The cables between the alternator and the battery posts will probably have to be upgraded to carry the higher charging current. At the higher charge rate, the batteries will become hotter, so you'll have to ensure adequate air circulation in the battery compartment, especially if you plan to sail in tropical regions. Consider installing two ducted fans, one to deliver fresh air and another, perhaps located above the engine, to remove heated air.

Inverter/Charger

An inverter converts DC electrical power, from your boat's batteries, into 110-volt

AC power, on which you can operate AC appliances. As people bring aboard more AC devices, from laptop-battery chargers to microwave ovens or power tools, an inverter has become essential equipment. Often, an inverter is combined with a battery charger used for charging the ship's batteries when connected to shore power or running a generator.

Boat Operations

A number of items are essential to the day-to-day operation of the boat and you should decide on which ones you will want.

Anchors

Several anchors of a variety of types and weights, together with a selection of rodes, are essential components of the offshore cruising boat's inventory. Exactly what you choose to take along depends on several factors, from the size of your boat to the nature of the seabed in the areas you expect to spend your time. I discuss this topic, and techniques for anchoring, in Chapter 21, *Anchors and Anchoring Techniques*.

Dinghy

Cruising vessels typically spend a lot of time at anchor, making a dinghy essential for ferrying people and supplies to and from shore. Its usefulness in keeping crew both young and old entertained when in port should also not be underestimated.

While your personal preference and needs will influence your choice of a dinghy, bear in mind also its practicality: how many people it will usually carry, how fast and maneuverable you want it to be, how you will store it aboard the yacht, and how much money you can allocate to its purchase.

An inflatable dinghy with a soft floor is very easy to roll up and store, but the pliable floor allows it to flex under way, which impairs its performance. Models with a rigid floor are more difficult to store on board, but will be faster and more maneuverable.

If there are children on board, it may be worthwhile to invest in a dinghy with a rigid fiberglass or aluminum hull for greatest range and performance. These rigid inflatable boats (RIBs) also boast the longest lifespan.

When choosing a dinghy, determine how and where you can store it aboard your boat. I recommend very strongly not to store the dinghies on transom davits when offshore. One breaking wave from astern could tear the dinghy loose, along with the davit and whatever it's mounted to. The dinghy should be deflated and stored in a locker. If there's room, it could be left inflated and lashed securely on the foredeck.

Dodger and Bimini

Crew exposed to the elements can suffer from discomfort and fatigue, which might lead to loss of enthusiasm. Providing protection from the sun, rain, wind, and spray is therefore essential on any vessel outfitting for extended passagemaking or cruising.

If you are fortunate enough to have a

rigid dodger built into the boat's design, you're ahead of the game. Any additions you make to the assembly should be supported on stainless-steel framing and supports. The dodger should not interfere with normal boom operations, but should be high enough that the helmsman can steer while standing.

The dodger should angle up from the coaming to attach and join with the bimini that extends aft. The dodger fabric can be permanent, but the bimini should be easily removable in heavy weather.

To permit the greatest visibility, the dodger should have heavy-gauge, clear-plastic windows, which should be supported by the framing, not by nylon webbing.

Barometer, Thermometer, and Clock

Each of these devices serves a function integral to the practice of good seamanship essential to offshore passagemaking. Aboard VOYAGER, we routinely monitor the barometric pressure and air temperature, keeping tabs of the weather experienced right on our boat as part of our "Single Station Forecasting." This information is then compared to graphs and charts downloaded from NOAA to formulate more accurate local forecasts. We also carry a submersible thermometer with which we monitor the seawater temperature.

Time is important to the mariner, and you'll need to keep track of several variations.

Anyone using the Nautical Almanac and Sight Reduction Tables will need on board an accurate clock that keeps Greenwich Mean Time (GMT), which is the basic reference for celestial navigation calculations. Universal Coordinated Time (UTC) and Zulu are the same as GMT and are used in schedules for weather forecasts and other wide-ranging communications. Using your short-wave receiver, you can check this time by tuning in to short-wave radio broadcasts from WWV 5,000, 10,000, 15,000, 20,000 kHz and from other sources. Radios built specifically to receive time signals are available from outlets like Radio Shack. Called Time Cube and similar names, they are pre-tuned to stations WWV and WWVH.

You will need another clock for Ship's Time. While your GMT timepiece tells the same time wherever you are in the world, you set Ship's Time to the local time for the Time Zone in which the boat happens to be. On VOYAGER, the ship's clock is mounted on a primary bulkhead visible to all and maintains our local time according to longitude. Time zones, beginning with that centered on the Greenwich Meridian, are 15 degrees of longitude wide. Each 15 degrees of longitude you traverse in a westerly direction retards Ship's Time by one hour—you set the clock to one hour earlier. Heading east, you advance the clock by one hour as you change zones.

Many sailors keep another timepiece that remains set to their home time zone. Some find it comforting to have that piece of home on board, and it makes it easy to schedule communications with family and friends at times convenient for them.

Foul-Weather Gear

Everyone on board should have foul-weather clothing available, individually selected for fit and comfort. Warm and cold climates call for different sets of gear for best results. The gear should provide adequate warmth, have a hood that seals the jacket from water, and should be made of breathable fabric to prevent the accumulation of moisture inside while it's being worn.

Water Filters

Water that is taken on in foreign ports, or which has been stored in tanks for extended periods, poses health risks due to microorganism proliferation. This may or may not be associated with the "tank taste" often found with boat tank water. Protecting the water stores prevents illness and extends the water capacity by keeping it palatable.

It is smart practice to filter water before bringing it aboard, and then a second time with a filter in the galley faucet. These filters are available from marine outlets, and you should find out the filtering capacity so you can estimate how many spare cartridges you'll need to carry.

Safety Equipment

Most of the other gear I consider essential falls into the safety category. I have listed these items here because they are essential equipment, but I discuss them more fully in Chapter 6, *Safety Equipment and Safety Measures.*

Offshore Liferaft

An offshore liferaft heads the list of safety equipment to be carried aboard. The distinction of *offshore* is important, because rafts built for the open ocean have design features and survival packs that exceed specifications used for coastal rafts. The raft has to be big enough for the whole crew complement and its certificate of inspection should be current.

When purchasing the liferaft, or at the time of a routine certification servicing, take the opportunity to compile a complete list of all the survival equipment it contains. If you can witness the inflation test, it is very informative to see the raft blown up. You'll get a feel for what it looks like exactly, how you get into it, how much room it has, and how the survival kit is stowed. The manufacturer should provide you with precise instructions on how to properly deploy the raft. Remember, this would usually occur in very difficult circumstances, and you want to know the exact procedure.

Abandon Ship Bag

What you place in your abandon ship bag depends to a degree on what comes along with the liferaft. The bag should be equipped with items to supplement the raft's contents and enhance your ability to survive.

Storm Trysail

Used to replace the mainsail in heavy weather conditions, when the wind strength exceeds what the deeply-reefed main can safely handle, the storm try-sail has to be extremely strongly constructed. The sail should be built specifically for your boat, and should generally not be larger than one third of the square footage of the mainsail. It should be similar in area to the storm jib or storm staysail you will set forward, to help balance the boat when under storm canvas. Ideally, the trysail will have its own dedicated luff track on the mainmast.

While the trysail can be used to continue sailing a course, it is especially suitable for heaving-to. Also, when motor-sailing in rolling wave conditions, which can subject the mainsail to abuse, I dampen the motion by setting the trysail instead. When at anchor, the trysail can be rigged on the backstay to serve as a riding sail to decrease the boat's tendency to fishtail.

Storm Staysail

In heavy weather conditions, it's sound seamanship to move the sail plan away from the boat's ends and inward toward its center of gravity. As well as reducing stress on the rig, this helps reduce yawing, the one single motion that most contributes to seasickness. To achieve this on VOYAGER, I had the storm jib con-

verted to a hank-on storm staysail, which sets on a removable inner forestay.

Sea Anchor

In the event a storm builds to survival storm conditions, the sea anchor is a valuable piece of gear. It can be deployed by itself, or used to complement the strategy of heaving-to. The most dangerous position for a boat to be in is broadside to large waves, especially when they are breaking. Stability studies show that any boat will capsize if impacted by a breaking wave with a height of 60 percent of the boat's length. In storm conditions, the boat must be maintained in an attitude that will prevent her exposing her beam to the waves. When hove-to correctly, the boat's bow will lie at approximately 45 degrees to the wind and waves. This is the most favored angle for coping with storm conditions, and allows the crew to stay in the relative safety and sanity of the cabin. When conditions begin to overwhelm the hove-to vessel, a sea anchor can help maintain this proper orientation to the waves.

Radar

For years, I wasn't certain the term essential applied to radar. Having done many deliveries on boats not equipped with radar, I became used to sailing without it. When it is available, though, radar is like a warm blanket on a cold winter's night.

The ability to locate traffic or a squall beyond the field of vision, and track it for avoidance purposes, is very comforting to have, and a valuable aid to good seamanship. When sailing shorthanded, especially solo, the radar alarm provides indispensable protection when no eyes can be on deck.

Radar offers the best means to assure safety when navigating in fog, and is especially useful in waters north of about 35 degrees North Latitude, where fog often occurs.

Since I've been sailing offshore much more with students rather than on deliveries, my opinion on radar has changed significantly. The safety element has made it essential equipment on VOYAGER, and I must recommend it for other offshore passagemaking vessels as well.

When looking into the purchase of a radar, take into consideration these important factors: Higher power gives a better return blip in heavy weather or wet conditions, generally with better detail; Liquid Crystal Display (LCD) monitors are more efficient, thinner, and easier to see in daylight; Cathode Ray Tube (CRT) monitors have the best resolution.

Radar Reflector

A radar reflector makes the boat more visible to other vessels' radars. Reflectors largely fall into two categories. Octahedral devices, such as the Davis, the Blipper, the Echomax, and the Mobri, are effective but, depending on their orientation to the sending radar unit, the reflected signal has null regions. The multi-element, or Luneberg Lens reflectors are used by the Navy and ocean-going ships. They work well on sailboats too, but are considerably more expensive and much heavier.

VOYAGER uses an inexpensive Davis Echomaster, hoisted on a flag halyard. For the price and its negligible weight, the Echomaster is hard to beat. When at sea, do not rely on other vessels seeing you on radar. Often, their radars are either not switched on or not monitored. Take a proactive attitude, and always watch for other traffic with all means available to you.

Binoculars

Binoculars are necessary equipment for their wide variety of uses, including spotting other vessels at sea. Try them out before buying, as individual preference is important here. Look at objects at various distances, making sure both eyes come into focus. The boat's binoculars should be in a designated location in the cockpit at all times, sheltered from the elements yet available at a moment's notice.

Spare Parts and Gear

Spares for each of the vessel systems are essentials of course. Because the spares list for every single boat will be different, it's not possible to provide a comprehensive list here. You should carry spares that will enable you to effect repairs to any of your boat's essential systems if need be and make safe passage to port. In my book, *Ready to Sail*, I provide a list which you can use as a starting point and reference.

Safety Harnesses and Tethers

All crewmembers should wear safety harnesses with tethers while on deck in heavy weather, between dusk and dawn, and at any time conditions or the skipper dictate. It is very important that the tether be of a length that does not allow its wearer to travel past the lifelines.

Jacklines

Jacklines must be rigged so that they provide a strong, taut, tethering point along the deck. On VOYAGER, we rig them from the stem to the cockpit, alongside the mast and inside the shrouds. On center cockpit vessels, the jacklines should also extend from the aft cockpit to the pushpit. They are located inboard so that the crewperson clipped on with harness and tether can reach any area of the deck to do a job, but cannot fall past the lifelines. Strong webbing is preferable to rope. It lies flat on the deck, so it doesn't roll underfoot and cause you to lose your balance, and it rolls up so it can be stowed tidily when it's not in use.

Speedometer, Depthsounder, and Wind Instruments

The depthsounder is absolutely essential on any boat for obvious reasons and the speedometer, usually provided with a distance log function, is invaluable for navigation and as a help when trimming sails.

True wind speed and direction data take the guesswork out of calculating that important information. This is espe-cially valuable when sailing downwind, where apparent wind can be substan-tially less than true, and less experienced crewmembers can be fooled. It is also very helpful to know the strength of gusts. When gust velocities are far greater than the prevailing wind strengths, sails should be trimmed according to those higher velocities.

Medical Kit

The medical kit should permit treat-ment of a wide variety of medical condi-tions offshore. How extensive the kit should be, and the nature of the medica-tions and supplies it contains, will be de-termined by such factors as how long you intend to be at sea or cruising, the number of crew aboard, and whether anyone sails with pre-existing condi-tions. The key is to be able to deal effec-tively with illness and injury that can occur offshore where help may be inac-cessible or days away.

List medications with their name, usage, and dosage schedule, and include with the kit first aid manuals or books with instructions on how to handle illness and injuries at sea. Before your departure, prepare a list of emergency medical con-tact numbers to use in case a more serious condition arises. These contacts can in-clude recommendations by your own physician and dentist, or organizations listed in Chapter 12 of this book.

VOYAGER's kit, which has been in the making for quite some time, with addi-tions and deletions as new products are developed, is discussed in detail in Chapter 12, *Health and the Offshore*

Sailor. Preassembled kits are available, for example at www.firstaidpak.com.

Scuba Gear and Tank

I began taking along my scuba gear after spending the better part of one morning in the choppy waters of Hawk Channel off the coast of Florida cutting a lobster pot line away from my propeller. That task would have been much easier, faster, and safer with scuba gear. It's also handy to have for inspecting and cleaning the bottom and propeller, setting and breaking loose stubborn anchors, finding items dropped overboard at anchor, helping others by retrieving lost articles, and for having fun. Snorkeling gear is great to have for playing, but when work needs to be done, you can't beat scuba gear.

Compass

The oldest, and since it was developed, the most valuable instrument on any ship; we still need a reliable, accurate compass on board. It is especially useful when steering the boat in the dark. Steering to data provided by the autopilot or GPS is very difficult, because their readouts are time delayed. I rely on my compass at night, since it gives almost instantaneous feedback on course changes.

Searchlight

When approaching land, a powerful searchlight can be an invaluable aid in searching the waters for navigation aids or unlit obstructions. It's also useful for signaling other boats and to shine on your own sails to make your vessel more visible to another. Many models are available and use a variety of power sources: disposable batteries, rechargeable batteries, and the boat's 12-volt electrical system. A 12-volt outlet is a useful addition in the cockpit, and makes using the searchlight more convenient. On VOYAGER, we keep the searchlight in the cockpit from dusk until dawn, ready should it be needed.

Masthead Tricolor Light

This is the best system of running lights for more than the obvious reason. First, the running lights at the masthead make the boat more visible to others. Secondly, the combination of side and stern lights in the tricolor is far more efficient electrically than individual running lights, using only about one third of the power. For this reason, it makes sense to wire the masthead tricolor as the primary choice for running lights. Since bow and stern lights are probably already installed on your boat, put them on a separate toggle switch so you can activate them if the tricolor fails.

Bosun's Chair

A safe, simple, and reliable method of monitoring or tending to problems aloft must be available. This is included in the safety section because a trip up the mast may well prove to be safety related. Having the bosun's chair fulfills only part of this requirement; knowing how to use it takes care of the other. The safety of the person in it is a top priority, especially at sea where there can be considerable motion aloft. A more complete discussion appears in Chapter 22, *Going Aloft in the Bosun's Chair*.

Lifesling

The Lifesling, and the technique developed for deploying it, has been shown both by experimentation and time to be a superior method of recovering a person who has fallen overboard. It should be included in the safety gear of any offshore boat, and all crewmembers must be educated in its proper use.

Equipment Required by Law

When sailing in waters that fall under the jurisdiction of the United States, and patrolled by the U.S. Coast Guard or other civilian authorities, Federal Law requires certain equipment to be aboard. Among the required items are fire extinguishers, a whistle, a bell, and visual distress signals. Specific information appears in Chapter 6, *Safety Equipment and Safety Measures*.

All in Perspective

A lot of available equipment doesn't appear on this list of essentials. People have sailed the oceans for so long without the luxuries we consider essential on land, so we should be able to strike a balance at sea. The more stuff we put on our boats, the greater the expense we incur, the more effort we have to put into installation and maintenance, and the more likely is the chance of a breakdown. At sea, the insidious menace of corrosion sooner or later takes its toll on everything metallic.

I recall a delivery, from Bermuda to St. Thomas, U.S.V.I. of an Irwin 52 that was equipped with everything. The owner was on board, and became a little distracted when the generator wouldn't start. He wanted me to service it, but I declined due to other responsibilities like navigation, maintaining the other vital systems, and managing us in 30 knots of breeze from just forward of the beam.

He persisted in his own efforts, without much luck, and received a "knuckle-buster" laceration on his hand while using the ratchet on a stubborn bolt. He then refused to take his turn on watch that evening, so another mate took over that chore.

By the next morning his preoccupation with the generator prompted him to decline all further scheduled watch duties until the thing ran. I finally assented to tend to it (the fuel line was obstructed), but made note of the distraction we'd experienced. Once the generator started, the owner shut it down to conserve fuel, and we never used it again!

CHAPTER 6

SAFETY EQUIPMENT AND SAFETY MEASURES

At sailing seminars, safety at sea and heavy-weather tactics are usually the most popular topics. People are fascinated with these discussions, as they should be. What many find surprising is how much time we spend on the psychological aspects of safety and how to present the subject to our crews so as to enhance their well being offshore.

Safety involves more than just equipment. Every member of the crew must adopt safety as a mindset, and constantly pay attention to the ever-present possibility of injury, sickness, or untoward events. Certainly the captain must provide training and instruction in the proper use of equipment, from fire extinguishers to the liferaft, but he or she should also teach a healthy respect for the power of the sea and the consequences of its whims. We must all be aware that at sea, on a platform in constant motion, fatigue, dehydration, and other factors increase the chances of our becoming ill or being injured. Always in the back of our minds must be the thought to prevent injury and keep ourselves free of illness. The adage, "One hand for the

ship and one hand for the sailor" sums up the concept.

We're able to control a great many things at sea, but apart from choosing the proper route and time of departure, there is nothing we can do about the weather. The best we can do is to make our craft and crew ready for what the ocean dishes out before departure and once we're at sea, to monitor conditions and adjust as necessary. We want all on board to be confident that we, and the boat, are prepared to handle any situation.

SAFETY EQUIPMENT

Much safety gear is necessary to outfit an offshore vessel. Many items are prescribed by regulatory bodies, both governmental and non governmental. The International Sailing Federation (ISAF) publishes safety requirements for boats entering races of various types. The United States Coast Guard mandates that all vessels carry certain items of equipment. The requirements for vessels 26 to 65 feet in length, a range into which most offshore cruising boats fall, are listed below.

United States Coast Guard Required Safety Equipment

- Personal flotation devices—One Type I, II, or III for each person on board, and at least one Type IV throwable device.
- Fire extinguishers—At least three B-I type approved hand-portable fire extinguishers, or at least one B-I type plus one B-II type approved unit. If a fixed fire extinguishing system is installed in the machinery space, at least two B-I type approved-hand portable fire extinguishers, or at least one B-II approved unit.
- Whistle—Boats up to 39.4 feet (12 meters): any device capable of making an "efficient sound signal" audible at one half mile. Boats 39.4 to 65.7 feet (12 to 20 meters): device meeting technical specifications of Inland Rules Annex III, audible at one half mile. (250-2100 Hz audible at one half mile.)
- Bell—Boats up to 39.4 feet: any device capable of making an "efficient sound signal." Boats 39.4 to 65.7 feet: a bell meeting technical specifications of Inland Rules Annex II with a mouth diameter of at least 7.9 inches. (A bell or gong, or other device having similar sound characteristics shall produce a sound pressure level of not less than 110 dB at 1 meter.)
- Visual distress signals—Orange flag with black square-and disc (Day); and an S-O-S electric light (Night); or three orange smoke signals, hand held or floating (Day); or three red flares of handheld, meteor, or parachute type (Day/Night).

Note: Most offshore vessels have the three red flares of various configurations. These are usually supplied in flare kits at marine hardware stores.

Think of the above as minimum requirements, especially for fire extinguishers, flares, and personal flotation devices.

Vessels with gasoline engines must meet special requirements for ventilation and other fire-prevention purposes.

- Ventilation—At least two ventilator ducts fitted with cowls or their equivalent for the purpose of properly and efficiently ventilating the bilges of every engine and fuel tank compartment of boats constructed or decked over after April 25, 1940, using gasoline or other fuel having a flashpoint less than 110 degrees F. Boats built after July 31, 1981, must have operable power blowers.
- Backfire flame arrester—One approved device on each carburetor of all gasoline engines installed after April 25, 1940, except outboard motors.

Note that these regulations do not apply to vessels with diesel engines.

TABLE 6-1

Safety Gear on VOYAGER.

Liferaft	Abandon ship bag
EPIRB	Radar
Radar reflector	Collision mat
Man overboard pole	Lifesling
MOB alert system	Preventer system
Harness/tethers	Jacklines
Type I PFD's	Storm trysail
Storm jib	Inner forestay
Storm anchor	Bosun's chair
Spotlight	Cockpit outlet
Emergency knife	Binoculars
Night vision scope	Bolt cutters
Emergency tiller	Emergency steering system
Automatic strobe light	Lightning protection

The Offshore Liferaft

Every vessel traveling offshore must have the means to enable the crew to abandon ship if the vessel is sinking or catches fire. On offshore sailing yachts, this normally takes the form of an automatically inflating liferaft. Such a liferaft must be large enough to accommodate the entire crew. It must be manufactured to withstand the rigors of the offshore environment and it must contain survival gear to match that mission.

Liferafts designed for offshore have two independent inflatable tubes. A pre-mium offshore raft has an insulated floor, ballast bags to prevent the raft from capsizing, a drogue, a self-inflating and supportive canopy, a system for righting the raft, and an entrance ramp.

Offshore liferafts come equipped with basic survival gear and provisions. When you purchase your liferaft (or when you lease it if that's what you choose to do), make sure you obtain a list of its contents so that you have no questions about what you will need to bring in your abandon-ship bag to supplement them.

Below is a list of items typically packed in a well equipped liferaft. It is your responsibility to supplement this list with the abandon-ship bag to enhance your chances of survival and of rescue.

TABLE 6-2

Contents of an Offshore Liferaft.

Floating anchor	Canopy lithium lamp
Thermal blanket	Reflective canopy tape
Floating knife	Waterproof flashlight
Rescue quoit with line	Whistle
Bailer	Seasickness meds
Sponges	Rain catching gear
Repair kit	Rainwater collecting pouch
Instruction manual	Water
Survival instructions	Graduated cup
Parachute rockets	Food rations
Signaling mirror	Fishing kit
First aid kit	

Liferafts come with either a storage bag or a canister. Many captains position the raft on deck, while others prefer to stow it in a cockpit locker where it's protected from waves. A six-person liferaft will weigh in excess of 100 pounds. It needs to be very accessible if you are to deploy that amount of weight over the lifelines on a heaving vessel in as little as 15 seconds.

If the raft is to be stowed on deck, it needs to be in a canister, which is a hard-shell container that, at least in theory, protects the raft from ultraviolet rays and water. (I've seen liferafts that had been left on deck all the time leak because of heat exposure.) The canister can be fixed into position by a number of methods. Usually, it's lashed to designated strong points on the deck, such as pad eyes, in a location where people will not step on it—it is not to be used as a stool. A liferaft in a canister on deck is far more subject to degradation from heat extremes and water ingress than one in a valise bag stored in a locker.

The main lanyard should be accessible through the canister or bag. It's vital that this lanyard be made fast to the boat to prevent the raft from floating away after it has inflated. The liferaft is deployed to leeward, and is inflated by a hard tug on the lanyard. Once the abandon ship bag, the crew, and other items are loaded, the lanyard is cut with a knife so the raft can drift away from the stricken vessel. A deck-mounted canister may be fitted with a hydrostatic release mechanism that automatically deploys the raft from the canister if you are unable to get to the raft before the boat sinks. Read and un-derstand all instructions for liferaft deployment and inflation.

Abandon-Ship Bag

You prepare an abandon-ship bag to complement the gear and stores packed in the liferaft. Among the most useful items are communications equipment, medications, additional foodstuffs and water, and, most important of all, at least one EPIRB.

For the bag itself, you can use a sail or duffel bag, or you can purchase a purpose-designed and made abandon-ship bag from a marine hardware store. These specialized bags contain room for abandon-ship essentials, are constructed of tough, water-resistant fabric, and they float.

The first thing in the bag should be at least one EPIRB. This device, in my mind, has revolutionized offshore sailing, and is indispensable.

TABLE 6-3

Contents of an Abandon-Ship Bag.

EPIRB(s)	Foul weather gear/ Survival suits
Sun block	Life jackets
Water	Portable watermaker
Canned food	Satellite phone
Can opener	Waterproof VHF
Flares	Xyalume sticks
Spear gun	Hats
Medical kit	

Other items you'll want to take with you in the liferaft, but are not necessarily stowed in the abandon ship bag, include:

- Yacht papers
- Ship's Logbook
- Handheld VHF radio
- Binoculars
- Hand-bearing compass
- Passports in a sealed plastic bag.

Always keep these items near the abandon-ship bag, even though you may be using them during the passage. They should be readily available to be added to the bag on very short notice.

Satellite Telephone

Another revelation in our offshore world is the satellite telephone. I have opted for satellite-phone technology over Single Sideband Radio (SSB) for two main reasons. With the phone, I am able to download data, send and receive e-mails or simply place a phone call to reach anyone at any time. The external antenna is simple and inexpensive to mount, and in the event of a dismasting, the antenna is not on the backstay and going overboard with the rig. I could still contact shore bases if I needed to. The phone would also go into the liferaft if we ever had to abandon ship. Together with the EPIRB, it would give us an even better chance of rescue as we could place phone calls to summon help and even to coordinate it.

I have had excellent results with Iridium and Inmarsat phones, and poor results with the Globalstar phone.

If you have a satellite phone, maintain its battery at a high level of charge at all times, and have a dedicated waterproof container that you can place it in. Along with the satellite phone, take the handheld VHF radio into the raft. If you use the external antenna for communications, be certain to take the portable antenna with the phone in the abandon-ship bag. I place the portable into the bag automatically before departure.

Radar

Many of the vessels I've delivered offshore were not equipped with radar, and for years I didn't consider it a priority item. Over time, I've changed my opinion because I've learned how using its capabilities can make a boat safer. We use it to detect other vessels in any visibility and to determine their bearings, distance away, and headings. Radar is of great assistance when we navigate in fog, rain, or dark. It also helps us to identify prominent land features and to locate squalls so we can take action to avoid them. Radar can now be integrated with GPS and electronic navigation charts, providing fingertip accessibility to a range of useful information.

All radar units work basically the same way. The scanner is mounted on the upper part of the vessel, most often on the mast or on a stern post or radar arch. As it rotates, it sends out radio waves in a circular pattern usually set to cover the entire 360 degrees around the boat. An object in the path of those waves, be it a ship, a rainsquall, or even a flock of birds, reflects the signal back to the receiving unit which processes and displays it on a monitor screen. The screen might be a cathode ray tube but many compact devices today have LCD screens.

The basic radar system is comprised of the display unit, the scanner, and connecting cables. Integration with the GPS, navigation software, and even satellite radio (within range of the radio signals), makes information such as position, heading, waypoints, seawater temperature, and MOB available on one screen.

The other side of radar is to give your boat its best chance of being detected by the radar of another vessel. Fiberglass sailboats make small targets at sea, and it's essential to accentuate your radar image with a radar reflector. It's interesting to note that, given a certain reflective capability, the returning radar echo increases by the fourth power of the diameter of the reflector. A reflector twice as large as another will provide a 16-fold increase in the reflected radar signal.

Installation and operation of radar are discussed in detail in Chapter 11.

MAN OVERBOARD

A great fear, among non-sailors especially, is that of falling overboard. In fact, it's a rather rare occurrence, and with the use of appropriate procedures and gear, it can be reduced to being a non-occurrence.

Aboard VOYAGER we have a simple rule: *Nobody falls overboard, ever!*

However, even with such a rule in place, accidents can happen, so every vessel, ocean-going or not, should have procedures to follow and equipment to deploy, just in case.

Recovery Systems

Aboard every boat a system must be available, and the crew trained to use it, in case an injured or unconscious victim must be hoisted from the water. In studies of MOB situations, it has been demonstrated that getting the boat back to the victim is easier than actually retrieving someone from the water.

A life ring of some type should be on hand at the transom. The *Lifesling* is an excellent choice for this duty. It is very buoyant, has a 125-foot length of polypropylene line attached, and is effective in retrieval. The Lifesling can be thrown into the water, and the boat maneuvered to bring the Lifesling to the victim.

A Man Overboard Pole is most useful when high seas make it difficult to maintain a watch on the victim. The overboard pole is comprised of a long pole with an International Code Oscar (Man Overboard) flag at its top and a weight at its bottom. This should be accompanied by an automatic floating strobe light, which is thrown toward the victim to provide a light source in the immediate vicinity.

Jacklines

When working on deck at sea you must be able to move around the boat and remain tethered at all times. Jacklines rigged on deck make that possible by providing strong, taut anchors to which you can clip a safety-harness tether.

After using rope line for years, and losing my balance as it rolled under my feet, I recognized the obvious value of webbing for this use. Webbing jacklines lie flat on the deck, are able to withstand more than enough shock loading, and are easy to stow after the voyage.

When equipping your boat for jacklines, use only solid pad eyes or the equivalent and install them near the centerline of the deck. Securely lash or shackle the lines to the pad eyes and run them inside the shrouds and over the cabin top to points just before the cockpit. Terminate the forward end far enough away from the bow that tethers won't extend overboard. I prefer to secure the aft end just ahead of the cockpit and run separate lines from the cockpit to the stern. Run lines on both sides of the boat the same way. Don't rig jacklines outboard. The principle behind rigging jacklines inboard is to prevent a tethered person from falling over the lifelines and being suspended off the deck in a dangerous position.

The safety harness and tether should be strong enough to support the wearer's weight at the end of a free fall of six feet or so. Most are made from webbing material. The harness should be adjustable to fit properly no matter how much clothing is beneath it. A crotch strap ensures that an unconscious wearer doesn't slip out of the harness.

Many of the new inflatable PFDs come with an integrated harness. Sailors tolerate these well because the PFD is not bulky, and the rig is easy to put on.

It's important, though, to regularly check the bladder for leaks and the inflation system to ensure it is still functional. The tether may become your lifeline, so check it for tears, frayed stitching, or clues that ultraviolet light has caused deterioration of the webbing. The tether should be the shortest length that allows access to the boat's perimeters while tethered to the jacklines, and no more.

Test your system by attaching the tether to a jackline, and then extend the tether to its fullest. You should be able to reach the toerail area, but falling over the lifeline would be impossible.

There should be a method to release the tether from the harness should that become necessary. Snap hooks of adequate strength are commonly used. The hook should hold the tether to the harness very securely, but also be easily released when necessary.

The captain must make the rules of harness use clear during the pre-sail briefing, and those rules have to be taken seriously. As a minimum requirement, harnesses should be worn whenever the wind reaches gale force, in rough seas, in fog, and from dusk until dawn. I have also asked crewmembers, depending on their experience, to hook in whenever they leave the cockpit area under any conditions. Children must certainly wear life jackets and harnesses when on deck.

Safety Line

When in 2003 I sailed VOYAGER solo from Tortola to Chesapeake Bay, I trailed a safety line so that, if I had fallen overboard,

I would have something to grab (Figure 6-1). I rigged a trip line which, when my weight came on the safety line was configured within the cockpit to 1) pull the engine shut-off knob and 2) disable the autopilot so that the boat would round up and lose her forward motion.

Trailing a line behind a vessel is a tactic utilized most often by solo sailors or by short-handed crews. In the latter case, the trip device could also be set up so that it would trigger a number of sound alarms, from ringing a bell to turning on an electrical sound device.

To make a safety line, you'll need:

- About 200 feet of ½-inch, yellow polypropylene line (i.e., floating line)
- A Styrofoam ball float like those lobstermen use to mark their traps
- At least two 5-foot lengths of ⁵⁄₁₆-inch or ⅜-inch elastic shock cord with a plastic hook at one end
- One or two ½-inch blocks on lanyards.

FIGURE 6-1

A safety line triggers several actions in the cockpit.

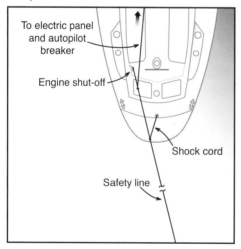

To electric panel and autopilot breaker

Engine shut-off

Shock cord

Safety line

Tie half hitches every six feet or so along the entire length of the buoyant safety line. These will give anyone holding onto it a better grip.

Attach the Styrofoam float to mark the outboard end of the line.

Two feet from the inboard terminal of the line, attach a shock cord to a knotted loop. The shock cord absorbs the normal drag on the trip line, and leaves the remainder of the line slack in the cockpit.

The cockpit end of the trip line is then connected to smaller lines. Each of these lines will perform a separate action, such as pull the engine stop, disengage the autopilot, or trigger an alarm. Setting up these operations requires some thought and it will probably take several tries to get all the lines to exert the necessary pull. You'll usually need the blocks to align the smaller lines so they pull in the desired direction.

Rigging the engine shut-off and disengaging the clutch on a windvane are actually easy. Shutting down an electrical autopilot takes a bit more thought and ingenuity. Unless the device is fitted with a pull knob, the usual approach is to run the secondary line to a toggle switch installed in the autopilot power line. The autopilot is shut off when the safety line opens the switch.

In practice, the added drag of a person's weight on the trip line overpowers the shock cord. The load on the line then goes on to the inboard end, and in turn onto the secondary lines which then activate the man-overboard responses.

While the task of reaching the boat and climbing aboard without help remains a daunting one, the safety line at least gives you a chance at surviving. The best course of action is always to avoid going overboard in the first place.

Electronic Overboard Alert

Recent developments have provided us with electronic crew monitoring systems in which the crew on deck wear sending units and a receiver on board monitors their signals. If a transmitter gets wet, its signal changes and the receiver alerts others on board to the emergency by sounding an alarm loud enough to awaken from sleep.

Emerald Marine Products Corporation, of Seattle, Washington, makes such a product, the Alert 2 Man-Overboard Alarm device.

All deck personnel carry a water-activated radio transmitter. A receiver unit on board "howls like mad" if activated to alert the crew of the overboard situation. The device also has the capability to shut down the engine and mark a position on the GPS.

These devices are ideal for night watches and during heavy weather conditions. Alert 2 is standard equipment on VOYAGER, and I also bring it with me on any vessel I take on delivery.

STORM SAILS

Storm sails are an important part of the safety equipment inventory. In the event that the weather deteriorates to the point where you have storm-force winds, you must have sails on board able to cope with the conditions. To manage

the boat, you have to match the sail area you set to the wind conditions. You must have a procedure in place by which, at appropriate times, you furl or remove the working sails and replace them with the storm sails.

I discussed the storm jib, staysail, and trysail in Chapter 5, *Offshore Essentials: Gear and Equipment*, where I stressed the need for these sails to be cut very flat and to have the strength to withstand heavy winds. A principle to follow when using storm sails is to bring their centers of effort, through which the force of the wind acts on the boat, inward toward the main mast. This decreases the amplitude of yaw and roll motions, and reduces stress on the hull and rigging.

Two-masters—yawls, ketches, and schooners—carry a variety of sails, and it's relatively easy to manipulate the sail plan to suit storm conditions. Sloops, being single masted, aren't so flexible. Most ocean sailors who sail single-masted vessels prefer the cutter rig with its two headsails. Sometimes they achieve a similar arrangement by adding a removable inner forestay on which to set a storm staysail. Such a stay can also control mast pumping and, when the wind and point of sail are favorable, accommodate larger staysails.

Adding an Inner Forestay

Ideally, an inner forestay will be parallel with the headstay. Where exactly it will fit best depends on several factors from the design of the mast to the layout of the deck and any support structure beneath it. Before you embark on a project like this, I recommend you consult with a professional rigger and, if possible, the original builder of the boat or the spar.

If the inner stay attaches to the mast more than about three feet below the headstay, you may need to fit running backstays to counter the load on the inner stay which will tend to bow the mast forward. Running backs are not normally necessary if the stay attaches higher up the mast.

Attaching the stay to the mast, sometimes the most difficult part of the job, can be done in one of several ways: to a fitting welded to the mast, to a strap fastened to the mast with rivets or machine screws, or to a special box fastened into the mast. For your best solution, consult with the mast's manufacturer. On VOYAGER, a stem ball swaged to the stay locks into a special fitting inserted into the mast.

Wire for the inner forestay is usually two sizes smaller than the primary forestay, since it is not subjected to the same loads.

The attachment of the inner forestay to the deck has to be unquestionably strong. This can be accomplished in several ways, but essentially the stay attaches to a chain plate on deck that is either integral with a brace extending through the deck, or is bolted to such a brace below. This brace is in turn connected, by whatever means is most convenient, to a main structural element such as a bulkhead or the boat's internal framing system. How this last link is made will depend to some extent on the boat's interior layout.

The deck end of the stay should terminate in a swaged-on toggle which connects via a turnbuckle to another toggle attached to the deck fitting. All hardware should be corrosion-resistant, type-316 stainless steel.

If the inner forestay is removable, you can detach it when it's not needed, which will make tacking the jib much easier. You can accomplish this in a number of ways. Using a quick-release pin instead of the normal clevis pin in the deck fitting is an easy and relatively inexpensive solution. You'll need a turnbuckle on the stay so that you can slacken it enough to pull out the pin. A better way is to incorporate a forestay release lever such as that manufactured by ABI.

The ABI forestay release lever, which incorporates a turnbuckle, is an extremely strong device and very easy to operate. The clevis pin attaches to a deck plate, while the other end is swaged to the stay. This is the system used on VOYAGER, and I've used it on other boats in the past.

You'll need a halyard for your staysails, and the requisite hardware should be installed in conjunction with the stay's attachment to the mast.

If the stay is rigged to be permanent, you may fit roller reefing or use hanked-on sails. The most versatile arrangement

FIGURE 6-2
The ABI forestay release lever. *Courtesy of ABI*

is a removable stay used in conjunction with a hanked-on staysail or storm staysail. You can then remove the inner forestay, when sailing downwind with a spinnaker or when tacking upwind for example, and set it up when you wish to increase drive with a staysail or when you need to set the storm sail.

Storm jibs and staysails can also be constructed with a wire luff that allows the sail to be hoisted on a jib halyard independently of a stay. The sail can be tacked to the stem fitting or to an eye bolt installed on the deck. This is a very reasonable option for the storm jib, because the deck remains clear when the sail is not being used. Because a sail with a built-in wire luff can be difficult to hoist, setting one in higher wind conditions is usually a two-person job.

Storm Trysail

The storm trysail should be considered top priority equipment on offshore vessels. Its use isn't restricted solely to heavy weather conditions; it can be useful in other situations as well. In light air, when the boat is rolling in a seaway, you can strike and flake the mainsail and set the trysail to act as a stabilizer. By doing this, you'll protect the mainsail from wear, and stop the noise it makes as it slats back and forth. You can also use the trysail as a riding sail at anchor by setting it up the backstay and sheeting it forward.

When designing your storm trysail, the first thing to determine is the hoist height of the sail. The other dimensions and the length of the track needed on the mast follow from that. Factor in the stack height of the mainsail after it's lowered and secured to the boom, even though, in storm conditions, it's best to remove the mainsail from the boom completely. A rule of thumb is that the trysail luff should not be longer than one third the length of the mainsail luff.

The trysail is built to be very sturdy, and is usually made with heavier sailcloth, more stitching, and more reinforcement than the mainsail. It is also designed to be flatter, with far less draft. Its sheets, which should be permanently attached, run aft through blocks on either quarter, and then to the cockpit winches.

The storm trysail track is normally mounted on the port side of the mast, adjacent to the mainsail track. This is because boats have traditionally been designed with galleys on the port side. When hove-to, we prefer to be on starboard tack so that if hot liquids on the stove spill, they go toward the leeward side, away from the cook. Being on starboard also makes us the right-of-way vessel.

The track is made of ⅝-, ⅞-, or 1-inch stainless-steel stock. It's usually mounted with stainless-steel machine screws in holes that have been drilled into the mast and tapped. The screws should be only long enough to penetrate the track and mast wall, and not invade the mast interior. Sometimes, pop rivets can be used instead of machine screws, but that choice depends on factors that include your boat's size and the expected load on the track. It would be helpful to obtain advice on this from the spar's builder.

Whether rivets or screws are used, you should apply a product such as Anti-Seize thread lubricant to limit corrosion between the dissimilar metals.

By extending the trysail track downward to near deck level, you can have the sail bent on, protected in its sail bag, ready to be set when needed. You can do this at the start of a passage or when the forecast indicates rough weather is coming.

When the trysail is hoisted on the main halyard, the extended distance from sail head to masthead leads to a lot of halyard slapping against the mast. This causes more noise in a blow, when the decibel level is already high, and leads to chafe on the halyard and damage to the spar. To eliminate this problem, run a separate halyard for the trysail. Mount a cheek block onto the mast, aligned precisely with the trysail track. Fasten it in the same fashion as you did the trysail track, which would usually be with machine screws into threaded holes. Lead the halyard

through the check block and secure it at the base of the mast so it can be deployed quickly. Since this halyard will be external, to protect it from unnecessary exposure to the elements, I recommend running a messenger line through the cheek block with both ends secured at the foot of the mast. When you are preparing for departure on a passage, use the messenger to pull the halyard through the block, ready for use.

The trysail is loose footed. When heaving-to, the clew is led and secured to a point on the leeward quarter rail. The object is to provide the boat with some windward impetus to balance the forces driving it to leeward. Because the boat best manages heavy weather when taking the wind and waves from approximately 45 degrees aft of the bow, this is the position we strive to achieve when hove-to. While the boat will weave about, bearing off a few degrees and then heading up, it will maintain a safe orientation to the storm.

FIGURE 6-3

Storm Trysail and Storm Staysail Deployed.

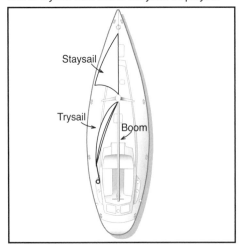

STORM MANAGEMENT

Sea Anchors and Drogues

Sailors may differ in their opinions about the best use of sea anchors, but most agree that they're valuable assets. In my view, the parachute type of sea anchor is a valuable addition to the storm-management arsenal. See Chapter 23, *Safety Procedures, Tactics, and Protocols* for an extensive discussion of storm management and the use of the parachute sea anchor.

To safely and effectively deploy a sea anchor, you need specialized gear which is vital to the anchor's performance. While you can obtain these items separately, I recommend you discuss your needs with the manufacturer, who will be able to package the sea anchor along with all the ancillary equipment sized to suit your boat. It is also more cost effective to get all of the gear at one time than attempting to piecemeal it together.

I believe that the most effective way to manage a boat in storm conditions is to reduce sail area appropriately and have able people at the helm to guide the boat's course. This is not always possible, though, and at some point it becomes advisable to let the boat handle the conditions while the crew takes shelter in the relative calm below decks.

In this case, the options are to heave-to or to deploy the sea anchor directly. The objective of either maneuver is to get the vessel to lie with its bow approximately 45 degrees to the wind and waves. In practice, the angle varies between 30 degrees and about 55 degrees as the boat reacts to the forces acting on it. The boat makes leeway, creating a slick in its wake that calms the approaching waves somewhat. Lying in this attitude, the boat is able to withstand tremendous forces, while the crew, safe below, takes nourishment, gets warm, and attempts to rest during the storm.

If you are hove-to, there may come a time when the boat falls off the wind, begins to make headway and sails out of its protective slick of calmer water. If adjusting the helm more to windward or

adding a touch of power to the trysail fails to add weather helm, it might be time to set the sea anchor to help maintain the proper attitude to the waves.

Running Off

Another way to handle storm conditions is to turn the boat and run before the wind and seas. A danger in this tactic is that the boat might attain excessive speed and bury its bow into a wave, possibly with disastrous consequences. While I wouldn't run with a storm once the boat became difficult to handle, those who use this tactic can gain some control by deploying a storm drogue on a long length of anchor line from the stern. This has the effect of slowing the boat and thus decreasing the chances of burying the bow.

A thorough discussion of storm tactics appears in Chapter 23 *Safety Tactics, Protocols, and Procedures.*

ADDITIONAL SAFETY MEASURES

Boom Preventer

The role of the boom preventer (Figure 6-4) is to make a catastrophic swing of the boom across the cockpit impossible. It's good practice to use a preventer as standard procedure when offshore, no matter the point of sail.

The preventer should be made with stout three-strand nylon line, at least ⅝-inch in diameter. So that the preventer tail needn't be uncleated from one side of the boat and re-led to the opposite side after a tack or jibe, use two lines, one on either side of the boat.

I will caution that the connection of the preventer to the boom must be very strong. My preferred way of achieving this, when possible, is to secure the preventer by tying it directly to the boom with a bowline or other suitable knot or hitch. This is only possible if the mainsail is loose-footed or is attached to the boom with slides. This is far more reliable than tying it to a boom bail. Also, don't tie the preventer to the boom end; fasten it at least a foot forward of the boom end.

Rather than attaching the preventer at a single point on the boom, you can create a bridle arrangement, with attachments near the end of the boom and just forward of its mid point. The preventer can actually be one continuous line, secured at its midpoint to the boom or to the bridle. No matter how they are attached to the boom, the preventer tails are led forward of the beam to blocks attached to the toerails, to cleats, or to some other secure point. From those blocks, lead the tails aft to the cockpit, where the leeward tail can be tensioned and secured to a cleat.

Don't run the leeward preventer tail to the primary winch because you'll be using that for the jib sheet. Don't lead it across the cockpit to use the opposite side primary either, because of the congestion it causes there. The preventer need only be taken to a cleat and snugged up manually; there's no need to winch it super tight.

Lightning Protection

There is no more helpless feeling than sailing into a thunderstorm with lightning bolts dancing all around your boat. You might be reassured, though, if prior to sailing you had installed a lightning rod, a Lightning Static Dissipator, or both, and had grounded the mast and other metal objects to the keel.

Turbulence in the atmosphere, created when cold and warm air masses meet, causes a difference in electrical charge to build up between the earth's surface and clouds aloft. When this polarity deepens and the disparity between positive charges aloft and negative charges at the surface creates a large enough voltage differential, the air becomes ionized leading to the release of the enormous electrical discharge we call lightning.

One way to protect a boat from this huge voltage is to attempt to prevent any static charge from building up on it.

FIGURE 6-4
Boom Preventer.

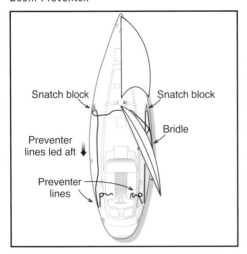

That is what the Lightning Static Dissipator (LSD) is designed to do. Mounted on the masthead, the LSD sheds electrons from the mast into the atmosphere, preventing a potential buildup. Alternatively, we must create a low resistance path for the strike to follow through the boat.

If lightning does strike a boat, it usually hits the masthead, and the bolt travels through whatever conductive material it encounters. This could be the stays or shrouds, leading to chain plates. It could also find its way through metallic elements to electrical wiring, electronic instruments, or to through-hull fittings. The danger lies in the damage that results to these vital components. To avoid such damage, we have to provide a direct pathway from masthead to ground, bypassing important vessel structures and equipment.

Start at the top by mounting a lightning rod at the masthead, making it at least six inches higher than any other structure on the boat, including the radio antenna. The rod must be pointed at its end to avoid the accumulation of electrons there.

An aluminum mast will adequately conduct the bolt downward. A wooden mast needs a #4 AWG copper cable connected to the rod to conduct the strike down the mast.

From the mast step, the pulse must be transmitted directly to ground. A metal hull itself can be the ground. A metal keel, centerboard, or dagger board makes suitable primary ground if not coated with an insulator such as fiberglass or epoxy. If the boat has no metal components of such a size in direct contact with the water, the alternative is to fit the hull with a ground plate at least one square foot in area. It must be of corrosion-resistant metal, preferably copper, bronze, or monel.

In addition to the central conductor, consider all other potential pathways. Using copper cables of at least #6 AWG, connect the chain plates and any other possible pathway to ground. Make the cable runs as straight as possible to provide a pathway of least resistance.

Protect the engine, also, by connecting it, again with #6 AWG copper cables, directly to the external ground. This will reduce the chances of a strike contacting the engine and traveling to the propeller shaft and stern tube, which could put the boat at risk.

The multimeter, an important component of the seagoing tool box, is useful for checking the connection of the boat's various fittings to ground, to ensure the lightning charge can follow the route we want it to take. Ideally, electrical impulses from metallic objects such as the engine, chain plates, pulpit or pushpit, and so on, will be conducted directly and unimpeded to ground. Test each path using the multimeter.

Select the ohmmeter function of the multimeter, connect one electrode to ground, and the other electrode to the test object. To verify that the starboard shrouds are grounded, for example, touch one probe to ground and the other to the shroud or chainplate. In a perfectly grounded system, the reading on the ohms scale is zero, or close to it, meaning that an electrical charge would pass from the shroud to ground with minimal resistance. A higher reading indicates some degree of impedance, in which case lightning might seek an alternative path which could result in damage to the vessel.

Diagram of Through-hull Locations

On a diagram of the hull, mark the locations of all seacocks and through-hull fittings. You should find such a diagram in the boat's owner's manual. Make any additions necessary, then put the diagram in a place where you can easily access it and refer to it in case you discover water leaking into the boat. Make sure all crewmembers know where the diagram is and that they can identify from it where all these important fixtures are located in the boat. A schematic for VOYAGER appears in Appendix 10.

When you go through the boat confirming the locations of through-hulls for marking them on the drawing, note also their sizes. Obtain a supply of softwood bungs, usually available at marine hardware stores, and attach one of an appropriate size alongside each through-hull fitting. In the event a fitting fails, you can hammer the bung into it to staunch the flow of water.

Secure the Cabin

When fitting out your boat for offshore work, make sure that every drawer, cabinet door, or any other storage access can be dogged down in rough conditions. Objects flying out of improperly secured lockers can create a hazard to crew, not to mention a mess when they end up on a wet cabin sole. Marine hardware stores stock a variety of latches designed for this purpose.

Floorboards, too, can become dangerous flying objects in a knockdown. Any that you don't have to lift to gain access to stores or equipment should be screwed down. Those that you do need to open when underway should be equipped with suitable locking catches. Make sure that you retain quick access to the bilge sump, bilge pumps, and any other essential equipment.

Some cooking stoves don't lock into their gimbals and can jump out in a knockdown. Make sure you can prevent that from happening.

In storm conditions, the boat should be made as waterproof as possible. Steps to take include fitting a latch on the companionway slide that can be operated from inside and outside, and providing for vents, cockpit speakers, and all ports and hatches to be sealed against seawater.

To understand the scope of the preventive measures you need to take, envision what would happen below if the boat were rolled through 360 degrees. Your goal is to prevent gear from coming loose and water from coming in.

Miscellaneous Safety Equipment

Other safety equipment, including binoculars, night-vision scope, heavy bolt cutters, searchlight, bosun's chair, and emergency knife are self-explanatory as to their purpose. They are all necessary items to have on board.

CHAPTER 7

SAILS AND SAIL REPAIR

A sailboat without its sails is nothing more than a powerboat. Their lift generates its motive power, and they have to withstand hours, days and even weeks of punishment in a sometimes brutal environment. It's only common sense, therefore, to pay special attention to ensure that they're always in the best possible condition and ready for sea duty. In this chapter I provide some basic guidelines on sail construction and maintenance to help you ensure that your sails are built to high standards and that you can keep them in good condition

THE OFFSHORE SAIL INVENTORY

Your sails drive your boat and are of paramount importance to your success when ocean passagemaking. Before sailing offshore, and especially if you intend to cruise extensively, take stock of your sail inventory, paying particular attention to the quality of the sails and their cut.

If the vessel will be used for extended cruising and subjected to the elements for long periods of time, the sails should be made of heavier material than is used for inshore sailing. Triple stitching of the main is a safety feature, and it should have three reef points.

When assessing your sails and making decisions about their condition and whether you need new or different ones, consult with a sailmaker who has knowledge of and experience with cruising sails. Many sailmakers who focus on racing have expertise, but perhaps not in making the types of sails you need. Racing sails are made for a different purpose than cruising sails, and often with different materials and techniques. Seek out a sailmaker who understands the benefits of hand-stitching fittings, such as sail slides, jib hanks, and reef points, and whose loft is capable of such handwork. Because you'll want your sailmaker to be your consultant throughout the outfitting process, and afterward for questions, suggestions, and additions, he or she should also be someone with whom you feel comfortable working.

Ideally, your sailmaker should join you on your boat for a sea trial, so he can get a feel for its dynamics, look at your current sails, see how they work on the boat and offer advice on how to get the best performance out of them. Be sure to describe your plans for the boat, your sailing style, and the cruising grounds you intend to visit. At the same time, the sailmaker should measure the boat to ensure that any new sails will be built to the right dimensions. If the current sails are a good fit, have him measure them, too, so you'll have an accurate record in case you need to make changes in dimensions or cut. For future reference, keep the dimensions in the Ship's Logbook, if possible with a copy of the boat's original sail plan or a reasonable sketch of it.

Dacron remains the best fabric for most offshore cruising sails. It's extremely durable, relatively easy to cut and sew, and it maintains its shape for years with proper care. Dacron can be flaked on the boom without damaging the fabric, whereas laminated sails must either be removed from the boom or furled. Older sails may need to be recut, since Dacron stretches a little with age. This stretching can cause more draft in the sail, making it fuller and more powerful, which increases weather helm and diminishes pointing ability. If your sailmaker is building a new sail, make sure he cuts it to allow for this stretch. Offshore sails should be triple-stitched with UV-resistant thread. The seams should be placed widely apart to allow room for restitching during repairs. A zigzag pattern gives the stitching greater surface area and has more integrity when the cloth edges are folded over before stitching.

High-tension sail areas like the head, clew, tack and reef cringles should be triple-stitched using several layers of fabric. These areas are usually reinforced with multiple overlapping pieces of fabric radiating from them to better distribute the loads across the sail. The corners of the sail are prone to chafe and should have leather chafe guards sewn in. Tears at hardware installation points often indicate a problem with the way the sail is set. Reef points tearing out indicate the tack and clew were not sufficiently taut to support the center points. Tears at jib hanks could mean the luff was not sufficiently tensioned. Try to set your sails in a way that minimizes the loading or chafe in any one spot.

The Mainsail

As the most important sail on the boat, the mainsail should be constructed to be durable and functional. The principal factor that determines how it is built and how it functions is whether it is configured as a traditional sail or a furling sail.

A traditional mainsail is the type that is normally stowed flaked on the boom and hoisted each time it's used. A furling mainsail is stowed on a roller furler, usually inside the mast but sometimes just aft of the mast. Furling systems that roll the sail inside the boom also exist but are less common.

Traditional mainsails are more efficient than their counterparts that furl into or behind the mast. They have battens that permit and control roach, which adds area to the top of the sail where more wind is usually available. Since most sailing is done in 15 knots of breeze or less, it makes sense to take advantage of the improved performance offered by a roached mainsail. Standard battens allow for this additional sail area, are relatively inexpensive, and permit the sail to be folded easily when it's taken off the boom.

While it's more expensive than a sail with standard battens, a fully-battened mainsail maintains its shape even better, resists luffing, and is easier to flake on the boom. The battens must be removed for folding the sail when it's taken off the boat.

The main disadvantages of full-battens are a tendency to chafe along the forward end of the batten and to bind against the mast track while being hoisted and lowered. These problems can be diminished by installing a fitting called an end receptacle at the luff end of the batten.

The foot of the mainsail is usually loose or it's attached by slides to a track on the boom. Both of these styles are preferable to a boltrope along the foot that slides into a slot in the boom. A sail attached in this way is subject to chafe, is prone to tearing, and is difficult to remove from the boom. Sail slides should be attached to the sail with webbing and hand sewn. Cringles for intermediate reefing ties should be high quality rings hand-sewn into the sail, not pressed grommets.

In-Mast Furling

I have always been leery of furling mainsails when I find them on yachts I am delivering, and I reduce sail cautiously for fear the mechanism could fail. New technology, though, has made furling systems more dependable. Although furling mains are easier to handle, they're smaller and less powerful than traditional mains. They must be cut with a straight or hollow leech, giving up the roach that would give them more power high up.

Masts with internal furling systems are larger in section and heavier than standard equipment so they offer more windage and weight aloft. They are also noisier in a breeze. It's usually not possible to add a storm trysail track to the furling mast. The sail can only have minimal reinforcement at the corners to allow for efficient furling. It doesn't have reefing points, so if the furler fails, the sail cannot be reefed.

Reefing

Single-line reefing is becoming more popular on conventional mainsails. When efficiently rigged, such a system allows one person to quickly reef the sail without leaving the cockpit.

To rig a single-line system, begin at the reefing cringle in the sail's leech. Feed the reefing line through the cringle and tie it to the boom with a bowline. Lead the other end through the boom toward the mast, then upward through the cringle (preferably through an eye on a strap). From the luff cringle lead the line downward to a block at the base of the mast and thence to the cockpit. The line should go through a clutch near a cockpit winch.

The procedure when reefing is to lower the sail on the halyard, bring in the reefing line until the cringles fore and aft are secured against the boom, and then raise the halyard to flatten the sail appropriately.

Boom Vang

A vang on the main boom gives you an extra control with which to adjust the shape of the mainsail. By pulling down on the boom, you can close the leech and reduce twist in the mainsail, which is especially useful when sailing off the wind.

A traditional boom vang is a simple block and tackle arrangement usually made up with a fiddle block at the boom end and another fiddle block with a becket and a cam cleat at the other end. This typically provides 4:1 purchase, making control easy. Modern rod or power vangs contain a spring mechanism which pushes the boom upward when the vang is eased. Because it supports the boom, this type of vang also acts as a topping lift. This makes it a good choice if you are fitting out, because you can eliminate the topping lift and the chafe it causes on the mainsail. These vangs are typically made of anodized aluminum, are very sturdy, and can be disassembled for maintenance.

Inspect your vang once in a while to make sure it's in full working order. With a traditional vang, check each segment of line for chafe and the blocks for corrosion, damage, or wear. A rod vang should be tested to ensure that it will support the boom and can also exert downward force. The weakest point of most boom vangs is the attachment point at either end. Pay special attention to the bail on the boom, which can become loose, and the fiddle blocks, which can become weakened with age.

The Headsails

Working Sails

Offshore jibs should be constructed as robustly as their mainsail counterparts. Most boats are equipped with roller furling on the working jib, and sometimes on the secondary or storm jibs as well. Most working jibs are 120 to 140 percent of the fore triangle in area on sloops, and 100 to 110 percent on cutter-rigged boats. Again, the specific dimensions should be arrived at in consultation with your sailmaker, based on your boat's characteristics and your sailing objectives.

The headsail should be constructed for strength and in a way that it will maintain its shape when partially furled. The roller-furling working jib should be effective in a wide range of winds, from a light breeze of six to eight knots to just upwards of 35 knots. Its versatility and effectiveness can be optimized with a padded luff, which reduces draft as the sail is furled. Without this padding, the sail tends to have deeper draft when furled and the headstay sags more. The boat heels more, suffers more leeway, and it becomes more difficult to balance the sail plan. The sail should have cover strips sewn along the leech and the foot to protect it from UV light when it's furled.

Light-Air Headsails

Every offshore sailing vessel should have a light-air headsail in its inventory. Such a sail is invaluable in breezes of four to eight knots, allowing you to make steady progress without having to rely on the engine. Fuel savings can be significant, and the sailing, in light air and usually accompanied by a low sea state, can be a wonderful experience. A variety of sails, from traditional spinnakers to asymmetrical spinnakers and reacher-drifter types, offer light-air choices to suit sailors of any ability or inclination.

Symmetrical spinnakers that have long been essential equipment on racing boats are rarely seen on other offshore boats. These powerful sails are used when reaching or running, with the wind anywhere from on the beam to dead aft. They set on a spinnaker pole which is controlled with a topping lift, a downhaul, and after guys. They must be jibed, not tacked, and are most easily set and doused with the aid of a snuffer.

Spinnaker sheets are led both sides of the boat, outside all the standing rigging and lifelines, to blocks at the quarters, from where they lead to the cockpit winches for easy control. The sail is hoisted on a dedicated halyard, which is configured at the masthead with a swivel to prevent chafe as it rotates with the sail.

Asymmetrical, or cruising, spinnakers are more popular on non-racing offshore boats. One reason is that they don't require a pole but tack to the stem. A line attached to the sail's tack runs through a block attached to the boat's stem as far forward as possible, and with it the height of the sail can be adjusted up or down, replacing the function of the pole with traditional spinnakers. The tack is pulled down with the wind near the beam, and progressively let out as the wind moves aft. Sheets are run similarly to those of symmetrical spinnakers. When jibing, the sail is usually doused with the snuffer, and then hoisted on the other side after the jibe is completed.

The reacher-drifter is a fuller, lightweight version of a large genoa, but cut flatter than a spinnaker. It is very versatile and can be used on virtually all points of sail in light air conditions. It needs no special hardware and no snuffer, and is a good option for sailors who don't want to deal with spinnakers.

In downwind sailing, jibs and genoas often benefit from being poled out. For this purpose it is always a good idea to carry a whisker pole or even a spinnaker pole when sailing offshore.

Storm Sails

Storm sails are an essential part of the offshore sailboat's wardrobe.

Storm Jib or Staysail

The storm staysail is usually about 25 percent of the fore triangle in area. It is constructed of 8- to 10-ounce Dacron and the hardware should be hand sewn into the sail. The clew should be cut high to clear waves, and must clear the mast when the boat is hove-to. An option for boats that cannot have an inner forestay is a storm jib that is hoisted over the furled jib. While workable, this means that the working jib is not removed which adds weight aloft and reduces the boat's stability. It can also be difficult to hoist over the furled jib.

An ideal storm sail is fully-hanked, and fitted to an inner forestay (making it a staysail). This allows the primary jib to be removed completely. If not removed, it should be furled tightly and the furling drum fixed so that it cannot rotate and allow the sail to unfurl.

Another option for the storm jib is one constructed with the luff on a wire that serves as a stay. At the tack fitting there is either a thimble or an eye which can be shackled to a deck fitting, and at the head is an eye to which the halyard attaches. Sails on wire luffs are difficult to hoist in high winds because the sail tends to be blown to leeward while it's being raised. The task usually requires two crewmembers.

A storm staysail, preferably hanked onto an inner forestay, is actually a better storm option than a storm jib. It brings the sail plan's center of effort aft from the bow, making it easier to balance the boat while also reducing the loads on the spar and running rigging. A storm staysail is constructed with the same design specifications as a storm jib, and is built from the same heavy fabric.

Storm Trysail

A trysail is standard equipment on any vessel that might encounter heavy weather. This specially-built sail is constructed of 10-oz Dacron with extra stitching, and is designed to be "bullet proof." Its area is designed in conjunction with that of the storm headsail so that the boat will be balanced when both sails are set.

The trysail is hoisted on its own mast track, ideally located on the side of the mast designated to be to leeward in storm conditions. If the galley is on the port side, the trysail would ideally also be on the port side so that any spill on the stove would splash to leeward and away from the cook. This arrangement has the additional benefit of putting the boat on starboard tack when hove-to.

The mast track must be very securely fastened. On VOYAGER, I used one-inch wide sections, fastened with machine screws into holes drilled and tapped into the mast.

Sheets should be permanently fastened to both sides of the trysail, coiled neatly in the sail bag for ease in deployment.

BASIC SAIL CARE

Make yourself familiar with every sail in your inventory. Before any voyage, check each one carefully and analyze possible wear or failure points. Inspect them carefully for stitching that's loose or worn, or where the thread holes have elongated in the fabric. Even the smallest tear requires a repair before you sail. By getting to know your sails, you'll be able to protect them, prevent needless damage, and prolong their usefulness by using appropriate trim and halyard tension.

Preventive Maintenance

Well before your departure date if you are planning a voyage, or at least after every season of sailing, examine your sails very closely for signs of wear and tear. To do this properly, you have to remove the sails from the boat, bag them, and take them to a suitable location where you can spread them out.

Pull each sail from its bag onto a clean surface. Examine the headboard, leech, foot, luff, and every seam. Check any slugs, slides, or hanks for wear and their attachments to the sail for damage caused by chafe or age. Look especially closely around cringles and other hardware, around windows, and inspect battens for weaknesses and their pockets for tears. Common places for tears on the main sail are low on the luff where the gooseneck catches a reefed sail, along the foot if excess outhaul is applied, and in the areas where the sail comes into contact with the spreaders. Tears in the vicinity of hardware often indicate problems arising from how the sail has been set. Tears around reef points indicate that they came under load when the sail was reefed, which they are not designed to do. This can happen when the tack and clew are not hauled sufficiently taut to support the belly of the sail.

You can take steps to prevent the gooseneck from puncturing the mainsail. When the mainsail is reefed, the luff cringle is placed over a hook at the gooseneck. This hook can sometimes pierce the area of sail beneath the cringle. Any holes caused in this manner should be patched from both sides of the sail—adding extra thickness to that area doesn't hurt.

One way to prevent the sail being damaged in this way is to use reefing straps. These are made of strong webbing led through the cringles and with a ring sewn onto each end. When the sail is lowered for reefing, instead of the sail cringle, a ring is placed over the gooseneck so the prongs can't hole the sail.

Another way to obviate this problem is to convert to a single-line reefing system, as described earlier in this chapter, making the gooseneck hooks redundant.

Inspect foot and leech cords for chafe or damage, and make sure that the mechanism by which you tighten them holds them securely. A flapping leech or foot is not healthy for the sail and does nothing for its trim. If the cords refuse to hold securely, have your sailmaker sew a new system onto the sail.

Telltales are valuable guides to sail trim, so be sure they're properly placed on the main and jibs, and replaced whenever you have the sail serviced.

Reefing Gear

Make sure the reefing lines are led properly and that they have not suffered damage from chafe or exposure, especially in areas where they are hard to see, such as where they run inside the boom. I once had the second-reef line part, during a blow at O-dark-thirty on a blustery, moonless night on an ocean passage. How loud that line popped, and the confusion that resulted from the flogging main sail was pretty surprising. That incident taught me to check reef lines where they run inside the boom by pulling them through so those portions of the line are visible. These lines tend to chafe where they emerge from the boom forward when the sail is reefed. Check all lines that run inside the mast or the boom, because it's unlikely that anyone else has.

To test the reefing system and the reefing lines, hoist the main and reef it down in sequence from the first reef to the last. Haul in on the lines hard, testing if they'll break when called on. Make sure that the foot of the main is brought down tight along the boom when reefed—leaving the sail off the boom allows excessive draft, and that's the last thing you want in high winds. The key to this is to make sure that the reefing line is snugly attached to the boom. If it's a loose loop you won't be able to haul the sail down against the boom. You can also haul the clew cringle down tight by passing a line or a length of webbing through it and wrapping it around the boom. This is a technique commonly used on racing boats.

Because of the distance it travels and the corners it turns, a single line used in this fashion can be subjected to considerable friction. Friction leads to chafe. Take care when pulling the line through the boom and applying tension that it can run as freely as possible. When taking the sail down, you can avoid some of the friction and chafe by going to the mast and pulling the reefing lines through the boom rather than simply hauling them in from the cockpit. An improvement you can make is to have small blocks built into the sail at the cringle locations. Running the reefing lines through these blocks instead of the cringles makes reefing and un-reefing easier and eliminates a source of chafe.

Battens and Batten Pockets

Mainsail battens are subjected to great abuse. This can be caused by the sail flogging, wearing against the spreaders, or snagging on the topping lift, running backstays or lazyjacks. They can be bent when the sail is flaked on the boom and even when the sail is improperly stored. You can't repair broken battens, they must be replaced. The leech ends of batten pockets can tear, loosen, or open up entirely allowing the batten to escape. Torn batten pockets are often a consequence of the batten not being snugly held in the pocket or of the sail being allowed to flog.

On many boats, when sailing downwind, the mainsail lies on the spreaders, which causes chafe. This is especially true on sails with full-length battens. To protect the sail and the batten pockets, add a sacrificial layer of cloth to each side in the areas where contact occurs.

Excessive tension in the outhaul, especially when associated with insufficient tension in the leech and luff, can cause long, sail-wrecking tears along the foot of the main. I've only seen this happen while racing in high winds and seas, but it's worth mentioning here. It's an area where old sails that have not been well cared for finally give out.

Headsail Problems

Jibs are prone to wear and tear at the clew and along the leech, where they snag on or rub against spreaders, steaming or deck lights, and the spinnaker track or radome. They also suffer chafe and rips just aft of the tack where they wear against lifelines and stanchions. Yankee cut jibs are less susceptible to this kind of damage. Again, the best way to protect these sails is to apply sacrificial patches to points especially prone to chafe.

Spinnakers can tear just about anywhere from snagging while being hoisted or doused, or during a jibe. Tears in spinnakers tend to be dramatic, as they can split wide open along a seam in big air. Inspect a spinnaker at every opportunity so as to avoid hoisting it with a small rip that can quickly become a catastrophic one.

Tired Sailcloth

Tears around cringles, where sails are reinforced to carry concentrated loads, indicate that the sail material has become weakened. If tears are also present in other areas of the sail, it may well be that the sail has reached the end of its life expectancy. If this is the case, the cloth will appear dull and dry, with areas of thin or torn fabric. Don't try to salvage sails in this condition; they deserve a well earned retirement.

Sail Repairs Under Way

If you intend to spend considerable time at sea, having the means and ability on board to mend sails is essential. You will be able to continue to use damaged sails, at least on a temporary basis,

FIGURE 7-1
Weakening at the clew cringle and poor condition of the Dacron and stitching. A new sail should be on the drawing board.

until you can get them to a qualified sail loft for permanent repairs. Fully stocked sail-repair kits are available at marine hardware stores and some sail lofts. Make sure yours includes a selection of cloths and hardware appropriate for making repairs to your particular sails. Table 7-1 lists recommended items.

Before you attempt a repair, first clean the damaged area of salt crystals, and make sure it's dry. Wipe it with rubbing alcohol if necessary. Remove all broken threads and torn pieces of sail. Next, cover the damaged area with adhesive-backed sail-repair cloth, applying it to both sides of the sail. On larger tears, or those in high-stress areas, reinforce the patches with stitching, using waxed nylon thread in an interlocking stitch pattern. This technique enables you to make a rapid, albeit temporary, repair, so that you can quickly put the sail back to work.

When prepping my own boat to sail offshore, I always take any damaged sails to a sail loft. I can make repairs on the water if necessary, but when I'm in port, I prefer to involve a knowledgeable professional. I recommend others do this, too, because a sail loft has the expertise and the materials and tools to do the job properly. For example, when repairing a torn area, or an opened seam, a typical method is called a cut-away patch. New, strong cloth is laid on one side of the sail to cover the damaged area and stitched in place. Then the damaged area is cut away from the other side, leaving a single layer of strong cloth with just a half-inch overlap around the perimeter of the patch. This is a difficult task to effect at sea.

TABLE 7-1

Sail-Repair Kit.

Sailor's palm	Sewing needles, assorted sizes, straight and curved
Seamstick tape, $\frac{1}{2}$"	Seizing wire, stainless, $\frac{1}{16}$"
Adhesive Dacron tape: 2" x 2 oz, 3" x 3.8 oz, 6" x 8 oz.	Tubular webbing, strapping, 1"
Spinnaker repair tape: 2"x 25'	UV resistant thread: V92
Waxed nylon thread	Stainless steel shackles: $\frac{3}{4}$", 1"
Leechline cleats, aluminum	Batten pocket elastic, 1$\frac{1}{2}$"
Dacron tape: 3" x 3.9 oz, 6" x8oz, 2" x 5 oz,	3" x 8 oz, 6" x 8 oz.
Replacement slides, slugs, hanks, protectors	Leech line Dacron, #505, $\frac{1}{8}$", Kevlar, Spectra
Shears, bent blade	Awl, 2$\frac{1}{2}$"
Seam rippers	Wire cutters

CHAPTER 8

COMMUNICATIONS

Give careful thought to the modes of communication you plan to use when you are at sea. How much and what type of equipment you install will depend on how often you want to be in touch with friends and family, or your business, at home. Further, you can decide between voice and e-mail, or you can equip your boat for both.

While choices are abundant in the electronic age, some equipment is necessary for the purposes of conducting the ship's business and for making contact with appropriate authorities, such as when arriving in a foreign port.

VHF Radio

A VHF radio is standard equipment on any boat. With it, you make contact with shore stations and other vessels. It operates in line-of-sight, so depending on the height of your antenna, that of the receiving station, and other factors, it has a range of approximately 25 miles. One VHF radio should be permanently installed, usually at the nav station, with its antenna at the masthead. A handheld unit makes a handy extra for use in the cockpit and to add to the Abandon Ship gear.

Radio Telephone Alphabet

Whenever communicating over the airwaves on anything but a social call on the satellite phone, it's customary to use the standard internationally recognized radio-telephone phonetic alphabet when enunciating letters or spelling out words. Each letter is represented by a specific word which clearly identifies it.

A	Alpha	J	Juliett	S	Sierra
B	Bravo	K	Kilo	T	Tango
C	Charlie	L	Lima	U	Uniform
D	Delta	M	Mike	V	Victor
E	Echo	N	November	W	Whiskey
F	Foxtrot	O	Oscar	X	X-ray
G	Gulf	P	Papa	Y	Yankee
H	Hotel	Q	Quebec	Z	Zulu
I	India	R	Romeo		

Place a copy of this alphabet near the nav station, where you can easily refer to it when using a radio. You'll present yourself as correct and seamanlike when you use the proper terminology over the airwaves.

Portable Computer

Computers have increasingly become standard equipment on passagemaking and cruising boats, where they are used for a variety of purposes, including navigation, communications, and entertainment. If you bring one aboard, give careful thought to where you'll install it or store it. While, in my experience, a computer is more likely to fail from being dropped or banged about than from corrosion, it should nevertheless be kept where it's accessible but it will remain dry as well as secure. If you mount it where you can easily use it, make sure it's out of harm's way. National Products, Inc. (www.rammount.com) sells a range of mounts that solve a variety of installation questions.

If you store your computer in a locker, provide ventilation so dampness won't collect around it. A laptop can be powered by a 12-volt adapter or by a small inverter that's dedicated to the computer to assure it of a clean power source. A small, uninterruptible power supply (UPS) will maintain power to a desktop (or other AC-powered systems) during voltage-drop periods and allow for an orderly shutdown if the inverter fails.

If you plan on an extended cruise, be sure to take along any CDs that came with the computer, especially the man-ufacturer's system recovery CD. Bring all your electronic navigation chart CDs, along with serial or security codes, so that you can reload them if you need to.

Make a list of all technical support phone numbers you may need. Bring along any written technical- or software-support information and all installation and user guides. Print out any additional information you might need from the vendors' websites.

Don't forget to include extra cables, adapters, and especially a long phone cable and computer network cable for getting connected in places where the data outlet and power plug are at opposite ends of a room. Carry extension serial or USB cables, a spare battery for the laptop, along with AC voltage and plug adapters.

When using the computer you want to enhance efficiency and decrease on-line time by making downloading information as simple and fast as possible. You can adjust some of the settings on the computer to interrupt time-wasting functions you don't need at sea.

Consult a computer technician for assistance in turning off the routine updates to computer software and services. These include automatic stock or weather reports, or new software versions. Turn off any service that moves data over the Internet without your asking for it.

Turn off the Windows Error Reporting function. Before you depart on your voyage, download the latest security patches and anti-virus updates, then disable all Windows Automatic Updates.

Re-enable these functions after the sea voyage, or at such a time as you are ready to re-connect to those services.

You can compensate for difficulty in viewing a laptop's LCD display screen by making the background pure white. This enhances the contrast between colorful icons and the white background.

Once the computer is working well with whatever devices you choose to connect to it, like GPS or a satellite phone, use the Windows System Restore feature to place that configuration in memory. If the computer setup changes or crashes, this utility will allow you to retrieve the desired configuration.

Single Sideband Radio (SSB)

If you want to be able to download weather information, maintain personal and business contacts ashore, or reach emergency numbers when sailing farther offshore, you will require long-range communication capabilities. A fundamental decision you will have to make, therefore, will be whether to install a Single Sideband Radiotelephone (SSB) or a satellite phone. These are discussed in Chapter 5, *Offshore Essentials: Gear and Equipment*.

If you elect to install an SSB, some recent developments mean that you can use it for more than simply receiving or transmitting voice messages. With the addition of a Pactor modem and specialized software to your PC laptop, you can send and receive e-mail via your SSB.

SailMail, administered by the non-profit SailMail Association, maintains a network of private coast stations in the

Maritime Mobile Radio Service via which its members can connect to the Internet from anywhere in the world's oceans for the purpose of sending and receiving e-mail. On its website (www.sailmail.com), the association provides a description of the service and information on how to subscribe, as well as advice on obtaining and installing suitable hardware and software.

Winlink is a similar service that allows voyagers to send and receive e-mails via the Ham Radio net. Information on this service is available at www.winlink.org.

These services are not identical. Sail-Mail uses the Marine Band radio frequencies, over which you can transmit business-related traffic. Because Winlink operates over Ham frequencies, it cannot be used for business communications but only for private correspondence and emergency transmissions.

Iridium and Inmarsat Satellite Telephones

Satellite telephones allow voice and data transmission without the extensive antenna installation procedures required by an SSB. In addition, because the satellite antenna is small and not usually mounted on the mast, you won't lose your ability to communicate in the event of dismasting. You could also take the highly mobile satellite phone into the liferaft, should you ever need to abandon ship. Having the means with which to communicate directly with agencies like the U.S. Coast Guard would certainly facilitate rescue.

To ensure that you can use the satellite

phone reliably in all locations, you should also take along a portable antenna, a spare battery, AC and DC charging adapters, and an international plug kit. Your accessory kit should include an adapter, data-software CD, and a module that attaches to the phone and connects it with a serial port on a computer. Using the USB port on a computer is not recommended, so if your laptop doesn't have a serial port, obtain a PC card from Radio Shack for better reception. The unit provides data in either the normal form or in a compacted form that decreases the download times. The portable phone's built-in antenna can be used for all functions, but offshore I recommend that you add an external marine antenna and antenna cable to improve access and convenience. On VOYAGER, this antenna is mounted on the transom post.

You can improve your capability when using satellite phones or an SSB for data communications by installing software from UUPlus or other providers in your laptop. Designed to work with slow connections such as these modes provide, it improves the reliability of data transfer and supports most satellite networks, GSM mobile phone networks, and Pactor II HF modems. You can find a full description of the software's capabilities at the UUPlus website, www.uuplus.com.

Inmarsat-C/GPS, developed specifically for offshore communications aboard oceangoing ships, combines voice, e-mail, and data capabilities with a built-in GPS. An Inmarsat-C unit can receive text messages that include updates to Notices to Mariners and world-wide weather forecasts and it can also be used for GMDSS distress communications.

Communicating When Ashore

I've found the AT&T International Calling Card very useful when making phone calls, especially from foreign countries. I have used this card on several voyages, and the only problems have been with the local phones, not with the card. You can apply for a card at 1-800-CALLATT.

Cruisers who have made their way to Europe or Asia may find that their best option for general communications is a GSM cell phone. Purchased locally, the phones, and the modems that connect them to laptop computers, can be used in different countries without incurring roaming charges. For each country, you simply purchase a new chip and register the phone.

Pocketmail is a service through which, using a proprietary device called a Composer (similar to a PDA), you can send and receive e-mail by way of almost any phone, including most cell phones. You type your message into the Composer, dial the PocketMail contact number, and place the composer up to the phone's microphone to send the message and receive any from your inbox. The service has toll-free access numbers for North America and some other parts of the world, and service is as low as $15 per month depending on the length of the contract you purchase. For a small additional per-message fee, you can send faxes. Full details of the service are available at the PocketMail website, www.pocketmail.com.

PocketMail would not be suitable unless you will have access to telephones or a cell-phone network whenever you want to send/receive e-mails.

More than ever before, Internet access and phone availability are becoming commonplace in Internet cafes, hotels, marinas, and other places. Yahoo or Hotmail accounts allow their owners to access e-mail from any computer that's connected to the Internet.

CHAPTER 9

SELF-STEERING SYSTEMS

Self steering is recognized as an essential element of any sailboat engaged in offshore passages or cruising, especially with a small crew. Steering by hand requires continuous concentration and effort, and the very real risk of fatigue makes it impractical except in emergency situations.

Most self-steering arrangements fall into one of two broad categories. An autopilot takes steering signals from an electronic control device and uses electromechanical or electrohydraulic means to move the boat's rudder. Windvane systems, which, on sailboats, pre-date their electronic counterparts, respond to changes in the apparent wind direction, mechanically converting deflections of the vane into movements of an auxiliary rudder or of a trim tab on the boat's rudder. Each system has its strengths and weaknesses, and many cruising boats have both an electronic autopilot and a windvane device aboard to take advantage of the best that each system has to offer.

WINDVANE STEERING SYSTEMS

The windvane steers a course relative to the apparent wind direction; if the wind direction changes, the boat's course changes with it. Small course alterations that occur in steady or oscillating breezes make little difference, but a persistent wind shift can cause the boat to be driven far off course. You need to monitor the boat's heading closely and make adjustments to maintain your desired course.

While a windvane is capable of steering a boat both upwind and downwind in moderate to fresh breezes, in light air it can have difficulty, especially downwind when the apparent wind decreases still further. Being dependent on the wind, a vane is not usually reliable in conditions that require motoring. It can also have difficulty holding course while sailing downwind in big waves.

Because they are mechanical devices, windvanes must be maintained to keep them in proper working order. Their parts must be free to rotate, and their gears must mesh properly with as little friction as possible. Constant exposure to wind, water, and sun takes its toll on the components, rendering them less effective or even incapable of functioning. It's also important to inspect regularly the vane device's physical attachment points. This is especially the case for the auxiliary-rudder type, which is quite heavy, and has to be securely mounted to reinforced points on the transom.

Windvane systems are generally sturdy and are able to withstand the elements well. Their obvious big advantage is that their operation requires no electrical power, just the wind.

The vane itself resembles that on a windmill and functions somewhat like it. To set it up to steer the boat, you put the boat on course, align the vane with the apparent wind, and engage a clutch device which holds it in a fixed position relative to the steering mechanism. When the boat changes direction, that exposes one side of the vane to the wind, the pressure from which, depending on the system, tips or turns the vane. The movement of the vane is translated into mechanical action to steer the boat back to where the pressure on the vane is again neutral.

One type of windvane steering employs a servopendulum to make adjustments to the boat's rudder, either through a direct connection to the rudder or the tiller or to the main steering system. Another type employs an auxiliary rudder. The reaction of the windvane to changes in the sometimes-capricious wind has to be amplified by the connected apparatus to generate enough energy and power to control the boat's course.

FIGURE 9-1

Examples of windvane steering systems. *Courtesy of Scanner International.*

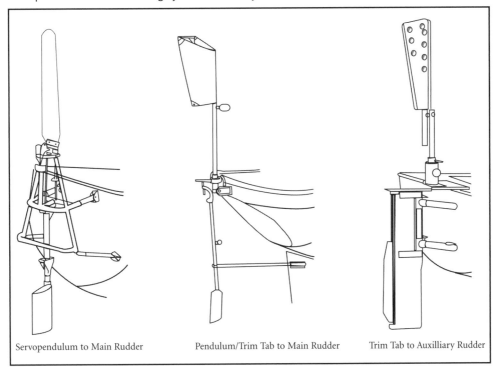

| Servopendulum to Main Rudder | Pendulum/Trim Tab to Main Rudder | Trim Tab to Auxilliary Rudder |

In the auxiliary rudder system, a trim tab is attached to the trailing edge of the auxiliary rudder. Movements of the vane are mechanically translated into movements of the trim tab. As the trim tab rotates, water pressure on it increases, generating enough torque to turn the auxiliary rudder, which causes a course correction.

The servopendulum is somewhat more complicated. The windvane is the servo. Deflections of the vane turn, through a system of gears, a slender auxiliary rudder, or oar. The resulting water pressure on the oar causes it to swing, like a pendulum, to one side. The force generated on the oar is transmitted via lines or linkages to the boat's steering system, or in some installations directly to the boat's rudder, to make the necessary correction to the boat's heading.

ELECTRONIC AUTOPILOTS

Electronic self-steering has evolved tremendously since early units began appearing on sailboats about four decades ago. Devices available today are more capable of holding a course in heavy seas, consume less electricity, and have become far more dependable.

The course to be sailed is set on a control panel, which might be located in the cockpit near the helm or belowdecks, or even in both locations. A fluxgate compass monitors the boat's heading and transmits that information to a small computer. When the boat goes off course, the computer, called the Central Processing Unit (CPU), activates an

electric motor of some type which ultimately causes the boat's rudder to be turned to effect a correction.

Electronically controlled autopilots come in a variety of configurations. Some mount on the steering pedestal and connect directly to the same shaft as the wheel. These types are normally not powerful enough to control a boat in ocean swells and a heavy sea. They are also quite vulnerable to being drenched in seawater, which, if it penetrates the CPU or drive motor, will knock the unit out of commission. Corrosion is also a worry whenever metallic parts are exposed to seawater.

On a vessel intended for offshore use, the autopilot is commonly installed below the deck, where it can be mounted securely in a dry area where it's protected from the elements. An installation of this type also typically uses a more powerful motor.

Autopilots employ a variety of drive mechanisms. A common type is the electric linear drive in which an electric motor controls an integral arm that extends or retracts according to the direction in which the motor turns. Another popular type employs a hydraulically driven arm. In both systems, the drive is connected to a tiller arm on the boat's rudder stock, or sometimes to the quadrant or radial drive used by the boat's primary steering system. Some drive motors operate through a rack and pinion system, where a gear on the motor's shaft meshes with a geared section on the quadrant.

Setting an autopilot to steer the boat is quite straightforward. When, steering by hand, you have the boat on the desired heading, you engage the autopilot, which will then steer to the corresponding heading transmitted by the fluxgate compass until given another command. It will maintain that course independently of wind direction. Should a large windshift occur, the sails may become enough out of trim that the boat loses drive. If the mechanism can no longer maintain the desired heading, an alarm sounds to alert you to the fact that the boat is off course. The autopilot will not follow large wind shifts, and will not allow the boat to sail far off the designated heading.

The obvious downside of electronic autopilots is their consumption of electrical power. This becomes a real consideration when the boat is able to sail for days on end without the need for engine power. At times like that you have to monitor the batteries' state of charge and run the engine periodically to recharge them. Each time you engage the autopilot, check its sensitivity setting. When sailing long passages, you can use the least sensitive setting so that the unit doesn't respond to every small course deviation. You want it to react more slowly when the boat's heading changes, because that will result in significant savings of electrical power.

Electronic autopilots are manufactured in distinct modular components. In the event that an autopilot fails, you restore operation by replacing the module that has broken down. For this reason, you should have replacement units available. You can do this either by installing a second complete autopilot that would be activated if the primary failed, or by carrying the second unit to provide the spare parts needed to restore the first unit to working order.

One goal of offshore route planning is to plot your courses so that the prevailing winds will be abeam or aft of the beam as much as practicable. It doesn't always work out that way, of course, but the self-steering system must be capable of holding true to a course in downwind conditions. My experience is that the electronic autopilots perform this function very well.

BALANCE THE BOAT TO STEER ITSELF

You can employ another method of steering that uses no electrical energy, requires no extra moving parts, and drives the boat while other steering gear and the helmsperson take a break from the action: If balanced correctly, and in the right wind and sea conditions, the boat will steer itself.

For several reasons, being able to set the boat up to do this is a valuable skill. Success depends on achieving balance between the forces acting on the sail plan and those acting on the hull, keel, and rudder. To achieve this balance, encourage your crew to learn how the boat responds to changes in how the sails are trimmed, and how they can adjust them until the pressure on the rudder is just so and it takes very little movement of the helm to keep the boat on course. The resulting straighter courses steered through the water are more efficient, and the reduced effort needed makes steering the boat less physically demanding on the crew. Similarly, the workload on a self-steering device is less, reducing wear and tear and, in the case an electronic device is used, lowering its consumption of electrical power.

A boat should normally be capable of steering itself on any point of sail from a close reach to about a beam reach. Waves approaching from aft of the beam tend to impact the stern first, lifting and accelerating it. The bow digs in and the boat wants to round up. The load on the rudder changes quickly and quite dramatically, the forces on the sails less so, with the result that balance is lost. This makes it impossible for the boat to maintain course when waves approach from much aft of the beam. With the wind from the proper quarter, though, you need only to balance the sail plan and provide enough power to keep the boat steadily making way against the wave action. A close reach is an ideal point of sail on which to do this.

A Matter of Balance

To attain balance, we're concerned with two opposing forces, one acting on the center of lateral resistance (CLR) of the hull and the other on the center of effort (CE) of the sail plan. In Figure 9-2, the CE of the whole sail plan is shown to be comprised of the combined CEs of the mainsail and the foresail. In the case of a ketch rig, the CE of the mizzen would be factored in as well.

The relative positions of the CE and the CLR determine whether the boat will exert weather helm, when it has a

FIGURE 9-2
Components of the Center of Effort.

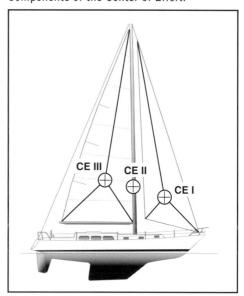

tendency to turn to windward, or lee helm, when the tendency is to turn to leeward. While the CLR remains more or less fixed (although heel angle and the hull's attitude in waves will change its position somewhat), you can move the CE by making changes to the sails you set and to their trim.

The CE of a sail is normally taken to be at its geometric center. On a triangular sail, this point lies at the intersection of lines drawn from each corner to the midpoint of the opposite side.

To find the combined CE of two sails, draw a line joining their centers. The combined CE lies along this line. To figure out where, a simple moment calculation is performed.

Taking moments about the CE of the mainsail CE(M), we have:

$$F \times D = T \times d$$

where F is the area of the foresail, T is the total area of mainsail plus foresail (F + M), D is the distance between CE(M) and CE(F), and d is the distance from CE(M) to CE(T).

The CE of a sailplan is taken to be the point through which the combined sail forces act. Their tendency is to heel the boat and push it to leeward. These lateral forces are countered by the boat's righting moment and the resistance to sideways movement presented by the hull and its appendages (keel and rudder) and taken to act through its CLR. Lift generated by the sail's shape has a forward component and a lateral component. It is the forward component that drives the boat forward.

Yacht designers aim, by careful placement of CE and CLR, to give a sailboat a small amount of weather helm when the standard sails are properly trimmed. To achieve this, the CLR is located aft of the CE. The distance between them, called lead, is critical: Too little lead creates weather helm; too much creates lee helm.

Some weather helm is desirable, because it causes the boat to head into the wind if the helm is unattended—a generally safe situation. Too much weather helm creates excessive helm loads. Lee helm is undesirable because in the event the helm is unattended, the boat will steer itself downwind and ultimately jibe.

An easy way to figure how changes in CE or CLR affect boat handling is to remember that when the centers move closer together, weather helm increases; moving them farther apart reduces

weather helm and may induce lee helm. Modern sloops tend to pick up weather helm as the wind builds. By taking a reef in the main, you reduce the force on the mainsail and move its CE forward, away from the CLR, both of which actions reduce the weather helm. Reefing a large, overlapping genoa will also reduce weather helm, and on many boats this is usually the first step to try when trimming for balance.

What Causes Weather Helm

If you sense an increase in weather helm while sailing, that usually means that the CE of the sail plan has moved aft or that the boat is over-canvassed—the forces on the sails have overpowered the countering forces on the hull.

FIGURE 9-3
Weather helm results when CE and CLR mover closer together.

The CE moves aft when

You have too much mainsail
The mainsail is over-sheeted
The mainsail-sheet car is too high on the traveler
You have too little jib
The headsail is under-sheeted
The headsail fairlead car is too far aft.

If the boat seems to have excessive inherent weather helm, it could be because the mast is stepped too far aft or that it has too much aft rake.

Short of making modifications to the keel, there's not much you can do to move the CLR. However, you can affect it to a small degree by trimming how the boat floats to its waterline. For example, if you trim the boat down at the bow by stowing extra anchors and chain forward, the CLR will move forward, and weather helm will increase.

If the boat has a swing keel or centerboard, adjusting its position will affect the CLR. By how much and in what direction it moves depends on the design of the hull and of the board.

What Causes Lee Helm

If you sense a tendency toward lee helm while sailing, that usually means that the CE of the sail plan has moved forward or that the boat is under-canvassed.

The CE moves forward when

You reef the mainsail
The mainsail is under-sheeted

FIGURE 9-4
Lee helm is the result of CE and CLR moving apart.

The mainsail-sheet car is too far down on the traveler
You are flying too big a headsail (or a spinnaker).

If the boat seems to have inherent lee helm, it could be because the mast is stepped too far forward or that it has too little aft rake, or that it has forward rake.

You can counter lee helm to some degree by taking actions that move the CLR forward. You can do this by moving the crew weight forward to trim the boat by the bow.

Trimming the Sails for Balance

When trimming sails, we aim to have a couple of degrees of weather helm. This tells us that the jib is working to provide drive through the water and it also gives the tiller or wheel the "feel" we need to help us steer efficiently. If there's too much weather helm, either decrease the pressure exerted by the mainsail or increase the power of the headsail. Start by moving the main traveler down the track, making the main flatter, or reefing. Increase drive of the jib or genoa by moving the sheet lead forward, tweaking trim, increasing the draft in the sail, or by going to a larger headsail.

Once the sails are balanced to the point where you need very little helm control, lock or lash the helm and make small adjustments to fine tune the sail. Very soon the boat will maintain the heading on her own, and your drivers, autopilot, and windvane can all take a break. I once sailed a crippled vessel over 400 miles this way, giving the crew of three a much needed break from constant hand steering.

The relatively narrow wind range in which boats can hold their own course certainly limits the use of this technique. Nevertheless, the principles of balancing the sail plan should be used at all times under all points of sail, whether the boat is being steered by a crewmember, an autopilot, or a windvane. Properly balanced, the boat sails at its most efficient, and the steering gear benefits from the reduced workload. The art of trimming a boat to steer by herself, or with minimal manual or mechanical intervention, is a great asset in a sailor's repertoire of talents.

CHAPTER 10

ALTERNATIVE ENERGY

At sea, all resources are precious, because they are limited by how much we can carry with us. This is true of food and of water, and it's equally true of energy. We use energy, usually derived from the fuel we carry, to propel the boat in the absence of wind and to generate electricity to power the various devices, from lighting to navigational instruments, that depend on it.

Anyone who spends time on the water quickly learns how important it is to conserve that energy—we don't want to run out of it before the voyage ends. We benefit in several ways when we discipline our energy consumption: We learn how to operate the boat efficiently, we consume less diesel fuel, and by not wasting energy we don't create unnecessary pollution.

The first step in achieving energy efficiency on board is to make every crewmember aware of its importance. Advised of the consequences of waste, they will appreciate the necessity of following rules that promote conservation. Simple procedures, such as turning off electronic devices when they are not in use and using lights as little as possible, go a long way to conserving battery power. You can save fuel by sailing the boat as well as you can and as much as you can,

so as not to use the diesel engine. As the boat's owner, you can take steps when equipping it to reduce demands on your electrical supply. One way is to replace incandescent lights with compact fluorescent bulbs, which use up to 70 percent less power. Some LED lights that have recently come on the market use even less power and create more appealing light.

While diesel fuel, burned in the main engine or in an auxiliary, is the primary source of energy aboard a sailboat, alternative means of making electricity are available. Solar panels and wind generators are reliable energy producers, and their use can significantly reduce the need to consume diesel fuel. Anyone contemplating spending long periods of time at sea or cruising should consider their potential. Supported by a conservative approach to power utilization, these non-polluting devices can generate most if not all of your normal onboard power needs.

Solar Panels

Photovoltaic cells, which usually have as their active component silicon combined with other elements, convert energy from the sun into electricity. Assembled into arrays, these cells can be connected to deliver a range of voltages. Solar panels designed for use on boats usually are wired to supply a nominal 12 volts DC (the actual voltage depends on the quality of sunlight falling on the cells), which is used to charge the ship's batteries. The batteries are protected against over-charging by a regulator connected between the battery and the solar panel. The regulator may also provide discharge protection, as draining the battery excessively will cause long-term damage. Sophisticated control systems are available which can monitor the charge, shut down power-draining equipment automatically if necessary to preserve the battery, and display information on voltages, charge rates, and discharge rates so you can check the status of your system at any time.

Calculating Electricity Usage

When calculating your expected electricity demands, you can focus on either the amp-hours per day (Ah/d) or the watt-hours per day (Wh/d) that you would consume in a typical day. The watt is a unit of electrical power, defined as the power in a current of one amp under a potential difference (voltage) of one volt. The power consumed by an appliance is calculated using the following formula:

$$watts = amps \times volts$$

All appliances come with information on their electrical requirements. These may be given in either watts or amps, and you can easily convert one to the other using the formula above. Since boats, when at sea or at anchor, are generally operating on 12-volt power systems, our calculations become simplified. I find it convenient to calculate the total amp-hours of power expected to be required in a day at sea.

The computation of how many amp-hours are consumed aboard in a typical day at sea might look like the following table.

	Amps	Hours/day	Amp-hours
Autopilot	4	18	72
Knot meter	0.1	24	2.4
VHF	1	1	1
Depth sounder	24	0.2	4.8
Radar	4	4	16
Running lights	3	8	24
Stereo	1	4	4
Freshwater pump	3	0.5	1.5
Total			125.7

(Radar is in energy-saving mode throughout the night.)

If you use other devices, calculate their demand and add the result to the total.

For an appliance that draws 2 amps of current and is used 6 hours per day, we calculate its energy consumption as follows:

2 amps x 6 hours = 12 amp-hours

Do a similar calculation for all the appliances used and total the results to determine the amp-hours the vessel will consume per day. With this total in mind, do some research to find the sources available to deliver that power. A range of solar units and wind power generators are available, in a number of configurations. Which device, or combination of devices, you choose, will depend on several factors. First, of course, is your estimated power needs, and then you have to take into account the reliability of sunshine or the wind in the regions you plan to sail. Then there are the practical considerations of how and where on your boat you will install the equipment. Also, you may have a personal preference for choosing one system over another.

Several companies provide descriptions of and information on alternative power solutions, as well as offering systems for sale:

Alternative Energy Store
43 Broad Street, Suite A408
Hudson, MA 01749
Phone: 1-978-562-5858
Toll-free: 1-877-878-4060
Website: www.altenergystore.com

e-Marine, Inc.
4960 SW 52nd Street, Suite 418
Ft. Lauderdale, FL 33314
Phone: 1-954-581-2505
Toll-free: 1-877-432-2221
Fax: 1-954-337-2287
Website: www.e-marine-inc.com

ExtremeGB, Ltd.
Nene House, Sopwith Way, Daventry, NN11 8PB
United Kingdom
Phone: +44-870-7485700
Website: www.sailgb.com

Best Marine Imports
Toll-free: 1-888-669-0633
Website: www.bestmarineimports.com

Another way to generate electricity when underway is with a towing generator, which can produce enough power to run your navigation instruments, lights, and radios while you are sailing. *Practical Sailor*, in its February 15, 2003 issue, gave its highest recommendation to the Redwing Towing Generator, available from Downwind Marine:

Downwind Marine
2404 Canon Street,
San Diego, CA 92106
Phone: 1-619-224-2733
Fax: 1-619-224-7683
Website: www.downwindmarine.com

CHAPTER 11

RADAR

In my books and speaking engagements I now list radar under priority equipment, and for good reason. Radar can provide position, range, and bearing information about other vessels in the vicinity of yours, it is a helpful aid in coastwise navigation, and you can use it to track and avoid thunderstorms. When I sail single-handed on VOYAGER, the Watchman function (a feature of Furuno products) allows me to rest with the knowledge that if any vessel approaches within a 12-mile radius, the radar will sound an alarm. I'll be up on deck with plenty of time to assess the situation and take action should it be necessary.

A schematic of a radar set-up (Figure 11-1) illustrates the component parts.

As well as a main power cable, the radar set has connections for additional system inputs. Raymarine, for example, has a proprietary system called SeaTalk which allows a variety of navigation information to be displayed on the radar screen. Position, heading, waypoints, and seawater temperature are all available, as is an MOB feature. Weather information obtained via Sirius Satellite

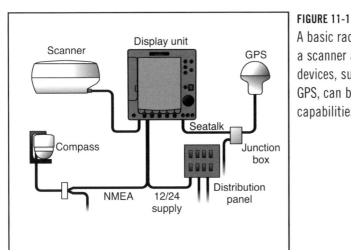

FIGURE 11-1
A basic radar system consists of a scanner and a display. Ancillary devices, such as a compass and GPS, can be incorporated to add capabilities. *Courtesy of Raymarine*

Radio, can be displayed too, but only in regions covered by the signals.

Radar units intended for use on sailing yachts operate on either 12- or 24-volt DC power. The scanner (antenna), which radiates the pulses and collects returning echoes, should be mounted in an elevated position on the mast, on a post or arch at the transom, or on the backstay. It should not be so high as to be affected by the boat's motion, which is amplified with height. A good spot for installation on the mast is usually near the lower spreaders—high enough to provide adequate radar coverage, but not to be adversely affected by pitch and roll. That location is also fairly accessible, with the spreaders providing a degree of support for someone going aloft to install or service the scanner. On sailboats, the scanner is usually enclosed within a plastic radome to protect it from becoming entangled with lines.

VOYAGER has a transom post with a platform that accommodates the radome and the satellite-phone antenna and is available for other items as well. It's much more accessible than if it were on the mast, and since radar problems can frequently be traced to cables leading to the scanner, maintenance is much easier, too.

If you choose to mount the radome on the mast, you should purchase a guard assembly to protect it from contact with lines and sails. Use the platform mounting kit supplied by the scanner's manufacturer and make sure it's tightly secured to the mast. The type of hardware you use will depend on the particular unit and on the configuration of the mast.

The radar should be on a dedicated electrical circuit protected by a thermal circuit breaker or fuse at the main panel. The scanner is connected to the display unit by an insulated, vinyl-coated cable that enters the rear of the display. This cable must be protected against chafe at any point at which it turns and where it passes through bulkheads and through openings such as in the mast or transom post. A connector in this cable allows scanner and display to be installed and serviced separately.

Once the system is installed, your maintenance should be limited to checking the electrical connections to the display and assuring that exposed cables are not damaged. Only a trained professional should repair malfunctions of the scanner, display, or cables. To test the system, simply close the main breaker to send power and depress the power button on the display. Hold the button down a few seconds until the unit beeps. The unit should then enter Standby mode and be ready for use.

The Radar Display

A radar display is an example of a Plan Position Indicator. The center of the display represents the position of your vessel, and a bright line, rotating in synchronism with the rotating antenna in the scanner, represents the radar beam. Beams reflected by targets appear on the display as points of light, or blips, that persist until the beam completes its revolution of the display and re-illuminates them.

The display can be set to a number of different ranges out from the vessel, and you select the range you want to view from the control panel. Typical ranges seen on small-boat radar displays are 0.5, 1, 2, 4, 8, 16, and 24 miles. Concentric rings displayed on the screen facilitate estimating the distance to a target. For example, on a 4-mile range setting, the rings might be at 1-mile intervals, making it easy to interpolate the range of a target that lies between two rings. At greater ranges, less detail is displayed than at closer ranges.

There is also a minimum range from the vessel at which no radar reflection is possible. This distance varies according to the radar unit and its set-up, but is usually from 50 to 150 feet. This is inconsequential at sea, but can be important when maneuvering in close quarters. The higher the antenna is mounted, the greater this blind spot becomes.

Radar displays usually include a bearing line that you can direct from the center to an echo. This bearing line will display the bearing (relative to your heading) to the other vessel or object and its range in nautical miles. This information is useful in a number of situations, including piloting and coastal navigation, tracking a weather disturbance in order to avoid squalls, and monitoring another vessel to maintain a safe distance.

When used for navigation, the bearing to a charted object and its range serve the same purpose as a visual line of position. In this situation, you can obtain a fix by a single radar observation, since you know both the bearing to an object and your distance from it. When you plot such a fix on a chart, you should circle it and label it with the time and the word "radar."

Rain squalls show up as menacing echoes on radar, and their range and bearings are valuable information. You can determine the squall's direction of movement by tracking it on radar and by observing the direction of prevailing winds. Once you know the squall's path, you can avoid it by setting a course that takes the most efficient route away from it.

When in active scanning mode, most radar units draw from 4 to 6 amps of power. They can also be placed into a power-conservation mode that is useful when no imminent threat to the vessel is present. On VOYAGER, I use it at night, when we're sailing along without generating power. I program the Watchman function of the Furuno radar to sweep the horizon every 20 minutes. If it detects a target vessel within a 12-mile radius, an alarm sounds. This is a real comfort, and solved the only trepidation I had about sailing singlehanded. Now I know I can rest without abandoning all principles of seamanship.

Radar and Collision Avoidance

The International Regulations for the Prevention of Collision at Sea (COLREGS) state implicitly that all means possible are to be taken to avoid risk of collision. This includes the use of radar in clear weather as well as in restricted visibility. Rule 7(c) states further that a quick glance at the radar is not sufficient:

Assumptions shall not be made on the basis of scanty information, especially scanty radar information.

The reason is that knowing only the direction of relative motion (DRM) of another vessel, or contact, is insufficient. You must also factor in the speed of relative motion (SRM) to complete the picture of your position relative to that of another vessel.

You do this by tracking the change in relative positions of your vessel and the contact over a specific period of time. Six minutes (1/10 hour) is a convenient period to use because the distance covered in 6 minutes multiplied by 10 gives the relative speed in nautical miles per hour (knots). By comparing the relative positions of the vessels over time, you can calculate both DRM and SRM.

You can track the position of a contact on the radar screen by making no-tations with a grease pencil at specific intervals of time. You can then transfer this information to a radar screen plotting sheet vector diagram, or you can construct the diagram on the display screen itself. (The grease pencil technique works well on the glass screen of a cathode ray tube, but may not be appropriate on modern liquid crystal displays.)

Figure 11-2 shows how the relative speed of your vessel and a contact is calculated by determining the change in relative positions that occurs in 6 minutes. The distance between the plots divided by the time (1/10 hour) gives the solution in knots.

On the radar screen in Figure 11-2, the range circles are 1 nautical mile apart. The positions of the target were plotted 6 minutes apart (and the time of each plot noted next to it). During that period, the plots show that the vessels closed by a distance of 2 nautical miles. The SRM is therefore:

$$\text{SRM} = 2.0 \ (\text{knots} / \ 0.1 (\text{hour})$$
$$= 20 \text{ knots}$$

If the radar range was set differently, and the circles represented 0.5 mile, the computations would be altered:

$$\text{SRM} = 1.0 / 0.1$$
$$= 10 \text{ knots}$$

In most situations, you can determine simply by watching the display screen the relative directions and whether a risk of collision exists. However, when you

FIGURE 11-2

Relative Motion Plotted on a Radar Screen

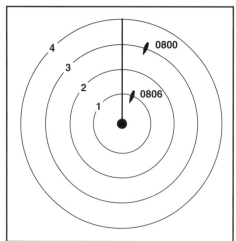

want a more precise determination, you can calculate the DRM by constructing a simple vector diagram. When you know both DRM and SRM, you can calculate the risk more accurately.

Assume for this example that your boat is moving at 6 knots. Calculate the distance you traveled in the period between the two plots on the radar screen:

6 knots x 0.1 hour = 0.6 nautical miles

Your vector is 0.6 miles long.

On the screen, you have point "R" at 0800 hours and point "M" at 0806 hours. The line R-M represents the vector of the relative speed of the vessels.

To represent your boat's track and speed, draw a line from R down the

FIGURE 11-3

Vector diagram of relative movement of two vessels.

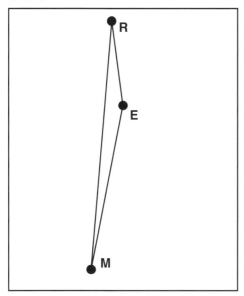

screen parallel to the heading line. (The display is in "head up" mode so your direction of travel is vertical on the screen.) At the point on this line that represents a distance of 0.6 miles, mark point "E."

Draw a line from E to M. The line E-M represents the speed and course of the target. Its length is its speed (approximately 14 knots) and its direction is its track.

In Figure 11-3, R-M represents the DRM for this situation. By extending the DRM toward your position (represented by the center of the screen) you can estimate the point of closest approach. Obviously, in this instance, there should be communication between the vessels, and avoidance action is necessary, because the vector lines R-M and E-M are very close to a line directly between the two vessels.

Vector computations like the one above have been rendered unnecessary by modern radar units that are equipped with software that can instantly indicate the contact's bearing, heading, speed, and the closest point of approach (CPA). The radar takes into consideration the relative courses and speeds of the vessels involved, and calculates where and when they will reach their CPA and the distance that will separate them at that point. Any CPA closer than 1 mile is cause for concern, and should prompt you to communicate with the other vessel and evaluate setting a course to avoid it.

Never rely on another boat's radar to detect you. On a recent passage, I observed a sail off my starboard bow.

After hailing the boat on VHF Channel 16, I learned that it was a Swan 68. I thought it remarkable that such a seamanlike vessel did not appear on our radar!

I recommend you assume the attitude that it is your responsibility to care for your own ship, and that includes avoiding close encounters. Maintain a vigilant lookout for other vessels, and be proactive in monitoring their positions. Do not hesitate to hail other vessels at sea to clarify their intentions, and to make sure they know you're out there.

PART 3

PLANNING FOR THE VOYAGE

CHAPTER 12

HEALTH AND THE OFFSHORE SAILOR

Before committing to an offshore passage or an extended cruise, do take into consideration the fact that you will be leaving an environment in which you have ready access to medical care at all levels and entering one which, as well as being removed from that access, exposes you to a higher risk of injury and illness. Prepare ahead of time by learning about your own health and that of all your crewmembers, including any pre-existing conditions or prescriptions they may have. Ensure that the skipper, or someone else on board, has basic knowledge of first aid and how to handle medical emergencies, assemble a comprehensive medical kit, and collect contact numbers you can use to obtain medical assistance if needed. Anyone intending to be away from home for extended periods of time should look into acquiring health insurance.

A great number of people making offshore voyages or cruising are middle-aged or older. They have reached the stage in their lives where these adventures are feasible because they have the time and the resources to acquire a suitable boat, prepare it, and sail away for an extended period. This age group is more prone to illness and even injury than younger sailors. Other predisposing factors for medical problems offshore include smoking, obesity, high blood-pressure, extra susceptibility to seasickness, poor general physical conditioning, and pre-existing conditions. Longer voyages or cruises, extended offshore passages, crowded boats, poor hygiene, and having children on board can all raise the likelihood that someone will at some time get hurt or become ill.

A boat in constant motion offshore creates an environment far more conducive to injury and illness than does a stable platform on land. Your crew must be made aware of this fact before sailing, and you should discuss injury prevention with them, stress its importance, and make sure they understand its implications. Emphasize that the motion of the vessel requires a steadying hand at all times, and that everyone has to measure their movements in advance of taking any step. It's uncanny how a wave can roll, yaw, or pitch a boat just when you've left yourself vulnerable. Keep yourself secure by always being aware of the boat's attitude. Look for firm handholds, take careful steps, and keep your center of gravity low. After a period of acclimatization, you'll find these precautions become second nature, and a normal part of life aboard ship. I'm certain that it's in part because I offer these precautionary words to my crews that there has never been a serious injury aboard a vessel I've captained offshore.

Nobody should ever use an ocean passage as an opportunity to quit smoking, give up drinking alcohol, stop taking anti-anxiety or antidepressant medications, or shake a drug habit. This is a sure prescription for trouble and even disaster. I once sailed with a dear friend who became irritable as soon as he joined the boat in Bermuda and continued that way throughout the entire passage to Green Turtle Key, in the Little Abacos. Awakened around 0600 the following day by sounds of activity on the boat, I made it to the deck just in time to see him walking down the road with his bags, heading for the airport. It was over two years later I learned that he had been addicted to cocaine, and was using the passage to cold turkey himself from its grip.

Protect the health of all crewmembers by requiring them to be examined by a physician and a dentist. The check-ups should take into account musculoskeletal pain, toothaches, cardiac abnormalities, diabetes, skin ailments, allergies, incontinence, phobias, and any other pre-existing conditions. If a condition is revealed that causes you concern, consult with a medical professional and obtain a thorough understanding of the ailment. Ask about its normal course or stages of progression, all symptoms, and what the prescribed medication does.

Also, learn about signs that might indicate a worsening of the condition, and what happens when medication is lost or runs out. Make certain that any ongoing conditions are treated before you risk making them worse offshore.

If you or any member of your crew have a pre-existing condition such as diabetes that requires chronic medication, have recently undergone surgery, or have allergies of any nature, you should, before setting sail, advise your doctor of the sailing agenda, and ask if there is a medical reason to preclude you from taking part. You should also contact the Medic-Alert Foundation (209-668-3333) emergency response service. Once you, and your medical information, are entered in its database, you will be assigned an identification number that will give you access to information about medical conditions and whom to contact should the need arise. You can also obtain a Medic-Alert bracelet or necklace, which conveys important information to providers in the event of an emergency.

Well ahead of your departure date, get advice about vaccination boosters or inoculations that may be required for specific destinations. Before you sail, fill all your prescriptions and obtain prescriptions for refills you will need along the way.

The skipper, and other members of the crew if possible, should become versed in all aspects of first-response medical care. This includes management of an unconscious person, fracture stabilization, minor wound care, and treatment of lacerations and burns, hypothermia, seasickness, dental pain, common eye and ear maladies, near drowning, and chest pains. These topics are covered in Appendix 8. It is the responsibility of the skipper to take CPR and emergency first aid courses for certification to have at least a basic knowledge in this area. This is the case even if a medical doctor is on board. For those intending to cruise or sail with children, special thought must be devoted to their care as well.

You can obtain information on training classes from a number of organizations, some of which are listed below.

American Red Cross

YMCA

Maritime Medical Access (affiliated with George Washington University)
Website:
www.gwemed.edu/maritime/maritime

Pacific Maritime Institute
Website: www.mates.org

Stonehearth Open Learning Opportunities (SOLO):
P.O. Box 3150, Conway, NH 03818
Phone: 1- 603-447-6711
E-mail: info@soloschools.com
Website: www.soloschools.com

The Maritime Institute of Technology and Graduate Studies (MITAGS):
692 Maritime Boulevard, Linthicum, Maryland 21090
Toll free: 866- 656-5569
Fax: 410-859-5181 or 443-989-3206
Websitewww.mitags.org

The US Coast Guard approved medical training course SALTS (Save A Life at Sea) is offered by a variety of providers around the United States.

THE ONBOARD MEDICAL KIT

A comprehensive medical kit is an important part of the outfit of a boat sailing offshore, where injury is more common and help may be hundreds or thousands of miles away. It's as important to have a basic knowledge of how to use its contents when needed. Self sufficiency in this respect is especially crucial when voyaging.

When assembling your medical kit, you may well wish to solicit the help of the doctors who examined you and gave you prescriptions. Describe to them your plans for extended absences and the need for prescriptions to cover the amount of time you'll be away. Ask for their recommendations on medications or supplies to include in your kit.

If you or any of your crew are taking prescribed medicine at the time you make your departure, you should bring them along, together with a list of the medications by name and with their dosage and frequency. Each member of the crew should also bring along the names and contact numbers of their doctors and dentists.

Books and manuals on medicine and first aid are vital components of the offshore medical kit. I've used *Advanced First Aid Afloat*, by Dr. Peter Eastman, and the National Ski Patrol's *Outdoor*

Emergency Care, by Warren D. Bowman, M.D., along with the latest manuals from the Red Cross CPR and first aid courses.

Advanced First Aid Afloat is a thorough reference for not only the common ailments and injuries, but also for some that are seen more rarely. It's easy even for people with no medical training to read and understand and it contains much information specific to children, making it a great resource for cruising families. It should be read and understood by anyone venturing offshore or planning to embark on an extended cruise.

Aboard VOYAGER, we have *Where There is No Dentist*, by Murray Dickson, which provides excellent advice for dental problems not covered in Dr. Eastman's book.

The following recommendations are my latest in a long, ever-evolving list of component items for the medical kit.

Supplies for the Medical Kit

Ace Bandage Wrap

Bandages—a variety of sizes for small cuts and grazes

Betadine surgical scrub—used to disinfect wounds in preparation for suturing or bandaging

Blades—surgical blades are supplied sealed and sterile. Number 10 blade is best.

Cast liner—padding to put under splints

Cotton—absorbent, sterile

Forceps

Gauze pads—sterile, 4-inch by 4-inch

Intravenous catheters—thin plastic tube with a removable metal component to pierce the skin and vein used to administer intravenous fluids (Experience is warranted in placing an IV catheter.)

Knife—surgical knife

Lactated ringers solution—for intravenous or subcutaneous injection; plastic bags contain one liter of solution.

Needle holder

Resusitube—used in CPR or mouth-to-mouth resuscitation; this device is demonstrated in all CPR courses.

Rib belt—to be used to support the chest in the event of fractured ribs

Scrubbing soap pads

Sphingomanometer—for measuring blood pressure

Steri-Strips—adhesive tape used instead of sutures to close smaller wounds

Stethoscope

Suture material—3/0 silk with a swaged-on needle in packaged, sterile units

Syringes—used for injecting medications. Plastic syringes are sold pre-packaged with needles attached, usually 3 to 5 ml syringes with a 22 gauge needle.

Thermometers—must include a below-normal-temperature thermometer

Universal arm splint

Complement the instruments and supplies listed above with the following medications:

Medications for the Medical Kit

Skin Ailments

A&D Ointment, 4 gm tube—used for chronic skin ulcerations and to prevent nosebleeds

Chiggard—or any one of the liquid products applied topically to treat chigger bites

Furacin cream—used in cases of wounds or burns as an antibacterial

Gyne-lotrimin or suppositories—for vaginal yeast infections

Hydrocortisone cream, 1%— applied as a topical to severely itchy skin

Lanacaine—useful for skin rashes that occur with prolonged saltwater exposure

Povidone—iodine for antiseptic skin cleansing, also used before suturing wounds

Prednisone 20 mg tablets—for severe allergy and sunburn

Silvadene—salve used for fungal infections

Tinactin or Lotrimin creams—for athlete's foot

Triple antibiotic ointment—for external skin infections or burns

Gastrointestinal

Activated Charcoal tablets— to absorb toxins

Antihistamines (Benadryl)— for mild seasickness and allergic reactions; also a mild sedative for insomnia

Atropine sulphate—a narcotic used for relaxing the GI tract or urinary bladder in cases of urinary bladder infection; supplied as injectable liquid in individual ampules

Compazine (prochlorperazine) 25 mg—used in cases of severe vomiting to control stomach spasm; also has a tranquilizing effect. This is available as an intramuscular injection or as a suppository. The injectable is used in cases of severe, intractable symptoms of seasickness. Compazine suppositories are considered by many as the most reliable remedy for the symptoms of seasickness.

Flagyl (Metronidazole) tablets 250-500 mg—for intestinal parasitism (Giardiasis, Amoebiasis)

Fleet enema kits

Gelusil—antacid for treatment of indigestion; available as tablets or liquid

IPECAC—to induce vomiting in cases of non-corrosive toxins

Lomotil—given to control diarrhea; tablets in blister packs for adults, liquid for children

Metamucil—laxative

Phenergan suppositories—for seasickness

Senokot—a mild laxative

Suppository packets—for more severe constipation

Tagamet tablets—for indigestion or ulcer

Transderm Scopolamine patches, 1.5 mg.—seasickness preventative medication

Antibiotics

Bactrim DS—antibiotic used to treat urinary bladder infections; 500mg tablets in bottles of 100

Bicillin AP 500 mg capsules and as a dry powder mixed with diluent—broad spectrum antibiotic, synthetic ampicillin (check for drug allergies before administering)

Cortisporin Otic (ear) drops—for external ear infections, like swimmers ear

Doxycycline—broad-spectrum antibiotic supplied in oral capsules; 100 mg capsules in bottles of 50 capsules

Erythromycin 250mg capsules—great for Staphylococcus infections, especially for patients allergic to Penicillin

Neosporine—ophthalmic ointment as antibiotic for eyes

Analgesics

Cavit—used as a packing for dental cavities

Demerol—used for control of more severe pain; a narcotic given by injection; supplied in 30-cc bottles, 50 mg/cc

Ibuprofen—analgesic, supplied as 200mg tablets

Pontocaine—used to control painful eye injuries

Tylenol #3—to control pain; contains codeine, a narcotic; 30 mg tablets

Valium—also your ace in the hole in cases of hysteria

Dehydration

Gatorade powder—although not strictly a medication, is invaluable as a replacement fluid in cases of heavy perspiration or fluid loss due to nausea or diarrhea

Pedialyte—a powder to be mixed with water to supply electrolytes in cases of heat stress

Sodium chloride enteric-coated pills—to combat losses from heavy perspiration

Anaphylactic Shock

Epinephrine HCl—used as an intramuscular injection in cases of anaphylactic shock such as is seen with insect bites, acute food allergies, or drug reactions

Small Lacerations

Super glue—holds small cuts closed until they heal

Triple antibiotic ointment

Heart Attack Kit

Aspirin 300 mg daily

Lasix (Furosemide)

Lidocaine Monoject 100 mg

Nitroglycerine patches

Oxygen

Percodan

Tenormin, propranolol, or other beta-blocker to control arrhythmias

Contents of this kit are to be used for those with heart disorders demonstrating visible and unmistakable signs of heart attack. If possible, they should be used while in communication with a medical facility.

Anyone who knowingly sails with a heart condition should have discussed it thoroughly with a physician, and should have the equivalent of this kit along with complete instructions on use of the drugs. Such a crewperson should also bring along a portable defibrillator, and have their head examined before sailing!

Miscellaneous Items
   Adolphs Meat Tenderizer (Papaya extract)—for jellyfish stings
   Household ammonia—for insect stings
   Hydrogen Peroxide—for cleaning skin wounds, or to induce vomiting
   Insect Repellent—products containing DEET, such as Cutters, are best
   Rubbing alcohol—for cleansing, disinfecting, and mixed two parts to one of white vinegar for swimmer's ear
   Tincture of benzoin—to promote adhesion of steri-strips and skin dressings

Before setting sail, instruct the crew as to the location of the kit, as well as the locations of commonly used supplementary items and the medical books and manuals.

HEALTH UNDER WAY

Crew who are healthy before the voyage are the most likely to stay healthy. Should the physical exams identify problems, they should be taken care of before sailing. Some chronic conditions or existing health problems may persist, though, and these deserve special attention.

Seasickness

The most common of all maladies aboard a seagoing vessel of any kind, seasickness can affect almost anyone. Because at best it impairs and at worst disables, it is a legitimate safety concern.

Anyone who wishes to be able to sail in comfort and really enjoy the experience must conquer seasickness. Those who truly can't overcome its effects will probably never become capable bluewater sailors. Some people are born with a seeming immunity and others become less susceptible to it as they increase their exposure to the offshore environment. The majority of people I've sailed with feel it to some degree, as I do myself.

Ultimately, we bring with us whatever predisposition we may have, but we can control to a degree some of the contributory dynamics. To lessen the chances of becoming afflicted, we must understand these factors so we can prevent or counter them.

At the root of seasickness is a difference between what our eyes perceive and our inner ear, or vestibular system, senses. If a boat's motion is primarily limited to one type, such as gentle rolling, there is a small degree of stimulation for the onset of symptoms.

As the motion becomes more exaggerated with pitch and yaw thrown in, the inner ear cannot accommodate the unfamiliar motions, and most people will start to feel nauseous. In my experience, yawing, because it is the type of movement to which we are the least accustomed, is the most responsible for symptoms. One reason that pilots usually make good sailors is that they are familiar with this motion.

I've also observed that, below decks, two activities in particular seem to bring on seasickness. One is concentrating the eyes on a specific object, such as when reading a book or attempting to plot a position on a chart. I've seen spinnaker trimmers, who by concentrating their vision on a specific area of the sail, become affected even though they're on deck. The other cause is bending over with the head downward, while performing maintenance chores for example. These are all activities that concentrate the eyes away from any port or hatch that might give a sense of the boat's motion relative to the world around it.

Many sufferers can control or alleviate the symptoms by going on deck and watching the horizon. A spell at the helm often helps. Symptoms tend to lessen as the senses of sight and balance become more aligned with reality.

For some, actually giving in to the urge to vomit brings relief as that appeases the emetic impulses from the brain. Others find relief in heading to their bunks to sleep or simply relax with their eyes closed. When they arise, though, they should quickly head back on deck.

The worst thing you can do is to give in to the symptoms. I've sailed with crewmates who retired to their bunks, missing watches, meals, and the rest of the ship's activities. They never overcame the illness, and stayed miserable for the duration of the passage. Oddly, I've never seen this happen offshore; only in the long Mackinac races on the Great Lakes. In order not to succumb, you have to continue sailing actively, stay busy, take medication, drink and eat in small amounts, and allow your system time to adapt to the new environment.

Fear is a contributory factor in seasickness. It can take hold at sea or, in some people, before leaving land. This is one aspect of a person's psyche that I always try to learn about before taking them on the ocean; do they have an innate fear of sailing far away from land? I've noticed this phenomenon arise when people realize that they have left solid ground far astern, and nothing but the wide ocean lies ahead. This can happen at any time, and for two of my clients setting off on ocean passages, the Ambrose Light, seaward of New York Harbor, has been the trigger. In both cases, I took note of their apprehensions, had private reassuring conversations with them, and in one case, stood watches with her the first night out. They both gained confidence and actually did very well after that.

People with that fear are very likely to suffer from seasickness. Other factors aboard can also induce it: cigarette smoke below in confined quarters, odors from leaks in the head or its hoses, kerosene or diesel fumes, and the smell of onions are examples. B-complex vitamins can upset the stomach and become a factor. Fatigue and dehydration not only contribute with other factors to cause seasickness, they are also consequences of it, and can increase its severity and prolong the symptoms. The effects of alcohol can contribute mightily for many people, and for this reason, I do not allow alcohol, or cigarettes, aboard VOYAGER.

Seasickness, unlike the flu, is not caused by any specific organism, but it can appear contagious among crewmembers. When one member is affected and begins to exhibit its signs, especially vomiting, the spread among the crew is sometimes dramatic. This may be due in part because conditions on board have become more conducive, but a psychological aspect also contributes. Any crewmember overcome with nausea and vomiting should attempt to make for the head or lee side deck if possible.

Discuss seasickness during your crew orientation sessions. Talking in a matter-of-fact way about its causes and ways to control it is very helpful. Remember that fear and anxiety are factors, so don't overdo it. In those discussions, develop policies that will limit or eliminate situations on board that provoke symptoms.

No smoking at all on board is the best policy.

Be very careful when using jerry jugs to fill the fuel tank, prevent leakage in fuel jugs, and be diligent in engine inspections to prevent fuel leaks.

Consume no, or at most very mini-mal, alcoholic beverages the night before sailing, and none at all when at sea.

Begin seasickness preventative measures at least four hours before sailing, and maintain them at recommended intervals. Compazine, in 25 mg. suppositories (not tablets), is the most effective seasickness remedy. Also consider Transderm Scopolamine 1.5 mg patches. These are both prescription medications and their potential side effects include dry mouth, loss of taste sensation, and blurred vision. It's good practice to try these medications out before you depart on an offshore voyage, so that you can recognize any side effects, and how much they affect you. For a week at sea, get 10 or 12 dosages of the Compazine. The Scopolamine patches are renewed every three days, so you'll only need three for a week at sea. You can use Dramamine non-drowsy both as a preventative and as therapy. Regular Dramamine may be preferred to encourage rest.

Keep well hydrated offshore. Many people benefit from increasing their hydration, beginning at two weeks prior to sailing. Increasing water intake to up to a gallon per day helps to reduce dehydration on the water.

Avoid coffee and other diuretics before the voyage, and during it if dehydration becomes a problem.

Avoid eating spicy foods when at sea.

If symptoms begin, take palliative measures immediately to forestall or prevent seasickness. These include going on deck, driving the boat, taking medication to control vomiting, lying down with eyes closed, and limiting food and water intake to small portions to avoid a full stomach.

If possible, try not to let crewmembers witness others vomiting. If vomiting occurs below, clean it up immediately.

The Medical Logbook

The Medical Logbook is separate from the primary Ship's Logbook. It is used to keep a record of medical problems of any nature, including illness and injuries of any kind, experienced by any member of the crew. It is also a place to note relevant medical information on everyone aboard.

Columns should be labeled:

Crewmember Name
Pre-existing conditions, allergies,
    medications, and dosages
Date
Illness
Injury
Medication given, dosage, and
    schedule used
Duration of treatment, and progress.

The Medical Logbook should be kept very carefully and accurately, with no omissions, because the information it contains may be invaluable in the event a condition must be referred to a medical doctor.

The Medical Logbook should also contain a list of all medications kept on board, their expiration dates, and their consumption. This helps you in keeping the medications current and in restocking them periodically.

This logbook is also the ideal place to record emergency numbers of doctors or medical facilities that you would contact in the event of medical necessity.

Medical Communications

Equipping the boat so that you have the capability to communicate with medical professionals from remote areas is part of your voyage planning. That is when you choose the mode of communication, whether SSB radio or satellite telephone, you will take on board.

For those with SSB radio, the Ham network probably works best. If possible, contact Ham operators or Ham radio clubs in your home locality and prepare them to receive calls from your station in the event of need. The Maritime Mobile & Seafarers Net, at 14313 kHz, is available 24 hours a day.

The U.S. Coast Guard is also a good contact, and can connect you with a local hospital or with CIRM, a worldwide medical consulting organization.

With a satellite telephone, you can direct dial any physician, hospital, the Coast Guard, or other medical resource of your choice. Make sure that you have the necessary contact information on board, preferably written in the Medical Logbook.

The Centers for Disease Control and Prevention (CDC) is host to a wealth of information on a variety of topics.

Phone:1-404-639-3534
Toll free: 1-800-311-3435
Urgent: 1-800-232-4636
Website: http://www.cdc.gov/

CDC also provides information about Certificates of Vaccination and health topics of specific interest to travelers.

Toll free: 1-877-394-8747
Website: www.cdc.gov/travel/

The American Association of Poison Control Centers operates an emergency hotline.

Toll free: 1-800-222-1222

The International Association for Medical Assistance to Travelers (IAMAT) provides information on the need for immunization, risks of diseases, and a valuable list of physicians who speak English in countries around the world:

IAMAT
1623 Military Rd. #279, Niagara
    Falls, NY 14304-1745
Phone: 1-716 754 4883
Website: www.iamat.org.

CHAPTER 13

HEALTH INSURANCE

The majority of people able to cruise are at least middle aged, and many are seniors. Statistically, people in these age ranges are more likely to have medical problems, either pre-existing or yet to develop, and medical insurance becomes very important. It is also a fact that extended cruising, including offshore sailing, is more conducive to illness and injuries than a sedentary life. Anyone with health problems is well advised to take account of this greater risk of illness or injury before committing to such an undertaking.

Health insurance costs more for those spending time away from home than does domestic coverage, and not all companies offer it for cruisers. Generally speaking, most companies will cover insured customers for emergency care abroad. Some allow extensions of the coverage under the Cobra Plan, although only for limited and specified time periods. Before entrusting yourself to any program, be sure to find out exactly what it will cover, for how long, and at what rate and deductible. Some cruisers will be content with emergency coverage only. For others, a better option is to investigate programs

designed specifically to cover those sailing abroad.

To qualify for most of these plans, you have to be considered an expatriate, which means you have to be out of the country for at least six months a year. You can enroll in an insurance program for expatriates over the Internet, and coverage can begin that same day. Expect to have to answer questions relating to pre-existing conditions. You may or may not be required to have a physical examination as a condition of insurability. Another consideration is that your sailing resume reflects experience commensurate with your intended plans. The most common exclusions for these policies include sexually transmitted diseases (STDs), immunizations, cosmetic surgery, contraceptives, and hazardous sports.

Payments can be made on an annual, semi-annual, or quarterly basis. Refunds are pro-rated for claim-free customers after receipt of a written request for the policy to be discontinued. There are no restrictions on hospitals outside the USA, and payment covers claims that are usual, reasonable, and customary (URC) according to industry standards. Maternity coverage includes pre- and post-natal checkups and normal deliveries.

Be sure to have all your specific questions answered before enrolling in any insurance program, whether it's domestic or for coverage abroad.

Plans offered by the following companies are examples of those available:

Lifeboat Medical Plan
Kuffel, Collimore & Company
1761 South Naperville Road, Ste. 105
Wheaton, IL 60187
Phone: 1-630-221-6000
Toll free (USA): 1-877-335-1234
Fax: 1-630-221-1453
E-mail: info@lifeboatmedical.com
Website: www.lifeboatmedical.com

eWay Health Insurance is affiliated with Blue Cross Blue Shield, and offers protection for travelers.
eWay Insurance Services
500 Esplanade Drive, Ste. 950
Oxnard, CA 93036
Phone: 1-805-983-6683
Toll free (USA): 1-800-227-6474
Fax: 1-805-983-4957
E-mail: info@eWayInternational.com
Website:
www.eWayInternational.com

IMG
2960 North Meridian Street
Indianapolis, IN 46208-4715 USA
Phone: 1-317-655-4500
Toll free (USA): 1-800-628-4664
Fax: 1-317-655-4505
E-mail: info@medexplan.com
Website: www.medexplan.com

Healthcare International (formerly Med-Help Worldwide) provides accident and health insurance for blue water sailors spending at least six months abroad. The coverage includes worldwide assistance in locating competent medical assistance, repatriation, and evacuation from foreign countries. The policies are available through:

Wallach & Company, Inc.
Post Office Box 480, 107 West
Federal Street
Middleburg, VA 20118
Phone: 1-540-687-3166
Toll free (USA): 1-800-237-6615
Fax: 1-540-687-3172.

Diver's Alert Network (DAN) provides coverage for emergency medical evacuation for anyone more than 50 miles from home, even if the injury isn't diving related. Annual membership plans begin at $25.

Divers Alert Network
The Peter B. Bennett Center
6 West Colony Place
Durham, NC 27705
Phone: 1-919-684-2948
Toll free (USA): 1-800-446-2671
Website: www.diversalertnetwork.org

The Seven Seas Cruising Association (SSCA) has several programs of health insurance for its members. The policies are available through:

Blue Water Insurance Company
Blue Water West
PMB 389, 2726 Shelter Island Drive

San Diego, CA 92106
Phone: 1-619-226-6702
Toll free (USA): 1-800-655-9224
Fax: 1-619-226-8513
Toll free: 1-866-795-3707

Blue Water East
1016 Clemons Street, Suite #404
Jupiter, FL, 33477
Phone: 1-561-743-3442
Toll free (USA): 1-800-866-8906
Fax: 1-561-743-8751
Toll free: 1-866-795-3707
E-mail: sales@bluewaterins.com;
  service@bluewaterins.com
Website: www.bluewaterins.com and
  wwwbluewaterinsurance.com

International SOS. On joining this organization, you will receive cards that contain your vital medical records. Membership entitles you to obtain medical advice via phone and medical referrals worldwide. If needed, the organization will arrange medical evacuation and pay for transportation expenses.

International SOS Assistance, Inc.
3600 Horizon Boulevard, Suite 300
Trevose, PA 19053
Phone: 1-215-942-8000
Toll free (USA): 1-800-523-8930
Fax: 1-215-942-8299
Website: www.internationalsos.com

The FAQs sheet provided by MedExPlan (and copied below from its website) will answer some questions you may have concerning this type of insurance. Please understand that this information is only valid for this one company, and may or may not apply to others. Use it to gain some insight into this insurance and to whom and where it applies. To obtain specific information, contact the individual companies directly.

MedExPlan FAQs

Eligibility:

Who is eligible?
Anybody under age 75 is eligible provided they are not Americans living in the USA.

What is my home country limitation?
The only restriction is that you cannot be an American living in the USA; otherwise there are no geographical limitations.

General:

What period of time can I be covered for and are the plans automatically renewable?
The policy is for one year and automatically and guaranteed renewable annually. You can continue to renew as long as the plan is available and you are eligible. The upper age limit for new applicants is 74. You will receive a renewal form by post as well as 60- and 30- day e-mail notices prior to your expiry date. You can renew on-line or by faxing the renewal form.

Will I be required to answer a medical questionnaire or have a medical exam?
We have medical questions on our applications that ask about pre-existing

medical conditions, but no physical exam is required.

Will my coverage be affected if I return home?

If your geographical area contains your home country, then there is no limitation and you can continue to renew. The only restriction is that Americans must reside outside of the USA 6 months per year, and have a residential address outside of the USA.

How do I apply and how quickly can I be covered?

You can apply on-line and get same day coverage paying by credit card. Or simply download an application form and fax or post it to us. If you are paying by credit card we can cover you immediately or on the date you specify up to 30 days in the future.

How can I pay?

You can pay annually by credit card (Visa, MasterCard, JCB, American Express), check, postal money order, or bank draft in US dollars. You can only pay quarterly or semi-annually with a credit card.

What will I receive after I join?

You will receive a plastic membership ID card for your wallet with policy number and expiry date. On the back of the card are the contact numbers for IMG Assistance emergency response in the event of a problem. You will also receive a certificate of insurance, the policy wording, claim forms and procedures.

Can I change the level or area of coverage?

Yes, but only at renewal. If you upgrade, wait periods for benefits such as maternity will apply anew. If you have a medical condition under treatment and want to change your geographical area to be treated in the USA or Canada, then this will be at our discretion.

Am I covered if I travel outside of my country of residence?

You get full coverage within your geographical area, with Area 1 Europe, and Area 2 worldwide excluding USA and Canada, and you get 30 days in the USA accident and emergency coverage for travel or holidays.

What is the refund policy?

You can cancel and get a full refund within 15 days of starting. If you are claim free, you can get a pro rata refund.

Can I seek treatment anywhere in the world?

Yes, so long as it is within the geographical area you paid for.

What is the compassionate/ reunion travel benefit?

Compassionate travel is a return home $3,000 benefit that allows you to go home if an immediate family member dies unexpectedly, or becomes terminally ill. It also allows an immediate family member to come to your bedside if you become hospitalized. Under the Medical Evacuation benefit, reasonable transportation costs for an accompanying person will be paid if deemed necessary by IMG Assistance. In all circumstances these benefits must be pre-authorized and coordinated by the IMG Assistance.

What are the major exclusions?

STDs, immunizations, cosmetic surgery, contraceptives etc. are excluded. These exclusions are standard with most policies.

Are hazardous sports excluded?

Hazardous sports are excluded. Please see the policy wordings for a complete list. Downhill skiing and snowboarding on trail is not considered to be a hazardous sport.

What is in-patient treatment?

This is when you are admitted to a hospital. It is usually for a serious medical condition.

What is out-patient treatment?

This is when you consult with a general practitioner (family doctor) or out-patient specialist (e.g. a cardiologist) without being admitted to a hospital. An example would be if you have the flu and visited your doctor's office for a consultation.

What is the difference between travel and medical insurance?

Travel insurance is usually for short periods but can be for up to three years and does not cover urgent or elective medical problems. It covers only accidents and emergencies. Travel insurance companies expect you to end your trip and return home for elective or urgent treatment, and some policies require you to return home before your planned return date once diagnosed. For example, if you were diagnosed with cancer while on a travel policy, there might be an urgent requirement to commence treatment, but it is not a life or death situation to get on an airplane and return home. Travel insurance is also not renewable.

CHAPTER 14

BOAT INSURANCE

The percentage of offshore and cruising boats covered by insurance policies has increased in the last 20 years. Only a limited number of companies, however, insure boats offshore, and many refer to that insurance as the "London Market," meaning Lloyds of London. Beware of this option, though, and ask questions about how and when you'll be paid in the event of a claim; there is a history of difficulty in getting reimbursed.

Your offshore and cruising experience will be a factor used to determine eligibility and rates of insurance coverage. Those with limited experience will benefit from taking training courses, including on offshore passages.

To obtain insurance, you may be required to hire an experienced, professional captain on your initial long-distance passages. You may also be required to supply the company with a current survey report for your yacht. You'll need to put together a sailing resume describing the waters you've traveled as well as a list of vessels you've owned and for how long.

IMIS Corporation offers a policy it calls *The Jackline*. Expressly designed for people who are doing extended cruising throughout the world, this policy is quite comprehensive. It is not available for boats that will be moored at a central location. The Jackline provides "all risk" coverage on a replacement cost basis up to an agreed value, and includes coverage for a range of other hazards including mechanical breakdown, ice and freezing damage, pollution liability, reef damage liability, loss of use expense, and professional crew liability.

A feature of the Jackline program of particular importance to cruising couples is that in most cases having only two crew aboard doesn't prevent you from obtaining coverage.

Insurance rates depend on a number of factors that are determined once you fill out the application forms. For offshore insurance coverage, you can expect to pay an average of 2 to 4 percent of the boat's insured value in yearly premiums.

International Marine Insurance
Services
462 Kent Narrows Way North
Grasonville, MD 21638
Phone: 1-410-827-3757 x19
Fax: 410-827-3758
E-mail: mail@imiscorp.net
Website: www.imiscorp.net

The following is a list of conditions that will exclude a vessel from being insured under the Jackline policy:

Vessels that are not registered in the U.S. unless at least one owner is a U.S. citizen or resident or unless the vessel is regularly moored in the U.S.

Vessels that are not anticipated to be used for extended cruising during the first policy term.

Vessels that have not been used for extended cruising during the past two policy terms and are not anticipated to be so used for the coming policy term.

Vessels that are not anticipated to be used for extended cruising during the policy term and will instead be regularly moored at a location between Georgia and Texas that is more than 150 miles from the regular residence of the owner.

Vessels that are not anticipated to be used for extended cruising and will instead be regularly moored at a location in the U.S. that is more than 400 miles from the regular residence of the insured.

Vessels chartered or otherwise used in commerce.

Vessels participating in any transoceanic race unless as part of a cruising rally.

Vessels that are constructed for or are primarily used for racing.

Vessels with carbon fiber masts unless the Non-Aluminum Spar Amendment and a 30% hull surcharge are applied.

Vessels that are over 25 years old.

Vessels with cement or wood hulls.

Vessels with metal hulls built prior to 1990.

Vessels with converted or customized hulls or engines.

Vessels built by Ocean Yachts prior to 1990.

Houseboats, homebuilt boats and kit boats.

Catamarans built prior to 1990 unless built by Prout.

Trimarans.

Risks that within the past five years were declined, cancelled or non-renewed by any insurer for any reason other than the insurer not covering a navigation area or the insurer withdrawing from covering such risks.

Risks with two or more losses in the past three years.

Risks where no crew of the vessel has at least five years boating experience or three years ownership experience with boats of similar size (less than 10' difference).

Risks where fewer than two crew have at least three years of coastwise experience including extended cruising.

Risks presently insured by Markel through another producer unless the risk was referred to IMIS by that producer.

Premiums proposed to be less than those provided for in the premium tables hereinafter incorporated.

Renewal premiums proposed to be

less than the expiring premium except for reasons of reduction in risk or exposure.

New coverage proposed to be backdated to take effect prior to the receipt by IMIS of a definitive order for the coverage.

Renewal coverage proposed to be backdated to take effect more than thirty days prior to the receipt by IMIS of a definitive order for the coverage unless a statement of no known losses is provided by the policyholder or incorporated into the policy and the date of such statement is not more than sixty days from the effective date of the renewal.

Hull coverage amounts in excess of $750,000.

Personal property coverage amounts in excess of $50,000.

Protection and indemnity coverage amounts in excess of $1,000,000.

Personal liability coverage amounts in excess of $300,000 unless the excess is underwritten by Essex Ins. Co.

Medical payments coverage amounts in excess of $25,000.

Policy periods of more or less than twelve months.

Changes proposed to the coverage provided by current editions of the Jackline policy, Travel Restrictions and Personal Property Schedule other than by approved amendment forms.

Surveys

Prior to binding coverage for vessels over ten years old IMIS must accept a current professional survey report on the vessel. New surveys are required every fifth year, except for risks requiring transoceanic coverage which must have been surveyed within the past three years. A statement from the policyholder or the surveyor attesting to the correction of major deficiencies identified in a survey report should be on file within sixty days of binding coverage and prior to any extended navigation.

CHAPTER 15

A GUIDE TO THE MARINER'S WEATHER

To the sailor, weather is everything. Safe, swift ocean passages are the result when we make the most of the good that comes our way and avoid the bad.

Understanding the weather—what causes it and why—and from that being able to predict what might be in our future is therefore without question a primary goal of mariners. We don't need to become meteorologists, but we must be able to make observations of our current weather at any time and combine them with information we obtain from outside sources so as to make educated forecasts on which to base our sailing decisions.

For any prospective voyage, the first of those decisions concerns the time of departure. We should neither leave port when unfavorable conditions loom, nor should we be caught unawares by deteriorating conditions once we're at sea. Good seamanship dictates, therefore, that we begin to monitor the weather along our proposed route several weeks in advance of departure and continue to do so for the duration of the voyage.

On shore, we are bombarded with weather forecasts and weather-related stories broadcast over television, radio, and the Internet. Once we get offshore, while our need for information becomes more specific, our sources become limited by the means we have available with which to access them.

From the United States, the National Oceanic and Atmospheric Agency (NOAA) broadcasts marine weather data and forecasts for reception by a variety of means. It provides voice transmissions over short-wave radio several times a day on a number of frequencies. It transmits the same information for reception via weather facsimile and also as data for processing in a computer. One of the important decisions you have to make when preparing for your offshore voyage concerns the way you wish to receive your weather information, which in turn will dictate the equipment you install.

You can receive high seas voice forecasts with a short-wave radio receiver. An SSB radio transceiver will give you access to those same transmissions and also provide a means for long-range communications. In conjunction with a weather fax, the SSB will allow you to receive the forecasts in text together with synopsis charts. If you use a satellite telephone, you can receive data files for downloading into a computer. I discuss these options more fully in Chapter 8, *Communications*. I recommend you have either the SSB or satellite capability, and back that up with a short-wave radio receiver.

It's never too soon to start learning about weather and weather forecasting, and you can begin by taking observations at home and correlating them with the weather that you experience. Acquire your weather data equipment early in your voyage preparations so that you can install it and any accessories you need and become familiar with how it all works together.

Several weeks in advance of your departure date, start downloading weather information. Practice interpreting it, and compare your predictions to what actually comes to pass. While you do this, you'll also be able to iron out any bugs in your system so that you can be confident it will work when it's needed. If you use an SSB, practice downloading on several frequencies to determine the times and channels that give you the best reception. By the time your departure date arrives, you'll have a firm handle on weather systems and their rhythms as they affect your home area and your intended route.

The more knowledge you acquire about weather and the more practice in forecasting the better. Competence will not come from one article on the subject but from continued study and practice.

I provide the information in this chapter as a foundation on which to build your skills, and I recommend the following resources for more extensive studies.

Reading the Weather, by Alan Watts
The Sailor's Weather Guide, by Jeff Markell
Mariner's Weather Handbook, by Steve and Linda Dashew
www.sailnet.com/collections/seamanship/weather/index.cfm

WEATHER FUNDAMENTALS

Earth's atmosphere is a complex, dynamic system which can surprise even meteorologists who study it all their lives. However, the forces that drive it are, if not utterly predictable, well understood, and if you, too, acquire a basic understanding of those fundamentals, you should be able to read weather charts, interpret them, and combine that information with local observations to make forecasts.

The topics we'll look at include:

- Air masses—where they come from and how they circulate and interact
- The Coriolis Force—how it affects wind direction
- Atmospheric pressure—its causes and its effects on weather
- Fronts—how they form and how they affect local weather
- Pressure systems—how they form, how they travel, and how they affect weather
- Thunderstorms—how they form, their characteristic clouds, and how they affect mariners

- Squalls—how they form, typical clouds, and what to watch for
- Prevailing weather versus weather systems
- Sea breeze, land breeze—how they form and how they differ from weather systems
- Clouds—types, names, how they develop, and what they indicate
- Tropical cyclones—how they form and how to forecast their movement
- Extratropical storms— how they form and how to forecast their movement
- Predicting and monitoring storms— how to use chart and local data to predict and monitor weather systems
- Fog—its different types, how it develops, and how to predict its forming
- Symbols on weather charts—the symbols used to depict various weather features
- Reading weather charts
- Surface and 500 Mb charts
- Storm avoidance techniques

Air Masses

What we call weather is the result of interaction between *air masses* of differing temperatures. Those air masses acquire their heat largely from the surface of the earth, and how they come to be at different temperatures is due to two characteristics of the earth.

The earth gains its heat energy from the sun, and because the earth is a sphere, that energy is distributed unevenly—the part of the surface facing the sun receives more than areas inclined away from it.

Further, the earth rotates, so that over the course of a day, different areas of its surface are being heated or are cooling down. Because the axis of the earth's rotation is tilted (at 23.5°) with respect to its plane of rotation about the sun, the areas of its surface that receive the most heat vary over the course of a year. The resulting seasonal changes add a further complication to the weather forecaster's task.

During daylight hours, the earth's surface heats up and warms the air in contact with it. On warming, air expands and becomes less dense and rises, creating an area of lower atmospheric pressure at the surface. Air from an adjacent area of higher pressure rushes in to balance it and surface winds are the result.

The effect of surface warming is especially important at the equator. It is constantly warm and is always an area of low pressure, with surface winds blowing toward that relative vacuum (Figure 15-1). Because winds from both sides of the equator converge in the area to fill in the void created by rising hot air there, this equatorial zone of low pressure is called the *Intertropical Convergence Zone*, or ITC.

Hot air that rises, for example in this equatorial zone, must go somewhere once it's aloft, and it does. It cools in the upper atmosphere, becoming a denser air mass of higher pressure and colder temperature, and settles to the surface toward another area of lower pressure.

FIGURE 15-1

Hot air rising from the equatorial zone flows to the earth's poles and is replaced by cool air flowing from the poles.

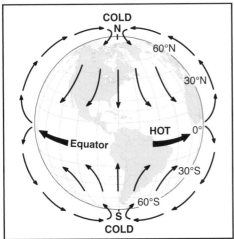

Air masses have different characteristics over land than they do over water. Land heats up much more quickly than water, and it cools more rapidly as well. The air over land will be much dryer than that over water, which retains water droplets from the underlying surface. The types of air masses found over those different earth surfaces are known as either *continental* or *maritime* masses, and they are further subdivided according to their locations in either warm or cold regions.

Major Air Masses

Maritime Polar (MP)
  cold, moist air
Continental Polar (CP)
  cold, dry air
Maritime Tropical (MT)
  warm, moist air
Continental Tropical (CT)
  warm, dry air

Each of these air masses has its own characteristics, and produces different weather as a result. For example the continental air masses will carry less moisture than maritime masses, and the warm air from tropical regions will carry more moisture than masses from polar zones.

The Coriolis Force and Winds

Figure 15-1 is a simplified representation of what would happen if the earth were stationary. The fact that the earth is a rotating sphere affects the dynamics.

The surface of the earth, and its atmosphere, moves at a greater velocity at the equator than it does at the poles. A point on the equator, where the earth's circumference is about 21,700 nautical miles, travels eastward at about 900 knots. The farther from the equator, the slower the surface velocity. At the poles, which are the ends of the axis of rotation, the surface has no easterly motion. Air originating at the poles and flowing toward the equator has no easterly velocity and therefore no easterly momentum. By the time it reaches the equator, it has been deflected toward the west, relative to the earth's surface (Figure 15-2).

The air rising from the equator and flowing toward a pole has easterly momentum, so as it moves northward it continues eastward relative to the earth's surface.

The deflected winds are a result of the Coriolis Force, which affects everything

FIGURE 15-2

The Coriolis Force deflects winds on the earth's surface.

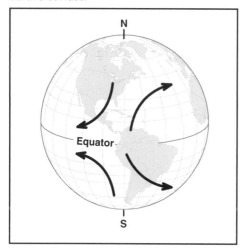

that moves on the planet in the same way.

The upper-left arrow in Figure 15-2 represents a polar wind. If it originated at 60° N Latitude, its initial velocity would be 450 knots toward the east—the speed of the earth's surface at that latitude. As it flows southward over the surface, which is moving eastward at a growing rate of speed, its direction relative to the surface of the earth is deflected. To an observer on the surface, it deflects to the right.

In the same way, the wind blowing toward the north pole from the equator, where the surface is moving eastward at 900 knots, is deflected to the observer's right as it passes toward the slower moving region.

In the Southern Hemisphere, the deflection of the winds is to the observer's left.

As described above, the equatorial area of low pressure created by rising hot air must be replenished from the areas of cooler, higher pressure air in the Northern and Southern Hemispheres. Figures 15-1 and 15-2 together show in simple form the origin of the winds that persistently flow into the equatorial region and are known as the northeast (Northern Hemisphere) and southeast (Southern Hemisphere) *Trade Winds*. Figure 15-3 shows how these are just two of several bands of winds that prevail at different latitudes.

A large portion of the hot air that rises from the equatorial region cools and settles toward the surface to form a region of high pressure at about Latitude 35 in both hemispheres. This is the area of relatively light, cool winds that plagued merchant sailing vessels. Their progress through them was often so slow that horses on board died from dehydration, from which the regions earned the name "the horse latitudes." It's this region in the North Atlantic Ocean that's characterized by the Bermuda High.

FIGURE 15-3

The earth's predominant wind systems.

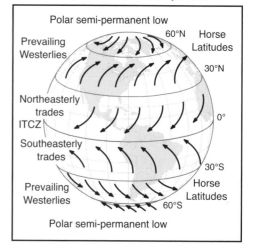

Air from these high pressure regions flows to regions of lower pressure to their north and south. In the Northern Hemisphere, the north-flowing winds, deflected by the Coriolis Force, become the prevailing westerlies that affect a good portion of the North American Continent and the North Atlantic Ocean. The south-flowing winds, similarly deflected, become the Northeast Trades.

Figure 15-3 shows the wind systems that predominate over the earth's surface. In addition to the low-pressure at the ITCZ, another zone of relative low pressure lies to the north of the horse latitudes (in the Northern Hemisphere), fed by the westerlies and by cold, high pressure polar air flowing southward. It is this cold, polar air flow that creates much of North America's harsh winter weather.

A similar situation exists in the Southern Hemisphere.

Atmospheric, or Barometric, Pressure

The earth's atmosphere is made up of air. Air has weight, and a one-inch-square column of the atmosphere weighs, on average, 14.7 pounds, so the pressure the atmosphere exerts on the earth's surface, called *atmospheric pressure*, is 14.7 pounds per square inch. The exact number at any point on the earth's surface will depend on the nature of the air mass above it.

A column of mercury 29.92 inches high exerts the same pressure, and in the English system of units standard atmospheric pressure is stated as 29.92 inches of mercury (chemical symbol Hg). The more common unit used internationally for atmospheric pressure, and the one found in NOAA products, is the *millibar*. (One millibar is 1,000 dynes per square centimeter).

Standard atmospheric pressure = 29.92 in. Hg = 1013 Mb

Atmospheric pressure is measured with a barometer, and is sometimes referred to as *barometric pressure.*

The measurement of atmospheric pressure has been important to mariners for centuries because it has a direct influence on weather conditions. High pressure is generally associated with cool, dry air and pleasant conditions. Low pressure usually indicates the presence of warm, moist, unstable air with unfavorable weather in the offing.

Air expands when it's heated, so warm air is less dense than cool air. A column of warm air consequently weighs less than the same height column of cool air, so measurements of barometric pressure can indicate the nature of the surrounding air mass.

No single barometric pressure reading, especially one that's near normal, provides information that's much use for forecasting. A series of readings taken over time, however, will show a trend in pressure, both in its direction and its rate of change, which we can use in our predictions.

The direction of change indicates what kind of *pressure system* is on the way; the rate of change helps us to forecast the strength of the system and of the winds it will bring. As shown in Table 15-1, a standard way to judge the intensity of an approaching low-pressure system is to mark

TABLE 15-1
Expected weather changes for a range of rates of fall in barometric pressure in a three-hour period.

Millibars	Inches of Mercury	Future Weather
3	.1	Low pressure may be approaching
6	.2	Depression nearing, expect force 6 winds soon
10	.3	Expect force 8 winds soon
12	.4	Expect near-hurricane-strength winds soon

the change in barometric pressure over three-hour periods. The more rapid the change, the more intense the system. Note that weather deteriorates as low pressure approaches, and is expected to improve with the advance of high pressure.

Highs and Lows

Individual air masses, as defined previously, are associated with regions of higher or lower atmospheric pressure. Circulation within pressure systems is characteristic, and very useful in making forecasts. High pressure systems are formed from descending (*convergent*) cool, dry air. Upon reaching the surface, the air moves outward across the surface toward low pressure. This outward (*divergent*) flow of air is deflected by the Coriolis Force toward the right in the Northern Hemisphere and leftward in the Southern Hemisphere (Figure 15-4).

Isobars

Lines shown on weather charts connecting points of equal pressure are called *isobars*. Their spacing is usually 4 Mb of pressure. They also indicate the wind direction at any point around the system. For example, around a high-pressure system in the Northern Hemisphere, the wind flows outward and to the right in a spiral fashion at an angle to the isobars of about 15 degrees (Figure 15-5).

High pressure at the surface can also take the form of a *ridge*. This feature is shown on a chart as a bold, jagged line emanating from a high-pressure system.

FIGURE 15-4
Winds blow outward from a high-pressure system and are deflected by the Coriolis Force, shown here for the Northern Hemisphere.

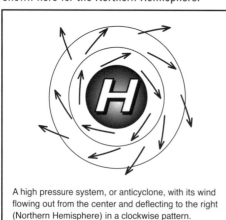

A high pressure system, or anticyclone, with its wind flowing out from the center and deflecting to the right (Northern Hemisphere) in a clockwise pattern.

FIGURE 15-5

The wind direction relative to the isobars around a Northern Hemisphere high-pressure system.

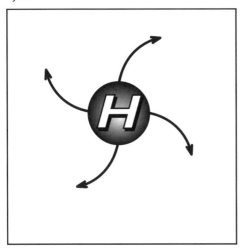

FIGURE 15-6

The wind direction relative to the isobars around a Northern Hemisphere low-pressure system.

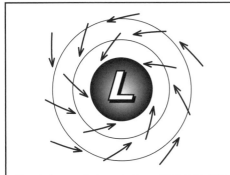

The winds around a low spiral inward and to the right in the Northern Hemisphere. If a low passes north of your position, the winds will veer from southeast to northwest. Backing winds indicate a low passing to the south of your position.

Ridges are occasionally associated with strong winds, especially in areas where the isobars are tightly curved.

Low-pressure systems also appear on weather charts as areas of concentric isobars. Because the lowest pressure is at the center, winds blow inward. In the Northern Hemisphere they are deflected to the right and again follow the isobars but at an angle of about 15 degrees inward (Figure 15-6).

A *trough* is an elongated area of low pressure around which the isobars can be tightly curved. Troughs are indicated on charts with bold, interrupted lines. The weather around a trough is similar to that around the low associated with it.

Buys Ballot's Law

The predictable nature of wind direction around the centers of high- and low-pressure systems allows us to estimate the direction in which they lie based on the direction of the wind experienced on the surface. This simple exercise, known as Buys Ballot's Law, is a valuable tool in your onboard weather predictions.

To determine the location of a high:

- Stand facing the wind in its prevailing direction.
- Extend your left hand to the side and forward.

When you refer to Figure 15-5, you can see that your left hand is now pointing toward the center of the high-pressure system.

- When facing the wind, the *high* is to your *left* and *forward*.

To determine approximately where the center of a low-pressure system lies:

- Stand facing the wind in its prevailing direction.
- Extend your right hand to the side and backwards.

When you refer to Figure 15-6, you can see that your right hand is now pointing toward the center of the low-pressure system.

- When facing the wind, the *low* is to your *right* and *behind*.

At sea, monitor wind direction among other weather measurements in your ship's Weather Logbook and use the information to assess your local weather conditions. Through Buys Ballot's Law, you can use changes in the wind direction to track the movement of weather systems relative to your position and update your chart with that information.

When a wind changes direction in a clockwise manner it is said to *veer*, or *clock*. When it changes direction in a counterclockwise direction it is said to *back*.

Fronts

As described earlier, air masses originate in four different states, each with its own characteristics that cause particular types of weather. These air masses can change, however, influenced by the surfaces over which they travel.

As air masses age, their temperatures increase, possibly making them warmer than adjacent air masses. Differences in temperature between air masses are key to the development of *frontal weather* along the zone where the masses meet. Frontal weather is characteristic to the type of *front* that forms, and knowledge of what to expect is of utmost importance to mariners.

A front is the boundary between adjacent air masses. The air within different air masses does not mix. Cool, dense air moving near the surface forces warmer air to rise up and over it. As the warmer air rises, it cools and cannot retain all of its moisture, some of which condenses to form clouds. The nature of those clouds and consequences they portend depend on a number of factors, such as the moisture content of the warmer air and how rapidly it rises. In general, the faster warm air rises, the more unstable it becomes and the more likely that precipitation will follow. Slow-rising warm air forms thin, wispy clouds very high up that carry little moisture and no threat of immediate storm activity.

The clouds formed from rising warm air are classified into a number of types, the presence of which alone or in combinations can help us forecast the coming weather.

If the northernmost (in the Northern Hemisphere) cold air mass pushes south against another warmer mass, the interface is called a *cold front*. This is typically the case, because cold air masses generally move more quickly than warm ones. If the southernmost (in the Northern Hemisphere) mass of high pressure, warmer in relation to its more northern counterpart, actually pushes north, a *warm front* forms at the boundary.

When neither the warmer nor cooler air mass pushes the other, specifically if no progress of 5 knots in either direction is made, the frontal boundary is termed *stationary*.

Very often, no organized frontal boundary develops, and the entire area is confused, with a portion acting as a cold front, some moving north as a warm front, and still another area behaving as a stationary front.

For the purpose of the following descriptions of fronts, we'll use Northern Hemisphere terminology.

The Cold Front

The most dramatic of the frontal systems is the cold front, formed when a cooler air mass pushes back warmer air. Especially in temperate regions, cold fronts arise when maritime polar or continental polar air masses travel from the high-pressure polar regions southward. Pushed by the Polar High, and influenced by the prevailing westerlies, they travel southeasterly.

As the cold, dense air moves toward the warm air mass, it forces the warmer, lower pressure air aloft in a steep frontal zone that causes rapid condensation and often dramatic cloud formation (Figure 15-7). This is characteristic of the cold frontal zone, with vertical clouds building into high cumulus cloudbanks. Fast moving cold fronts sometimes force the warm air skyward dramatically, causing great turbulence and resulting in cumu-

FIGURE 15-7

Schematic of a typical cold-front boundary and the pre-frontal squall line.

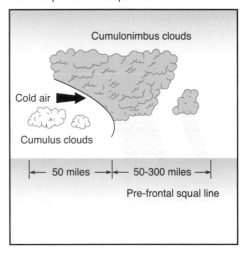

lonimbus, or thunderhead, clouds with thunderstorms.

In Figure 15-7, cold air, on the left, is moving eastward, forcing the warmer air to rise rapidly into the cooler upper atmosphere. There, the moisture it contains condenses fast, forming thunderhead clouds and short-lasting stormy weather with heavy rain, gusty winds, lightning, and possibly hail.

A line of squalls can develop ahead of the frontal boundary, and portends the event to come. These pre-frontal squalls tend to form when there is a large temperature difference between the air masses and the warmer air mass is laden with water. This is commonly seen when cold fronts pass over oceans where warm, moist air abounds.

When you see such a line of squalls at sea, be ready for immediate action, as the strength of the wind may take you by surprise. Drop the sails and watch the water to windward; it will tell you when the wind and rain are approaching. VOY-AGER was recently hit with such a thunderstorm squall line, and experienced winds over 60 knots. We were prepared, however, and used the engine to direct the bow into the wind. These squalls generally pass rapidly, and this one lasted less than two minutes.

These pre-frontal squalls can contain the same weather as the front itself, namely thunderstorms with high winds. When passing through a line of squalls, take note of the temperature. If there is no significant change, you know the cold front itself has not passed, and is still to come.

The frontal line itself arrives with a sudden burst of wind, and rain can come down in sheets. The sea surface appears to "boil" and differentiation between sea and sky is blurred. A wind change occurs rapidly when the front passes, veering to the west or northwest in the Northern Hemisphere, while backing in the Southern.

The seas will often become confused, since the newly formed wind waves may be from a different direction than the sea swells. The barometric pressure rises with the passage of the front, because the cold air mass has a higher pressure than that of the warm mass it is overtaking. After the front passes, which can take as little as 15 minutes, the skies usually brighten, dotted with cumulus clouds as the cool, dry air overtakes the region.

While fronts move at greatly varying speeds, you can use 20 to 30 knots as a rule of thumb for cold fronts, although they can move as fast as 50 knots. That's

FIGURE 15-8

Symbol used on weather charts to denote a cold front.

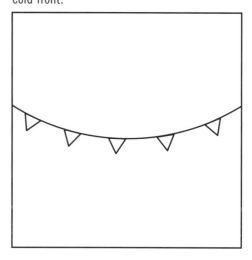

why they tend to pass quickly, and why we need to watch for them closely.

A cold front is shown on weather charts as a curved line with tooth-like projections pointing in the direction of frontal movement (Figure 15-8). On colored charts, the teeth are usually in blue.

The Warm Front

Warm fronts (Figure 15-9) arise when the warmer air mass pushes back the cooler mass. These warm air masses usually originate when maritime tropical air pushes northward against a weaker cool air mass, or an older high pressure system that has become warmer moves to the north. Warm fronts move generally eastward as well, due to the prevailing westerly winds.

The warm air in these systems meets cooler air at the frontal boundary, but is not forced upward violently. Air in the

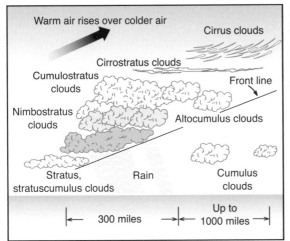

slower-moving warm front rises slowly over the cooler air, forming a very shallow angle from the frontal zone extending out ahead of the direction of frontal movement.

At the upper right of Figure 15-9, a very thin, high layer of ice-crystal cirrus clouds that are very delicate and lacy in structure form several hundred to 1,000 miles ahead of the warm front. They are the first indication of an approaching warm front and the depression that might follow. By observing these cirrus clouds, located at 30,000 feet or higher in the atmosphere, you can determine the direction of the jet stream and upper-atmosphere winds, but they may be obscured by lower-level cumulus and stratocumulus.

As the front nears, a gradual thickening of the high-level ice crystals forms the sheet-like cirrostratus clouds, recognized by the halo they create around the sun or the moon.

Next come the lower, denser altostratus, blocking out the sun and ac-companied by a drop in barometric pressure.

Passage of the front is immediately preceded by very low, dark, sheet-like stratus and nimbostratus clouds. Because the clouds are formed from slowly rising warm air, there is no thunderstorm development, but rather a steady rain is often seen at the front and extending outward until the clouds reach higher elevations. This can extend several hundred miles ahead of the front, explaining why warm fronts often bring rain that lasts for several days, with a low, thick, gray cloud cover. When the front finally passes, the drizzle will stop, although low stratus clouds often persist for a while. A wind shift is associated with warm fronts—it will veer up to 45 degrees—but it's gradual, without the bluster of cold frontal passage.

A warm front is shown on weather charts as a curved line with rounded nodes pointing in the direction of frontal movement (Figure 15-10). On colored charts, the nodes are usually in red.

FIGURE 15-10
Symbol used on weather charts to denote a warm front.

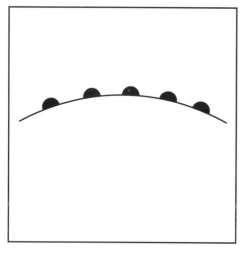

The Stationary Front

A stationary front develops when neither the warmer nor the colder of two air masses advances by pushing the other back. When this stagnant situation exists, the weather is quite like that of a warm front, with mild conditions stretching out over great distances. This stalemated situation can change, either back to its original form, or even revert to the opposite, when the other air mass takes control. On weather charts, a stationary front is depicted with alternating symbols of cold and warm fronts on either side of the front line. (Figure 15-11).

Depressions

While there is little mixing between air masses, we have seen that interaction at their boundaries creates considerable turbulence as air of the warmer mass is forced aloft by that of the cooler mass. When the Coriolis Force is factored into this turmoil, the stage is set for rising, unstable air to adopt rotation. This is the setting for the formation of *depressions*. Because depressions generate the most significant storms we face at sea, this is a phenomenon all mariners need to understand.

Figure 15-3 shows that in both hemispheres, at the interface between the base of the polar zone of high pressure and the semi-permanent zone of low pressure, the winds flow in opposite directions. This is what imparts the original impetus for fronts in their respective zones to interact and to begin to rotate.

Numerous features control the development of depressions. Among them are differences in humidity, temperature, and pressure between the air masses, additional energy of high-altitude weather systems, the effect of land and water, and

FIGURE 15-11
Symbol used on weather charts to denote a stationary front.

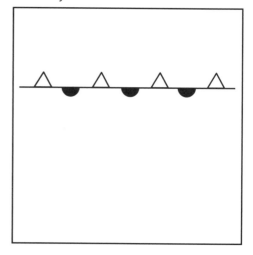

the sun's energy. Not all depressions become major weather systems, because for that to happen many factors must work in concert.

Air masses of different types and characteristics and with opposing wind directions begin to interact (A) (Figure 15-2). If an area of distortion forms along the frontal line (B), an airfoil effect results, accelerating the winds flowing to the north and creating "lift" and a zone of lower pressure.

The situation sometimes stalls at this stage, causing only some cloudiness and rain before it dissipates. However, if conditions are right for dynamic development, the distortion forms a wave, warm air rises and rotates, and the isobars curve around the central zone (C). When the wave is formed, the winds along the two sides of the original front act much like a breaking wave, toppling as its base is interrupted. They follow the isobars, which eventually tighten to complete the low pressure development (D), with its characteristic circulation, counterclockwise in the Northern Hemisphere, as shown, and clockwise in the Southern Hemisphere.

Note the isobars, which are straight between the individual fronts and curved around the rest of the system. These intra-frontal isobars are a key indicator of the direction the whole system will be expected to travel.

The system continues to mature, as the faster moving cold frontal zone travels toward the warm sector. As it catches up with the warm front, the two conjoin (E). This is the beginning of occlusion. The formation of the *occluded front* sig-

nals that the system has begun to weaken. The occlusion usually begins at the depression center, and radiates out from there (F). The symbol for an occluded front is alternating warm and cold front symbols facing the same direction, that of the cold and warm fronts that created it (Figure 15-13). On color charts it often appears as purple.

In an occlusion (Figure 15-12 E, F), the cool air from behind the cold front pushes forward, and wedges itself beneath the air in the warm sector. This causes rain in the warm front to decrease because much of its energy is dissipated already. Persistent warm-frontal rains, with decreasing winds, accompany passage of the occluded front, then become more intermittent. The barometer ceases to fall, or falls very little, and the air temperature stays constant.

Occluded fronts are characteristically features of aged depressions, and indicate that they've lost much of their power and destructive capabilities. Mariners shouldn't drop their guard when they form, though, because just as it appears the system is beginning to dissipate, a secondary low can form off one of the trailing fronts. The newly formed low pressure system can retain some of the energy of the previous one, and gather additional strength from the maritime equatorial air present at sea. This is what happened in the 1979 Fastnet Race, when the fleet was beset by a secondary low that became a monster of a storm.

Figure 15-12 depicts the classic steps involved in the development of an *extratropical cyclone*, in which the temperature

FIGURE 15-12

Sequence of events that results in the formation of a depression.

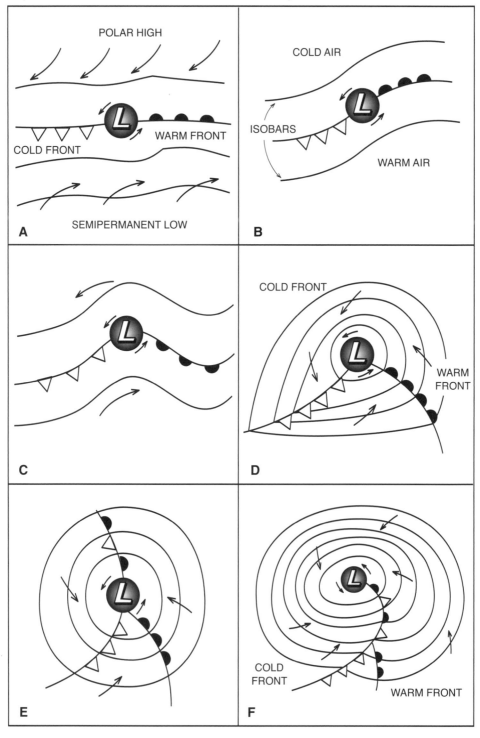

FIGURE 15-13
Symbol used on weather charts to denote an occluded front.

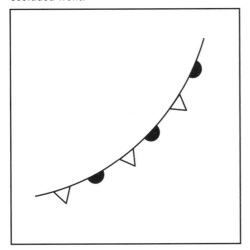

FIGURE 15-14
Weather at various locations within a Northern Hemisphere extra-tropical low-pressure system.

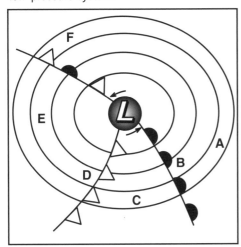

within the core is colder than outside it. These systems, which form outside the tropics, are also referred to as depressions, as low-pressure areas, or simply as lows.

The weather conditions experienced vary according to the location within the cyclone (Figure 15-14).

A) Warm front approaching
Cirrus with cirrocumulus, cirrostratus with lower stratocumuplus, cirrus with low cumulus, cirrostratus with lower stratocumulus, altostratus, stratus/nimbostratus. Rain begins with altostratus cloud cover, barometer dropping slightly near the warm frontal zone, with stratus/nimbostratus clouds, steady rain, wind veering slowly.

B) Warm front passage
Wind veering further to the southwest, air temperature rises, clouds decrease, and rain eases. The barometer steadies, but doesn't rise yet. Winds usually get lighter, wind waves subside. Sea swells diminish much more slowly.

C) Warm-air sector ahead of the cold front
Stratus layer becoming cumulus, rain ceases, wind shifting, barometer steady, temperature steady. Typical cold-frontal clouds are seen in the west.

D) Cold front passage
Boisterous heavy breeze, sudden wind veer to the northwest, temperature drops.

E) Cool sector
Cool, clear skies, diminishing winds from north, eventually giving way to prevailing patterns, seas calming, barometer has risen.

F) Occlusion area

131

Cloudy with heavy rain, very similar to warm front zone. Winds are from north to northeast, and heavy, with seas to match.

Negotiating an Extratropical Cyclone

If you were on the North Atlantic Ocean with an extratropical cyclone, as depicted in Figure 15-14, approaching from the west, you would expect your weather to reflect that segment of the system in which you were sailing.

At Point A, with the storm coming straight toward you, cirrus clouds appear overhead, gradually become thicker and lower as the system approaches (see Figure 15-17 for illustrations of the clouds described). Note that the highest cirrus clouds are moving easterly, driven by the prevailing upper-level westerlies, but your prevailing westerly surface breeze has given way to winds governed by the system. They are now coming from southeast to south. This is an important point: When a low approaches, the wind comes from your left side as you face the upper-level wind direction. After the storm passes, the winds will come from your right side, as you face the same direction.

Ocean swells may change early in the progression, causing confused seas if their direction differs from previous swell directions. The change in wind direction alters the local wind waves, giving the ocean a totally new feel.

Within a few hours, cirrus clouds will give way to cirrostratus. Turbulent air aloft interacts with the thickening clouds there, imparting a tumbling effect to

form cirrocumulus, the clouds of "mackerel skies." Barometric pressure begins to fall, slowly at first, but more rapidly as the low pressure nears.

When the warm front portion of the system is about 300 miles off, clouds will continue to thicken and get lower, altostratus usually being the predominant type with some altocumulus. Winds build steadily and continue to veer with the approach of the front. Precipitation can begin at any time when stratus and nimbostratus become the predominant clouds. Winds become south to southwesterly, the barometer continues to drop, and the rain gets heavier by the hour. Precipitation fog may develop as the cold rainfall contacts warmer air below. Winds continue to build, up to Beaufort Force 8, and waves build accordingly.

As the warm front passes, things steady up. The wind is still strong, but the barometer and temperature are steady and the rain eases up.

You know the cold front has yet to pass, so you stay in storm mode. Winds will pick up again, continuing to veer, as cumulus clouds form, darkening the skies to the west and northwest. Squall lines may precede the cold front, giving a taste of what's to come. When the front passes, it's accompanied by heavy showers, thunderstorms, strong winds with frequent gusts, and very confused seas. The wind veers abruptly toward the northwest quadrant, the barometer rises, and cooler temperatures confirm passage of the cold front. Waves quickly become northwesterly in accordance with the post-frontal wind direction.

They can become dramatically large, sometimes upward of 30 feet in height, especially if counter to an ocean current. Sky cover usually proceeds from cumulostratus or stratus to rapidly clear, with crisp, cool weather in control. Smaller cumulus may dot the blue skies. When the frontal passage is particularly rapid and violent, the sky sometimes becomes dotted with small, circumscribed, "popcorn" cumulus clouds.

Tropical Cyclones

Depressions that develop in the tropics are called *tropical cyclones*. They are also referred to, depending on geographical location, as hurricanes or typhoons.

Tropical cyclones differ from those of extratropical origin in a number of ways. Mainly, tropical cyclones have warm cores and do not have associated warm and cold fronts. They can also become a great deal more intense, which explains why they are viewed with dread by mariners.

Tropical cyclones form over the oceans and usually originate in the regions between 5 and about 20 degrees Latitude on either side of the equator. Barometric pressure decreases from the periphery inward, with the lowest levels at the center. The winds spiral inwardly in a counterclockwise direction in the Northern Hemisphere, clockwise in the Southern. The temperature at the center of a tropical system is always warmer than at its periphery.

When winds at the center are below 34 knots, the system is classified as a tropical depression. When the winds are between 35 and 64 knots, it is termed a tropical storm, and when the winds exceed 64 knots it qualifies as a hurricane, typhoon, willy-willy, or cyclone, depending on the part of the world it's in.

A major goal when planning a route for a voyage and its timing is to avoid tropical cyclones. They occur in the North Atlantic from June until November, in the eastern North Pacific from May until December, and at any month of the year in the western North Pacific. The South Pacific and South Indian Ocean zones are at risk from September until May, while May and September are the most active months in the Bay of Bengal and Arabian Sea areas.

Tropical cyclones often develop near the equatorial latitudes where the trade winds of the two hemispheres converge. Interaction with the ITCZ results in bending of the isobars, called at that point a *tropical wave*. Most tropical waves simply travel along with the prevailing winds, failing to develop further. When the wave does mature, and isobars around it close into loops, a tropical depression is formed. When a number of features in the surrounding environment are just right, the depression can develop, perhaps ultimately into a hurricane.

Many of the contributing factors are understood, and research continues to determine others. Among the known needed elements are high sea-surface temperature and winds aloft that contribute to, rather than counter, the system's development.

Signs and Symptoms of a Tropical Cyclone

The progression of events that herald an approaching tropical cyclone is fairly typical and predictable. It resembles that described above for extratropical storms, with the changes in sea swell, cloud development, and barometric pressure, except that the swells and pressure changes are of greater magnitude, reflecting the greater intensity of the systems. (Tropical cyclones are geographically smaller than many of their extratropical counterparts, but they can contain winds of far greater strength.)

In the hours when the full-fledged cyclone is within about 150 miles, the winds become sustained at over 64 knots, torrential rain blows in horizontal sheets, and the sea is covered with wind-blown spume as waves reach heights of 40 feet and more with breaking crests. The barometric fall is far more rapid and deeper than in an extratropical low, dropping to 950 millibars or even lower.

If the storm center, or *eye*, passes over you, the rain and wind cease and blue skies appear overhead. The seas become very confused and particularly dangerous. When the storm's fury suddenly returns, its wind and rain will come from the opposite direction until the storm passes.

Your weather chart and data gathering, augmented by your onboard observations, are never so valuable as when one of these monsters threatens. You have to take all possible measures to identify, track, monitor, and predict the path of a tropical cyclone so that you can plan evasive maneuvers and ready the ship for the coming storm conditions.

Thunderstorms

When sailing near land in hot summer weather, the risk of encountering thunderstorms is often present. Severe thunderstorms with lightning, thunder, and hail commonly occur on humid days when the land heats sufficiently.

Warm, moisture-laden air, further heated by the hot land, rises. As it cools aloft, the air sheds the moisture it can no longer hold and it condenses to form mountainous cumulus clouds that rise vertically, the unstable air billowing to elevations that exceed 30,000 feet. The tops of these clouds are flattened by upper level winds blowing in the direction taken by the clouds, forming the anvil shape typical of the thunderhead, or cumulonimbus cloud (Figure 15-15).

Powerful updrafts pull surface air into the clouds from all directions, while

FIGURE 15-15

Updrafts and winds associated with thunderstorms and sea squalls.

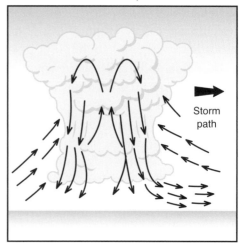

Storm path

downdrafts of cold air descend rapidly back down through the clouds.

While they are caused by a different mechanism than those encountered out at sea that accompany a rapidly moving cold front, they can be every bit as violent.

Winds around thunderstorms can be severe. Outlying air is aspirated into the vortex, so winds blow toward the storm from all directions. Close to the storm, powerful downdrafts blow down and away from it. If you sail into a downdraft you'll experience a sudden wind shift and wind speeds of up to 50 knots.

When you see mountainous cumulus clouds forming during daylight hours, be on the lookout for thunderstorm development. Be alert to the following indications of the stages of the storm's development and decay:

- Unstable, boiling appearance at the uppermost levels
- Flattened, anvil shape at the top when the clouds reach the upper winds
- When the top appears fuzzy without the boiling appearance, generation ends
- When "false cirrus" appear to stream out from the front of the anvil, the storm has lost its power.

Waterspouts

Waterspouts form at sea in much the same manner as tornadoes do on land. They are tightly confined zones of very low pressure, whirling counterclockwise in the Northern Hemisphere, usually developing in association with the instabil-

ity of thunderstorms. They may be seen with their funnel shape developing downward from the base of cumulonimbus clouds. Waterspouts are composed of water droplets formed from condensation, not from seawater drawn into the funnel. They're short-lived, not as powerful as tornadoes, but threatening to sailboats with canvas still up.

Squalls

Squalls at sea are created in the same way as the thunderstorms seen over land on hot summer days (Figure 15-15). The two primary ingredients of squalls are humidity and heat.

Heated by the sun, the ocean's surface imparts warmth to the overlying, moist air, which begins to rise. As the air rises to cooler altitudes, the water vapor condenses and releases energy, which causes the air to continue rising, more water condenses, and large cumulus clouds begin to take shape.

Before long, the water vapor forms enough droplets aloft that they begin to fall toward the surface. As the now cold water droplets fall, they encounter drier air, and some of the water evaporates, cooling the air further and making it denser.

The cool, dense air descends, creating the sometimes-powerful downdrafts of squalls at sea. The tallest cumulonimbus clouds can generate microbursts, where condensed water droplets become very cold, and then impart that cooling to descending drafts of air. That air, now even colder, becomes even denser and descends faster, gaining surprising velocity as it approaches the surface. Microbursts occur in squalls at sea and in association with thunderstorms on land.

It seems logical, and from personal observation, probable, that squalls form at least partly due to the heating of islands, which contribute to the heated air. At sea, it often appears that some squall-inducing cumulus clouds arise over land, so keep that in mind as well.

Squalls usually occur in the late afternoon or evening, so when at sea, observe any cumulus clouds as they develop during the afternoon hours and take note of their positions just before dark. At night, the tops of squall clouds will blot out the stars.

When you suspect a cloud is to windward, be alert to changes in the wind's direction and turn on the radar, which can help you estimate the size and intensity of a squall by the amount of rain clutter on the screen. If the outdraft from the squall is contrary to prevailing wind direction, you will experience a lull as the squall approaches, a sure sign that something's in the wind. The crew should be on their guard and ready to take sails down when the squall gets close.

Working a Squall to Advantage

Squalls are certainly worthy of your concern, and it's wise to prepare for the bigger ones by taking sails down. However, you can also use the winds and rain associated with sea squalls to your advantage.

The quick rain showers provide relief from tropical heat and wash down the boat with fresh water, and you can collect the rain to supplement the water stores.

In squalls, the wind blows in a direction about 15 degrees to the right of that of the prevailing wind (in the Northern Hemisphere). If you are sailing in a southerly wind, therefore, expect the wind to come from the south-southwest after the squall hits.

Figure 15-15 shows air being drawn into the squall from all directions at only moderate speeds. The cold air aloft picks up speed as it descends downward and emanates from the bottom with more velocity, fanning out over the surface. In the leading edge of the squall, the exiting downdraft wind supplements the prevailing wind, adding to its velocity, so it's there you'll encounter the strongest winds. This is the downwind, or leeward side of the squall. On the windward side, winds coming out of the squall blow into the prevailing winds and in effect cancel one another out. This explains the wind lull that occurs subsequent to a squall's passage. The former, prevailing winds fill in only when the system is well past.

For sailors, the best winds associated with squalls are usually on the north side in the Northern Hemisphere, to their south in the Southern Hemisphere.

If you can position your boat to lie in front of the squall as it approaches (assuming it's not too large and threatening) you can use its stronger winds to sail faster. Figure 15-16 illustrates where the best winds are located around a squall in the Northern Hemisphere. Positioning your boat in the area of strongest winds can provide a real boost in your sailing speed.

You can also determine from Figure

FIGURE 15-16

Winds about a squall at sea in the Northern Hemisphere: The squall moves pole-ward of the equator and the strongest winds lie ahead of it, light winds behind it.

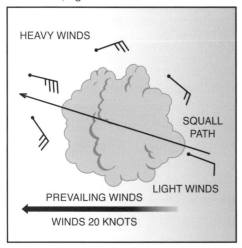

HEAVY WINDS

SQUALL PATH

LIGHT WINDS

PREVAILING WINDS

WINDS 20 KNOTS

15-16 the path you'd take to avoid a heavy squall. Instead of sailing to get ahead of it, you'd head away, toward its equatorial side, where the winds are lightest.

Line Squalls

Line squalls form in much the same way as described above, except that they are associated with frontal activity and can extend for greater distances.

Line squalls can be associated with the zone between adjacent high pressure systems, where plenty of cool, dry air is converging to the surface. These systems should be watched closely, because the squalls they produce can be more powerful than those that arise due to simple convection of warm air.

Safety against a string of line squalls lies toward the equator.

Cloud Types and Characteristics

One of the most valuable tools in your onboard weather forecasting is an ability to recognize cloud formations and an understanding of how clouds form and what weather conditions their presence signifies. Part of your voyage preparation should include the study of clouds.

Pay attention at all times to the types of clouds present, their direction and speed of movement.

Cloud formation begins when moisture is added to the air by evaporation from the earth's surface. Heated, moist air rises by a number of mechanisms. At altitude, moisture in vapor form is cooled and condenses into water droplets which then form clouds.

Various types of clouds (Figure 15-17) form in different weather systems as differing amounts of water droplets condense at various rates and altitudes. The relative barometric pressure and moisture content of the air are also factors in the types of clouds that develop and at what altitudes they form, which in turn provides the observer with valuable information about the mechanism by which they were formed.

Most clouds can be described using four basic classifications. Their names, taken from Latin words, generally indicate the level that the cloud occupies aloft.

- **Nimbus**—Low, unorganized clouds, thick with water vapor; associated with rain

- **Stratus**—Layered, dense with moisture, at lower altitudes
- **Cumulus**—High, puffy clouds associated with fair weather; very high, towering cumulus clouds generate thunderheads
- **Cirrus**—Very high clouds composed of ice crystals, usually a feature of the jet stream and indicative of its direction of movement.

These names can be combined, or used as suffixes or prefixes along with others to identify other cloud types.

- **Cirro**—suggests a cloud at great altitude (30,000 feet or more)
- **Alto**—is used as a prefix to indicate a cloud in the middle altitude ranges
- **Nimbo**—means the cloud is associated with rain

Clouds at High Altitude—30,000 Feet and Higher

Cirrus

Wispy, delicate, often strikingly beautiful against the blue sky; also called *mares' tails.*

Cirrus clouds with hook-like appendages are highly suggestive of an approaching warm front. Observe the speed at which the cirrus clouds move. Located at the altitude of the upper winds that drive weather systems, they indicate storm movement. The intensity of the associated low is often proportional to their speed of approach.

Because the jet stream is usually at a similar elevation, we can use the movement of cirrus clouds to estimate its di-

rection and speed. As described above, cirrus is the earliest indicator of warm frontal activity up to 1,000 miles distant and on the way. It can also herald extratropical cyclones or hurricanes.

Cirrostratus

A high (30,000 feet and higher) cloud made of ice crystals appears as a thin veil, creating haloes around the sun and moon. It indicates an approaching warm front with its associated low-pressure system. Frontal passage should be expected in 12 to 24 hours.

Cirrocumulus

Ice crystals at high altitudes that form masses thicker than cirrus clouds. Developing at high altitudes, they're often tumbled by upper level winds and take on the appearance of the mackerel fish—whence the expression *mackerel skies.* These clouds are indicative of upcoming frontal activity.

Jet contrails, not to be confused with clouds, can be used to derive the direction of a jet stream. When the ice crystals of contrails remain with little movement, they indicate that warm, moist air is present as the warm front approaches, and could indicate rain in 48 hours or so.

Clouds at Middle Altitudes—10,000 to 20,000 Feet

Altocumulus

Thinner than cumulus, altocumulus tend to be individual smaller clouds packed closely together, with sky showing between them. They are typical of the lowering cloud patterns seen as a warm front approaches.

Altostratus

Denser sheets that obscure the sun, moon, and stars. This lowering, thickening cloud system indicates that warm frontal approach is now within hours. Precipitation can commence in association with altostratus, beginning as a light, misty rain.

Low Altitude Clouds—3,000 Feet and Below

Stratus

A uniform, low, grey cloud also called *high fog* and usually accompanied by light rain or drizzle. These are seen at the frontal boundary, and after frontal passage, as conditions are changing.

Nimbostratus

Low, dark, moisture-laden clouds that blot out the sky, seen at and just before a warm frontal passage. The rain present may actually fall from altostratus clouds above, and emerge through the nimbostratus layer.

Jet Streams

The *jet streams*, located typically above 35,000 feet in altitude, are currents of air born of extreme temperature differences between the poles and the equator. The several different components of the jet stream are known as the subtropical, the polar, and the arctic zones.

The subtropical part carries warm, humid air from the tropics toward the polar regions. This air is a key component in the power of the jets. The polar jet, or middle part, is located farther toward the poles, and it bears colder air from that region. When the middle jet's path curves toward the equator, the cold air mass it bears contacts warmer air from the subtropics, which increases the potential for frontal-wind development. The arctic flow is the source of the polar jet's coldest air. Because they introduce air to regions that have air

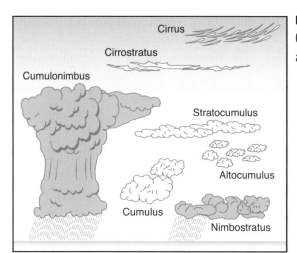

FIGURE 15-17

Cloud types and the relative altitudes at which they form.

139

masses of different characteristics, the paths taken by the undulating jet stream components are fundamental to the development of weather systems.

The jet stream is of particular interest to mariners sailing during the winter months. For example, if you are heading toward the tropics from a subtropical region, there is the potential that threatening weather will develop if the jet stream is toward the equatorial side of your route. Always try to leave when the jet stream is located poleward of your route.

Jet stream information is available from the weather services. You can check for it visually by looking for fast-moving cirrus clouds.

Fog

Fog occurs when airborne moisture is cooled to its condensation temperature, or *dew point*. This is the temperature at which the air contains all the moisture it can hold under its present pressure. It is also referred to as the saturation point. Warm air holds more moisture than cooler air, so the dew-point temperature for warm air would be higher than for cooler air.

Lowering the temperature will cause air to reach its dew point. Fog is generated when the air temperature falls below the dew point or if the dew point rises to the air temperature. The difference between the air temperature and its dew point is called the dew-point spread. When its value is less than 5 degrees Fahrenheit (2 degrees Celsius), fog is likely to develop.

An instrument called a sling psychrometer can be used to determine the dew point at a given time. The device consists of two thermometers attached to a rotating arm. One thermometer is fitted with a moistened cover (sock), called the wet bulb, the other thermometer is called the dry bulb.

When the device is rotated, moisture evaporates from the wet sock, taking heat with it and lowering the temperature of the wet bulb. When the wet bulb temperature stabilizes, the difference between wet and dry bulb temperatures is noted and used to calculate the dew point by reference to a table (Appendix 9).

The sling psychrometer and dew point table should be standard equipment on vessels that frequent waters where fog develops often. Alternatively, modern handheld weather instruments are available which have a dew-point function.

Radiation Fog

Radiation fog usually develops in the evening when land, heated by the day's sunshine, cools rapidly. This causes cooling of the air just above the surface. If it reaches its dew point temperature, the moisture condenses into fog. This is primarily a land-based fog, and only concerns those sailing near the coasts or on inland lakes or rivers.

Radiation fog dissipates when sunshine begins to heat the surface, allowing the warming air to take up more moisture. Wind that develops in the morning also helps to move the fog over warm land and to mix it with drier air aloft.

Advection Fog

Advection fog, also known as sea fog, is caused by air movement close to the surface. This usually occurs when warm, moist air moves over cold water, as when moisture-laden winds blowing over the Gulf Stream are heated, and proceed over the cold waters off the New England coast. Advection fog is also seen in the Great Lakes areas, when cold autumnal winds blow over the still-warm waters of the Lakes. Sea fog also forms when a warm front passes over cold water.

Advection fog usually develops when the wind carrying warm air is less than 15 knots in strength, since stronger winds take the air higher up to form stratus clouds. Stratus clouds can also extend downward toward the surface to create advection clouds. Sometimes, with advection fog in place, heating of the surface by sunlight warms the cloud, which rises in elevation off the surface to form a stratus layer.

Usually with advection fog, a discrete fog bank is seen moving horizontally across the surface. The bank can grow to be several hundred feet thick and resist dissipation by even 25-knot winds. It can persist for several days, and can present a real hazard to sea traffic.

Precipitation Fog

Precipitation fog may be the most common type of fog, since it's created during rain when the moisture is cold. The cold water droplets cool the air as they descend, causing some of the air they pass through to reach its dew point and cause its mois-ture to condense out. Precipitation fog usually clears when the rain ceases, but if the air is very warm and moves over cold water, advection fog can develop.

Sea Smoke

Sea smoke appears much like steam rising from a cup of hot coffee. It forms when very cold air drifts slowly over water that's much warmer. The cold air at the water's surface takes on heat and moisture from it and the moisture condenses as it rises into the cooler air above, hence the steaming appearance. Sea smoke readily disappears under the sun's warming influence.

Up-Slope Fog

Up slope fog is probably most familiar to skiers, who commonly see fog developing as air pushed up the mountain slope gradually cools to its dew point and its moisture begins to condense.

Weather Chart Symbols

Symbols used on weather charts have become uniform for the most part. For specific information about chart symbols, contact the issuing weather bureau.

NOAA's Tropical Prediction Center and Ocean Prediction Center also use the following symbols:

L indicates the center of a Low
   pressure area
H indicates the center of a High
   pressure area
L indicates the location of a Tropical
   Depression.

Reading Surface Weather Charts

An important part of weather forecasting is reading surface weather charts and trying to envisage the dynamics behind the static, two-dimensional representations.

Even though you might be familiar with the symbols in general use, it sometimes takes practice to recognize and understand their meanings on physical charts.

Isobars are very important symbols. They indicate pressure gradients, the directions in which systems are traveling, and zones where winds are stronger than expected.

Isobars are normally spaced to represent 4-millibar changes in barometric pressure. Isobars spaced well apart indicate low wind speeds because there is little pressure gradient to supply energy. The more closely spaced the isobars, the greater the expected wind speed, as pressure is changing over a smaller distance.

Just as wind over a sail moves faster on the convex side, significant curvature in isobars around a high can cause wind to accelerate around the bending by as much as 25 percent over the charted speeds. Contrarily, around a low, wind speed is decreased when affected by curved isobars. Alterations in wind speeds around isobar curves are more dramatic when they occur at higher latitudes than at lower latitudes.

FIGURE 15-18

Surface weather chart downloaded from NOAA: The symbols are characteristic of those used on surface meteorological charts. High pressure near Bermuda is seen to control the weather, with a ridge extending westward. Note the winds flowing either along the ridge or away from it.

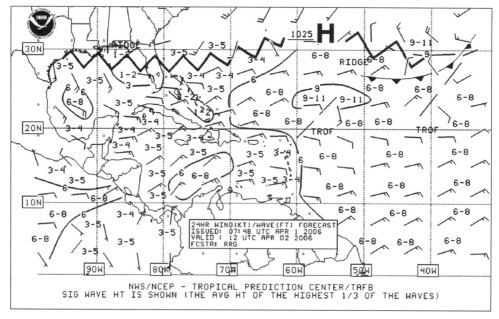

Weather charts usually have wind arrows to indicate wind speeds and direction around weather-making systems. If there are no arrows, wind speeds can be calculated by determining the distance in nautical miles between isobars, and referring to a chart, where the other element is your latitude.

Another phenomenon of interest occurs when adjacent pressure systems come close together, squeezing the isobars of both systems, creating winds of greater force within that area. These important features of weather charts are known as *compression zones* (Figure 15-19).

Low-pressure systems usually move at faster rates than high pressure does, and can actually overtake the slower-moving highs, forming compression zones. This is a situation we must watch for, since winds can be significantly stronger than those predicted in the absence of such compression of isobars. Winds will increase, even though the barometer remains unchanged, when that isobar has become compressed by another system.

The chart in Figure 15-19 has several features of interest to a sailor. In the region where isobars curve around the low, the winds will be diminished in strength by about 10 percent from the expected straight-line values. Meanwhile, in the region where the isobars curve tightly around the high, in the vicinity of a ridge that extends from it, the winds will be significantly stronger. The close proximity of the two features has created a compression zone, where higher winds can be expected across the steeper pressure gradient.

FIGURE 15-19

High- and low-pressure systems can affect wind fields that lie between them.

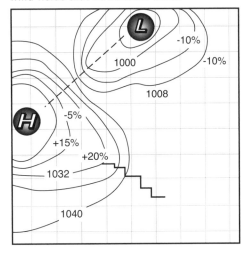

Thermal Winds

Heating of land during the day creates *thermals*, or updrafts of warmed air. The air drawn into the area, blowing from the sea toward land, is called a *sea breeze*.

As cooling takes place in the evening, the sea retains more heat than the land. Drawn by weak thermals over warm water, the wind reverses direction and becomes a *land breeze*, blowing away from land toward the sea.

Sea and land breezes can counteract prevailing or system winds indicated on a weather chart.

In the same way, mountains, valleys, expanses of treed tracts, or spaces between islands affect the direction and speeds of local winds. These are factors controlling local weather that can't be accounted for on weather charts, and underline the need to combine weather chart information with observations of local conditions when making predictions. These factors are not considerations on the open ocean.

UPPER ATMOSPHERE INFLUENCES

While the discussion so far has centered around weather at the surface of the earth, it has touched on the effects of altitude on temperature and on the influence of the jet streams. It's therefore clear that knowledge of what happens in the upper atmosphere will enhance our understanding of weather and our ability to predict it.

Winds at high altitudes are stronger than surface winds, ranging from 30 knots to upward of 50, and 100 to 250 knots in the jet streams. These are the winds that direct the movements of surface systems.

Moreover, disturbances at high altitude actually stimulate the development of surface low pressure systems. Data indicating that such conditions exist aloft proves very helpful in predicting what is primed to occur, or if already happening, what might get more powerful, in the weather on the surface.

To provide a picture of what's happening in the upper atmosphere, meteorologists create charts that follow activity taking place at elevations where the barometric pressure is 500 Mb. To have as complete a picture as possible of the weather, you should download both surface and *500 mb charts*. By studying 500 mb charts generated over the course of a few days, you will see patterns emerging just as they do on surface charts. Because the systems aloft create and influence those on the surface, this is valuable information.

500 Mb Charts

A surface chart is easy to follow because it's essentially two-dimensional—the isobars represent pressure at the surface.

Reading a 500 mb chart requires a different view, because the contour lines represent altitudes at which the atmospheric pressure is 500 mb (approximately half what it is at sea level). So, while the chart might look flat, it is in fact more like a topographical map. The lines are *height contours*, depicting the height at which the pressure is 500 mb, and they are labeled in meters of height. Higher elevations indicate that the air below is warmer, lower elevations that it is colder. The average altitude on a 500 mb chart is 18,500 feet (5,600 meters), higher in warm atmosphere (almost 6,000 meters), and lower in cold atmosphere (4,700 meters). Height contours are often separated by 60 meters of elevation and with the last digit omitted—564 indicates 5,640 meters.

A mass of warm air is lighter and under less pressure than colder air, therefore its 500 mb pressure level will be higher in altitude than that of a corresponding mass of cold air.

There is one important similarity between isobars and height contours though. When 500 Mb contours appear close together, that implies that the temperature gradient between them is steeper, and so will be the pressure gradient in the same region. Just as with surface isobars, whenever the lines are closer together, the gradient between them is steeper, and more wind is expected.

Winds high above the surface, apart from the sub-tropical jet stream, flow in a general direction of west to east. Their paths aren't straight though. They meander from the poles toward the equator, driven mainly by differences in temperature and by the Coriolis Force, which affects them more dramatically at higher latitudes.

On the sample 500mb chart (Table 15-2), the centers in the high latitudes are virtually all lows, because these are areas of cold air masses with high barometric pressure and consequently low-level height contours.

Toward the equator, over Central America, the air is warmer, the 500 mb height contours are at higher elevations, and the centers are highs.

The terminology leads to some confusion because similar terms are used to describe what appear to be different concepts on surface and 500 Mb charts.

Upper level ridges and troughs are major weather-makers of concern to mariners because of their influence on surface systems.

There are two types of upper level troughs. *Long-wave troughs* of cool air under higher pressure extend from the polar regions outward toward warmer air nearer the equator. These long waves of air encircle the globe, moving very slowly, and are responsible for much of the weather occurring over months of time.

TABLE 15-2

Expression	Surface Chart	500 mb Chart
Ridge	A zone of high pressure denoted by a bold, jagged line extending from a surface high. Ridges are occasionally associated with strong winds, especially in areas where the isobars are curved. Circulation around a Northern Hemisphere ridge is clockwise (anticyclonic).	An area of relatively warm air at high levels (like a mountain ridge) at which the barometric pressure is 500mb. Ridges generally extend toward the poles from the tropics, and circulation around them, in the Northern Hemisphere, is clockwise (anticyclonic), akin to high pressure systems at the surface. They aspirate warmer air from the tropics.
Trough	An area of low pressure, denoted by a bold, dashed line emanating from an end of a low around which the isobars bend sharply. The weather around a trough is similar to the low, or the associated fronts.	Areas of colder temperatures with denser air under more pressure. Their 500 Mb levels are lower than ridges because cold air remains at lower levels at increased pressure. Troughs generally extend from the poles toward the tropics and circulation around them, in the Northern Hemisphere, is anticlockwise, (cyclonic) like low pressure systems at the surface.

Short-wave troughs represent the same cool, dense air systems as their longer cousins, but appear as much shorter troughs on upper-level charts, move much more rapidly within the prevailing westerlies, and interact with lower-level low pressure systems to help create and intensify those systems.

A warning sign of potentially serious development is when the 500mb height contours close to form a 500mb low.

Convergence and Divergence

Air around a surface low is drawn in toward it and enters it. In this phase it is described in meteorological terms as *convergent*.

When this warm air, spiraling upward in the vortex of the low reaches altitude and disperses, it becomes *divergent*.

If air at the top of the column had nowhere to go, the vortex would lose momentum, and the system would fall apart. For the system to persist, conditions aloft must promote the divergence. Customarily, a short-wave trough or high-altitude low will not only accommodate the updrafts from a surface low, but will pull air upward in the vortex of the surface low to create and sustain the surface system.

Figure 15-20 is a schematic of how this works: An upper-level short-wave trough, with its cool descending air, creates a vacuum that pulls divergent air from the top of an adjacent surface low, making it more powerful.

When height contours around an upper level trough circle around and close, they form a *500 mb low*. That's

FIGURE 15-20

An upper-level low draws divergent air from the top of a surface low so that warm surface air can converge and be drawn in.

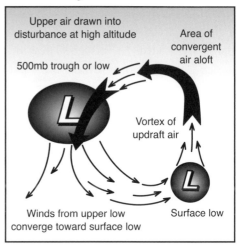

Upper air drawn into disturbance at high altitude

Area of convergent air aloft

500mb trough or low

Vortex of updraft air

Winds from upper low converge toward surface low

Surface low

when it causes maximum surface development. The surface low would remain potent as long as the trough above stayed in that relative position. Because a 500 mb short wave usually moves more quickly than a surface low, it steadily draws nearer the surface low, finally reaching a position overtop of it. When the upper level downdraft opposes ascending air in the surface low, the short-wave trough stifles the updrafts of air from the surface low which then falls apart because it has no source of energy. Such is the life cycle of many low pressure systems encountered at sea.

When downloading surface and 500 mb charts, compare systems on each chart for correlations. A short-wave upper-level trough or upper-level low to the west of a surface low signals great potential for the surface depression to deepen and become powerful. Also, the lower the trough's altitude, the colder and denser is the air within it, and the greater its potential for producing a storm. As long as the trough remains separated from the low, pulling air away from the top of the low, and feeding it back on the surface, the system will stay intact. When the trough approaches and positions itself over the low, the surface system will begin to disintegrate.

This concept is important enough to be worth reiterating: *Whenever an upper level short wave trough or upper level low is positioned to the west of a surface low, be aware of the potential for rapid deepening of the low into a more severe storm.*

Upper-Level Wave Interactions

Much of the time, the surface of the ocean is affected by two different wave systems. Long, regular ocean swells born of disturbances far away interact with local, wind-driven waves of different amplitude.

Similarly, in the upper atmosphere, long and short atmospheric troughs exist together. Just as ocean waves and swells combine crests and troughs to amplify their intensity or neutralize it, so do upper level atmospheric waves.

If a 500 mb chart shows an atmospheric short wave nearing a long wave, look for a new wave pattern to develop, depending on the directions of their respective winds.

Short-wave troughs can combine their forces and become more powerful generators of weather below in the same way. Whenever two atmospheric short waves get closer together, and their

winds come into phase, the potential exists for severe weather development if a surface low is in the region to the east.

Short-wave troughs most commonly flow around the globe within the strong westerly winds that circulate eastward in the mid latitudes. When the 500 mb height contours align close to that east-west axis, *zonal flow*, or a *zonal pattern*, is in place. In these conditions, when short waves are associated with surface lows, the westerlies move the systems rapidly eastward, at a rate of approximately half the speed of the upper level winds.

When the flow of upper-level winds becomes more pole-to-equator oriented, it's called a *meridional pattern*, because it lies closer to the direction of the longitudinal meridians. This creates a more direct path for atmospheric polar air, in lows or troughs, to intermix with warmer tropical air, increasing the chances for storm development at the surface. This is another feature to look for when comparing 500 mb charts with their surface counterparts.

A *ridge blocking pattern* occurs when a static high-altitude ridge blocks the easterly progression of short waves (Figure 15-21). When the waves contact a blocking ridge, they're usually directed poleward, but sometimes they persist against the ridge, force it up, and sneak underneath. Once under the ridge, the short waves travel toward the equator (southeasterly in the Northern Hemisphere). They're then at low altitude, and in prime position to relate with a surface low.

In figure 15-21, the height contours are compressed where the blocking ridge pattern has arrested the progression of

FIGURE 15-21

The effect of a ridge blocking pattern on a short-wave low.

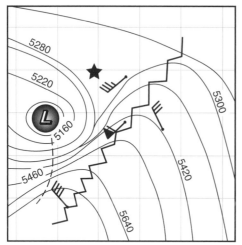

the short wave and is directing it toward the surface low, which will then have the impetus to progress from a nondescript system to a full-blown gale.

A 500 mb ridge oriented east-west (Figure 15-20) is a feature that would be expected to prevent atmospheric short waves from affecting surface lows for those sailing in the Caribbean. The short wave troughs would have to undercut the ridge to gain access to the region.

Cut-Off Low

A strong meridional pattern of flow can carry an upper-level low from the pole farther toward the equator, away from the westerlies, where it can become disassociated and is then called a *cut-off low*. This results in a mass of cool air aloft, very different from the warm air below, creating a steep temperature gradient. The instability causes rain and

squalls or thunderstorms. These scenarios usually last three or four days before the upper level low dissipates or is picked up by the westerlies and escorted out of the area.

Reading 500 mb Charts

When interpreting 500 mb charts, you follow a similar process as when you study their surface counterparts. You must remember that they represent air masses and systems that exist far above the surface, their components are at varying elevations depending on air temperature, they're in constant motion, and they are responsible for creating most of the weather you experience below. Look for upper-level features, especially troughs and ridges, that can interact with lower-level systems, causing weak disturbances to become much stronger very quickly.

Monitor meridional flow, ridge blocking patterns, streams affecting the westerlies, or systems within the westerlies, because they can all impact the weather you will encounter.

It should now be apparent that accurate weather prognostication depends on knowing the relationship between what is happening aloft and surface features below. It is essential to gain access to both the surface wind and wave charts and the 500 mb charts, set them side by side, and compare the systems at both elevations. You should begin doing this well before your sailing date so that you can get a feel for the patterns that exist and where the significant developments are.

Important features to look for:

- Atmospheric lows and troughs that approach the area of surface lows
- 500 mb troughs that close and form a low, with maximum potential to affect surface lows
- Any development at altitude that would force a 500 mb low or short-wave trough toward equatorial warmer air or an existing surface low
- Converging upper level wind streams, where polar air is pumped into the westerlies
- Short-wave troughs combining with long waves
- Meridional streams
- Blocking ridge systems
- Cut-off lows

SINGLE-STATION FORECASTING

Using information about the weather at your location, gathered on your boat, to formulate weather predictions is called *Single-Station Forecasting*. Combine the information you record on board with that obtained from weather charts, buoy reports, and other sources such as HF-radio broadcasts and Internet downloads. Your own observations will enable you to confirm forecasts you receive and to modify them to reflect conditions where you are.

The skills you acquire through Single-Station Forecasting will become especially valuable, and essential, should you find yourself unable to access weather downloads due to equipment failure or because you are sailing in an isolated area with poor reception.

The basis of the practice is to keep a weather log to document changes in various important weather parameters. Weather data should be entered in the Weather Logbook at least every three hours when at sea and hourly whenever a storm is approaching. It's usual to analyze the data when you have at least six hours of it. Use a log similar to the Weather Logbook we use on VOYAGER.

The Weather Logbook

Weather forecasting begins on board with the systematic recording of the weather conditions you are experiencing. You use the information gathered to confirm that the weather you are experiencing conforms to the forecast, or not, and to help you anticipate what's in the offing. (See Chapter 29 *Logkeeping* for a page from the Weather Logbook we use on VOYAGER.)

Your observations should provide the following information:

- Changing cloud types
- Upward movement of clouds
- Changes in wind direction, whether it's backing or veering
- Changes in barometric pressure
- Temperature
- Alterations in the sea state, both sea swells and wind waves
- Changes in visibility

Always take advantage of opportunities to communicate with shipping in your area. It's not only very interesting, but information from their sophisticated weather apparatus is always helpful. I always make it a practice to contact other vessels spotted at sea by hailing them on VHF Channel 16.

Forecasting Hints

To make weather forecasts at sea using only your local information, follow these logical steps (in the Northern Hemisphere):

- Use the prevailing cloud types, temperature, barometric pressure, wind direction and strength, wind waves, and sea swells to infer whether the type of air mass in the upcoming system is Maritime Polar, Maritime Tropical, Continental Polar, or Continental Tropical.
- Determine your vessel's position within the air mass, using wind direction and Buys Ballot's law:
  1) Locate the center of a low pressure system by facing the wind, and extending your right arm back and to the right.
  2) Locate the center of a high pressure system by facing the wind, and pointing your left hand to the left and forward.
- Also determine the storm center (depression, or low) by adding 115 degrees to the direction of your true wind. For example, if true wind is from 90 degrees, the center of the low pressure center is near 205 degrees.
- Determine the direction of movement of the air mass by observing the wind direction (Figures 15-6 and 15-14).
- Note any changes in direction and

period of sea swells that indicate the storm's direction of movement. Changes in their period or height indicate whether the storm system is moving toward or away from you.

From your observations, and any other data available, determine if there is a significant possibility of upcoming heavy weather. Continue to monitor and log the data until it confirms or confounds your forecast.

Apply the Rule of Persistence, which states that the movement and changes in intensity of pressure systems can be extrapolated six hours into the future, based on their history, with great reliability. That accuracy diminishes gradually thereafter.

Follow several additional key guidelines when making your prognostications:

- Lows tend to move in a direction parallel to the winds and isobars of the warm-sector winds (between the warm and cold fronts), with a speed of approximately 80% of those winds.
- Low-pressure troughs tend to move somewhat easterly, toward the position of the preceding high-pressure ridge.
- The rate at which a surface low-pressure system deepens accelerates as the cold front approaches the warm sector. The rate slows when the occlusion process begins.
- The speed of a low system's movement decreases when its fronts are occluded.

If you establish that a low is approaching, determine where its center is located, and what sector of the system will affect your vessel. Anticipate whatever weather is typical for that quadrant and base your storm avoidance tactics, if called for, on that information. Tracking your local weather conditions will also help you to predict a storm's course and duration. Use the same techniques to anticipate warm and cold fronts and their associated weather.

Obtaining Weather Information

Weather File Downloads

Well before setting sail, locate the sources from which you will be downloading weather charts and forecasts, decide what information you want to access, and practice obtaining it.

For example, to obtain files from NOAA, you will need software in your computer to decode the data you receive. Send an e-mail to the NOAA FTP server (ftpmail@ftpmail.nws.noaa.gov) with a script requesting the files.

While sailing the western North Atlantic and Caribbean, I send the script in the left hand column below to receive the weather file listed in the right-hand column.

Message sent to NOAA:	To Receive:
Open	
cd fax	
get PPAE00.TIF	24 Hour Surface
get PWAE98.TIF	24 Hour Wind and Wave
get PPAE50.TIF	24 Hour 500 mb
get PPAI50.TIF	48 Hour 500 mb
get QDTM85.TIF	48 Hour Surface
get PJAI98.TIF	48 Hour Forecast
get PPAM50.TIF	96 Hour 500 mb
get PWAM99.TIF	96 Hour Surface
get PJAM98.TIF	96 Hour Wind and Wave
quit	

Upon receipt of the request, NOAA automatically sends the information. You make your Internet connection with the receiver, and download the data when you want it.

The importance of downloading current and accurate weather charts cannot be overstated. I strongly recommend that you check out UUPlus for your laptop software packets. UUPlus is a reputable company providing software to select, download, un-encode, and display weather chart information. The program also allows use of the Internet and provides e-mail capability. I have selected UUPlus software for my laptop on VOYAGER based not only on their professional software, but the caring service they make available.

Forecasts by Radio

NOAA broadcasts Offshore and High Seas reports which you can receive via SSB or with a short-wave receiver. The audio reports on SSB receiver are computer-generated and delivered by "Iron Mike," a voice synthesizer ("Perfect Paul" retired in April 2007). The same reports are available in text form on the Internet.

I have long maintained that if you don't have SSB, you should definitely have a short-wave receiver, and this is where it's used. I've sailed for years, without problems, guided by weather from these audio transmissions and Single-Station Forecasting only. They've also come in handy when satellite phone reception with Globalstar failed.

NOAA publishes schedules for voice and weather-fax HF transmissions on its website (www.noaa.gov/wx.html).

In the summer of 2007, the U.S. Coast Guard, which transmits the voice and fax HF broadcasts generated by NOAA, intimated it would shut down these services at some point in the future due to obsolescence of its equipment unless public demand was strong enough for it to continue.

NOAA on the Internet

NOAA provides a wealth of information over the Internet. Go first to the home page to see just how extensive it is (www.noaa.gov/wx.html).

From there, proceed to Marine Weather, where you'll find links to the Ocean Prediction Center (www.opc.ncep.noaa.gov) and information on how to access a variety of products, from voice forecasts to surface and 500 mb charts.

Weather Routing Services

A number of companies offer private weather information that includes pertinent weather chart data, along with their interpretations of those data. Depending on what kind of arrangement you wish to sign up for, they can even customize weather forecasts and sailing-course suggestions on a daily basis. Use of such a service is particularly advantageous for those lacking experience or for those embarking on long passages or along routes known for inclement weather.

Routing Sources for Weather Information

Jenifer Clark's Gulf Stream Analysis, at www.gulfstrm@erols.com
Commander's weather at www.commandersweather.com
Weather Routing Inc. at www.wrix.com
Other useful sources of weather information are:
Caribbean Weather Center at www.caribwx.com
Starpath at www.starpath.com
Steve Dashew's website, SetSail. www.setsail.com/links/weather/html
Herb Hilgenberg South Bend II HF/SSB Frequency 12359.0 broadcast at 2000UTC

CHAPTER 16

VOYAGE ROUTING

Voyage routing entails the thorough planning of all aspects of your proposed passages. This includes the timing of departures and arrivals, the courses you will follow, the plotting of waypoints, and accumulating all the charts and publications that you will need both for planning and along the way. With these preparations, you will give yourself the best chance for success.

Timing a passage correctly hinges primarily on choosing the time of year when conditions are likely to be most favorable. Precisely when you leave port will depend on circumstances that prevail when your departure date arrives. The key factor in both decisions is weather.

When researching to begin your routing, the major factors to take under consideration are weather patterns, ocean currents, prevailing winds and waves, and the chances for encountering storms. The best single source for this data is the Pilot Chart for the ocean area where you'll be sailing.

Pilot Charts are published individually for every month of the year, and each chart provides a wealth of information on sea and weather conditions averaged over many years of reporting for the month it covers. In every section, 5 degrees of Latitude by 5 degrees of Longitude, is a wind rose indicating the average strengths and percentage of the time that winds blow from every 45 degrees around the compass, along with the percentage of time winds are calm. The charts show the set and drift of ocean currents, and delineate zones where wave heights exceed 12 feet for 10, 20, 30, and 40 percent of the time. They also show Great Circle courses between major ports, lines of equal magnetic variation, information about the frequency of gales, tracks of extratropical and tropical cyclones, air temperature, atmospheric pressure, and visibility.

Because they contain so much useful information, the Pilot Charts are the first reference to use when planning a voyage. You should supplement them with a number of other publications, the preeminent among them (though very expensive) being *Ocean Passages for the World*. I have used *The Atlantic Crossing Guide* by Phillip Allen since 1987, along with *World Cruising Routes* by Jimmy Cornell which has also proven valuable.

Tide and Current Tables, Light Lists (or Lists of Lights), Notices to Mariners,

Navigation Rules, and Coast Pilots for all areas of the voyage are essential publications to have on board. These are all available on line at various sites. Just search for the appropriate title, and several sites will appear.

See for example:

- www.tbone.biol.sc.edu/tide—for tide and tidal currents
- www.navcen.uscg.gov—for Notice to Mariners, Navigation Rules, Light Lists
- www.nauticalcharts.noaa.gov/nsd—for downloadable Coast Pilots

Celestial navigators will need HO 249 Volumes I and II (or HO 229 volumes for the latitudes of the voyage), a current Nautical Almanac, and plotting charts.

When routing for long ocean passages, the relevant Gnomonic chart is very useful for plotting Great Circle courses. Draw your intended course line on the Gnomonic chart, then pick points located at convenient intersections of latitude and longitude and transfer them to a Mercator ocean chart. Connecting these points from departure to destination gives you the Great Circle route on the Mercator chart. This is the rhumb line, or shortest distance course. Actually making that course at sea is a different matter, but it's a useful guideline for your route planning. After you've drawn this course, study the Pilot Chart for the prevailing winds and sea states, as well as ocean currents. Make alterations to your rhumb line course as necessary to take advantage of chances for good conditions and to avoid bad

ones. Once you have charted your final route, you can determine waypoints and enter them into the GPS. Remember to write the waypoints down in the Ship's Logbook, or in a separate navigation log.

For transferring positions from plotting sheets or from GPS readouts, you will need the appropriate small-scale (1:3,500,000) ocean chart, an example of which is *Chart #108, North Atlantic Ocean Southeast Coast of North America Including Bahamas and Greater Antilles.*

Larger scale (1:80,000) charts of areas along your routes that may serve as storm refuge or emergency ports are also essential as back-ups. For example, when making a passage from Nassau, Bahamas, to Norfolk, Virginia, NOAA *Chart 11539 New River Inlet to Cape Fear* is useful for the information it provides on possible refuges along the United States East Coast.

You'll also need large scale charts (1:5,000 or 1:17,500), used for the approach to landfall, and harbor charts. Cruising guides of island chains like the Bahamas are extremely useful, and are priority items as well.

Charts are available as paper charts or in electronic format. I have chosen to stay with paper charts, and I recommend that you have them on board even if you navigate primarily with electronic charts. You can still use them should your electronic system fail for any reason.

Be prudent when using GPS and electronic charts. Do not put absolute faith in your position as indicated on an electronic chart when you are anywhere near land. While most of the time GPS position data is accurate in terms of Latitude and Longitude, the charts may be based on survey data dating back many, even scores, of years when techniques were less accurate than they are today. Consequently, a GPS position may indicate you are in safe water when in fact you are not. Before making any final approach to land, confirm your position with respect to that land with the use of more traditional navigation methods. Use coastal navigation and piloting skills, depth contours, and the local buoyage system to assure you'll make a safe landfall.

You can employ a professional consulting service to help you in your route planning. Several companies offer services through which they provide you with weather information and suggest course changes to make to use the weather, both current and forecast, to your best advantage. Depending on the arrangement you agree to, you might simply receive their weather prognostications or you can contact them via SSB or satellite phone for a consultation. If you install the appropriate software in your computer, you can download their proprietary weather charts and forecasts.

Professional Routing Assistance

Jenifer Clark specializes in analysis of the Gulf Stream, providing invaluable routing information to sailors leaving the East Coast of the U.S.A.

Jenifer Clark's Gulf Stream
3160 Lacrosse Court, Dunkirk, MD
   20754
Phone: 1-410-286-5370
Fax: 1-410-286-5371

Website: http://users.erols.com/
   gulfstrm
E-mail: gulfstream@comcast.net

Commanders' Weather provides comprehensive weather routing and forecasting for a wide range of enterprises.

Commanders' Weather Corporation
154 Broad Street, Suite 1517, Nashua,
   NH 03062
Phone: 1-603-882-6789
Fax: 1-603-882-666
Website: www.commandersweather.
   com
E-mail: commandersweather@
   compuserve.com

The Float Plan

The final aspect of route planning is the formulation of a Float Plan. This is a written outline of your planned passage or voyage. It contains information about the vessel, all its crewmembers, and details of the intended route and estimated times of arrival. See Appendix 5 for the Float Plan that I've used. I invite you to make copies of the plan for your own voyages.

Fill out the Float Plan just prior to departure. All the information it contains must be current and accurate. Give the plan to the person looking after your interests at home and, if possible, to someone at each destination or landfall on the voyage. Notify your contacts at home and at your next destination at the time of each departure and upon your arrival. Provide them with the date of departure, the expected duration of the passage, and your estimated date of arrival at the next port of call. The Float Plan is not filed with the Coast Guard.

Communicate any problems you encounter en route with one or both pertinent shore contacts. Inform them as to the nature of the problem, of any injuries or illness on board, or damage to the vessel, and advise them if you expect to be delayed.

Instruct your shore contacts that, in the event they don't hear from the vessel past the latest agreed-upon date of communication, they are to get in touch with the nearest Coast Guard or Navy facility and alert them of the situation. The authorities at that point will use their discretion as to the most appropriate procedures to be taken.

CHAPTER 17

PREPARING THE CREW

Crew selection and training can be as important to successful voyaging as any other factor. When thinking about the crew you would like to assemble, take into account the nature of the passages involved and how you intend to sail the boat. Choose your crew based on those considerations and on the needs of the boat. Under most circumstances, it's best to sail with the minimum number of people it takes to handle the boat properly for the intended passage or cruise. The best crews are usually made up of people who are eager and willing to learn and keen to contribute to the adventure as members of a team. They should be ready and able to participate in all aspects of voyaging. Do bear in mind, though, that a group of people confined to a small space and subjected to the stress and motion associated with being on a boat at sea, and the possibility of fear, fatigue, and lack of proper nutrition, can be a recipe for trouble, even when those crewmembers are familiar with each other.

The master of a vessel is ultimately responsible for the well-being of its crew, both at sea and in foreign ports. If you have any doubt that a potential member of the crew will serve well on board and behave properly on land, you'd probably be wise to find someone else.

Be vigilant when selecting crew. Ask any prospective crewmember for a written resume of his or her sailing background and of life experiences that might be pertinent to the voyage. Interview each one in person and try to assess their honesty, fitness, purpose for making the voyage, and their plans for after it's completed.

Come to an agreement with each member of the crew regarding their compensation, your expectations of their abilities, their duties on board, any contributions they will make to the ship such as food, and their responsibility to return home at their own expense. Make it clear that, as captain, you are legally responsible for everyone aboard and their effects, and therefore you do not permit alcohol, drugs, tobacco, or firearms on board your vessel. Once you have made these agreements, put them in writing, with each party keeping a copy, and enter each agreement and its date in the Ship's Logbook.

Our protocol on VOYAGER requires us to provide all crewmembers with a great deal of information prior to sailing. Part of safety at sea is that all members of the crew are able to function as able seamen and contribute to the team effort. Experience has shown that should some members be unable or unwilling to pitch in, others are forced to bear the burden, leading to disharmony and fatigue.

Crew wellbeing contributes to safety, therefore our orientation begins well in advance of the sailing date when we send each member of the crew lists designed to prepare them for the offshore experience.

One such list, Checklist for Personal Gear and Clothing (Appendix 1), is intended to ensure that crew bring appropriate clothing and certain items of personal gear.

The other list, Crewmember Responsibilities and Duties (Appendix 4), enumerates the tasks each member of the crew will be expected to handle at sea. This provides them adequate time to practice or to learn new skills prior to sailing.

Two days before the intended date of departure, the crew assembles and commences to prepare the vessel according to protocols. If I am sailing a vessel other than VOYAGER, the entire inspection is carried out, according to the checklists drawn up for each boat system.

While the inspection process is less extensive in scope on VOYAGER, with which I am very familiar, we nevertheless go over all systems thoroughly. Crewmembers are free to observe and contribute to the vessel inspection process.

During the preparation phase, crew should be asked to perform specific chores, such as filling the water tanks,

loading jerry jugs with fuel, and stowing their belongings below neatly.

As for the Crew Preparation, that is an entirely separate matter. The philosophy behind crew orientation and instruction is summarized in this excerpt from *Ready to Sail*:

> Educating each member of the team provides him/her with the tools necessary to contribute fully. Psychologically, persons receiving this information benefit by gaining in confidence; feeling secure in the knowledge that they are able to handle their responsibilities and that the vessel is thoroughly prepared. The value of crew personnel in this frame of mind is beyond accounting.

On board, with everyone assembled, I issue handouts that outline the topics that will be discussed, both on shore and at sea. The crew orientation and instruction has evolved over the years. It began when I would jot down notes and items I wanted to discuss with crews aboard delivery vessels or racing yachts. That cockpit chat has now become a seminar with an actual curriculum designed to fully prepare all crewmembers for their sea voyage.

This chat is a discussion of what each person should know about the vessel, its gear, our guidelines and rules, and how we intend to operate at sea. Just as someone starting a new job benefits from being given a thorough understanding of the associated tasks and what is expected of them, we aim to provide our crew with the information they need so that they can be at their best, and enjoy themselves the most. I recommend this protocol to all skippers.

We begin with a table which lists items in the boat that the crew must be able to locate and operate. We go over each item separately, giving demonstrations as required.

TABLE 17-1 ITEMS ABOARD ALL CREWMEMBERS NEED TO LOCATE AND OPERATE.

Life preservers	Cooking stove
Signal flares	Medical kit
Fire extinguishers	Engine key
Horseshoe ring	Lifesling
Emergency knife	Binoculars
Flashlights, spotlight	VHF radio
Electric panel	Windlass
Battery isolation switch	Abandon Ship bag
Watch schedule	Drinks and snacks

The following is a list of procedures with which each member of the crew should be familiar. The skipper should ensure that everyone on board is able to perform the following tasks:

- Be able to don a safety harness quickly in dim light. Understand the jackline system and be familiar with the rules concerning the need for life jackets and harnesses on.
- Make sure that nothing drags behind the boat at any time.
- Start and stop the engine.
- Use the throttle and gear shift.
- Understand the Standby and Auto functions of the autopilot, how to change course and how to immediately take manual helm control from the autopilot.
- Know how to position the boat on a course and select the course for windvane control. Know how to instantly disengage the windvane clutch to regain manual steering.
- Operate the VHF radio.
- Understand the posted watch schedule.
- Understand the clean-up procedures after meals.
- Understand the daily maintenance and monitoring of ship's systems and gear.
- Know the location and how to install the emergency tiller.
- Know the location of the Abandon Ship bag
- Know where the EPIRB is located and how to operate it.
- Be able to read latitude and longitude, speed, track and bearing on the GPS.
- Be familiar with how to use the radar, and know how to place it in energy-saving mode.
- Reef or furl the mainsail.
- Furl the headsail.
- Deploy the storm sails and rig for heavy weather.
- Understand how to grind and release the winches.
- Maintain proper stowage belowdeck.
- Operate manual and electric bilge pumps.
- Know where the diagram of seacocks/through hulls/fire extinguishers is located.

- Know the location of the toolboxes and spares.
- Know where the collision mat is located, and how to deploy it in an emergency.
- Make certain that any existing medical conditions are known for each crewmember.
- Understand and implement the deck logbook.

Night Watch Rules

Aboard VOYAGER we also have a set of guidelines for the night watches to follow, both to ensure the safe operation of the vessel and for the comfort of their crewmates asleep below.

- Be courteous toward those off watch.
- Keep sound levels down—no loud talking or music.
- Don't drag tether ring on deck; carry it above the deck.
- Keep flashlights in their designated locations.
- Keep the binoculars in their designated location.
- Keep the spotlight in its designated location.
- Leave the toilet seat down to prevent it from slamming.
- Maintain nighttime lighting below decks.
- Observe 360 degrees around the boat at least every 15 minutes.
- Understand the basics of COLREGS lights and what they indicate about another vessel's course.
- Know where Granola bars, crackers,

other snacks, and chewing gum are located.
- Be familiar enough with the stove to be able to heat water for warm drinks.
- Note course, speed, weather parameters, and special notes in the Deck Logbook once per watch or as necessary.
- Do not start the engine unless absolutely necessary, and if possible inform the off-watch crew before doing so.
- If a question arises concerning the operation of the vessel or its position relative to another vessel, land, or another object at sea, do not guess about how to deal with the problem; wake up the appropriate person.
- Understand the watch schedule as posted, and be able to comply with it.
- Standing orders are to call the Captain or First Mate whenever a vessel is sighted, any unusual sound is heard, a low, dark cloudbank, rain squall, or waterspout is sighted to windward, there is injury or a medical condition arises, or for any other reason that creates uncertainty or concern.

Regular maintenance and constant monitoring of the vessel and its equipment are essential elements in our efforts to make our passages safe ones. We discuss these topics, which are covered in detail in Chapter 24, *Monitoring and Maintenance at Sea*, so that every member of the crew can both take part and feel they are contributing.

If the list of items we discuss with

crewmembers seems ponderous, that only serves to demonstrate how important it is. As we make our way through the items listed in our discussions, I have noticed how the attitude and behavior of the crew change. Individuals who are anxious, or are questioning their own sanity in taking on such an adventure gain confidence and begin to anticipate our departure more eagerly. That is what we seek, a confident, able, and willing group of sailors who will make the voyage a success.

As we proceed, and the crew absorbs and understands the details of how gear is used and where it's located, we turn our attention to focus on specific emergency situations, beginning with the overboard emergency.

Everyone needs to understand the procedures outlined, and be ready to follow them should the situation arise. We always end this conversation with the message that the best overboard procedure is to make absolutely certain it is

never needed by being conscientious about safety at all times.

In the cockpit chats or at offshore preparation seminars, I stress the use of the deep beam reach and quick stop methods of returning to a person in the water, as described in Chapter 23, *Safety Tactics, Protocols, and Procedures*. Using diagrams to illustrate the techniques, we explain step by step how we return to the victim and how we deploy the Lifesling to retrieve the victim from the water. We also make it a point to discuss the protocols for rigging for heavy weather, responding to flood or fire, and the procedure for abandoning ship.

We conduct our cockpit chat in an atmosphere that encourages questions and suggestions. Everyone should be made to feel at ease about speaking up; there is no such thing as a bad question. As well as educating and providing guidance, the goal of our chat is to build confidence and a sense of camaraderie in our crew.

CHAPTER 18

MEAL PLANNING AND PROVISIONING

Normally, the person who will be the primary cook on board takes charge of planning meals for the voyage and doing the provisioning. Meal planning involves determining what foods will be available for each meal throughout each day and calculating the quantity of each food item to stock. Provisioning is the process of procuring the items on the grocery list, bringing them on board, and stowing them according to a well thought-out plan.

Begin your meal planning by figuring out how many meals you expect to serve during the course of the voyage. This will depend on how many crew will be aboard and how long you expect to be at sea. To calculate the total number of meals, multiply the number of crew by the number of days at sea, then multiply the result by three.

A crew of five on a 14-day passage would therefore require a total of 210 meals, 70 each of breakfasts, lunches, and dinners. Plan also to put aboard a variety of snack foods and beverages.

Once that figure of 70 breakfasts is determined, the meal planner decides what foods the meal will consist of. The menu might include such items as oat-meal, dry cereal, bread with peanut butter, and eggs. The next step is to determine quantities of each item to procure for the passage, adding a factor of at least 10 percent to be on the safe side. Do this for each meal until your shopping list is filled out.

With this list complete, you can begin the provisioning. In my experience, the tendency is to buy more food than is needed rather than less. People often have smaller appetites at sea than they do on land. I recommend you subject your meal planning technique to a trial run. You can do this while spending a few days away from shore, either on a short cruise or while simply lying at anchor, with a complement equal in number to your proposed crew. During this entire trial period, eat all your meals on board. By all means get off the boat if you want to, but don't eat any meals ashore.

Unless you have refrigeration aboard, avoid taking fresh provisions. Some exceptions to this are eggs, potatoes, onions, and other items that have a long shelf life. Take ample quantities of canned and dried food, along with staples such as flour, rice, and pasta. You'll find dehydrated products like milk and

Gatorade powder and dried foods such as potatoes and macaroni and cheese useful at sea. So that the cooks in your crew become accustomed to working with these and other products they might not normally use, such as pancake mix, flour, packaged oatmeal, and various bulk foods, include them in your planning and provisioning rehearsal.

Your provisioning will include condiments and essentials such as salt, pepper, mustard, sugar, cooking oil, baking powder, and, if you intend to bake bread, dried yeast.

Preparing meals at sea is usually a challenge, and is sometimes next to impossible. Unless the cook is experienced and adept, and willing to produce elaborate meals, food should be prepared according to the following principles: Meals should be easy to prepare, serve, and eat. They must be nutritious and tasty, they should create little waste, and their ingredients should store well. In general, carbohydrates make a valuable contribution to the diet at sea because they're relatively easy to digest and they provide a ready source of energy.

Foods to Take Offshore

Select foods from different categories. Use the following as the basis for planning:

- Canned goods are easy to store and have a long shelf life.
- Freeze dried foods are always fresh, taste good, retain all nutrients, are very convenient to store, and don't require cooking.
- Bulk foods, such as flour, cereals, pastas, rice, potatoes, crackers, nuts, beans, and oatmeal should be stored in Tupperware or plastic bags with zip closures.
- Dried fruit, like raisins, dates, prunes, and oranges, can be added to other foods such as cereals or eaten as snacks. Dried tomatoes, for example, can be worked into many different meals. Instant dried milk is necessary in the absence of refrigeration, and makes sense even with it.
- Pumpernickel bread and pitas actually last quite well when wrapped and kept cool.
- Breads can be made either in a pressure cooker or a bread machine while under way.
- Vegetables can of course be canned, and they'll then have extended shelf lives. Fresh vegetables that last well include tomatoes, potatoes, onions, garlic, green beans, carrots, and cabbage. Cabbage, carrots, and potatoes survive the longest, so it pays to consider them often in meal planning.
- Fruits in general don't keep as long as vegetables, but some that do are acceptable. Always select fruits that have not yet ripened, and are not bruised, and store them securely in a cool area where they can't be jostled. Unhusked coconuts can last several weeks. Apples will last up to a month if washed and wrapped individually in paper towels. Hard, green mangoes will last a couple of weeks if stored properly. Green pineapples can last up to a week if stored with the stalk still on and in a cool, dark

area. Watermelons actually last well when kept cool.

■ Eggs can keep for months if they're fresh and unwashed. Lengthen their storage time by coating them individually with Vaseline, and by turning them over every couple of days.

■ Meats spoil quickly, so what you can take depends on whether or not you have refrigeration. Always pay close attention to keeping chilled or frozen meats from spoiling. Canned products are the safest, and a wide variety is available including ham, tuna fish, chicken, Spam, and corned beef.

Offshore Cookware

Cookware that I have found to work well on board includes a pressure cooker, Pyrex baking dishes, nesting pots (that fit one into another), a large frying pan with high sides, and a stainless steel kettle for boiling water. I recommend against Teflon, which degrades at sea.

Easy Offshore Meals

Seagoing breakfasts very often consist of PBJ on bread, cereal or oatmeal with re-constituted powdered milk, fresh or canned fruit, and coffee or tea. My standard breakfast is peanut butter and orange marmalade on bread; it's been that way for over 20 years!

Soups are great lunch fare. Heat-and-eat lunches in Styrofoam cups are ideal for offshore meals. Also, vegetables that store well on board, like potatoes, onions, and beans can be combined with a broth to make great, chunky-style soups or nice batches in the pressure cooker (see below). Sandwiches are easy to prepare for lunches and can be made with canned tuna, chicken, or Spam.

Dinner is often the one meal in the day at which the whole crew gathers together. People are rested from the watches of the previous night and are preparing for another round, so a nice meal fits into the schedule well.

Pre-prepared dinners of pasta, and thick, hearty stews are handy to have aboard if you have refrigeration. In the days leading up to departure, you can make them on land, seal them in plastic bags, and freeze them. To prepare one on board, you simply take it from the icebox, place it in boiling water, heat it and served it in bowls; with a nice hunk of bread you have a pretty good meal. I also like Dinty Moore stews for ease of preparation, their longevity on board, and because they taste great. Both rice and spaghetti fit the offshore credo well.

Of course, fish, ham, and hot dogs are all possibilities, if conditions allow for their preparation and they've been kept from spoiling. Hot dogs are actually easy to store in the icebox, and easy to cook by boiling in water. They can also be chopped into chunks and added to the vegetable soups.

I like making instant mashed potatoes mixed with all types of vegetables. This provides a healthy meal that everyone enjoys, and it's easy for the chef.

Whenever fresh fish are brought over the transom (don't rely on it!), they enliven the menu tremendously. You can sometimes attract flying fish to the boat by lighting it at night. The fish will hit the sails or cabin top and fall to the decks, especially if you're sailing in a moderate seaway.

Salads make a dinner a bit more nourishing and elegant. The ingredients are all easy to stow but they don't last long unrefrigerated. If you don't have refrigeration, plan on eating salads only on the first two or three days, and provision accordingly.

To summarize, the best choices for the ship's stores are most often canned goods of all types, heat-and-eat soups, dry, dehydrated, and bulk items, certain vegetables, eggs, crackers, and meals you've prepared, sealed, and frozen in advance. Foodstuffs brought aboard must store easily, last well, be easy to prepare, and create a minimum of waste.

Offshore Snacks and Beverages

Healthy snacks provide a boost to both energy and morale for the watch on deck. Snack foods that keep well include Granola or energy bars, trail mix, and dried fruit. Bring, too, an assortment of crackers because they can help ease the queasy stomach. Jiffy Pop popcorn is a nice treat for the crew, and it's a good source of fiber. Marshmallows placed in the ice box or refrigerator will keep them smelling fresh by absorbing food odors. They still taste good in spite of performing that useful task.

Many people on offshore passages develop a bad taste in their mouths. Queasiness, seasickness medications, and dehydration can all contribute to

the sensation. I've found that chewing gum works well to dispel it, and it also helps watchkeepers stay alert at night.

Favorite drinks aboard usually include coffee, hot chocolate, and tea, but caffeinated drinks should be avoided if dehydration is a problem. Soft drinks of some type are needed, but carbonation can also contribute to an upset stomach. A better choice might be canned juices or products like Gatorade or Kool-Aid. You should always have powdered Gatorade on board to provide electrolytes in cases of dehydration.

Water Management

When planning for your voyage, take into account the water consumption needs of the crew for the time you will be at sea. On average, each individual consumes between two quarts and one gallon of water per day, depending on the temperature and their level of exertion. Make sure your tanks are of sufficient capacity for the duration of your time at sea with enough to spare for another week or so.

Proper water management is critical when sailing offshore. Water is never to be wasted, and must be used sparingly until you are assured of reaching your landfall. To conserve water, wash dishes in seawater and rinse them in measured amounts of fresh water. On VOYAGER, I place a plastic container in the sink bowl, with a line drawn about two inches from the bottom. I then make it my goal to rinse all of the dishes with less water than the line indicates.

It is not necessary to bathe daily when at sea. Every two or three days will suffice, and even then, you can save water by washing with seawater and rinsing with fresh.

Refrigeration

Opinions differ on the need for refrigeration offshore. While VOYAGER has engine-driven refrigeration, I usually elect not to use it because I can't justify the fuel consumed by running the engine an extra hour or two per day to keep ice available. Many people do use refrigeration and manage their fuel and electrical budgets so as to keep it running. Provision according to your capacity to keep perishables fresh.

In a well insulated ice box, block ice with cubed ice keeps most items cold and safe to eat for at least four to five days in the Caribbean, and longer in more northern waters. This is an acceptable alternative to refrigeration. Be sure to consume the more perishable items early in the passage.

The Pressure Cooker

A pressure cooker is a great asset in the galley. It makes possible a greater variety of dishes and cooking with it is often safer than with open pots or pans. With it, you can efficiently prepare large batches of stews and soups for the whole crew, and when the lid is sealed down it eliminates the risk of hot liquids splashing onto the cook.

To use the pressure cooker as an oven,

place a spacer or trivet between it and the stove burner. This spacer should be at least a half-inch high, and can be made from a can with the top and bottom removed. Place a metal pan inside the pressure cooker, allowing at least half an inch between it and the cooker's sides for air to circulate. Before using a pressure cooker, always refer to the instruction booklet for safety precautions and suggested cooking times. The most important rule is to never open the sealed lid until the pressure has gone down.

Culinary Disclaimer

I have to admit that my expertise is in areas other than the culinary aspects of sailing, so here I'll recommend you research the numerous books that have been written for seagoing cooks. Among others, *Kitchen Afloat: Galley Management and Meal Preparation* by Joy Smith is chock-full of information on food-related questions for sailors while *The Great Cruising Cookbook: An International Galley Guide* by John C. Payne contains recipes from all over the world and extensive chapters on galley equipment, provisioning and storage. Choose books that have recipes that appeal to you and that make sense for the type of sailing you do. Look especially for recipes that are easy to prepare, that don't produce much waste and garbage, are cost-effective, and that use ingredients that store well and are nutritious, and, above all, tasty.

CHAPTER 19

FINAL VESSEL PREPARATIONS FOR SEA

By now, the inspection of the entire vessel has long been completed and all the appropriate checklists filled. All defects discovered in the course of the inspection have been repaired, and inspected once more, with special attention paid if you didn't do the work personally.

All equipment deficiencies noted on the checklists have been addressed. Items such as glassware have been removed, PFDs updated, the flare kit is current, and lee cloths are in place on all bunks. It's these details that you turn your attention to as your preparations enter their final stages.

You want the boat's bottom to be clean, because a hull freed of barnacles and growth pays dividends in improved performance. Often times, crew are available, eager, and willing to pitch in, and this is a good way to let them contribute.

Once you're at sea, you'll follow a routine monitoring and maintenance program designed to keep all gear in working order, and to catch problems early before they have a chance to escalate. As you prepare to leave, you'll go through that whole list and more. While you're still connected to shore and sources for parts and equipment, you can attend to a number of essential, pre-departure tasks.

Engine and its associated systems

Check the charge of all house and dedicated engine batteries. If a battery shows low voltage, check it with a voltmeter and write down the voltage level. Start the engine, run it up to a speed at which it charges the batteries (usually around 1,000 to 1,100 rpm), and note the time. Make sure the battery isolation switch is on "both."

As the engine runs, periodically check the battery voltages to monitor how well the alternator brings them back. Bear in mind that batteries readily charge to about 80 percent of their capacity, but the final 20 percent takes much longer. When the batteries are reading around 12.5 volts, note how long it took, and you'll have an idea of how long you need to run the engine to effect a charge. If you have completed an estimate of the amp hours needed per day, as described in Chapter 10, *Alternative Energy*, you can estimate how many times a day and for how long you need to run the engine to recharge the batteries.

When the charge test is complete, check the raw-water intake filter, and clean it out if necessary. Move next to the raw-water pump. Remove the faceplate and check the impeller. Unless it has been very recently changed, pull it out and put in a new one. Save the old one if it's in good condition, and add it to the engine spare parts inventory.

Dip some diesel fuel from the bottom of the tank. Examine it closely for sediments. Using a flashlight, inspect the inside surfaces of the tank. Look closely for microbial growth. Check the sediment bowl at the bottom of the tank or primary fuel filter. If you detect water or sediments, you should empty the fuel tank, scrub it, flush it, and fill it with fresh fuel.

Change the primary and secondary fuel filters. Keep the old ones if they're in good condition and store them in plastic bags.

Change the oil and oil filter. Take note of the condition of the oil for signs of engine trouble. Examine the engine bilge one last time for water, oil, or anything that shouldn't be there.

Examine the engine belts, running your hand over them to feel for cracks, frayed areas, or slackness. Replace any belt that doesn't look like new, including any that drive auxiliary systems like a refrigeration compressor, for example, which has a belt that is tighter than most.

Check the coolant levels. There's no need to change the solution out as long as it's clear of debris. Just top it off with fresh coolant to keep the level nominal.

Check the transmission fluid and top it off if necessary.

Start the engine one last time. Pay attention to how fast it kicks over and runs, feel for abnormal vibrations, and listen for abnormal sounds. Check the exhaust for smoke and to make sure water is flowing normally from the exhaust (meaning that you put the impeller in correctly!). Observe all the engine instruments for a while, to make sure the battery is charging and the temperature and oil-pressure gauge readings are normal.

Make sure the dock lines, especially the fore and aft springs, are secure, and have a mate slip the transmission into gear while you observe from below. Watch the shift mechanism as it moves from neutral to forward and then back to neutral and into reverse.

Watch the propeller shaft as it spins; it should be smooth and vibration-free. Check the stuffing box one last time while you're right there. Be sure you know where the engine throttle is located, as well as the transmission shift lever, in case the cables fail.

Fuel and Water

If you will be carrying extra fuel in jerry jugs to supplement the tank capacity, first make sure the jugs are clean inside. Fill them with clean diesel fuel. To ensure it is clean, run some of it through a filter and examine the filter element. Replace the caps tightly on the jugs and bring them on board. If there is room for the jerry jugs in cockpit or deck lockers, they are safer stored there than lashed to the stern pushpit, against the lifelines, or anywhere else near the periphery of the boat. I have also stowed fuel, lashed down very securely, beneath a dinghy on deck. Always store jerry jugs in the upright position.

If you plan to make stops along your route before you head into the ocean, you might as well wait to top off the fuel tanks until you are at your port of departure.

If you choose to bring extra water in jugs, this is the time. Bring along as much as you can store without it taking the place of other essentials. You can store it in jerry jugs, but by using smaller containers you can take advantage of smaller stowage compartments. Store containers securely to prevent them from being jostled and punctured.

Water is a precious commodity at sea. Fill the water tanks only after visually inspecting them for algae or dirt. An extra precaution you can take is to filter the water before it goes into the tanks. A suitable in-line water filter is available from West Marine. You should also have a water filter installed on board to kill microorganisms and improve the taste of tank water.

While you fill the tanks, check the external vents for escaping air, and watch the bilges for signs of leakage. Also, flip on the pressure-water switch at the panel, just to be sure it's pumping water. The pop of a stainless tank alerts you that it's almost full. Top the tank off by running water slowly near the end, until the water no longer disappears from the deck fitting. Secure the deck screw cap on after each tank is full but do not over tighten it and be very careful not to strip the threads.

Ship's Systems

The bilges should be dry before leaving on an offshore passage, so that you know that the subsequent appearance of water suggests a leak, from a seacock, a through-hull fitting, or the stuffing box, and you will set about tracing it. Bilge pumps should be located where they are easily accessible and preferably not where you have to empty the contents of a storage bin to reach them.

Check the running lights, stern light, deck, steaming, spreader, anchor, tricolor, and compass lights, and any other external lights. Test all interior lighting and appliances such as wall fans.

Turn on all the instruments and check the displays to make sure they are receiving and processing signals.

Deck Preparations

Leave the anchor on the bow in case you choose or need to use it. At your last stop before leaving the shore, stow your secondary anchors safely, preferably somewhere low in the boat. Take the primary anchor off the bow, and secure it where it won't snag running rigging but can be fairly easily readied for use when you approach land. If your boat has an anchor well, that's a good place to stow it. While doing so, make sure the drain hole is clear of obstructions.

Leaking deck hatches can make life below miserable. If you're not sure of their integrity, or if a wet passage is in the cards, it would be prudent to seal the hatches from outside the boat. Duct tape placed around the whole hatch, bridging the hatch rim and deck, is very effective. This does entail, at voyage's end, cleaning the deck and hatch rim with acetone to remove the tape remnants, but that's better than water below. Another way to prevent water intrusion is to tie the right-sized line firmly in the gap between the hatch lid and the deck ring. You can supplement this method with caulking. If you use caulking material designed for household window use, it will peel right off at voyage's end. Pay attention to toe rails and wooden cap rails. Their junction with the deck can be porous, and water will stream below, sometimes far away from the leak. This can be confusing especially if you are not used to sailing offshore. Boats that never leak on the lake or bay suddenly become wet offshore.

Galley Preparation

Check the fuel supply for the galley stove, whether it's propane, butane, or CNG. Turn on the tank valve, and from below, open the main solenoid to allow gas to flow. Next, turn on the manual valve in the galley, if there is one, so that gas has access to the entire system. Once all the valves are open, watch the fuel gauge for any sign that gas is leaking from the system. If the gauge indicates no decrease in pressure over a period of several minutes, turn off the valves. If necessary remove the tank, or tanks, and have them topped off with cooking fuel.

While your preparations on deck are being completed, the member of the crew in charge of meals should be stowing the provisions. A logical way to do this is to start in the galley, putting the most-used items and those needed early on the voyage close at hand, and those for later use in the less accessible lockers and bins.

The galley is the center of much activity, and needs to be well organized and kept in good order. If you need convenient extra storage space for snacks and other oft-sought items, you can easily sling a net or two from the overhead. A product called Scoot Guard is handy to prevent items from sliding on counter tops.

Paper towels can be cut in half on their rolls, making them last longer and take up less space. Dishes must be dried after washing, and stowed safely after meals. Do not leave dishes in the sink to dry; they'll likely wind up strewn all over the boat. Have a place for the dish towels to hang and dry.

Keep a large thermos in a secure place in the galley. You will use this to keep beverages hot for the night watches.

Prepare a plan for handling garbage. Waste and scraps should be cleaned meticulously after meals. If your passage is to last a week or less, you can store waste in plastic bags for disposal at the next port. Unfortunately, some islands simply take garbage out to sea and dump it, which means that despite your best intentions, your garbage will join it. Garbage in plastic bags can float, and not only is this kind of pollution unsightly, it's also a hazard to marine animals and other vessels. If you have reason to believe this will be the case at your destination, you can improve the outcome somewhat: First remove all plastic (it's illegal to dispose of plastic into the ocean), collect your trash in paper bags, weigh them down to be sure they sink, and dump them at sea.

Eve of Departure

Go over the navigation station to make sure all the instruments are functioning and that you have the tools you need for chart work. Check to be sure that your supply of flags will include every foreign country on the itinerary, the national flag of the ship's registry, and an International Code Q flag. By this time you should also have on hand all the charts, books, and navigation publications you will need and, if you plan to use one, your laptop computer with all the necessary software installed and running. Make sure there are fresh batteries in the handheld GPS and VHF, deck flashlights, and life-jacket strobe lights and that you have an ample store of replacements.

I always have some items I've found very useful on board. I keep an emergency knife fixed to the companionway rail. This should be a multi-purpose knife, and most important, it must have a very sharp, serrated blade. This will be necessary should you ever have to cut a line or a crab pot from the propeller. It once took me over an hour, diving over and over again with a hunting knife, to finally hack through a crab pot line that I'd picked up in Hawk's Channel, off Florida; a serrated blade is much better. Keep a knife sharpener in the tool kit and use it to ensure the blades are always ready for use.

A good supply of spare line of different sizes is essential in case you need to replace a reefing line, spinnaker guys, or jib sheet, for example. Shorter lengths of ⅜-inch and smaller line are useful for any number of odd jobs that crop up. An electrician's fish tape is invaluable if you ever have to replace a reefing line that has snapped inside the boom. These are available at Home Depot, and can make a difficult job very simple.

Several flashlights should be available, with fresh batteries. Always have two flashlights in the cockpit after dark, stored in the same place every night. A pair of binoculars should also be close at hand in a dry location but readily accessible.

I like to keep a couple of towels right on the saloon sole so that whenever water gets below, it can be wiped up right away before someone can slip on the slick, wet surface.

Crew Briefing

When the crew assembles, focus your attention on familiarizing them with the boat and with your protocols for managing it.

Everyone should arrive at least a day in advance, to overcome any jet lag or travel problems and to get accustomed to the new surroundings. A good way to start their time together is around a meal, followed by a tour of the boat and her gear and where everything is stowed.

Each member of the crew should have a bunk, where they stow away their gear. Once they are settled in, you can assign the final pre-departure tasks, so that all the last communications and preparations are taken care of calmly and without anxiety.

Encourage the crew during this time to drink lots of fluids so that they start out well hydrated. On the day before setting sail they should avoid caffeine and alcoholic beverages, and should get as much rest as possible. This is a good time to remove jewelry and clip the fingernails too.

Seasickness patches or medications should be started four hours before departure.

Zero Hour

Fill any gaps in the ice box with block ice. Block ice will keep food cold for several days in a refrigerator even if the refrigeration isn't activated. It serves a double duty, because when the ice melts, it can be used to replenish water already emptied.

Top off the fuel tanks, and record the tanks' full capacities in the log book, along with the engine hours.

Pump out and thoroughly flush the holding tanks and turn the head Y-valves to the seagoing position. Make sure wood bungs are tied to every seacock and through hull in the boat.

Notify your shore contacts of your departure time, fill out the Float Plan and transmit it to the designated parties. Note your departure time in the Ship's Logbook.

In the preceding hours, you will have discussed the entire Crew Preparation Guide with the crew. Everyone on board should understand and be willing to abide by it. They should make one last visit to a shoreside facility for showers, to visit the head, and to make any goodbyes.

If the final weather update is favorable, and the tide is headed out, then start the engine, cast off the dock lines, stow the fenders, and let the fun and adventure begin!

PART 4

BOAT HANDLING AND SHIPKEEPING

CHAPTER 20

MANEUVERING UNDER POWER

Having the ability to maneuver a sailboat under power in any situation with confidence is a valuable asset. Such a skill is acquired through practice and experience, but its foundation is an understanding of how controlling a boat's motion is affected by characteristics of the hull, the rudder and by the action of the propeller on the water.

Sailboats by nature are more difficult to maneuver than powerboats. Their relatively low engine revolutions, single-propeller configuration, deep draft, and displacement hulls are all factors. You can't always count on the engine alone when negotiating narrow channels, in docking or undocking, or when traversing a heavily traveled harbor. You have to use forethought and common sense to work with, rather than trying to fight against, such external factors as cross-winds, currents, powerboat wakes, and where the sun is.

Some years ago, I was accustomed to maneuvering racing vessels and a light-weight 28-foot sloop. The first VOYAGER was a heavy Vagabond 42 ketch with very different handling characteristics. I had to learn to think ahead before starting a maneuver and assess every factor that could influence its outcome. I learned valuable lessons, which I was then able to pass on to my students.

FORCES IN PLAY

Four factors govern the effects an engine has when steering and maneuvering a sailboat: the direction in which the propeller turns, the angle at which the propeller shaft exits the hull, the actions of water flowing out of the propeller, and the position of the rudder.

Propeller Hand

The direction in which the propeller rotates has a turning influence on the hull. Propellers are described as being right- or left-handed. When viewed from astern of the boat, a right-handed propeller rotates in a clockwise direction when propelling the boat forward. Most sailboats have right-handed propellers; that means when the boat is in forward gear, the propeller spins in a clockwise direction and thrusts the water aft. In reverse gear, the propeller spins counterclockwise and pushes the water toward the bow.

Shaft Angle

On most sailing yachts, the propeller shaft proceeds aft from the engine and exits the hull at a downward angle. The shaft angle causes the spinning propeller to exert different forces on the descending and ascending sides of the propeller; the blades on either side are at different pitch angles. When the right-hand propeller is in forward gear, this difference in propeller angle causes stronger propulsion on the starboard side, resulting in the stern clawing its way to starboard in forward gear. When it's in reverse, the stern moves toward port. The net result of this unbalanced propulsion, termed "unequal blade thrust," is the stern tending to move to starboard in forward gear, and to port in reverse.

The water flowing out of the propeller is called the propeller "discharge current." A right-hand propeller in forward pushes its discharge current back and down on the starboard side while the port side current travels upward and back. This port discharge current hits the rudder and hull and pushes them, and the stern, to starboard. This is the other reason you notice the boat has a slight tendency to steer to port when motoring ahead. In reverse gear, the opposite occurs. The turning propeller pushes water on the starboard side against the hull, pushing the stern to port. This is a major consideration when backing a vessel.

The net result of propeller discharge current is that in forward gear, the current impacts the port side hull and rudder, pushing the stern toward starboard (Figure 20-1), and in reverse, the current forces the stern to port as it impacts the starboard side (Figure 20-2).

Figure 20-2 demonstrates the forces applied with a right-hand propeller in reverse gear. The port side blades now have greater pitch and bite, and pull the stern toward port. The discharge currents are also reversed; port side discharge is forward and down, causing no secondary action while the starboard discharge is now forward

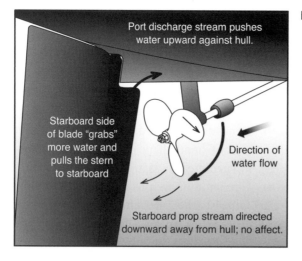

FIGURE 20-1

Port discharge stream pushes water upward against hull.

Starboard side of blade "grabs" more water and pulls the stern to starboard

Direction of water flow

Starboard prop stream directed downward away from hull; no affect.

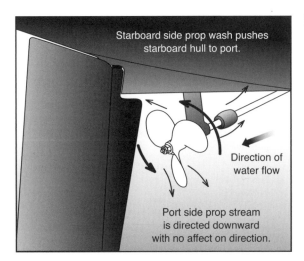

FIGURE 20-2

Starboard side prop wash pushes starboard hull to port.

Direction of water flow

Port side prop stream is directed downward with no affect on direction.

and up, striking the hull and pushing the stern over toward port. The forces of increased blade pitch to port and the starboard discharge stream also pushing the hull to port result in a rather strong tendency for the stern to move to port when backing, at least until enough sternway is gained for the rudder to gain steerageway.

The Rudder

The fourth important contributor to how a vessel responds under power is the rudder.

Water flowing past the hull, and water in the propeller discharge stream impact the more exposed side of the rudder. When the steering wheel is turned to starboard, the rudder turns so that its starboard side is exposed to the discharge stream. This pushes the rudder to port, with the result that the boat turns to starboard. When the rudder's port side is exposed to the discharge stream, the stern is forced to starboard and the bow turns toward port.

For the boat to have steerage, there must be water flow past the rudder, i.e. the boat must have way on through the water. It will not respond to the helm if drifting or riding in a current. This is why, when maneuvering in close quarters, it's important to understand how to use engine thrust and the effects of unequal blade thrust (also referred to as "prop walk") to push the stern in the desired direction when the rudder otherwise has no effect.

When the boat has way on and the rudder is turned, the boat turns with a pivoting motion. When the boat has forward motion, the pivot point is located roughly a third of the boat's length aft from the bow. When it's going astern, the pivot point is about one third of the boat's length forward of the stern (Figure 20-3). This is an important consideration during close quarters maneuvering. When in forward gear, turning to port, the starboard quarter kicks out to starboard. When backing and the wheel is over to port, the bow swings to starboard.

FIGURE 20-3

Pivot points when a boat has forward and sternward motion.

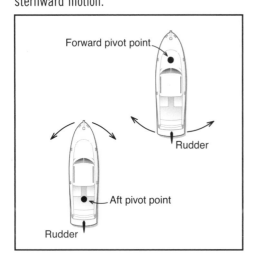

FIGURE 20-4

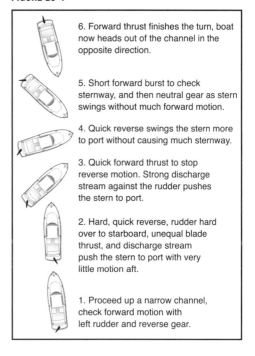

6. Forward thrust finishes the turn, boat now heads out of the channel in the opposite direction.

5. Short forward burst to check sternway, and then neutral gear as stern swings without much forward motion.

4. Quick reverse swings the stern more to port without causing much sternway.

3. Quick forward thrust to stop reverse motion. Strong discharge stream against the rudder pushes the stern to port.

2. Hard, quick reverse, rudder hard over to starboard, unequal blade thrust, and discharge stream push the stern to port with very little motion aft.

1. Proceed up a narrow channel, check forward motion with left rudder and reverse gear.

TIGHT QUARTERS MANEUVERING

The U-Turn

In one particular maneuver, that of turning the boat 180 degrees in a narrow channel, you can use the principles of unequal blade thrust and direction of discharge stream to your advantage. As you head up the channel, check your forward motion with reverse gear, and then pivot the boat with minimal forward or reverse motion. Most sailboats have right-hand propellers, so a turn to starboard uses the prop walk to good effect.

As the boat loses its forward motion, apply full right rudder to initiate the turn and apply a short burst of engine thrust in reverse. At this point, both the rudder's response to the boat's residual forward motion and the effect of unequal blade thrust are working together to pivot the boat in the same direction.

Before the boat can begin moving astern, apply another burst of forward power. Now, the discharge stream pushing on the rudder continues the pivoting action.

Another burst of power in reverse arrests forward motion and continues to swing the stern around.

Arrest sternway with another burst in forward gear, and then shift into neutral while the boat continues to pivot under its own momentum.

Apply a final burst of forward thrust to finish the turn, throttle back, and bring the helm back to amidships to steer down the channel in the opposite direction.

Note that throughout the maneuver, the rudder remains in the same position. The turn is effected by applying short bursts of power and using the discharge streams they create before they cause much forward or reverse movement in the boat.

Getting the Feel

All boats have their idiosyncrasies and all behave a little differently. The prudent skipper practices boathandling for as many situations as possible, both to acquire the necessary skills and to learn how his boat responds to a variety of circumstances. Practicing this 180-degree turn and the maneuvers below will give you a good feel for your boat and how it maneuvers.

- From a stopped position, determine how many boat lengths it takes to achieve enough speed to gain steerage (called bare steerageway). Do this in forward and reverse gears.
- Determine how much distance is required for the boat to stop from two knots of boat speed.
- Practice checking headway by using reverse power.
- Back the boat in a straight line.
- Back the boat and turn to port and to starboard.

DOCK LINES AND DOCKING MANEUVERS

Knowing how to use dock lines is very valuable whenever you have to maneuver a sailboat at a dock, along a wall, or into or out of a slip. Miscues and missteps can cause damage, not to mention embarrassment. You can control a boat's

movement in many ways, according to where you attach the dock lines, both on the boat and on the dock.

Terminology of Dock Lines

Each line arrangement commonly used has a name. Figure 20-5 illustrates the terminology of dock lines used to secure a vessel—where they lead and what they are called. Dock lines are used in various ways and combinations depending on the situation. To be prepared for any situation that might arise, you should acquire a thorough knowledge of how they work and when to use them. (Figures 20-5 to 20-11).

Approaching a Dock or Wall

When approaching a dock or wall, your first line ashore should be an aft bow spring line attached to the boat approximately at its pivot point. With the

FIGURE 20-5
Terminology of Dock Lines.

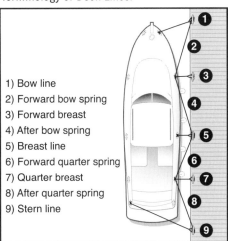

1) Bow line
2) Forward bow spring
3) Forward breast
4) After bow spring
5) Breast line
6) Forward quarter spring
7) Quarter breast
8) After quarter spring
9) Stern line

FIGURE 20-6

Dock line to use when approaching a dock or wall.

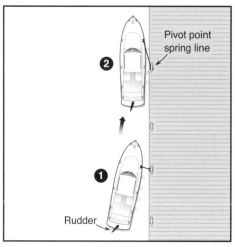

FIGURE 20-7

Approaching a dock shorthanded.

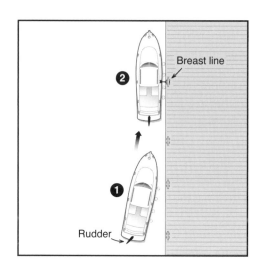

rudder turned to steer the boat away from the dock and the engine at idle speed in forward gear, the boat is "hinged" laterally toward the dock and the remaining dock lines can be positioned at leisure. This is especially helpful when the wind is blowing off the shore.

Docking Shorthanded

When approaching the wall, have an amidships breast line ready and attach it quickly to a cleat or bollard (Figure 20-7). This prevents the boat from drifting away and allows more time to secure bow, stern, and spring lines. This is particularly helpful, along with the pivot point spring line, when singlehanding. I usually don't leave a breast line on once other dock lines are in place. Notice the short scope of the breast line in Figure 20-7; a falling tide could tighten the line and damage the boat.

FIGURE 20-8

Springing the stern off a dock against the wind.

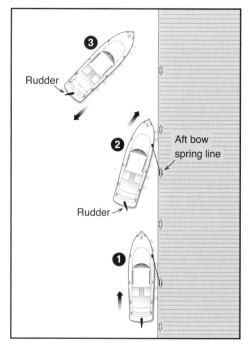

FIGURE 20-9
Springing the bow off a dock against the wind.

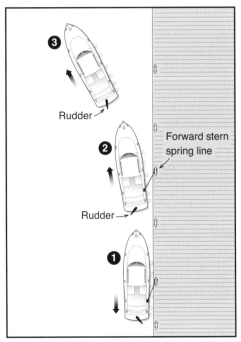

FIGURE 20-10
A breast line to an anchor holds the boat off a dock.

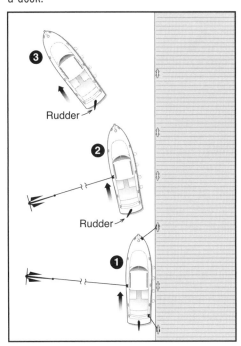

Leaving a Dock in an Onshore Wind

This can be a challenging situation, especially in a strong wind, but you have two techniques to choose from. Which you use will depend to some extent on your boat's own characteristics.

Use an after bow spring and with the rudder turned toward the dock, ease the boat forward with the engine (Figure 20-8). The stern will swing out and you can use reverse gear to pull away from the dock. Placement of a fender at the bow is mandatory.

You can also use a forward stern spring and the engine in reverse engine with rudder toward the dock (Figure 20-9). This is the tactic I often use leav-

ing the fuel dock in St. George, Bermuda, where the wind almost always bears against the dock. Note the fender placed at the quarter.

An Anchor to Windward

Kedging off the dock by winching in a breast anchor line draws the boat away from the dock (Figure 20-10). Once clear of the dock, you can either head forward with hard left rudder, or transfer the anchor line toward the bow to assist in turning the bow against a strong breeze, along with left rudder.

Deploying a breast line to a kedge anchor is also a nice way to keep you off a

FIGURE 20-11

Using a spring line when backing into a slip.

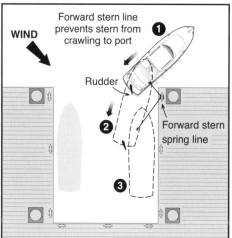

dock. It's especially useful when you'd prefer not to get too close for various reasons, such as when a wall is foul with pests or extrusions or when a heavy swell or wave action is present. Once the anchor is deployed, you might as well use it to help get off the wall when it comes time to leave. If using a kedge in a busy area, tie a line to the anchor stock, attached to a float to warn other vessels of the anchor line.

Backing Into a Slip in Windy Conditions

This is actually a situation to avoid if you can. When the wind makes a maneuver difficult, choose an easier method that presents less risk. Here's an example of a boat that should have been docked bow first, because it is more maneuverable in that direction (Figure 20-11), but the technique is valuable when you need it.

Wind is forcing this boat against the

piling, with the bow being pushed strongly to leeward. At this point, any action is ineffective because the wind is too strong. The only way to salvage the situation without causing damage to the starboard side is to use lines. A forward stern spring to the piling (1) controls the stern when the engine is reversed, allowing the boat to be maneuvered backward into the slip. A fender is used between the boat and the piling. The person tending the spring line must be able to control sideslip of the stern while slacking the line as the boat moves backward.

Notice how the stern line is led to the piling in situation 1. This is done by a crewmember on the dock. As the engine provides reverse thrust, the stern is kept from kicking to port, and the hull is kept away from damage. The boat creeps astern as the line is eased by the crewperson. In situation 2, the boat moves aft as the spring eases. A port side bow line, tended from the dock on that side, would also be helpful in this situation.

Tips for Maneuvering Under Power

- Approach all docking situations at slow speed.
- Before approaching a dock, study the situation. Consider wind and current, available room, your boat's handling traits, depth, and all other pertinent factors. Decide on your strategy, explain it to your crew so they know their duties, and make sure the dock lines are in place and the fenders are out before you begin your final approach.

- Before the point of no return, shift between forward and reverse gears to make certain the transmission engages properly.
- Do not be afraid to abort a landing if you have miscalculated. Turn around and re-think your approach.
- To pivot your boat in a very short distance, you must have little or no way on. If you wish to turn the bow to port, for example, give full left rudder and apply high engine revolutions in a short burst. The ejection current will impact the rudder while unequal thrust impacts the port hull to push the stern to starboard. Use very short bursts of power to avoid producing headway.
- Be very careful when shifting gears. The engine must be at idle when changing gears. Shifting at speed will damage or ruin the transmission.
- The judicious use of fenders can save a lot of gelcoat. Have fenders positioned and have one of the crew serve as a rover, hanging a fender over the side but ready to move it as necessary.

- Check for trailing lines before starting the engine.
- Inspect the propeller and shaft whenever the boat is hauled. Look for damage to the blades, a loose propeller shaft, damage to the strut or skeg, and check the condition of the zinc anode.
- If leaving a dock with one dock line looped around a piling, be certain it will release easily when you want it to. It's very easy to have the line snag on projections or crevices in the piling and hang up.
- Always approach a slip under minimal headway. Try to have about one knot of boat speed when the bow passes the front pilings so it's under control and easy to stop. Placing an after bow spring line, breast line, or after quarter spring is also easier when there is little headway.
- Never approach a dock expecting to reduce speed at the last moment with reverse engine thrust.
- Remember the number one rule of docking a sailboat. Any docking you can walk away from is a good one!

CHAPTER 21

GROUND TACKLE AND ANCHORING TECHNIQUES

Anyone who has dragged anchor, or has had to fend off another boat that was blown down toward them, understands the importance of ground tackle. There's nothing as comforting after a long passage as the security you feel lying to a well set and reliable anchor. Achieving that level of confidence in your ground tackle begins with outfitting the boat with the best anchors, rodes, and hardware available. Opinions vary, and debates rage over which anchors work best, but we must make our own choices based on our own boats, where we sail, and the conditions under which we'll likely be setting the hook.

ANCHORS AND ASSOCIATED TACKLE

Anchors

Yacht anchors in general fall into two broad categories: the heavy plow type and the lighter anchors with flat flukes.

The CQR, Delta, and Bruce are examples of the plow type. Their flukes, shaped like those of a plow, bury into the bottom initially because of the anchor's heavy weight. They generally hold very securely, and are the most suitable on cruising boats that anchor in a variety of bottom types and sea states, where security and reliability are the most important considerations. A windlass is very helpful when raising and lowering these heavy anchors.

Inland or coastal sailors who prefer not to weigh down their bows with heavier tackle often choose lighter types of anchors. The Danforth, which is made of high-tensile steel, and the Fortress, which is similar in concept and design but made of aluminum, are the members of this class most commonly seen. These anchors have flat flukes with pointed tips that pivot and dig into the seabed when the shank comes under load. Because they are lighter, they can be easier to handle, but they must be tended more closely when being raised because their configuration makes them more awkward to stow.

When selecting anchors for your boat, determine first what class will be the most appropriate. You will need several anchors, so you should take at least one of a different type to prepare you for different holding conditions. Once you know which types you want, determine their appropriate weights according to your boat's size and displacement. Anchor manufacturers publish tables to help you make the right selection.

The table, provided courtesy of Fortress Marine Anchors, shows the estimated load on an anchor on boats of different lengths in a range of wind strengths. These numbers should be used only as a guide, because boats of similar lengths can be of very different configurations—those with high freeboard or superstructures will have greater windage, for example, and therefore be subject to higher loads. Compensate for such factors by acquiring anchors one or two steps up the holding power ladder.

The Anchor Rode

The anchor line, or rode, will be a combination of nylon line, usually three-strand rope, and chain, or all chain. Nylon is used both because of its strength and because of its great elasticity, which reduces the shock loads it will transmit between the anchor and your boat's fittings. An all-nylon rode is too light to impart an effective horizontal pull on the anchor, so a length of chain is usually connected between the anchor and the nylon. The weight of the chain holds the rode down so that the pull on the anchor is horizontal, enabling it to set properly. The chain also protects the line against chafe from the sea bed.

TABLE 21-1

Anchor rode tension for boats of different sizes and in a range of wind strengths.

WIND SPEED	BOAT LENGTH in FEET							
	20ft	25ft	30ft	35ft	40ft	50ft	60ft	70ft
15 kts	90	125	175	225	300	400	500	675
30 kts	360	490	700	900	1,200	1,600	2,000	2,700
42 kts	720	980	1,400	1,800	2,400	3,200	4,000	5,400
60 kts	1,440	1,960	2,800	3,600	4,800	6,400	8,000	10,800
WIND SPEED	BOAT LENGTH in METERS							
	6m	8m	9m	11m	12m	15m	18m	21m
15 kts	41	57	79	102	136	181	227	306
30 kts	163	222	318	408	544	726	907	1,225
42 kts	327	445	635	816	1,089	1,452	1,814	2,449
60 kts	653	889	1,270	1,633	2,177	2,903	3,629	4,899

If you regularly anchor in 25 feet (8 meters) of water or less, use 6 feet (2 meters) of chain. For greater depths, use 6 feet for every 25 feet of water depth. For example, use 24 feet (7 meters) of chain if you regularly anchor in 100 feet (30 meters) of water.

Anchor manufacturers will also provide charts to assist in selecting size and length of anchor lines. The longer the anchor rode, the closer to horizontal the pull on the anchor (Figure 21-1).

Anchor chain is available in a range of sizes—bigger boats generally need heavier and stronger chain—and is galvanized to prevent corrosion. All-chain anchor rodes are customarily seen on larger boats that spend a lot of time at anchor and in a variety of depths and holding conditions. Chain rodes are heavy, and deliver a nice horizontal pull on the anchor. The only way a chain anchor line can dampen shock loading, however, is by having sag along the length of chain that pulls taut when the boat is lifted by a wave. This is a major disadvantage of chain, and calls for the

attachment of a snubber (Figure 21-2) at the boat end to absorb some of the shock.

A snubber is a length of nylon line, sometimes with a mooring line compensator added, which you connect to the chain anchor rode after the anchor is set. You can do this by tying it with a rolling hitch, or with a hook spliced into the end of the snubber line. The attached snubber is then made fast to a cleat. Since the snubber is able to stretch, it absorbs the shock loading of the chain.

The snubber line should be long enough so that if the anchor rode must be let out in a blow, the snubber can be let out along with it.

Connecting Anchor and Rode

Ground tackle consists of more than anchors and rodes. It includes the several items of hardware used to connect the anchor rodes to the boat and to the anchors. These cannot be overlooked, since the weakest link in any chain will be the one to fail.

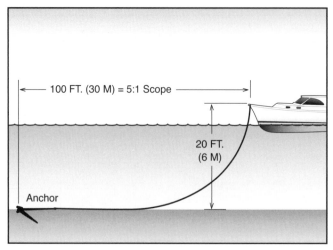

FIGURE 21-1
A longer anchor line applies the load to the anchor in a direction closer to the horizontal. *Courtesy of Fortress Anchors.*

100 FT. (30 M) = 5:1 Scope

20 FT. (6 M)

Anchor

FIGURE 21-2
Anchor chain snubber.

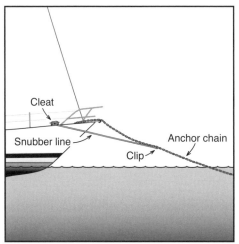

Both ends of the nylon part of a rode are usually spliced around a thimble. The bitter end is shackled to a secure attachment point in the chain locker or anchor well. The working end is connected to the anchor shank, or more usually to the chain, with a swivel shackle or swivel and shackle.

All of this gear is subject to high loads and corrosion, and should be inspected routinely to assure it's in good working condition. Shackles sometimes become pitted with corrosion and need replacing. The shackle pin is also subject to great physical wear when the anchor is in use and should be secured with stainless steel wire to prevent it from unscrewing. It's also good practice to apply waterproof grease or silicone to the threads of shackle pins to protect them from corrosion and ensure they can be undone when necessary.

Check eye splices in the anchor line for signs of damage or weakness. Nylon line that's stained by rust from a thimble may be weakened and you may need to splice in a new eye. Thimbles are usually constructed of galvanized steel or stainless steel, but some may be composed of bronze or plastic. Watch for corrosion if the swivel or shackle to which it connects are made of different metals. Make sure that the thimble is secure within the eye of the splice. If the thimble isn't properly seated, it may slip out when the line becomes taut, which will lead to accelerated chafe of the anchor line. If the thimble is improperly matched to the line diameter, or if the eye is chafed, the thimble may work loose.

Swivels need to operate freely, and corrosion and physical damage from excessive line loads may prevent them from doing that. If a swivel has seized up, you may be able to free it by applying penetrating lubricant and twisting the two ends in opposite directions. If you succeed, remove debris from the components with gentle wet sanding. If the swivel remains frozen or the working surfaces are pitted and damaged, you're better off replacing it. If you find any weakness in your ground tackle, it's time to replace the faulty component.

Anchor Windlass

Many vessels are also equipped with a windlass, without which some ground tackle would be very difficult to hoist when well dug in. Windlasses are either operated manually or powered by an electric motor. Electric windlasses can usually be hand operated in case of electrical failure. Various types of windlasses are manufactured to suit different deck arrangements and sizes of anchors and chain. The most versatile models are capable of handling rope or chain, and make it easier to deploy twin anchors.

The cables that conduct electricity to the windlass usually connect to the battery isolation switch. A toggle on the main panel or a combination circuit breaker and on/off switch usually supplies power to the windlass by activating a solenoid. The power cable itself is usually protected by its own fuse or circuit breaker. The cables run forward within the electrical harness to a junction box housing the solenoids which power the windlass in response to signals from foot-operated button switches or a handheld control unit.

TECHNIQUES FOR ANCHORING

Preparing to Anchor

A discussion of ground tackle would not be complete without mentioning an oft-neglected piece of anchoring equipment, the nautical chart. The chart tells us, among other valuable bits of information, the depths, bottom contours, restricted areas, and what type of bottom to expect. It makes no sense to blindly drop anchor, hoping for good holding when you can select the optimum areas by simply consulting the chart. *Chart #1* explains all the symbols found on nautical charts.

Once you've selected the most suitable spot in which to anchor, you'll want to know the depth. Use the chart as a guide in selecting the spot, and use the depth meter to find the depth both where the anchor drops, and where the boat will lie after backing down. Calculate the scope you need according to the depth where you will deploy the anchor. Next, calculate the expected depth at high tide. To that depth, add the height of the bow rollers above the water to find the basis on which you will calculate your scope. Scope is the ratio of the length of anchor rode you deploy to the height of your bow roller above the sea bed.

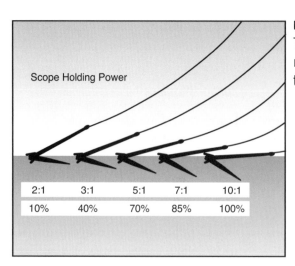

FIGURE 21-3
The weight of a chain rode does most of the work holding a boat to its anchor.

How much scope you let out depends to some degree on the anchor you use, the type of rode, the nature of the holding, and the weather conditions. I recommend at least 5:1 scope for security.

If we calculate that the depth at high tide will be 15 feet, and the height of the bow roller to the water is 5 feet, our total basis is 20 feet. For a scope of 5:1, the length of line to let out would be:

$$scope = 20 \times 5$$
$$= 100 \text{ feet}$$

Make sure that the anchor you use can give the performance you need. A "lunch hook" should be able to hold your boat in a 15-knot breeze. A primary, or "working anchor" should hold in up to 30 knots of wind. A "storm anchor" is for winds up to 42 knots. As the wind speed doubles, the holding requirement quadruples.

Holding power is a factor of scope almost as much as it is of the anchor itself. The key is to provide a horizontal pull on the anchor so that the flukes dig in at maximum efficiency. If the rode is inadequate, you won't achieve that optimum horizontal pull. Most anchors that drag do so because insufficient rode has been let out, the result being that the boat pulls upward on the anchor, dislodging it. With inadequate rode, even a terrific anchor won't hold in adverse conditions. Referring to Figure 21-3, note the increased holding power as rode increases. At 3:1, you will give up a significant amount of holding power and may have difficulty setting the anchor.

Setting the Anchor

Once you've identified the spot at which you'll anchor and determined the scope you'll need, the actual process of setting the anchor begins. Make sure that the anchor line or chain is free to deploy once the anchor is lowered. Head the bow into the wind or current, whichever will have the most influence on how the boat lies once anchored. Stop all forward way, and begin backing the boat slowly. At this point, the bow crew releases the anchor, and the boat continues to power backward as the crew notes how much anchor line is deployed. Once the desired scope has been let out, the boat ceases backing. The deck crew "snubs" or secures the anchor rode to prevent more from paying out. A nylon rode is usually made fast to a stout bow cleat. Chain is often left on the windlass at this point but it's good practice once anchored to remove it from the gypsy and secure it elsewhere to avoid subjecting the windlass to shock loads.

Once the line is snubbed, I recommend power setting to dig the anchor's flukes deeply into the bottom. By using this technique, you improve your chances of drag-free anchoring. Back down very slowly. When backing down initially, you will get accustomed to feeling the anchor if it drags across the bottom instead of setting. The person at the bow can feel it in the anchor line, which quivers slightly as the anchor bumps along. Even at the helm position, you can sense a very slight shaking of the hull underfoot.

When the anchor digs in and the line grows taut, slowly increase the load with your engine, setting the anchor deeply into the bottom. You can often feel a discernible jerk when the boat pulls directly against the anchor. The anchor line should remain taut even when the boat is backed hard. If it slackens, you'll have to repeat the procedure. When you are confident the anchor is set, ease the throttle. With the power off, the residual tension in the anchor rode will pull the boat slowly forward until the line becomes slack.

If the anchorage is crowded, power set your anchor at 5:1 scope, then shorten the line as required. I always anchor far enough for at least 7:1 scope overnight. After setting the anchor satisfactorily, monitor the boat's position until you're certain she won't drag in the current or foreseeable conditions. Select two prominent features on land, and periodically check their relative bearings as the boat settles into position. The boat will probably fishtail around a bit, but should maintain those general bearings. Another method is to note the position on the GPS and monitor that closely for a while. This is particularly useful at night, when objects on land are harder to see.

Setting one anchor very well is adequate for most anchoring situations. To accommodate areas of poor holding, expected shifts in wind direction or tidal currents, or for changes in water flow in tidal rivers, other techniques are indicated.

Using Multiple Anchors

Setting twin anchors off the bow with an angle of 45-degrees between them (Fig-ure 21-4) increases security against increasing wind or swell. Set the primary anchor (1) and then pay out scope as you motor the boat laterally and a little forward to a position parallel with the first anchor (2). Begin moving backward, drop the second anchor, and pay out 7:1 scope (3). When adequate line is out, power set the second anchor, and move the boat toward the first anchor to settle between the two (4).

The second anchor should be deployed in the direction of any expected wind shift or change in current, but don't let the angle between it and the first anchor exceed about 60 degrees.

Another technique that employs two anchors is the Bahamian moor (Figure 21-5), which is your best protection

FIGURE 21-4

Twin anchors set in a Vee from the bow.

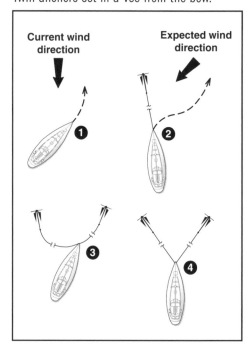

against changing currents. Begin facing up-current, and set your primary anchor. Continue to fall back, paying out scope as you go. When you reach the limit of scope, either drop the second anchor or take it back farther in the dinghy.

When the second anchor is down, motor forward against the current toward the first anchor, taking in the slack in the primary anchor rode while paying out line to the second anchor. When you've allowed enough rode in the second line, set the second anchor very securely with a good power set that pulls hard on the second anchor without dislodging it, and then settle back and lie to the first anchor while the current flows in that direction.

Monitor your position on number-one anchor to be sure of a good set, bearing in mind that you have not confirmed the set of number two. This is one instance where an anchor watch is in order for the period during which the current changes in direction, as indicated by the tide tables. This may well be during the night, so make sure to designate someone to be responsible for maintaining watch as the boat turns to lie to the second anchor, and to verify that it holds well.

Lying Between an Anchor and the Shore

The Mediterranean moor (Figure 21-6) is most often used to enable boats to lie stern to a dock or wharf. The anchor is set off the bow, with adequate scope, and the boat backs up to the dock, to which it is secured with mooring lines. It's a tricky technique, especially in a crowded harbor, because you have to set the anchor securely while having little room for maneuvers or mistakes. The anchor must be firmly power set, because it must keep the boat off the dock. A similar technique can be used to anchor close to a beach. Once the anchor is set, two lines are taken from the stern to shore, and tied to something very strong that can't pull out.

Using an Anchor in Other Situations

Use of a breast line (Figure 21-7) is sometimes necessary when lying against a dock. Lower the anchor into the dinghy, take it to windward, and deploy it at a distance from the yacht that will

FIGURE 21-5
In the Bahamian moor, the boat lies between two anchors set in a line fore and aft.

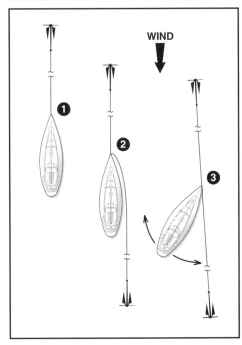

FIGURE 21-6

The Mediterranean moor holds a boat stern to the shore.

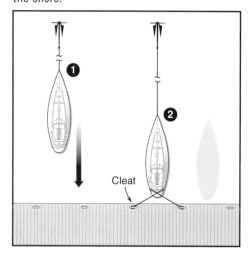

technique so that they will swing in a similar manner.

Methods used to limit how much a boat swings to its anchor include deploying a second anchor off the stern and hoisting a riding sail, which might be a special sail that sets on the backstay or the trysail sheeted amidships.

Ensuring a Good Set

When anchoring, a reliable rule of thumb regarding holding power is, "When in doubt, let it out." While this is true in many situations, it isn't always so. If an anchor that is fouled drags and cannot reset properly, letting out more line won't help it set.

If plenty of scope is already out, and the anchor drags and will not set properly, there is most likely another problem. The best thing to do in that case is to bring the anchor back up for a look,

give adequate scope. Make the boat end of the rode fast to a cleat amidships. An anchor set on a breast line in this way will hold the boat off the dock against the wind and prevent it from being damaged by waves pushing it against the wall.

When using this technique in a busy harbor, it's good practice to attach a float to the anchor stock, to warn other boats of its presence. Use a sentinel to keep the line deep if the situation warrants it.

The Etiquette of Anchoring

Boats already in an anchorage when you enter it have *right of first arrivals*. They have chosen their anchoring spots and their methods of anchoring. Others arriving later should make every attempt not to encroach within their swinging radius, and to use a similar anchoring

FIGURE 21-7

Using an anchor to set up a breast line.

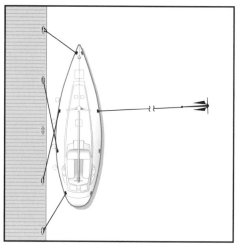

and start over. Bruce anchors, for example, can dredge up a ball of clay from the bottom that can prevent them from resetting. Check the chart again, and see that nothing is wrong with the anchor before you redeploy it.

There are several ways to increase the horizontal pull on the anchor. The most obvious is to attach a length of chain at the end of a nylon rode. As mentioned above, many offshore sailors and cruisers use all-chain rodes. In some areas, where rock and coral are prevalent on the bottom, that's really the only option.

Another way to induce sag in the anchor line is with a sentinel. This is simply a weight that slides down the anchor line after it's deployed. A retrieval line attached to the sentinel lets you adjust its position and bring it back aboard before you raise the anchor. The weight pulls the anchor line downward, so that it pulls at a more efficient angle on the anchor.

A sentinel can be as simple as chain in a plastic bucket, molded concrete with a hook on its top, or a bronze casting. Just don't forget to tie the retrieval line to it.

lowing the boat to glide forward. When the anchor line is up and down, the stock is pulled upward, breaking the flukes free of the bottom.

Hoist the anchor until it clears the water. If it's covered in mud, clean it before bringing it on deck. Dunk it in and out of the water, or wash it with seawater from a bucket, or from a wash-down hose if the boat is so equipped. When it's clean, carefully maneuver the anchor over the bow rollers and into position.

You can break a stubborn anchor loose from the bottom in several ways. The first one is to maneuver the boat over the anchor, snug the rode on a cleat and use the boat to pull the flukes out. If that fails, you can motor the boat in a circle around the anchor and pull on it from a number of directions.

If the anchorage is known to be foul, before you anchor, rig a trip line. Tie one end to the crown of the anchor and attach a fender as a buoy to the other end. To break the anchor free, retrieve the fender with a boat hook, cleat the trip line securely, and pull the crown with the boat.

Retrieving the Anchor

When it's time to raise the anchor, one person is stationed at the helm, and one at the bow. Start the engine, and make sure the windlass solenoid is in the "on" position. The helmsperson slowly motors the boat toward the anchor, directed by the bow crew, who takes in slack in the anchor line.

When the boat approaches the anchor, the throttle is placed in neutral, al-

Picking up and Dropping a Mooring

Many harbor areas have permanently installed moorings. Moorings are identified by buoys, sometimes called mooring balls, that are attached by chain to a concrete structure under the water or to a secure anchor device that is screwed into the bottom. The buoy usually has a mooring pendant attached which sometimes has its own float for identification and as an aid in picking it up.

As when anchoring, you maneuver the boat toward the mooring ball against the wind or current, as appropriate, and let it glide slowly on near approach. As the boat comes close, the bow crew grabs the pendant with the boat hook. The pendant usually has an eye spliced into its end, for placement over a bow cleat. When the pendant is cleated, let the boat swing to leeward on the mooring. It often pays to wear rubber gloves when grabbing the pendant—they're usually slimy and may have barnacles attached that can cut bare hands.

In some harbors, the mooring design provides a second pendant for the boat's stern. A line connects the bow and stern pendants. Once the bow is secured, find the connecting line, and follow it hand over hand while walking toward the stern. As the connecting line is pulled short, it brings the second pendant up, and that is cleated at the stern.

Moorings are usually on quite short chains, which eliminates the large swing radii of boats on anchors and allows more boats to fit into the harbor area. Since moorings are very secure, once the pendants are cleated, there is normally no need to post an anchor watch, though it might be advisable if the wind builds to gale force with a sea to match.

To cast off a mooring, start the engine and move slowly toward the mooring ball to relieve tension on the pendant. The bow crew removes the pendant from the cleat, and releases it. When free of the mooring, allow the wind to blow the bow clear of the mooring buoy, then engage the propeller and steer for a clear lane to open water.

When pendants are cleated to bow and stern, begin by casting off the leeward pendant, usually from the stern. Keep the gear shift in neutral and allow this pendant to sink to avoid wrapping it in the propeller. When clear of the pendant, nudge the bow forward so the forward pendant can be released, and allow the wind to push the bow away from any potential entanglements.

CHAPTER 22

GOING ALOFT IN THE BOSUN'S CHAIR

When the need arises for a trip up the mast, the vehicle most commonly used is the bosun's chair. Done the right way, these excursions not only allow you to accomplish your tasks, but can be fun too.

Before you, or anyone else, goes aloft, inspect the bosun's chair. Make sure the fabric is not torn or abraded, the pockets have no holes in their bottoms, and the two D-rings to which the halyard attaches are secure in their webbing straps.

When seated in the chair, you should fit snugly and comfortably. The chair should have a crotch strap to prevent you from slipping out.

Whenever ascending the mast, take the tools you need for the job in hand and a few others, in case while you're up there you discover situations requiring minor repairs and adjustments. I recommend you take a sailing knife, sail tape, an adjustable wrench, a multimeter, pliers, straight-slot and Phillips screwdrivers, Teflon spray, a line to lower should you need anything else from below, and, because the view is usually worth capturing, a camera. You might want to have a small bag ready on deck into which you can place very small items, such as light bulbs or screws, and which you can attach to the line you lower from the chair.

Take any other items you need, but take care to stow them all safely in the chair pockets. Make sure, too, that you know where they are and that you can reach them easily. Falling items can be deadly to someone on deck, so once the halyard is made up, no one should remain directly below the person aloft. On a medium- or small-sized boat, the people on deck should restrict their movements to a minimum—shifting weight on deck can rock the boat and cause sudden movement aloft.

Make sure any halyard used to hoist a person aloft is in very good shape. Depending on where the job is, use a jib halyard or the main halyard for the hoist but never trust the shackle alone. As a precaution, using a bowline backed by a half-hitch, tie the halyard through both the D-rings on the chair in addition to attaching it with the shackle.

For extra security, attach a second jib or spinnaker halyard to the chair and have a mate keep it snug and around a winch, as the climber ascends. The primary halyard should be taken to a substantial deck winch, with the end properly tailed.

Before starting your ascent, climb to the boom, then help the grinder by pulling yourself up by grasping the shrouds and walk up the mast with your feet.

When you reach your destination, those tending the halyards should secure them using all means available—in line clutches, with extra wraps around the winches, and to cleats—to ensure they cannot be inadvertently released.

When it's time to descend, the deck crew takes up tension on the halyards, opens the clutches, and take wraps off the winches, leaving one or two so as to maintain control. They then lower the chair smoothly, without jerking motions, until it reaches the deck.

Going Aloft at Sea

Ascending the mast at sea is a far different proposition than it is on smooth water at the dock. Even small motions of the boat are accentuated at the masthead, making going aloft more difficult and treacherous. You therefore have to take steps to make the boat's motion as steady as possible.

To avoid rolling and yaw motions and maintain a relatively constant heel angle, put the boat onto a close reach. Use engine power to maintain a steady speed if necessary. At very slow speed the boat will wallow and be at the mercy of waves; if the boat is going too fast it will pound as it bashes into waves. Maintain a moderate speed that results in the least amount of motion. Whatever the job, it should be postponed if steep waves, confused seas, or high wind velocities will make going aloft too dangerous.

To reduce exposure, the crewmember going up has to complete the task as quickly as possible. So that he and everyone else understand what to do, you must discuss the job beforehand and assign duties. The person going aloft should wear long pants, shoes, and sailing gloves for protection.

The boat's motion may make it difficult for the ascender to assist the winch grinder by climbing—it may take all his efforts to hang onto the mast so as not swing away from it, and back into it, as the boat rolls. The grinder will just have to earn his keep.

In case the rolling motion is violent enough to keep slinging the climber away from the mast, attach a strong line to the climber that can be tended from the deck to steady him. To prevent this situation, some climbers tie a loop from themselves around the mast after reaching the top.

Sending someone aloft at sea requires special care. So that it is carried out in the safest way possible, the crew has to work closely as a team.

CHAPTER 23

SAFETY TACTICS, PROTOCOLS, AND PROCEDURES

The purpose of this important chapter is to explain the implications of sailing in heavy weather and to describe procedures in such a way that any crew on any boat will understand them and be able to put them into practice when necessary to cope with extreme conditions. The recommendations made in the chapter are based on research, conversations with other sailors, and personal experience, and in my opinion describe the best courses for action in the situations described. These are the procedures we use and teach on VOYAGER.

I suggest that you provide these protocols to your prospective crew in written form well ahead of your proposed departure date, and that you discuss them in the crew briefings you hold immediately before departure. It is important for everyone to understand and adopt them.

Storm Avoidance—Tropical Cyclones

When a storm threatens at sea, you have to make some very important decisions. You have to decide if your best course of action is to make for harbor or if you must attempt to put the vessel in the most advantageous position at sea where you will have the best chance of survival. Being caught on the open ocean in a cyclone is the last choice anyone would make, but under some circumstances, it's the only option available.

In order to reach safe haven, you must have adequate time to travel the required distance and to prepare the boat to weather the storm once you get there. The worst of all possible scenarios would be getting trapped over the shallow waters of a continental shelf or anywhere near a lee shore without maneuvering room. If there's any possibility you'll not make port before the storm hits, your best strategy for increasing the odds of survival is to seek deep water with plenty of sea room.

As soon as you learn of the existence or threat of a storm, plot its position on a chart and begin to track its movements along with your own position. Continue to download weather data, to obtain all information possible. You can supplement this information with NOAA Offshore and High Seas broadcasts over short wave, and through direct communications with shore facilities or other vessels. As the storm nears and chances

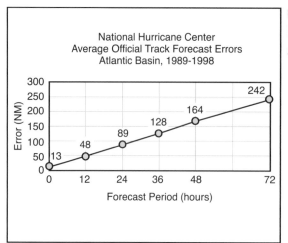

FIGURE 23-1
Hurricane track forecast errors increase along with time.

of losing your data source increase, your onboard observations become more pertinent to the situation and you should begin to update them at least hourly.

Movements of tropical cyclones in the Northern Hemisphere are guided by high pressure centers and winds aloft. They are formed and fueled by high altitude lows that also influence their paths. Storm avoidance tactics are based on knowing the storm's expected track, so monitoring its position is vitally important. Figure 23-1 demonstrates the fact that hurricane path prediction errors increase linearly with forecast period in hours. Since you expect forecast tracking error, you must account for that as you formulate your avoidance strategy.

Your goal is to avoid the 34-knot storm radius. If you can keep your vessel out of this zone of Force 8 wind, you should be able to safely negotiate the storm. Figure 23-2 illustrates the 34-knot radius of a forecast hurricane track and how we relate tracking error to it.

This is done by applying the 1-2-3 Rule of Storm Avoidance.

The 34-knot radius is a dashed circle surrounding the hurricane's core. The rule states that we add 100 miles to this radius on the 24-hour storm path prediction. This is illustrated by the outer ring around the 24-hour position. We add 200 miles to the 34-knot radius on the 48-hour predicted position and 300 miles to the 72-hour predicted position. Your strategy will be to avoid these extended radii, keeping your vessel within more manageable winds, so as to safely negotiate the hurricane.

In the event that weather downloads from satellite telephone or single side-band radio are impossible, try the short wave radio broadcasts and rely on your own weather skills. A change in sea swells will be your first indication of distant storm activity. Swells coming from the direction of the storm will initially be low, farther apart than normal, and gradually become higher. Cloud types

FIGURE 23-2

34-Knot Radius extended outward to accommodate errors in track prediction (NOAA).

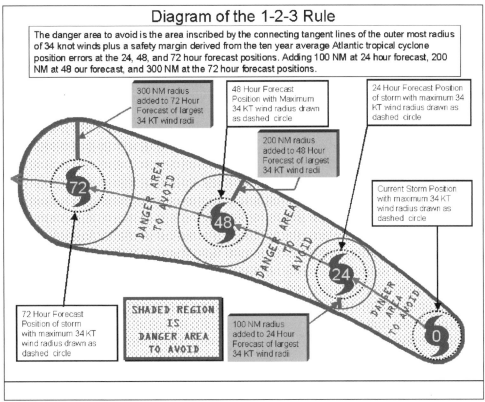

progress from the cirrus, cirrostratus, and alto type clouds, with thickening and lowering very noticeable. Rain accompanies the altostratus and altocumulus clouds.

As barometric pressure begins to drop, monitor its rate very closely. See Table 15-1 (Chapter 15, *Mariner's Weather*) as a guideline to categorize the intensity of the storm. Notice that the more rapidly the barometric pressure drops, the more severe the expected weather. A fall of 10 to 12 millibars in a three-hour period indicates that hurricane force winds are to be expected. As the cyclone nears, the barometer continues to drop even more rapidly, helping to determine the time frame of its arrival. An increase in wind speed of more than 25 percent in association with other indications is very significant, especially if the wind backs.

The first clouds that directly indicate the outer hurricane bands are the altocumulus or cumulonimbus types, seen to extend outward up to several hundred miles ahead of the hurricane wall, also termed the bar of the storm. This ominous, dark wall of clouds represents the hurricane's inner wall.

When observing a hurricane in the northern hemisphere from overhead, facing the direction of movement, the right side is called the dangerous semicircle because the wind strengths in that region are the sum of the storm's winds added to its speed of movement. If the hurricane winds are 85 knots, and the storm moves at 15 knots, winds on the right side are actually 100 knots (Figure 23-3). Winds on the left side are calculated to be 70 knots; the hurricane force of 85 knots minus 15 knots, since the storm movement opposes the storm wind direction. This is called the navigable semicircle.

Once you've determined a storm's position and forecast track, and you've applied the 1-2-3 Rule, mark your boat's position on a chart in relation to the storm's semicircles. A vessel at sea should not attempt to cross in front of a storm's path, even to reach the navigable semicircle, unless there is more than adequate time to do so successfully. Make accurate computations regarding the storm's speed and direction of movement versus your vessel's maximum speed and the best course you can steer; storms can travel much faster than sailboats. Bear in mind the swells that build in front of a hurricane's path; large swells cut down a vessel's speed. Avoid ocean currents whenever a storm threatens. Monitor the ocean temperature, and maneuver away from the warmest currents, like the Gulf Stream.

Another method by which you can determine in which quadrant a boat lies is by observing changes in wind direction. Referring to the positions denoted in Figure 23-3, apply the following rules:

Consider a vessel that is hove-to, in the Northern Hemisphere:

A) wind is veering (dangerous semicircle)
B) wind is backing the ship (navigable semicircle)
C) wind direction unchanging (directly in storm path).

Any vessel caught within such a storm system should use tactics based on the information in Table 23-1. This is also illustrated in Figure 23-4.

The vessel at A is in a precarious situation. The dotted arrow indicates that it should head for the navigable semicircle on the fastest broad reach possible. There

FIGURE 23-3

A hurricane can be roughly divided into a "dangerous" semicircle and a "navigable" semicircle.

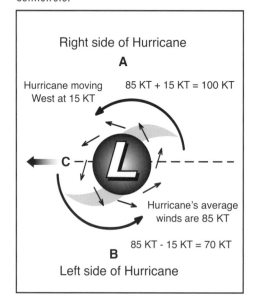

Right side of Hurricane

A

Hurricane moving West at 15 KT

85 KT + 15 KT = 100 KT

C

Hurricane's average winds are 85 KT

85 KT - 15 KT = 70 KT

B

Left side of Hurricane

TABLE 23-1

Storm avoidance tactics.

Vessel location	Navigation action
Ahead of tropical cyclone	Put the wind at 160° relative to the ship on the starboard side making best course and speed into the left semicircle of tropical cyclone.
Right semicircle of tropical cyclone	Put the wind at 045° relative to the ship on the starboard side attempting to make best course and speed to clear the system. Wind and wave can drastically reduce ship forward speed in this region.
Left semicircle of tropical cyclone	Put the wind at 135° relative to the ship on the starboard side making best course and speed to increase separation between ship and tropical cyclone.
Behind the tropical cyclone	Maintain best riding course and speed to increase separation between ship and tropical cyclone.

are various sailors' terms describing the situation for the vessel at RF (Right Forward). None can be included in this text! This boat will be facing the brunt of hurricane force winds in the dangerous semi-circle. It should be sailed on a close reach away from the worst conditions, and all aboard pray that the system diverts southward! The goal of your tactics is to avoid being in this position at all costs.

RR (Right Rear) illustrates a boat that apparently weathered the worst of the system. It is probably hove-to with or without a sea anchor. The crew may now decide to fore-reach out on a starboard tack or continue in a passive storm mode and wait out the storm.

A vessel positioned anywhere between these two should get on a starboard broad reach and make hull speed away from the worst of the semicircle.

LF (Left Forward) is near the 34-knot radius and should also make hull speed on a starboard broad reach to relatively better conditions away from the harshest winds. LR (Left Rear) is in the best

FIGURE 23-4

Vessels in various positions within a storm system.

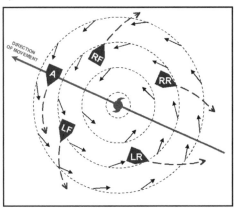

situation of all, and should also broad reach away from the storm.

PREPARING FOR HEAVY WEATHER

If while at sea you learn of approaching heavy weather, you can take steps ahead of time to prepare for its arrival.

Rigging for Heavy Weather

- Reduce sail early to the appropriate sail combination.
- Make storm sails ready.
- Secure all deck gear.
- Fill fuel tanks from jerry jugs if necessary.
- Secure companionway slides and ensure hatch can be closed and sealed from the deck. There should also be a mechanism ready to secure the hatch from below.
- Batten down hatches and ports.
- Don and clip on harness and tethers at all times while on deck, wear PFD and overboard alarm.
- Set up lee cloths.
- Secure all latches below decks to prevent spillage.
- Clear passageways below.
- Prepare a warm meal, put warm drinks in thermoses.
- Obtain position fix, communicate position and situation to land contacts.
- Charge batteries.
- Ensure that a furled genoa cannot unfurl accidentally.
- Determine and review storm tactics.
- Begin heavy weather watch schedule.

- Close all unnecessary through hulls and seacocks.
- Perform the entire routine maintenance and monitoring protocol.

I must stress how important it is, as the weather conditions deteriorate and especially if the forecast is severe, to be ahead of the storm with your preparations and with specific actions. Aside from the steps indicated above, your procedures for handling the boat should be in place. You should have a plan by which you reduce sail in a predetermined sequence. You should make each change promptly, as doing so becomes more dangerous as conditions worsen.

Reducing Sail

By sailing on a wide variety of boats, I've learned to my advantage how different vessels behave. The wind strengths at which sail has to be reduced and by how much vary according to the characteristics of every individual hull and its rig. It therefore becomes incumbent on the master of a vessel to learn the traits of that particular boat. Sail reduction is also done in a different sequence on sloops and cutters than on ketches.

Given the spectrum of hulls and rigs, use the recommendations that follow as guides to sail reduction. You can fine tune them as necessary for your own boat's characteristics.

Your goal at all times is to match your sail plan to the wind strength. If you manage to keep these two in balance, the only way you can be overpowered by wind is by a microburst gust. These are so short-lived they pose a minimal threat to the well-managed sailing vessel. I find it beneficial to have the information below readily accessible for review and for crew discussions. Always reduce sail early, regardless. Wind speeds are in true wind.

Reducing Sail in a Sloop or Cutter Rig Upwind

15 knots	First reef in main, possibly genoa 10-percent furled
22 knots	Second reef in main, genoa 20-percent furled
30 knots	Third reef in main, genoa 40-percent furled or removed and stowed below
35 knots	Deep-reefed main down traveler or dropped in favor of dropped, storm jib or storm staysail deployed
40-50 knots	Employ active close-hauled upwind steering, or heave-to
50 knots +	Continue concentrated, active steering or heave-to, with sea anchor if necessary.

Reducing Sail in a Sloop or Cutter Rig Downwind

20 knots	First reef in main, maintain full genoa
25 knots	Second reef in main, furl genoa 15-20 percent
30 knots	Third reef in main, furl genoa 30 percent
38 knots	Third reef in main, or trysail; genoa furled or removed; storm jib or storm staysail deployed
44 knots	Storm trysail and storm jib or staysail.
50 knots +	Actively sail the waves downwind, deploy drogue to maintain safe speed. Alternatively, head upwind and sail close reached, or heave-to. Never risk sailing too fast downwind under bare poles.

Reducing Sail in a Ketch Rig Upwind

16 knots	First reef in main, mizzen full, genoa furled 10 percent
22 knots	Second reef in main, first reef in mizzen, genoa 20-percent furled
28 knots	Main down, single reef in mizzen, genoa 30-percent furled
35 knots	Main down, double reef in mizzen, genoa furled or removed, storm jib or storm staysail (preferred) deployed
40-45 knots	Actively steer close-reached upwind, playing the wind and waves, or heave-to
50 knots +	Actively steer or heave-to, deploy sea anchor if necessary.

Reducing Sail in a Ketch Rig Downwind

20 knots	Full mainsail, drop mizzen, full genoa
25 knots	First reef in main, genoa 10-percent furled.
30 knots	Second reef in main, genoa 30-percent furled
35 knots	Third reef in main, furl genoa 100 percent, deploy storm jib or storm staysail (storm staysail preferred)
40 knots	Drop mainsail, sail on storm jib or storm staysail
48 knots +	Actively sail under storm staysail, deploy drogue if necessary, head up and close reach, or heave-to.

Running with the Storm

Heading off the wind with waves from astern (scudding) is a tactic that has been recommended since the days of clipper ships. Sailing with the wind and waves decreases apparent wind, and stops the pounding that can occur when sailing into the waves. Scudding can only be used when you have plenty of sea room, and when the seas build, it requires a skilled hand on the helm. It's very advantageous when the boat's heading coincides with the direction to your desired landfall, but if it means sailing in the wrong direction, the boat can be driven hundreds of miles off course. This is not my preferred tactic, unless it gains valuable distance toward my destination, and then only until the boat becomes difficult to handle or the seas coming from astern become threatening.

When running before a gale, the potential exists to generate high boat speeds. With that comes the possibility of burying the bow in the face of a crest as the boat surfs down a wave, or of falling laterally off a wave if descending it at a shallow angle. The concentration and effort needed to steer in these conditions can cause fatigue, especially if the crew lacks people capable of doing so safely.

Your speed downwind can be controlled by dragging long warps from the stern. The most effective means of controlling the boat in severe conditions is to tow a drogue (Figure 23-5).

FIGURE 23-5

Trailing a warp or drogue.

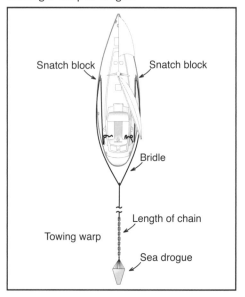

The technique for trailing a warp as shown in Figure 23-5 is particularly useful because it can provide some steering control. For that reason, this same technique can be used to assist in steering in the event of rudder failure or loss. The dragging of warps can be combined very effectively with a balanced sail plan to steer a boat without its rudder.

Attaching the warp to the boat with a bridle not only divides the load between two points on the boat for more security, it also makes it possible to maneuver the boat. To further increase drag, you can attach to the bridle a drogue, a length of chain, or additional warps.

The warp is attached to the mid point of the bridle line. The ends of the bridle lead through snatch blocks on either side of the boat near its point of maximum beam and then to the primary winches. To use the arrangement for steering, maneuver the trailing warp to cause drag in the direction you wish to turn. Do this by easing one side while taking in slack on the other. A length of chain is useful to keep the warp submerged, and to provide increased drag.

If while scudding you find that breaking waves begin to poop the boat from astern, the crew becomes overly fatigued, a lee shore looms, or speeds and handling are uncontrollable, it might be time to reduce sail and turn the boat to drive it forward into the wind and seas.

Forereaching, or Driving the Waves to Windward

This is my favorite tactic for coping with heavy weather (Figure 23-6). Actively guiding the vessel upwind allows it to face the elements at it was designed to do. Sailboats are constructed to efficiently head forward through the water, so the preferred method of coping with heavy weather conditions is to head the boat into them. The tactic of "driving the waves" keeps the bow facing both wind and sea, and is easier on the steering mechanism than scudding downwind.

This tactic involves heading the bow up, or higher into the wind, as the boat ascends a wave, and then bearing off to go down the back of the wave in a controlled manner. As the boat ascends to a wave crest, where wind velocities are highest, head up to feather the sails into the wind. Once over the crest, control the boat's speed as it traverses the back side of the wave into the trough, to prevent the bow from plowing into the next

FIGURE 23-6
Driving the waves to windward.

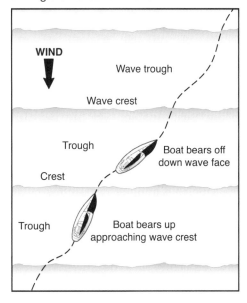

205

wave. Be careful not to bear off too much down the wave because the boat can fall off onto her beam. This up and down steering may sound complicated, but once you get a feel for the helm and the boat it becomes more automatic. After a short while, most people feel very comfortable steering the boat in this manner. That kind of confidence is valuable, because driving at night depends more on feel than it does on sight.

You can use this technique of actively steering the boat up and over the waves when under sail or when motoring. If you use the engine, keep at least a deeply-reefed main or the trysail up to stabilize the boat and improve your control of it. On most boats I've sailed, it's possible to balance the sail plan so that the boat actually steers itself on a close reach, which this is. Another advantage of this technique is that the storm conditions pass sooner than when running along with the storm, thus decreasing exposure of the boat and crew.

Like running off downwind, fore-reaching requires the active participation of the crew, who will also be exposed to the elements, unless the vessel has a pilothouse. As the storm wears on, fatigue can eventually set in. Before this becomes an issue, consider heaving-to.

Heaving-To

Heaving-to is another time-tested tactic that should be in every sailor's repertoire. It can be employed in storm conditions, in man-overboard situations, to provide a controlled motion in which to eat or relax, or simply as a way to stop

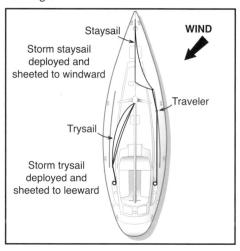

FIGURE 23-7
Heaving-to.

Staysail

WIND

Storm staysail deployed and sheeted to windward

Traveler

Trysail

Storm trysail deployed and sheeted to leeward

the boat to await daylight before making landfall.

The easy way to heave-to is to tack, preferably from port to starboard, while leaving the headsail sheeted in so it backwinds. Let the mainsail tack, and by adjusting the mainsail traveler and the helm, let the boat find a steady, balanced orientation at about 45 to 60 degrees to the wind and seas. The boat will hunt a bit, heading up and then bearing off, but it will maintain a safe and comfortable attitude while making leeway. The leeway is crucial in high wave conditions, because it dampens the oncoming waves before they impact the boat.

To get the boat to lie at the ideal angle, you have to balance the amount of mainsail you have set (or the trysail) with that of the headsail. In my experience, if anything, the foresail can be a bit less in area, and should be as flat as possible. Some boats actually heave-to best without a jib up at all. On any particular boat, you should determine the best combination by experiment.

Once the boat is stabilized, seas are dampened as the boat makes leeway, and the motion below becomes much more tolerable. The crew is able to get below, take in some food, and rest, while the boat takes care of itself.

In heavy weather and especially in extremely big seas, avoid exposing the boat beam-on to the waves. Most rollovers reported have occurred when the boat was caught broadside to an unusually large cresting sea which had enough momentum to pick the boat up and drive it to leeward, tipping it beyond its ability to resist capsize.

Heaving-To With a Sea Anchor

If the wind and seas continue to build, the hove-to boat may begin to head off too much at the bow, and risk becoming exposed beam-on. It may be possible to correct its attitude by moving the main (or trysail) up the traveler, steering higher, or reducing the area of the foresail. When heaving-to alone no longer works to maintain the boat at the optimum angle, the next option is to deploy a sea anchor to keep the bow into the wind and seas. Aboard VOYAGER, I have a Fiorentino ParaAnchor for just such an eventuality.

A sea anchor is in essence a parachute deployed on a long line that maintains a constant forward pull to keep the boat's bow into the storm. Such an anchor must be strongly constructed of high quality nylon and webbing with rein-

forced seams. It must also be properly sized for your vessel. Manufacturers publish tables in which they match vessels of different types and sizes with appropriate sea anchors.

While it's fairly obvious that you wouldn't want your sea anchor to be too small, it's a little less intuitive that it should not be oversized, either. In high wind and wave situations, too powerful an anchor could create excessive shock loading, which could lead to possible loss of the sea anchor.

The sea anchor is attached to its matching, appropriately sized nylon rode with a swivel that is shackled to an eye and thimble in the line. The diameter of the nylon rode should be the same as that of the boat's primary anchor rode. The usual recommendation for parachute anchor rode length is 10 feet of rode per foot of vessel. Rodes need to be of great length because they have to absorb considerable shock loads.

A disadvantage of sea anchors is that the boat can be driven backward by a wave, causing rudder damage. This situation occurs most frequently when boats ride to a sea anchor in wind and sea states below those of survival levels. The rode must be taut at all times. If too much rode is deployed, allowing it to sag with slack, then a larger wave can drive the boat back against the rudder. All of the rode should only be used in wind conditions strong enough to keep constant pull on the entire line. The best way to protect the rudder is to lock it amidships.

I recommend getting all of the sea anchor's associated hardware, illustrated below, along with the sea anchor directly from the manufacturer. This way you will have all the necessary parts, correctly sized for your boat, in one package. You can piece the hardware together, but at no great savings.

To rig the bridle (Figure 23-8), attach a snatch block forward at the stem. The parachute rode is made fast at the bow and led through this snatch block to avoid chafe. Attach a second snatch block aft, near the cockpit. A control line that will be tended at the primary winch is fed through that block and attached to the parachute line with another snatch block. The parachute rode attaches with a shackle to a swivel on the parachute.

With this arrangement, by adjusting the control line, you can control the angle of the parachute in relation with the boat, keeping the boat at a safe and somewhat more comfortable angle to the weather. Also, as the boat makes leeway, the slick created tends to flatten the waves as they approach to provide a dampening effect.

Figure 23-8, below, demonstrates a vessel in a hove-to attitude with parachute sea anchor deployed to maintain an optimum position.

When conditions deteriorate to the point that you have to adopt storm tactics, first heaving-to and then adding a sea anchor are the best alternatives in what may turn out to be a survival situation.

Sea Anchor Alone

Turning to a sea anchor at the onset of storm conditions is a viable tactic, and may be the primary choice of action for some sailors. The parachute anchor must be deployed before the conditions become severe; it is much more difficult afterwards. The advantages are that the sails are stowed and protected from damage, the crew is spared fatigue, and the boat is maintained in the correct attitude to withstand wind and waves.

When riding out a prolonged storm, there is a great risk of chafe to the sea anchor line at its attachment points and across the deck. Chafe prevention is

FIGURE 23-8

Courtesy of ParaAnchors by Fiorentino

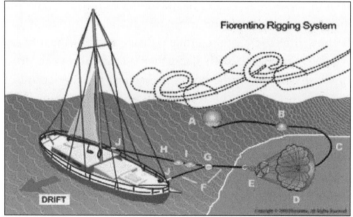

A. Retrieval float
B. Trip line support
C. Trip line
D. Parachute anchor
E. Pararing, to which the parachute lines attach, and is itself swiveled to the anchor rode
F. Anchor rode
G. Snatch block
H. Pendant line for bridle control
I. Support floats for pendant line
J. Chafe gear

therefore crucial to the success of this tactic, and you have to take the appropriate steps when you first deploy the sea anchor, so that during the storm you only have to be concerned with monitoring the chafe points.

Lying Ahull

I mention this technique last because of its limited application.

When you take down all the sails and allow the boat to fend for itself, it will generally lie nearly beam-on to the wind and waves. This is really only a useful tactic in calm seas for riding out a squall of short duration. I take all sails down and lie ahull only when a squall that I expect will contain strong winds approaches the boat, and then only when sea swells are very moderate in size. When larger waves are present, I reduce sails to accommodate strong gusts, and prepare to head into the wind. Usu-

ally I turn on the engine just before the squall hits.

Never expose the boat beam-on to large seas. Studies show that any boat will roll over when struck abeam by a wave whose height is 60 percent of the boat's overall length. Even in a less dangerous sea state, the uncomfortable, dangerous, and terrifying motion below makes lying ahull a bad proposition.

In true survival conditions, the best way to keep boat and crew safe is to actively steer, either heading off downwind or forereaching upwind as in Figure 23-6. Fatigue does become a factor, but skilled, well-conditioned crew driving the boat to advantage, avoiding dangerous waves and playing the wind gusts and waves, have the best chance of coming through safely.

If the course heading is downwind, reduce sails as indicated, and steer the waves while making speed toward the destination. The key is to avoid falling off the side of a wave onto the beam and to prevent the bow from slamming into an upcoming wave.

Steer up the wave crests, and then bear off a bit near the top to maintain control down the other side of the wave. Steer down enough to prevent the wave from catching the boat beam-on, but avoid heading down too steeply. When sailing this way downwind, the apparent wind is less, and thus easier to handle, although the wind and water are still very loud. The decrease in apparent wind can be very deceptive, so don't be lulled into a false sense of security that the conditions are moderating.

When the destination is upwind, I choose to keep the boat headed in that

FIGURE 23-9

Lying ahull.

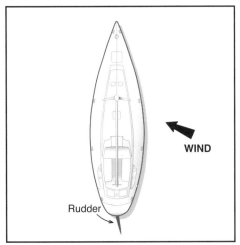

WIND

Rudder

general direction by driving upwind on a close reach. Reduce to storm sails early in the game, and take over steering from the autopilot or windvane so that you become accustomed to the conditions and the feel of the boat. Give everyone who steers a spell at the helm so they, too, can get used to the rhythm.

Again, drive up the waves, and then bear off on the back sides. This is a better tactic in severe conditions than any of the passive techniques, because with the latter, the boat is not maneuvered to cope with the waves and wind gusts but its orientation to them is set and is left to withstand the elements as they come.

In storm conditions, your mind set has to be that for as long as they persist, your purpose is to guide the boat through them. You concentrate while at the helm, and sleep when off. Determined people can carry on for days like this. I would only resort to other methods (heaving-to would come first) when the crew is too exhausted or seasick to continue.

Another consideration when coping with a storm is the noise it makes. It's one of the first changes you'll notice as the wind reaches 40 knots and above. The sound of the wind on the sails, spars, and rigging, and of the ocean itself prevents normal conversation in the cockpit. People only feet apart must shout to be heard.

This din seems to amplify the force and reality of the storm in peoples' minds, and heightens apprehension in the crew. I realized long ago that although a storm might be loud, that doesn't make it worse. I tell my crew that noise can't hurt them, but fear and indecision can.

Reduced Visibility and Fog

Sailing or motoring in reduced visibility and fog can present as great a danger as storm conditions. The seas are generally calm, sometimes with swells but not waves, since when fog prevails, winds are most often very light. An exception can be in warm waters like the Gulf Stream, where fog can develop when fast moving cool air encounters the warm water (advection fog). This is the moving fog bank seen to engulf areas like San Francisco Bay.

Fog tactics include obeying Rule 5 of the International Regulations for Prevention of Collisions at Sea (COLREGS). This rule states in part that "Every vessel shall at all times maintain a proper lookout by sight and hearing as well as by all available means appropriate in the prevailing circumstances and conditions so as to make a full appraisal of the situation and the risk of collision."

Rule 19 is specific for conditions of reduced visibility:

Rule 19
Conduct of Vessels in Restricted Visibility
(a) This rule applies to vessels not in sight of one another when navigating in or near an area of restricted visibility.
(b) Every vessel shall proceed at a safe speed adapted to the prevailing circumstances and conditions of restricted visibility. A power driven vessel shall have her engines ready for immediate maneuver.
(c) Every vessel shall have due regard to

the prevailing circumstances and conditions of restricted visibility when complying with the Rules of Section I of this Part.

(d) A vessel which detects by radar alone the presence of another vessel shall determine if a close-quarters situation is developing and/or risk of collision exists. If so, she shall take avoiding action in ample time, provided that when such action consists of an alteration in course, so far as possible the following shall be avoided:

    (i) An alteration of course to port for a vessel forward of the beam, other than for a vessel being overtaken;

    (ii) An alteration of course toward a vessel abeam or abaft the beam.

(e) Except where it has been determined that a risk of collision does not exist, every vessel which hears apparently forward of her beam the fog signal of another vessel, or which cannot avoid a close-quarters situation with another vessel forward of her beam, shall reduce her speed to be the minimum at which she can be kept on her course. She shall if necessary take all her way off and in any event navigate with extreme caution until danger of collision is over.

Rule 35 describes the sound signals vessels are required to use. Bear in mind that when a boat with sails up also uses the motor, it is considered a power driven vessel.

Rule 35
Sound Signals in Restricted Visibility
In or near an area of restricted visibility, whether by day or night the signals pre-scribed in this Rule shall be used as follows:

(a) A power driven vessel making way through the water shall sound at intervals of not more than 2 minutes one prolonged blast.

(b) A power driven vessel underway but stopped and making no way through the water shall sound at intervals of no more than 2 minutes two prolonged blasts in succession with an interval of about 2 seconds between them.

(c) A vessel not under command, a vessel restricted in her ability to maneuver, a vessel constrained by her draft, a sailing vessel, a vessel engaged in fishing and a vessel engaged in towing or pushing another vessel shall, instead of the signals prescribed in paragraph (a) or (b) of this Rule, sound at intervals of not more than 2 minutes three blasts in succession, namely one prolonged followed by two short blasts.

While sailing in fog or reduced visibility, especially while in a sea lane or other busy area, broadcast a Securite message on VHF Channel 16 to alert others of your position.

The procedure is to broadcast:

1. "Securite, Securite, Securite" (Pronounced see-cure-i-tay)
2. "This is the Sailing Vessel _____."
3. "Our position is _____."
4. "Our course is _____."
5. "We are sailing/motoring in reduced visibility."
6. "Any vessels in this area please respond on Channel 16."

PROTOCOLS TO FOLLOW IN EMERGENCIES

Every vessel venturing offshore should have protocols in place to cover a range of emergencies. When a covered emergency arises and the crew reacts according to the established protocol, confusion and indecision will be minimized. The best way to ensure your crew understands the reasons for these protocols and will be able to act on them effectively is to set them down in written form. So that everyone is clear about what's required of them, discuss the protocols with the crew prior to sailing.

Crew Overboard Procedure

- The first responder shouts, *"crew overboard"* as a call for all hands on deck.
- One person is designated as the "spotter" and points to the victim, never taking his eyes off him.
- The MOB Pole and/or Automatic Floating Strobe Light and/or any buoyant objects available are deployed as close to the victim as possible.
- Enter MOB on the GPS, note position of victim and retrieval heading on overboard alert system.
- The boat is placed on autopilot *standby* or the windvane disengaged, and one person takes control of the helm and directs sail maneuvers.
- The *Quick-Stop* method is initiated as the first preference. The second

option is the *Deep Beam Reach* maneuver. If sailing downwind, immediately heave-to, sort out the sails, make sure no lines are trailing overboard, turn on the engine and head back toward the victim.

- Deploy the Lifesling as the boat maneuvers toward the victim.
- Approach the victim to leeward, maneuvering the Lifesling close.
- Luff sails, check the transom for lines, start the engine, transmission in *neutral.*
- Retrieve victim by whatever means necessary.

There are three recognized sailing approaches for returning to the site of a person overboard. These are the Figure-Eight, the Deep Beam Reach, and the Quick-Stop maneuvers. The Figure Eight (Figure 23-10) has been the choice of instructors for quite some time because it's easy to teach and to comprehend, and no jibes are involved. I hesitate to recommend it wholeheartedly because it's relatively slow, and takes more time than other techniques to get back to the victim. The procedure is as follows:

Figure-Eight Maneuver

1. Shout "crew overboard", assign a spotter, throw flotation, lifering or MOB pole, and mark the position on the GPS.

2. Steer onto a beam reach for about five boat lengths.

3. Tack, and either furl, luff, or douse the jib.

4. Bear away to a broad reach.

FIGURE 23-10

The figure-eight maneuver.

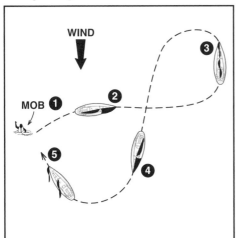

FIGURE 23-11

The deep beam reach maneuver

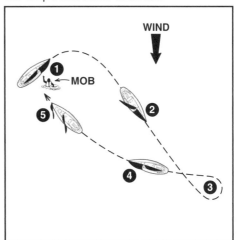

5. Begin to head up to windward as you approach the victim.

6. Luff sails near the victim and throw a line for retrieval.

The Deep Beam Reach Maneuver

The Deep Beam Reach technique (Figure 23-11) is similar to the figure eight, but returns the boat to the victim more quickly. Fewer maneuvers are involved, and the boat doesn't get as far away from the victim. Note the absence of a jibe. The technique can be initiated from any point of sail, although from a downwind course, the first heading would be a close reach.

1. Shout "crew overboard", assign a spotter, throw flotation, lifering or MOB pole, and mark the position on the GPS.

2. Steer down to a deep beam reach (broad reach), trimming sails accordingly for speed.

3. Tack after two boat lengths, and then luff, douse, or furl the jib.

4. Steer toward the victim.

5. Luff sails to reduce speed when approaching the victim.

6. Throw a line for retrieval.

The Quick-Stop Maneuver

From the victim's point of view, the most favored approach is certainly the Quick Stop (Figure 23-12), because it's the fastest and takes the boat the least distance away. This maneuver, however, probably requires the most ability and practice to perform correctly since it involves almost constant turning and sail handling throughout.

1. Shout "crew overboard", assign a spotter, throw flotation, lifering or MOB Pole, and mark the position on the GPS.

2. Immediately head up and tack, don't bother to tend the jib.

FIGURE 23-12

The quick-stop maneuver

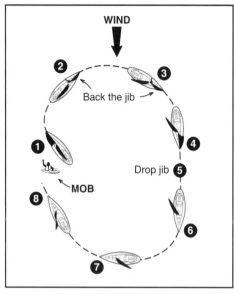

3. Sail down for two boat lengths while a hand forward either luffs, furls, or douses the jib.

4. Steer downwind until the victim is abaft the beam.

5. Jibe.

6. Head up and approach the victim on a close reach, luffing all sails.

7. Throw a line for retrieval.

Any of the above techniques can be employed when sailing downwind with genoa and mainsail up. However, when a spinnaker is flying, you have two choices. You can immediately heave-to, with the spinnaker blowing back into the rigging, or you can continue downwind until the chute is doused before maneuvering to retrieve the victim. I instruct offshore students to opt for immediately heaving-to, since it decreases the distance the boat sails away from a victim. If the maneuver is carried out promptly, the boat may yet be close enough for throwable flotation to be within the victim's reach. In any case, extra precautions are always warranted while sailing downwind, especially in big breezes with waves to match, and when you're going fast.

Once the spinnaker is sorted out (it doesn't have to be pretty), the boat has to be taken back to the victim in the fastest way possible. Inasmuch as the person may well be directly upwind, if I were in the water I'd like them to use the engine to return to me as quickly as possible.

As soon as you are sure no lines are trailing in the water, turn on the engine and begin maneuvering toward the victim. Approach the victim from leeward, and when the boat is near enough, place the shift lever into neutral.

There are other circumstances that require the engine be engaged, such as in very light airs or when heavy winds and big seas impair the boat's maneuverability.

Retrieving an overboard victim

Everyone on board should be familiar with the method of bringing a person back aboard that has been established for the boat and for which the boat is prepared. The most highly recommended retrieval system is the Lifesling, which combines a flotation collar with a harness. Once the boat has been maneuvered close, the victim dons the Lifesling, and can be hauled aboard from there. On VOYAGER, we keep handy a block and tackle that is useful in many situations. It is made up with, at one end, a fiddle block with a becket and a cam cleat, and at the other end, a fiddle block with a snap shackle.

When used in a victim retrieval operation, the fiddle block with becket is attached to the end of the main boom, the other fiddle block is lowered to the victim who attaches the snap shackle to the Lifesling. The tackle line can be hauled manually or taken to a winch to hoist the victim aboard. It is locked in place by the cam cleat. Guy lines are attached to the boom so its motion fore and aft can be controlled.

The Lifesling Retrieval Technique Under Power

The Lifesling can also be deployed while the boat is maneuvered with the engine, using the following technique:

1. Shout "crew overboard", assign a spotter, throw flotation, lifering or MOB pole, and mark the position on the GPS.
2. Clear all lines from the water, start the engine, and douse or furl the jib.
3. Toss the Lifesling overboard to leeward as the boat is tacked through the wind.
4. Circle the victim until he is able to grab the Lifesling line.
5. Head toward the victim and place the transmission in neutral to stop the propeller.
6. Victim puts on the Lifesling.
7. Pull the victim toward the boat, and assist in hauling aboard.

No consensus exists on whether it's preferable to approach the victim from

FIGURE 23-13

Maneuvering with the engine to deploy a Lifesling.

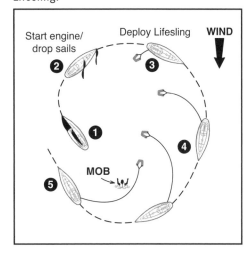

windward or from leeward. That decision depends on the sea state, wind direction and strength, lighting, the number of people on board, and the personal preference of the person at the helm. I have always preferred approaching from leeward. This keeps a luffing jib out of my line of sight and eliminates the concern of the boat blowing down onto the victim, which could happen when approaching from windward.

It has been pointed out, though, that retrieval of a victim is easier when the boat is to windward, when it cuts down the wave action affecting the victim. Of prime importance is maneuvering close enough to bring a person back on board, whatever side that may be.

If the victim is injured or unconscious, retrieval becomes much more difficult, and will necessitate someone going into the water to render assistance. After shedding bulky clothing that absorbs water and donning a life jacket and a tethering line, that person enters the water with the Lifesling in hand. He/she assists the victim by positioning him/her into the Lifesling, supporting the head at all times to maintain an airway.

The block and tackle will be necessary to hoist the person from the water. The rescue line is attached to the Lifesling, and the working end to a cockpit winch for retrieval. A French bowline knot or the bosun's chair can be employed in lieu of a Lifesling.

A discussion on near-drowning and immediate care of the non-breathing victim can be found in Appendix 8, *Medical Problems and Emergencies Offshore*.

Locating the victim is more difficult at night. Since people can fall overboard in the dark too, I urge sailors to practice these skills at night. Attach a personal strobe light to a fender, heave it overboard, and discover how different these maneuvers become with limited visibility. I found that my skill level during the daylight increased once nighttime maneuvering had been mastered.

If a MOB victim is lost from view, and has not been spotted by the time the boat has returned to the area where the victim was thought to have gone overboard, the best hope lies in conducting a systematic search.

In the example illustrated in Figure 23-14, the boat tacks and initiates a technique to return to the MOB position. Finding no victim, it begins a search pattern, moving in windward and leeward directions to minimize the boat's rolling motion. Each leg is measured at one quarter of a mile, at the end of which the

FIGURE 23-14

Rescue search pattern.

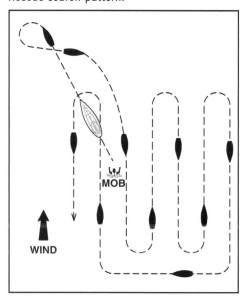

boat makes a gradual turn to return in the opposite direction. Once a reasonable area has been covered in that lateral direction, the boat returns toward the initial spot and begins the windward leeward legs toward the other direction. Not finding a victim after several passes, the boat would then begin legs with the wind on the beam to ensure the area had been covered completely.

Flooding Emergency Protocols

1. Person detecting the emergency shouts "Flooding at the bow," or whatever location.

2. Stop forward motion of the boat; heave-to or shut off the engine and drift, or anchor.

3. Assess the damage and degree of flooding.

4. Control flooding below with pil-

lows, sleeping bags, cushions, etc. shored against the damaged area.

5. Activate all bilge pumps as needed; use engine water intake hose if necessary.

6. Position collision mat from the deck.

7. Get underway if possible. If flooding cannot be controlled, ground the boat if feasible, and/or initiate Abandon Ship Protocols.

Deploying a Collision Mat

A key element of our strategy to relieve flooding is to position a collision mat of waterproof material over the damaged bow area from outside the boat. This mat can be previously fabricated of sail material in a triangular shape with all three sides measuring three feet long and with a grommet in each corner. Lines should be tied to each corner, and left there permanently, stowed with the mat and ready for emergency use. The mat is lowered over the stem to cover the damaged section of the bow, and then

FIGURE 23-15

Collision mat.

pulled up tight and secured with the lines.

Once the collision mat has been rigged, the boat can resume forward motion; in fact water pressure on the hull then actually helps to keep the shroud in place over the damage.

Fire Protocols

1. Person detecting the emergency shouts "Fire" to alert the crew.

2. The boat is maneuvered so the flames are blown to leeward.

3. Fire extinguishers are manned to fight the fire at once.

4. All hands should know the locations of fire extinguishers from our discussions and from the boat schematic.

5. If the fire is in the engine compartment, the engine is turned off immediately.

6. Propane is turned off at the tank.

7. Electricity is turned off at the battery isolation switch or battery posts.

8. If fire is uncontrollable, begin Abandon Ship protocols.

Abandon Ship Protocols:

1. Person detecting the emergency blows the horn or calls "Emergency on deck" as a call for all hands on deck.

2. The boat is immediately hove-to.

3. All hands put on lifejackets and foul-weather gear or survival suits.

4. Coordinate efforts to save the boat, depending on the emergency, for example, firefighting or stopping a serious leak.

5. Two people are designated in charge of deploying the liferaft, assuring that the

lanyard is tied, and that someone has a knife.

6. Raft is removed from the deck or cockpit locker and put into the water to leeward.

7. At the captain's orders, the raft is inflated by pulling the lanyard sharply.

8. One person enters the raft, ready to receive people, the abandon ship bag, food, water, etc. and to aid crew in boarding.

9. Captain decides when the ship is lost, and crewmembers enter the raft.

10. Mayday is called on Satellite Phone or SSB, and VHF. Activate EPIRB (only one initially).

11. All EPIRBS are placed into the liferaft, along with pre-designated gear in the abandon ship bag.

Once all personnel and gear are in the raft, cut the painter and shove away from the sinking vessel. It should be understood that this would happen only as a very last resort when the vessel is headed down, and only at the captain's orders.

Lightning

Lightning presents a situation in which we have virtually no control, except to prevent electrocution and damage should the boat be struck. Lightning protection should be installed during the boat preparations.

When squalls threaten, and lightning is seen in the skies to windward, keep tabs on its progression. Radar can show squalls graphically, and with it you can determine how far off they are and the direction in which they are moving. It can also give you an idea of their severity. You can calculate how far away a lightning strike is by counting the seconds between the lightning flash and its resulting thunder clap, when the sound reaches the vessel. Each six seconds of delay represents one mile. When this interval is becoming progressively shorter, you know the lightning is getting closer, along with the wind and rain.

The best procedure to follow when lightning is in the area is to get below decks and avoid touching anything metal. Disconnect all electrical appliances and equipment from the circuit breakers to isolate them from static charge.

When lightning is nearby, all hands should be off the deck. Lying ahull is a viable tactic for riding out the majority of squalls, since they so often occur in conditions of moderate waves.

CHAPTER 24

MONITORING AND MAINTENANCE AT SEA

Routine monitoring and maintenance of the vessel and its systems is a key aspect of good seamanship. A seemingly minor breakdown in one area can initiate a series of other problems, and only constant vigilance on the part of the crew will ensure that all systems and equipment remain in working order. All on board must be constantly on the alert against chafe on the sails or their sheets, signs of fatigue in components of the rigging, symptoms of trouble in the propulsion system, and depletion of water and fuel reserves.

Before beginning a passage, print out the monitoring and maintenance checklist (see the end of this chapter) and go over it with your crew during orientation. As you come to each item on the list, demonstrate the procedures and point out locations of each item described (this is especially important for the engine). Post the checklist where everyone on board can refer to it and incorporate its procedures in their daily chores.

Every time an inspection or maintenance task is performed, a notation should be made in the deck logbook. Anything found to be abnormal should be brought to the skipper's attention so

that he can initiate immediate corrective measures. No abnormality should be ignored.

A brief discussion of each item on the checklist follows.

State of Battery Charge

In order to best monitor the state of charge of the ship's batteries, it helps to have a basic understanding of the electrical system and how power requirements of electrical and electronic equipment are measured.

First, a few definitions:

- Electrical current is measured in *amps*
- The force, or potential difference that drives the current is measured in *volts*
- The amount of work done in the circuit is measured in *watts*
- These three constituents are related by the formula: watts = amps x volts

Some appliances are rated by the watts they consume while others are rated by the current (amps) they draw. The above formula helps us to relate these values.

Because battery capacity is measured in amp-hours, it's usually convenient to convert wattage ratings into the associated amperage.

Because most boats utilize a 12-volt electrical system, the example calculations use 12 volts. If your boat has a system other than 12 volt (24-volt systems are becoming more common on larger boats), the calculation method remains the same, just substitute the different voltage.

To calculate the current drawn by a 40-watt light bulb operating on 12 volts, for example, we would rearrange the formula:

$$watts = amps \text{ x } volts$$
$$becomes$$
$$amps = watts/volts$$
$$amps = 40/12$$
$$= 3.33 \text{ amps.}$$

The bulb would draw 3.3 amps. In one hour of operation, it would use 3.3 amp-hours.

To determine the amount of battery power needed on board every 24 hours, compile a list of the appliances used during that period of time with the amps they consume and the length of time they will operate. Calculate the amp-hours each one will need and add them up to arrive at your approximation.

Your next step is to compute the available battery capacity and how much charging they will need to maintain that capacity. For this purpose you only take into account house needs, not engine starting, which is handled by a dedicated engine battery.

For a typical day at sea, the computa-

tion may look like those in the figure below:

TABLE 24-1

Daily electrical consumption at sea.

	Amps	Hours/day	Amp-hours
Autopilot	4	18	72
Knot meter	0.1	24	2.4
VHF	1	1	1
Depth sounder	24	0.2	4.8
Radar	4	4	16
Running lights	3	8	24
Stereo	1	4	4
Freshwater pump	3	0.5	1.5
Total			125.7
(Radar is in energy-saving mode throughout the night.)			

In this example, the total power you require per day at sea is 125.7 amp-hours. Given the premise that you will sail as much as possible, using the engine only when motorsailing is necessary and to charge batteries, how often and for how long will you need to run the engine to provide the power needed?

Here, some further information about batteries is helpful. Deep-cycle batteries readily charge to about 80 percent of their capacity readily, but achieving 100-percent charge takes much longer. This is a function of battery construction. If you plan on running the engine as little as possible at sea, it becomes prudent to count on only 80 percent of your total battery capacity. On occasions when you have to motor for hours at a time because of a lack of wind, the batteries should be expected to receive a full charge, which is actually healthy for them every so often.

An important characteristic of batteries to take into account is that their working life is drastically reduced if they are deeply discharged on a regular basis. For that reason, you should limit their discharge to 50 percent of capacity. If you stick to such a regimen you will prolong their life a great deal, but you must factor it into your charging calculations.

If you can expect a maximum charge of 80 percent and a minimum of 50 percent, you have only 30 percent of your batteries' capacity with which to meet your electrical needs. This leaves little room for error, and you must bear in mind that to avoid continual deep discharging, you will have to make up for any electrical usage beyond your estimate with additional charging.

One deep-cycle 8-D battery has a capacity of about 200 Ah. Thirty percent of 200Ah is 60Ah, just about half of the calculated daily consumption. It's for this reason that 400 Ah is considered by many a minimum battery capacity for an offshore sailing yacht.

The alternator, mounted on the boat's engine, generates power for charging batteries, and you need to know how long it will take the alternator to recharge the batteries with the amphours you consume each day. This is most easily done if you have a battery monitor, a device that measures the current flowing out of or into the battery and displays the state of charge on a small screen.

Discharge the batteries to the point that the gauge indicates they are at 50 percent of their maximum charge. Run the engine at no less than 1,000 rpm and monitor the batteries to ascertain the time required for the alternator to pull them back to full charge.

Anyone outfitting for extended ocean passages or cruising should consider installing a high-output marine alternator (see Chapter 5: *Offshore Essentials: Gear and Instruments*). Charging times can be decreased by up to 50 to 60 percent by replacing the normal 40- or 50-amp standard alternator with a high-output alternator.

Engine

Monitor the engine and its ancillary components according to how much they're used. On a windy passage in which the engine is run only to charge batteries, check its fluids—engine oil, transmission oil, coolant for the enclosed cooling system—on a daily basis. At the same time, examine the belts visually and feel their tension manually. Examine all hoses for any signs of cracking or leaks, and peek at the raw-water intake strainer.

As a part of standard operating procedure, whenever the engine is started, observe the exhaust discharge. Watch for abnormalities in the flow of the exhaust water and note if there is smoke and what color it is. Listen for vibrations or abnormal noises when the engine engages the propeller shaft, and observe the transmission and drive shaft while it is engaged. Check for fuel or oil leaks, broken belts, leaking of the stuffing box, or anything else obvious.

When the engine is run for hours on end, the schedule has to change. The engine should be inspected at least every two hours while it is running to catch any problem early. You won't be able to check the oil or other fluids while the engine runs, but you can inspect all components visually. I recommend shutting the engine down every six hours to carefully check the seawater intake filter and the levels of the engine oil, coolant, and transmission fluid. Be careful to avoid touching the hot engine. Note each observation in the deck logbook.

Any time the engine begins to sputter, an alarm sounds, it lacks water in the exhaust, it begins to vibrate suddenly, or it makes abnormal noises, it should be shut down immediately, or as soon as the vessel circumstances permit. Once the boat is secured, examine the engine thoroughly and attempt to diagnose the problem.

Fuel Reserves

On any extended sailing venture, be it a cruising vacation on the Great Lakes or an offshore passage, fuel consumption plays a major role. Your onboard tankage is finite, and so that you're not caught out at the end of the voyage when the use of the engine might be critical, you should conserve fuel as much as possible. Maximize your sailing. Run the engine only as necessary to charge the batteries and to make miles when the wind doesn't cooperate. When planning a voyage, calculate your boat's fuel range both in miles and in terms of engine hours. See Chapter 4, *The Proper Ocean Sailing Vessel* for how to do this.

Your actual fuel range will be affected by the direction and strength of the winds you encounter, by the sea state, by currents, and by the boost provided by motor sailing. These factors combine to confound your pre-voyage calculations, making all the more important to monitor your fuel consumption while en route.

The easiest way to maintain an estimate of your fuel consumption is to record the hours that the engine operates. Note in the deck logbook the times at which the engine is started and shut down, the rpms at which it was run, and also record the number from the engine-hour meter. If you have tank gauges, monitor them. If not, dip the fuel tanks periodically to see how your estimate matches reality.

You should have a good idea before you leave how many hours a day you'll have to run the engine to charge the batteries. Keep this number in mind when figuring how long to motor in a calm spot, for example. And make sure to keep at least 10 hours of fuel in reserve for getting safely into port once you've made landfall.

Water Reserves

From the moment you leave the dock at the start of an ocean passage you have to manage on a finite supply of potable water. Before you depart, discuss water usage with your crew so that everyone understands the importance of conservation and agrees to abide by the ship's rules.

The governing factors in water usage

are your boat's water tank capacity and the expected duration of the passage. Using a guideline of one half to one gallon of water per person per day, it's a simple matter to calculate the expected water requirements for that period of time. When planning a voyage, be very conservative in your water estimates to allow for slow passages, water leaks, warm temperatures, or over-usage.

It's prudent to carry additional fresh water in jugs in case the tank water becomes fouled. This also provides a backup against running short due to a passage taking longer than expected.

Use one water tank at a time and dip it periodically to monitor how quickly it is being used. Be alert to the possibility of losing fresh water to dripping faucets or leaks from the tanks and plumbing into the bilge. Keep the pressure water system turned off except when water is being used.

Bilges

Close, routine scrutiny of all bilge spaces is part of the daily round. Table 24-2 calls for monitoring "at least six times daily." The bilges should be inspected every four hours, or at least once per watch. That period should be reduced to once an hour during heavy weather, at any time after a leak has been located, or whenever the engine is used for an extended length of time.

LPG Reserves

No cook or crew wants to run out of cooking fuel. The tanks should be filled and the system inspected carefully for leaks as part of routine vessel preparation before the beginning of the voyage. During the passage, use cooking fuel sparingly.

Remember, the gauge on the tank does not provide a measure of the available fuel, just the tank pressure. As a guide for fuel usage, a crew of four, using the stove three times per day, will use a 10-pound propane tank every two weeks.

Food Reserves

If the meal planning and provisioning were correctly done, there should be ample stores available for the number of crewmembers (see Chapter 18, *Meal Planning and Provisioning*). Usually, one person is in charge of this important duty, and that person should have the best idea of where items are stored, what's been consumed, and what remains.

It's a good idea to create a food log, using the meal planning calculations and provisioning lists as a basis. Break the log into columns for each day and each meal. If the meal planning sheet included specific meals for each day, simply crossing off each meal after it's been eaten will indicate what foodstuffs have been consumed.

Lights

Running, deck, steaming, anchor, compass, stern, and tricolor lights are the most important to the safe operation of the vessel. Every light should be tested at dusk each night and again before first light, so that any failed bulb discovered can be replaced in daylight. Lights below also contribute to safety and are important amenities. Replacement bulbs for each type of light are essential parts of the spares inventory.

Running Rigging

Chafe, wear, UV rays, and snagging are all banes of running rigging. Check all lines on a regular basis to catch abnormalities before they can lead to failure. Use binoculars to examine hoisted sails and rigging aloft.

Standing Rigging

Even when the boat is at rest, its standing rigging is under load. At sea, it's under continually changing loads, and components can fail with little outward indication of weakness. A thorough inspection of every component of the rig is essential before any passage. Most rigging failures are a consequence of cumulative damage caused by repetitive loading and unloading, vibration, shock loads, and corrosion.

Your monitoring procedure should include inspections of all shroud and

TABLE 24-2

Monitoring and maintenance checklist

Task	Schedule
State of battery charge	At least twice daily
Engine	At least twice daily, or as needed
Belts, hoses, fluids, oil, transmission fluid, coolant, stuffing box	As per circumstances
Raw water intake strainer	As per circumstances
Fuel reserves	At least daily, or as dictated
Water reserves	As per circumstances
Wet-cell battery fluid levels	At least weekly
Bilges	At least six times daily
Propane reserves	At least weekly
Food reserves	At least weekly
Lights	At least once daily
Running rigging	At least twice daily
Standing rigging	At least twice daily
Sails	At least twice daily

stay terminals at their chain plates, including each connection and piece of hardware. Look for any abnormality, such as bent clevis pins, kinked rigging wire, loose cotter pins, and cracks in hardware, fittings, or spars. Use binoculars to check the mast, spreaders, and rigging higher up.

If you discover a problem, consider the option of placing the boat on a tack that relieves stress on that component so that you can effect an immediate repair. Run a halyard to the toerail or other strong point on the affected side to provide additional support until repairs can be made. You should have on board tools with which to repair shrouds or stays, along with a method to fashion new terminals, and replace or repair defective hardware.

Sails

Sails are subject to chafe and wear in all wind conditions. Don't be lulled into assuming all is well simply because the wind is light or moderate and the boat is sailing well. At sea, and especially under sail, the boat, the rig, and the sails are in constant motion. Prolonged repetitive motion, no matter how slight it appears, can cause wear at specific locations which eventually leads to failure.

Monitor the sails at all their corners and in any areas that make contact with another part of the boat, such as the spreaders, shrouds, lifelines, and the bow pulpit. Also keep an eye on reef points and any areas that appear suspect.

If you find any damage in the sails you should make repairs as soon as possible to prevent further deterioration. This may require not using that sail for a time, or that you set another to replace it.

The goal of monitoring and maintenance is to find problems in their very earliest stages and deal with them before they become more serious. It's a normal, vital aspect of ocean voyaging, and should become an integral part of your and your crew's activities on every day you are at sea.

CHAPTER 25

SHIPKEEPING AT SEA

Shipkeeping is a term similar in meaning to housekeeping, and refers to activities aboard ship that promote neatness, proper storage, and cleanliness and by which we maintain our home afloat in safe, livable conditions. Being offshore in the confines of a boat can be challenging in itself, but it's much more so when the environment on deck and below is allowed to become messy and smelly.

One simple tenet to follow when sailing offshore is that seawater belongs in the ocean and we should take every precaution to ensure that that's where it stays. When it makes its way inside the boat, the salt attracts moisture and we quickly find ourselves living in musty, dank surroundings. Listed below are some of the precautions I use on VOYAGER to prevent seawater from gaining access below.

Keep the Living Quarters Dry

- Before departure, inspect the deck, hatches, and ports to detect and remedy leaks. Watching for drips during a gentle rain or when lightly spraying water on deck is ineffective. The best way to detect leaks is by spraying the deck and hatches with a strong stream of water from a hose that more closely reproduces the effect of ocean spray and can be more revealing.
- Keep forward hatches and ports closed at sea.
- Prevent wave intrusion through opened hatches and ports. These should only be opened when waves and spray from the hull are not a threat.
- Carefully monitor the open companionway. It should be closed if waves or spray are making their way aft.
- Rinse wet foul-weather gear with fresh water and hang it below to dry. When conditions permit, drying on deck is preferable. In heavy weather, designate one area below for the drying of gear. If available, a head on the windward side works well, especially if a shower is available for quick rinsing.
- Seawater-soaked clothing, shoes, and boots will stay damp until rinsed with freshwater and thoroughly dried.
- If conditions permit, rig a clothesline inboard from forestay to mast.

Clothing hung on the lifelines only dries if it doesn't get splashed with spray.

- Bring along a large supply of clothespins.

Laundry

Doing laundry on a sailboat at sea is a cumbersome exercise, it uses valuable freshwater, and often the results are mediocre. Fortunately, it's not usually necessary except on long ocean passages. Offshore sailing doesn't entail the sweaty, vigorous grinding activity seen on race boats, and clothes therefore do not need washing after a single wearing.

Dry, soiled clothes can be stored in plastic bags and taken ashore for laundering in the next port. Salty clothing has to be rinsed before it's stored because otherwise it will become mildewed and smelly. Clothing can also be rinsed in fresh rainwater any time the skies cooperate, without taxing the water stores.

When it does become necessary to do laundry, you'll need a bucket of fresh water for the scrubbing part. Use biodegradable liquid laundry soap. Use another bucket of fresh water for rinsing, and then hang the clothes out to dry.

When you take laundry to a Laundromat on shore, always add a splash of bleach to remove any mildew or mold spores and to control dank odors.

Personal Hygiene

Showering is likewise unnecessary every day. When taking a shower, bear in mind the need to conserve water, especially in the early stages of a passage. A freshwater rinse is essential after swimming or being doused by a wave, though, because saltwater will cause a nasty rash and sailors' sores if left on for even a few hours. It is for that reason I recommend you keep Lanacaine in the medical kit.

When showering below, spray yourself with fresh water and then shut off the shower. Soap up with liquid biodegradable soap and shampoo, and then rinse with fresh water quickly and efficiently. Boat showers are not the half-hour luxury-spa affairs many are used to!

Don't use large, fluffy towels for drying. A small towel with a short nap dries faster and is easier to clean on laundry day. Each person should have their own towel, and they're hung up to dry after use.

After people have showered, the head should be sprayed with Lysol, which is allowed a few minutes to kill germs, and then rinsed.

Galley

The galley is a busy locale on an offshore vessel. It's not only used for the preparation of regular meals, it's also the source of mid-watch and midnight warm beverages. It can become cluttered and soiled in no time, which makes it both difficult for the next watch to use and potentially hazardous.

Your own onboard routines for keeping the galley shipshape will be determined by such factors as the numbers in your crew, how your galley is laid out, your cooking and eating schedule, and how much freshwater you carry aboard.

Aboard VOYAGER, I have developed routines that work for us.

After every meal, the clean-up takes place immediately and no dishes or cookware, clean or dirty, are to be left in the sink. For washing dishes, we use seawater, for which there is a foot pump in the galley, and biodegradable liquid dishwashing soap. For rinsing, we place in the sink a plastic container approximately one-quarter filled with freshwater. We scrub the dishes with a pad or bristle brush, rinse off the suds with seawater, and place them in the bowl of freshwater. They're rinsed, dried, and stowed right away, and when we're done, we hang up the dishrags so they can dry too.

Heads

The mere idea of dismantling a head and its plumbing to remove a clog is stomach churning, never mind the reality of having to do so at sea. Fortunately, most head problems can be prevented by proper maintenance and thoughtful operation.

Before departure, test and thoroughly inspect the marine toilet. Look for worn valves and pump parts, weeping connections, and faulty pump parts. Replace any defective components prior to sailing and be sure to carry repair kits with all the necessary parts as well as hose clamps and spare hoses. In the toilet system, use only hose designated as "sanitary."

Make sure everyone on board knows how to operate the toilet and understands its limitations. Post instructions in the head compartment to remind people that no paper products other than toilet tissue can be expected to pass through the toilet hoses. Provide biodegradable toilet paper and instruct crewmembers not to try to flush too much at a time—a clogged toilet hose creates a nasty, smelly problem at sea, and when the discharge hose is taken off to be un-clogged, odors can linger.

To maintain the head in proper working order, lubricate the pump on a regular basis. Flush cooking oil or toilet lube through the toilet occasionally, and apply it to the pump's shaft to avoid excess wear and to prevent it from squeaking.

Avoid household cleaning products and especially those used to unclog the toilet. They can damage components and hoses and dissolve the lubricants.

Control odors by pouring white vinegar into the bowl, pumping it through, and allowing it to remain in the system for at least an hour.

Garbage Management

The disposal of waste at sea is regulated locally by countries that border the seas and globally by international treaty. It is illegal to dispose of plastic of any sort into any international body of water.

Once on the open ocean you can dispose of all biodegradable waste, such as food scraps, directly overboard.

On passages of 10 days or less, garbage does not usually present a problem as it's not too difficult to stash it in plastic bags for disposal at the next port. However, if garbage at your destination is simply taken out to sea and dumped—and it often is—then proper disposal from your vessel is an option.

Firstly, to decrease the amount of waste you'll have to deal with, all food wrappings, Styrofoam, cardboard cartons, and other surplus packaging should be removed and taken off the boat during the stowing phase of provisioning. Take measures to produce as little trash as possible, and then, if you plan to store it aboard, compact it before putting it in a storage bag. Crush aluminum beverage cans and remove the bottoms of tin cans so you can flatten them.

Personal Stuff

Singlehanded sailors offend nobody with their personal habits. On a compact vessel with a crew larger than one, however, one person's laxity is everybody else's problem.

Everyone can contribute to orderliness below by keeping their own berths and stowage areas neat and tidy. To prevent accidental slips and injury, all aisles and passageways through the boat should always be kept clear, and common areas, such as the galley and saloon, should be maintained free of clutter and personal effects.

General Comfort

A perennial source of odors below is the engine room. Diesel fumes in particular, when they permeate the confined quarters, produce a persistent, acrid smell that creates poor living conditions and contributes to seasickness.

You can minimize engine-room smells by starting out with a clean engine and by following the monitoring and maintenance routines to detect any oil, water, or fuel leaks before they become larger problems.

Salt deposits on deck accumulate on clothing and skin. In the absence of an occasional cleansing rain, it pays to quickly rinse the cockpit area with fresh water every couple of days as needed to make it more people friendly.

Nature's Pests

As you sail toward warmer climates, you need to become more vigilant about keeping your vessel free of pests, which can be in the air and in the sea or they can come from land. Airborne insects are in general not a problem at sea, but become bothersome as you near land. When fitting out, be sure to equip all openings with screens to deter flies and mosquitoes from getting aboard.

Barnacles and other forms of marine growth are the problem in the water, so be prepared to clean the boat's bottom from time to time.

Cockroaches are the biggest nuisance from the land, and can be most difficult to eradicate once they populate a boat. Preventive measures include not lying close alongside shore, along with careful inspection of all consumables brought aboard, especially fruits and vegetables. Avoid bringing aboard cartons or packing containers that have been stored in warehouses.

Numerous products are available to eradicate roaches, but none seem to work with one application. Success comes only when you are persistent about the job over a period of several weeks.

Rats will come aboard across dock lines or by hopping directly on deck if you spend much time tied up.

Maintaining livability in our home at sea is integral to the enjoyment of a voyage. Good shipkeeping habits help maintain high morale among the crew and make the boat safer. In essence, it pays to keep the boat, from stem to stern, ship shape.

CHAPTER 26

BOARDING BY THE COAST GUARD

It was a dark, moonless night as we motorsailed across the Florida Straits, bound for Fort Lauderdale from North Cat Cay. The starboard engine of TITAN, the Catana catamaran we were delivering from Tortola, had just shut down, and I was below in the engine compartment sorting out the problem.

I could feel the vibrations of the big diesels more than hear them, and figured a cruise ship or big fishing vessel was passing by. From deep in the engine compartment, where I was attempting to ream out the fuel line, I watched as an eerie red glow, reflecting off the open hatch, invaded the space below. The diesel vibration became more pronounced, and then the low, rumbling sound of the big engines became audible.

Peering aft out of the compartment in which I was wedged, I could make out the bridge structure of a vessel with a large davit arching over its deck bathed in that eerie, red hue. While I studied the apparition, trying to identify it, a spotlight suddenly shone directly at me, blinding me.

A voice boomed out from the mystery ship. "This is the United States Coast Guard. You in the engine compartment, climb up and stand on deck. We are sending a launch. Maintain your course and speed, and prepare to be boarded."

After the unusual entry and introductions, I was able to relax because I'd been boarded before. Most boardings aren't this dramatic, especially during daylight hours when the white cutters with diagonal, red bow stripes approach. Even then, though, being boarded can be unnerving, especially when you're unfamiliar with the procedure.

In waters near sensitive ports, like Miami and Fort Lauderdale, every vessel is tracked by radar. Whether you're actually boarded or not seems to be a matter of chance, or perhaps it depends on a set of criteria known only to the U.S. Coast Guard. I've certainly been across the Straits of Florida and not been boarded, but the odds seem to be in favor of it.

The USCG protects our shores from smugglers of all kinds of contraband, from illegal immigrants to drugs. In more recent times, terrorists and weapons of mass destruction have been added to that list. The service can hardly be blamed for fulfilling its task; in fact I appreciate very much what it's doing.

Hearing the authoritative tone of

the message, I scrambled up out of the starboard compartment to the deck, and watched as a hard-bottom rubber dinghy with big engines was launched and manned.

Boarding follows a standard procedure. Two personnel always stand ready at a gun mounted on the deck of the cutter, which maintains a constant position off your quarter. During the operation, observers using binoculars are in constant radio communication with the boarding party.

The launch, driven by a boatswain, carries at least five armed coastguardsmen to conduct the boarding. They approach from the starboard quarter, and come alongside on their own; they do not want assistance from anyone on your boat. One at a time, they come aboard and assemble in the cockpit; when all are aboard; the launch detaches and maintains surveillance from aft.

The officer in charge introduces the party members, and meets all your crew. He (they've been male on every occasion I've been boarded!) sets up an office in the saloon or cockpit, and briefly interviews everyone on board, captain first. While waiting to be interviewed, crew are expected to remain in the cockpit as much as circumstances permit.

The rest of the boarding party begins a systematic search of the vessel. They are very thorough but are careful not to be disruptive or to cause damage. On every occasion I've been boarded, everyone has been very courteous and professional. Their military conduct, though, doesn't always veil the fact that these are young people trying to do a job. One officer in

this particular incident was a kid from Minnesota, far from ocean swells, and he battled seasickness the whole time he was aboard. I offered him some non-drowsy Dramamine, but his commanding officer declined. "It's all part of being a Coastie," he said with a playful smile on his face, "and he's getting over it."

If there is contraband of any kind, I believe they know all the spots to look. Drawers, cabinets, bunks, settee compartments, the refrigerator, ice chest, sea bags, the abandon ship bag, the nav station; anywhere something could be hidden is looked into. They will examine water and fuel tanks with a boroscope, and even peer inside the mast.

In this instance aboard TITAN, a crewman straight away lowered himself into the engine compartment I had been working in, thinking, perhaps, it was a great spot for stowaways. All he found was a toolbox, some diesel fuel that had spilled, and a clogged fuel line. I asked if he wouldn't mind bleeding the engine, but he politely declined.

The officer in charge will want to see the Ship's Logbook, along with a list of all crewmembers and their passport numbers. The log seems especially important, since it documents your travels, dates, and ports of call, supporting what you've told him. Hand over the Float Plan too, that's something smugglers won't bother to produce, and it helps prove your case. Be prepared to produce the vessel's documentation papers, and all other ship's papers. You'll be asked about the nature of the voyage, whether it's for business or pleasure, and your previous ports of call. Be ready to produce customs documents for entry and departure at each port you've visited. You'll also have to produce all the safety equipment—life jackets, flares, horn, bell, fire extinguishers, etc.—required of vessels in U.S. waters. Be courteous and friendly, and you will be treated likewise.

After interviewing the skipper, which may only take a few minutes if your paperwork is in order, the officer will ask each member of the crew, passport in hand, a few questions.

The inspection will probably extend well past the crew interviews. On one occasion when VOYAGER was boarded, I chatted in the cockpit with the boarding officer for over an hour while the search was carried out. The searchers were just pulling the boroscope out to examine the water tanks when word of a vessel in danger of sinking interrupted proceedings.

When the search is completed, the boarding party informs the cutter that the boarding has concluded and summons the launch, which makes its way alongside. At this point, you may offer assistance by holding lines. The party will board the launch one at a time, and then the launch speeds off back to the cutter and you're free to resume your passage.

Unless you have something to hide, you should have no reason to be anxious when a launch brings a U.S. Coast Guard boarding party toward your vessel. In my experience, the documents they pay the most attention to are passports and the Ship's Logbook. If your log confirms the story you've related, you're pretty much in the clear, and the rest is just a formality.

Be polite, do whatever they ask, and enjoy the experience.

PART 5

UNDER WAY

CHAPTER 27

DEPARTURE AT LAST

For some people it has been a long process, but the day eventually comes when the long and exciting tasks of selecting, and outfitting the offshore sailing yacht are behind you. Your chosen shipmates are assembled, suitably equipped according to the advice you have given them, and fully aware of their responsibilities in the days ahead as you embark on your voyage together. You have familiarized all aboard with the boat, its systems and equipment, your protocols in various situations, and the rules by which you sail. You have routed your voyage properly, paying attention to timing and weather to best ensure the safety of ship and crew. Your final preparations have ensured that nothing has been overlooked; the boat is fully stocked with water, provisions, and fuel. Your communications systems are in place, your schedules for weather downloads and on-board (Single Station) weather observations in hand, and you have thought out your strategy for navigation. You have finalized the Float Plan and filed it with appropriate land-based contacts.

After sharing a light meal (a heavy meal is best avoided just before departure as it may not sit well), everyone has been given the opportunity to say their farewells, and make a final visit to the lavatory.

In short, you are ready to sail. For all aboard, the moments that follow will be filled with a mix of emotions, as the boat leaves her final slip or anchorage and makes way toward the ocean.

Everyone is excited at the certain prospect of adventure. Some may be feeling relief that the long months or years of preparation are finally over and their dreams are being realized at last. In others, anxiety and fear may be percolating beneath the outward show of eagerness and anticipation. These emotions are all normal and expected, and are probably present in each of us, to one degree or another.

As a captain in charge of the crew's well-being, when an offshore passage commences, I try to discern what each member of the crew is feeling. Understanding this can give me clues as to how each person will fare once we get several days or more into the passage. The reality of life at sea can erode the veneer of good spirits and camaraderie in some people, revealing aspects of their personalities that make them difficult to sail with. This is a fact of offshore sailing that every captain must be aware of, and he/she should be prepared to talk with any crewmember having difficulties adapting to life offshore.

Excitement and anxiety during the beginning hours of a passage raise adrenaline levels with the consequence that people often have difficulty sleeping on the first night at sea. This, the need for our bodies to become accustomed to the vessel's motion, and disturbed sleep cycles, can cause fatigue from which it is sometimes difficult to recover in the days that follow. As the boat sails away from land, in waters where the effect of the continental shelf accentuates wave action and rebound waves from the shores contribute to a mixed wave pattern, the boat's motion can be uncomfortable. As a result, it's not uncommon for sailors to experience queasiness quite soon after the passage begins. For this reason, it's advisable to take anti-seasickness medication several hours before setting sail, so that it's in the system and ready to counteract symptoms.

During this phase of the passage, which usually lasts about 48 hours, meals should be relatively small, and should not include spicy foods or anything that's likely to aggravate an already upset stomach. Hydration is very important, but carbonated beverages, caffeine, and certainly alcohol should be avoided at this time. Juice, water, or Gatorade are better choices to provide hydration while avoiding ingredients that promote dehydration or queasiness.

With the boat set on its proper heading, balance the sail plan to provide as smooth a ride as possible. While this is always good practice, as it makes sail trimming quicker and easier and lightens the helm, it's especially important at the outset of the passage while crew are adjusting to the boat's motion. If possible, crewmembers should stay on deck, to give their vestibular systems that control balance time to adapt to the motion. Staying busy and observing the horizon between bouts of activity are also helpful.

At some point in this settling-in period, each crewmember should take a trick at steering, to get a feel for the helm and how the boat responds. This is also advantageous because everyone gets attuned to the feel when the sails are properly trimmed. This gives them a basis of comparison for when the sails are inevitably out of trim. From that, they'll recognize the signs that indicate adjustments are needed and they'll learn how to make them to restore the proper balance. Naturally, the autopilot or windvane systems benefit from the sails being properly trimmed, it eases their workloads and they are able to maintain courses more accurately.

I have found that, for me, the business of conducting an offshore passage is actually easier than managing day-to-day life on land. My attention is focused on relatively few matters and the annoyances of everyday living take a back seat to the routines that are fundamental to safe voyaging. Navigation, weather, monitoring and maintenance, shipkeeping and logkeeping, and staying healthy are the concerns of offshore voyagers. Mind-ing them may be easier at some times than others, given the unpredictable nature of the offshore environment, but for the most part passagemaking consists of paying careful attention to those matters.

One of the most important things to do in these first hours is to step back emotionally, take stock in the situation, and realize what it is you're actually doing. Opportunities to sail on a vessel at sea may be commonplace for a lucky few, but for most people they are exceedingly rare. When the chance comes to actually fulfill such a journey, try to give yourself a moment to stop and smell the seawater, so to speak.

The sooner the crew settles in to begin the routine of sailing, the better. Everyone needs to get used to standing watches at specified times, including night watches that initially may be difficult for those not used to being awake during those hours.

Regular watches commence at the beginning of the voyage. You should discuss and settle on the schedule in advance of departure and post it in a conspicuous place for all to see. The crew should understand the rules of watchkeeping, and know how to perform all the tasks and duties entailed. In the following chapter, I cover guidelines for watchkeeping and suggest possible watch schedules.

By now you are well underway, and land is perhaps no more than a fleeting memory. The excitement and anticipation of departure, along with the activity of the first few hours at sea usually leave people hungry and thirsty. It's time for the cook, or whoever is on the galley roster that day, to make a light meal for all hands. This can consist of sandwiches, soup, and a beverage, enough to allay the hunger pangs and keep everyone comfortable and in good spirits. A good meal aboard meets the following tenets: It's nutritious, easy to prepare, convenient to eat, creates little waste, and requires little cleanup afterwards.

After this meal, the crew who are not then on watch should take the opportunity to go below to get some rest. Sound sleep might be elusive, but that doesn't matter. Getting away from the excitement and concerns of running the ship is restful in itself and will stave off fatigue. If sleep descends, all the better. The first couple of nights of taking shifts on watch are tiring for many people, and rest during the day is helpful.

All on board should maintain a cheerful outlook, show eagerness to pitch in to help when needed, and be courteous and forgiving of others. We can all tolerate a little discomfort and a little self censoring for a few days if it means keeping the boat free of disagreement and strife. When all aboard share a positive attitude, the whole crew benefits from the more pleasurable adventure that unfolds.

CHAPTER 28

WATCHKEEPING

Daily routines for monitoring, maintenance, and shipkeeping are an important ingredient in the successful accomplishment of offshore passages. Because these tasks, and the conduct of the vessel itself, go on 24 hours a day, an established watch system is essential to ensure each member of the crew is assigned a fair share of duties as well as sufficient time in which to eat, sleep, and rest.

Different boats place different demands on their crews and individual crewmembers bring a range of competencies and experience on board. As skipper, it's your obligation to assess the needs of the vessel and the abilities of the crew and draw up a watch schedule that meets both. An essential aspect is that no matter his/her skill level, each crewmember should feel an integral part of the team effort, and in return should be willing to contribute conscientiously to the operation of the vessel.

Once you have established the watchkeeping schedule for the voyage, you must ensure that all hands understand and agree to abide by the rules that make it work smoothly. This agreement at the outset reduces errors, confusion, and conflict among crewmembers. Each person entrusted with the care of the vessel while other crewmembers are resting should be fully versed in its operations and procedures and know when to call for help. At no time can the vessel be placed at risk because one person hesitates to ask for assistance. In many instances, the duty of the watch is to be alert to all that's going on both on board and around the vessel, notice if a problem arises, and then to get help in coping with it.

On Watch Duties

The two principal duties of the person or persons on watch are to sail the boat and to keep a lookout. If the boat is on self steering, they can perform other tasks, too, if and when there is a need.

Aboard VOYAGER, I have some set rules for the watch to follow so that the skipper or the following watch know what has been going on.

At least once per watch, record in the deck log:

- Course, speed, and weather parameters—wind, sea state, barometer, etc.

- Duties performed and observations taken.
- Special events, such as ship sightings, weather changes.

Do not start the engine unless absolutely necessary, and inform the off-watch crew if possible before doing so.

If a question arises concerning the operation of the vessel or of its position relative to another vessel, land, or other object at sea, do not guess about how best to deal with the problem but wake up the appropriate person immediately.

Standing orders on VOYAGER are to call the Captain or First Mate whenever:

- A vessel is sighted and is nearing our position.
- A low, dark cloud bank, a rain squall, or a waterspout is sighted to windward.
- Any unusual sound is heard.
- There is injury or a medical condition arises.
- Any other situation creates uncertainty or concern.

Watchkeeping Systems at Sea

The watchkeeping system you adopt for a particular passage depends on a number of factors. First of all, you have to assess the experience of each crewmember and their ability to handle watches offshore. Certainly everyone must contribute, but the system must fit the crew in a number of ways.

For example, some people can stand a two-hours-on, two-hours-off schedule for extended periods of time. These are usually experienced sailors who are able to handle any responsibility during their watch and yet are able to "turn it off" when it's time to rest below decks.

Others, unaccustomed to less than eight hours of unbroken sleep each night, simply wear down after a few days at sea. In these circumstances, adhering to an inflexible system can lead to fatigue and sometimes difficulties with the affected crew and those who have to cover for them.

Another important factor is the nature of the passage itself. Voyages that cross oceans are in some ways much easier than passages made near the coast or shipping lanes. In the absence of traffic and the need for constant, focused vigilance, being a dot on a big ocean simplifies the sailing. However, in the event of mechanical breakdowns or heavy weather, those passages become more challenging and test the will and stamina of some sailors.

I have sailed with people who were perfectly capable on watch as long as they stayed on deck. Whenever they went below, seasickness quickly took hold and made them practically useless. This has occurred on two occasions, despite the administration of various preventive medicines.

In those instances, I had to adapt the watch schedule, because those individuals could never be counted upon to serve as cook or navigator, or even to perform the belowdecks monitoring and maintenance routines.

Loss of self-steering capabilities can require drastic alterations to a watch schedule because people have different tolerances for steering by hand. Some can only stay focused at the helm for an hour or so, while others are able to drive for hours on end.

In rough weather conditions, or in the cold, I modify the system to limit the time spent on deck in one watch. In those circumstances, either a team of two people forms a watch, or another watch is on standby ready to lend assistance at a moment's notice. If we adopt a two-person-team watch system, I always pair a crewmember with more experience with one who has less.

Barring unusual events, two time periods are the most demanding on almost any passage. These are the first and last 24 hours. The beginning of every passage can be especially stressful. Whenever the vessel is near shallow water and other traffic is around, piloting and maintaining a safe position relative to other vessels demand everyone's full attention. Until you gain the deep ocean, away from continental shelves, rebound waves can create confused seas and uncomfortable conditions on board. At the voyage's early stages, too, high adrenaline levels, anxiety or fear, unaccustomed motion and noise and disruptions to the diet all combine to prevent sleep. The first couple of nights at sea can exact a heavy toll on some people. Being awake on night watch disturbs the circadian rhythms, causing a form of jet lag from which recovery can be difficult.

I have found it of great benefit to discuss these phenomena before departure, to make everyone aware of the important roles rest, food, and hydration play in combating them. It's incumbent on any skipper to stress the importance of taking rest during daylight hours to combat fatigue, and to urge crewmembers to consciously resist the onset of seasickness.

It is also incumbent on the skipper to make every member of the crew feel that they are an essential part of the group effort, and that their contributions are needed. It is beneficial, for example, to keep everyone involved in the procedures established for monitoring and maintaining the boat while underway. One tool I use to keep people engaged is the deck, or rough logbook, in which crewmembers are expected to legibly write their observations on a number of items during their watches. This information is subsequently transferred to the Ship's Logbook and becomes part of the official record of the voyage.

I first adopted one of my basic watch-keeping systems in the early 1990s, and I have amended it several times. It works very well with crews made up of competent sailors who have been presented with the pre-voyage orientation and seminar. This works wonders to get everyone on the same page, understanding their roles and responsibilities, and cognizant of the Ship's Rules. When they sense the excitement and anticipation that I feel for the voyage, they in turn become confident, willing, and able.

I call this schedule the 12:12 because 12 hours are covered by two-hour watches, and 12 are covered by watches of four hours (Table 28-1). I extend the 1800 to 0600 watches to four hours in order to allow for a maximum of nighttime rest for the crew. It also makes only one watch at night totally in the dark. Because it's

TABLE 28-1

The 12:12 watch schedule.

DAY	06-08	08-10	10-12	12-14	14-16	16-18	18-22	22-02	02-06
1	A	B	C	D	A	B	C	D	A
2	B	C	D	A	B	C	D	A	B
3	C	D	A	B	C	D	A	B	C

TABLE 28-2

Three-hour watch schedule.

Day	Cook	06-09	09-12	12-15	15-18	18-21	21-24	24-03	03-06
1	A	B	C	D	B	C	D	B	A
2	B	C	D	A	C	D	A	C	B
3	C	D	A	B	D	A	B	D	C

TTABLE 28-3

Double-up 12-12 watch schedule.

DAY	06-08	08-10	10-12	12-14	14-16	16-18	18-22	22-02	02-06
1	A	B	C	D	A	B	C	D	A
2	B	C	D	A	B	C	D	A	B
3	C	D	A	B	C	D	A	B	C

this watch that can sometimes arouse the most anxiety, I try to position the most apprehensive individuals as A. In that slot, they won't stand the 22-02 watch until the third day out, by which time we hope they have become more confident and less anxious.

Table 28-2 shows a more traditional system, with all watches 3 hours in length and a cook designated on a rotating basis. The cook also pulls the final night watch, 0300 to 0600.

This watch system works well if all hands are able to serve as cooks, and if all hands can eat that cooking!

The system shown in Table 28-3 is an adaptation of the 12-12 system. It employs two teams of two people, usually set up to pair a strong person with one of less experience. This is the schedule we adopt on VOYAGER in gale-force winds. Conditions dictate the arrangement, but usually one person is on deck while the other stays below but ready as needed.

Note that there is no cook, as full, prepared meals don't happen under severe conditions. Everyone is encouraged to maintain their seasickness medications, drink Gatorade often in small amounts, and to maintain energy by nibbling on Granola bars, energy bars, candy bars, crackers, and the like.

In storm conditions, unless the boat is hove-to or lying to the sea anchor, two hands must be together in the cockpit, harnessed-in, with Type-I life jackets on, and wearing an Alert 2 MOB alarm at all times.

I have one last system in my inventory of watches and it's the one I use on ocean passages when I have a qualified First Mate and advanced sailors on board. In effect, it's the 12-12, but with the captain available at all times, and during one of the night watches to discuss the watch, responsibilities, and to point out the wondrous world of the ocean at night.

Handling Broken Watches

I have experienced several occasions when people have become disabled by seasickness. In one instance, after the boat fell off a large wave onto her beam-ends, a crewmember lost all willingness to drive on his watches. (We had lost autopilot steering early during the onset of a three-day gale.)

If watch system #3 is in effect, the skipper simply steps in to cover the disabled person, while taking all steps necessary to restore his or her ability to return to duty.

In the event that one of the systems using individual watchkeepers is being employed, all watches would be extended to four hours, and a four-on, eight-off regimen put in place for as long as needed. If heavy weather is involved, we would switch to a 2-hour on, 4-hour off regimen, with the next in line acting in a stand-by capacity.

On VOYAGER, if fatigue became an overriding factor, or if conditions worsened to the degree that sailing was no longer prudent, the boat would be hove-to.

The Etiquette of Watchkeeping

There is more to watchkeeping than paying attention to the world around the boat and the onboard systems that keep it functioning. We all have to keep in mind that while we're on duty, the rest of the crew is trying to rest.

An important duty of the watch on deck is to treat the watch below with courtesy. The reverse is also true, and this begins with being punctual from the get go. Many people are shy about rousting others from sleep when it's time for their watch, let alone having to make several attempts to prize someone out of a warm bunk. The best system is one in which people set their own alarms 15 minutes ahead of their scheduled time on deck. This gives them time to gear up, take a small snack or get a warm drink, and get on deck to be briefed on the ship's status and get their bearings before taking control. One sure way to get on crewmates' bad sides is to be difficult to awaken and late for watch.

After dark, the boat should be lit only dimly belowdecks so the off watch can rest and to preserve the night vision of the watch on deck. Certainly if a problem arises or there is a need for more light, it is appropriate, but normally the boat should be kept under low lights.

All efforts should be made to keep noise to a minimum. Doors and hatches below should be secured against slamming, toilet seats should always be down, and sinks should be empty. Goods stored in drawers or cupboards should be stowed so they don't roll around. Crew moving about below should do so as quietly as possible.

On deck, two primary noisemakers are winches being ground, which usually can't be helped, and the metal ends of tethers being dragged along the deck. It is understood that the engine should not be started during the nighttime hours unless absolutely necessary. Batteries should be charged during daylight hours, and only a failing wind or other strategic need, such as to avoid collision or to power off a lee shore, would necessitate the engine being started. Keep in mind that everyone below trying to rest will certainly be awakened by the engine turning over. If the boat is motorsailing before nightfall the engine is already running, and should continue to run as long as it's needed. That's a very different situation than starting it during the nighttime hours.

Night Watch Rules

I have developed a set of rules for night watches on VOYAGER. When everybody lives by them, which is not a hardship, the nights pass quietly and pleasantly for the whole crew.

Night Watch Rules

- Be courteous toward those off watch—no loud talking or music.
- Don't drag tether rings on deck but carry them above deck.
- Keep flashlights in their designated locations.
- Keep the binoculars in their designated location.
- Keep the spotlight in its designated location.
- Set the toilet seat down at all times to prevent it from slamming.
- Maintain night lighting below decks.
- Observe 360 degrees around the boat at least every 15 minutes.
- Understand the basics of COLREGS lights and what they indicate about another vessel's course.
- Know where Granola bars, crackers, other snacks, and chewing gum are located.
- Be able to heat water on the stove for warm drinks.

Truly compassionate sailors also look out for the well being of the next watch up by preparing a fresh pot of coffee or hot cocoa. This ensures they begin their watch with a warm feeling, both physically and emotionally. Passagemaking pursued in this spirit makes voyages even better.

CHAPTER 29

LOGKEEPING

Skippering a sailing yacht on an ocean passage is a challenging exercise in management. Between navigating, keeping an eye on the weather, ensuring food and water supplies last, and that the vessel is properly operated and maintained, the skipper has a lot on his plate. One way he can keep track of how the voyage is going is by maintaining a detailed record of what happens on board and what goes on around the boat. This record is the Ship's Logbook. More than a journal, this document can serve as a lesson book for future voyages, and

TABLE 29-1

Example page from the Weather Logbook.

Date Time	Temp Dir	(Wind Data) Kts	Change	Gen Vis	Wx	Barometer Pres	Change	(Wind Waves) Dir	Ht	Period	(Sea Swell) Dir	Ht	Period	(Clouds) Type	Dir	(Clouds) Type	Dir

above all, it can stand in a court of law as an official record of a vessel's voyages.

While the Ship's Logbook is the official record, the information it bears may derive from a number of separate logbooks kept on board. In the following pages, I describe those we use aboard VOYAGER.

The Weather Logbook

The Weather Logbook is used to record local weather conditions observed from our boat. On VOYAGER, we track those conditions on logs such as the one on Table 29-1.

Entries in the One Station Weather Logbook are made at a minimum of once each watch period. Whenever conditions deteriorate, calling for closer monitoring, observations are recorded at more frequent intervals. Each person making entries into the weather log should be certain that those entries are correct. Crew not versed in cloud types, for example, should not guess at what they see or simply copy the notes of the previous entry but should get verification from a knowledgeable crewmate.

The Galley Logbook

Maintained by the person in charge of food stores, the Galley Logbook is a record of what foods have been consumed and what remains available. This log is more necessary on longer passages with larger crews involving more consumables. Freshwater consumption and reserves are also monitored in this log.

The Engine Logbook

An Engine Logbook is kept specifically to tabulate engine hours, oil, oil filter, fuel filter, air filter, impeller, hose and belt changes, and other maintenance or repairs undertaken. Data in this log is especially useful in calculating fuel used per engine hour—vital in estimating fuel range. It's more convenient to have a separate engine log than to make the entries into the general Ship's Logbook as it makes the information much more readily accessible when needed.

The Medical Logbook

The Medical Logbook is used to maintain a record of supplies and medications in the medical kit. It also contains medical information on crewmembers, such as allergies, pre-existing conditions, medications needed and brought aboard, and contact numbers in case of medical necessity. If a member of the crew sustains an injury or becomes ill, that is recorded in the Medical Log along with treatment and medications administered.

The Deck Logbook

Entries in the Deck Logbook, sometimes called the Rough Log, are made by the crew during their watches. The Deck Logbook can be set up to monitor any number of parameters, but they usually include wind direction and speed, cloud cover, heading, course changes, speed, hours of engine use, sails deployed, and the trip log. Findings of ship-monitoring routines are also written in this log as are any exceptional events.

Positions in Latitude and Longitude should be entered with a notation to indicate if they were taken from the GPS or from celestial fixes by the navigator.

Course and speed are entered hourly, and their times noted, as well as all course changes, with old course, new course, and time of change very plainly noted. These DR parameters are there as recourse in the event of the loss of electronic navigation.

Several different people will make notations in the Deck Log, and all entries should be legible and easily understood. The captain or navigator will transfer these notations into the Ship's Logbook.

The navigator may use the Rough Log but may prefer a separate navigation notebook. He or she will record celestial observations and fixes, contacts with other ships that yield positions, bearings on charted objects that provide a fix, and all DR information pertinent to celestial navigation.

While sailing in waters affected by tides or currents, a column should be available in the Deck Logbook for recording the set and drift of the tidal stream or current. This information comes from the Tide and Tidal Currents books.

The Ship's Logbook

The Ship's Logbook is an important legal document. It is a compilation of all information used to run the ship and the vessel's official record of each passage. It is usually maintained by the skipper and it includes all deck log entries with other important parameters. It should cover weather, communications, navigation, monitoring and maintenance, illness of or injury to crew personnel, and all notable events.

The Ship's Logbook record for the voyage should begin before departure, with a list of the members of the crew along with their passport numbers and personal information including contact numbers. The time and date of departure is entered when the vessel leaves harbor, which marks the beginning of logkeeping for that passage.

A Ship's Logbook should have hard covers and be horizontally lined. To fit all the appropriate information, the book should be at least 8 by 13 inches. Columns should include all those in the Deck Logbook, along with room for navigation and weather information. You can obtain a plain ledger book from a business store on which you construct your own columns and headings, or you may prefer one of the proprietary logbooks that are available at marine outlets. These come with many pre-labeled columns and can be adapted to suit your preferences.

It may take some trial and error to establish your own ideal set of column headings, but the Ship's Logbook should include at least those listed below.

Ship's Logbook Column Headings

- Ports of departure and destination
- Date

- Time of entry
- Position fixes
- Course—note whether from GPS, ship's compass, or autopilot compass.
- Speed
- Trip log
- Current
- Wind direction and speed
- Barometer
- General weather conditions
- Cloud cover
- Temperature
- Engine hours
- Fuel reserves
- Maintenance
- Fuel taken on
- Water taken on
- Engine/Sail combinations
- Remarks and observations

Boarding Pass

Many years ago, the United States Coast Guard made the importance of the Ship's Logbook crystal clear to me during my first boarding experience. The lieutenant in charge was very interested in examining the log, which recorded the chronology of our voyage from the Great Lakes to New York Harbor, Bermuda, Green Turtle Cay, North Cat Cay, and into the Straits of Florida where the boarding occurred.

He scanned each page of the logbook, and based on that was assured that our intentions excluded smuggling of aliens or drugs into Miami. The search of our vessel continued, but he knew we were clean, and we enjoyed a relaxed chat in the cockpit while his crew checked the boat.

CHAPTER 30

MAKING LANDFALL

One of life's special pleasures is making landfall on a distant shore at the conclusion of a successful offshore passage.

The most important factor contributing to a successful landfall is your navigation. Knowing your position with accuracy makes entry into a harbor easier and safer by reducing the stress brought on by indecision and anxiety. The worst thing you can do is approach unfamiliar waters without knowing exactly where you're going or what conditions to expect. Whenever approaching a port from sea, especially for the first time, you should be fully prepared with large scale harbor charts, tide and current information, the Light List, and information on local waters from the Coast Pilot or cruising guides. While still several miles out, try to raise the local harbormaster or customs officials by VHF radio to announce your presence, establish rapport, and begin a dialogue. Sometimes, authorities at your destination will contact you first, having tracked your approach on radar. Bermuda is a prime example. Bermuda Harbor Radio usually makes this first contact, and its operators are extremely helpful in supplying directions and guidance as you draw close.

On your way to your harbor approach, plot your position frequently. If you're within 30 miles or so of an island destination during the night, you may confirm your navigation by observing the island's "industrial over-glow" created by lights reflecting off clouds above it.

Consider the port's configuration with regard to tides and currents. Many harbors should not be entered during an ebb tide, which makes the waters confused and difficult to navigate. For example, the *Coast Pilot for the U.S. Atlantic Coast: Cape Fear to Key West*, states the following about the Beaufort Inlet, N.C.:

> Tidal currents along the Beaufort Inlet Channel attain velocities of up to about 2 knots. They usually set along the channels, but, at the entrance to Morehead City Channel, they usually set across the channel near the end of the flood period and beginning of the next ebb. Heavy swells build up in Beaufort Inlet Channel with northerly or southerly winds, making boating hazardous and entry or departure of

ships difficult during unfavorable tidal conditions. Thus approach to Beaufort Inlet Channel should be during flood or slack tidal periods.

Familiarize yourself with the aids to navigation. Major ports often have a large structure several miles out from the harbor, an example being the Ambrose Light in the approaches to the New York Harbor.

Study your harbor charts, paying close attention to the buoys, channel depths, prominent features on land, and the numbering of successive buoys. Identify and respect the sea lanes used to marshal ship traffic into busy harbors. Know how the approach is made, and be aware that within the lanes those ships have the right of way.

Don't attempt to enter an unfamiliar harbor in darkness. While still at sea, adjust your speed so as to make landfall during daylight hours. If you do near the port at night, the safe approach is to stay out until morning by heaving-to, drifting, or motoring in safe waters. Use appropriate lights to identify your position and status to others, and continue normal watches just as at sea.

Standing off may not be necessary if you are entering a well-marked harbor with adequate, easily identified landmarks and with which you are familiar. Fort Lauderdale, for example, has excellent buoyage, numerous large buildings on shore for reference points, and a well-lit channel.

When you are within 25 miles of your destination, be prepared with your VHF tuned to Channel 16 in case an agency from that port contacts you by radio. Be courteous and willing to establish a working relationship, and comply with any instructions they may give.

Before entering any harbor, estuary, or river where you might have restricted maneuvering room, bring the primary anchor up to its ready position. As you make your final approach, you'll want to ready the dock lines and fenders. Have the Q-flag attached to its halyard for hoisting to the starboard spreader as you approach. This is a benchmark moment in your passage, signifying the safe conclusion of your time at sea, and the beginning of a new adventure in a new destination.

Your national ensign should also be in position at the stern.

Preparing for Clearance Formalities

Once you arrive in port, contact the customs office and make arrangements. Be aware that you have made official contact with their soil when your anchor hits the bottom in their harbor.

Before setting off on your voyage you will have used the Internet and other resources to obtain information about how to complete entry formalities for the countries you plan to visit. For example, the Website www.islandhopping.com gives all pertinent information on customs procedures for the Bahamas and most of the Caribbean islands. You'll want to know where to go on arrival, what you are expected to do, and how much money to take with you to cover the entry, exit, and other fees.

On arrival, make the boat neat and shipshape so that customs officials get the right impression when they arrive on board. Crew should all shower and put on clean clothing appropriate for meeting local officials. It's not a formal affair, but conservative, modest apparel conveys the right message.

Customs personnel may be able to visit your boat right away, there may be a wait, or you might be asked to go to the customs office instead. The procedure varies, as each country has its own way of handling these matters. As a rule, only the captain of the vessel is permitted off the boat until all formalities have been satisfied, but to be certain, ask the officials how to proceed.

Make sure to abide by local protocols to start your visit off on the right foot. You want to avoid any problems, because as guests in the country you are subject to its laws and should also respect local customs and social conventions.

Have all of your ship's documents on hand for inspection by officials. Be sure to have a crew list of everyone on board with their passport numbers. I always produce the Float Plan, also.

Make a list of any stores that might be subject to duty, especially unopened bottles of alcoholic beverages. Duties are usually waived for ship's equipment and small quantities of liquor and tobacco that are obviously for consumption on board. However, label containers of spare parts, identifying them as *Spares, Yacht in Transit*. Otherwise, they may be subject to duty.

Declare all medicinal drugs, and produce a prescription for each stating the medication's name, number of tablets, and for whom they're intended. In lieu of a prescription, you should have that information in a note from the prescribing physician.

Produce all weapons for inspection. Authorities in some countries will confiscate guns, some will hold them for the duration of your stay, others allow them to remain aboard as long as they're declared. Any weapon that is discovered and not declared is subject to seizure, so be sure that doesn't happen. That's also a quick road to their doghouse, where you don't want to be.

Port fees are usually collected at this time, varying in their description and amount per person on board. Some nations may require you to purchase a cruising permit if you will be staying in their waters. Also, be prepared to pay harbor dues, ship's dues, charges for forms, entry taxes, and even departure tax.

When you have cleared customs and fulfilled any other clearing-in obligations, bring the Q-flag down. If you are in a foreign country, hoist its colors as a courtesy flag in its place and continue to fly it until you leave that country's waters.

At the conclusion of the clearing-in procedure, you'll be advised of berthing areas, moorings, or anchorages where to take your vessel.

Once you have securely moored or anchored your boat, you'll be free to explore your new harbor.

FINAL THOUGHTS

Begin your voyage project by making the boat and its gear truly reflect your sailing style and plans. Outfitting should assure that gear and instrumentation essentials are installed. Avoid excesses that only add time, expense and effort to the project.

A very thorough, systematic approach to the voyage project assures a seaworthy boat and crew, while avoiding the pitfalls of harbor paralysis. When the final goal of realizing your dreams are kept in mind, voyage preparation is the means to an end, not the end of your dreams.

CHECKLIST FOR PERSONAL GEAR AND CLOTHING

PERSONAL GEAR

- Flashlight, crew light, or head lamp, eg. Pelican Mitylite, West Marine.
- Anti-seasickness medication of your choice
- Sunscreen
- Aspirin, ibuprofen, acetaminophen, etc.
- Lanacaine
- Personal grooming supplies
- Spare eyeglasses/sunglasses/repair kit/safety strap
- Camera and film
- Sleeping bag, lightweight with stowage bag
- Clothing appropriate for restaurant dining
- Personal medications
- One bed sheet
- Two small MSR Packtowl towels (REI)
- Passport and driver's license
- Favorite CDs
- List of allergies or medical conditions
- List of contact persons and numbers
- A PIN number for your Visa or Mastercard

COOL WEATHER

Foul-weather gear

- West Marine's Lightweight Breathable, or Third Reef. Jackets must have a hood.
- Other clothing
- Cotton T-shirts
- Helly Hansen undergarments
- A Patagonia long-sleeve top
- Patagonia fleece pullover jacket
- Patagonia long pants. Jeans are difficult to dry.
- Fleece pants
- Polartec Orca Hat
- Ski gloves
- Underwear
- Footwear
- 1 pair of new, white-soled boat or sneaker shoe for boat use only
- 1 pair of non-leather, comfortable shoes for shore excursions
- Thongs or sandals
- Waterproof, breathable socks, like Sealskinz MTV from REI
- Rubber deck boots

WARM WEATHER

Foul-Weather Gear

- Light weight, breathable foulies, like Trailwizard from Hally Hansen or Equatorial Lightweight gear from West Marine. Jacket must have a hood.
- Other Clothing
- Nylon lightweight running shorts
- Patagonia Baggies shorts
- Patagonia Gi II Pants
- 2 cotton T-shirts, and Versa Duel sleeveless running shirts from Hally Hansen

- 1 lightweight, short-sleeve, collared dress shirt
- Light-colored, lightweight, long-sleeve shirt for sun protection
- Sun cap
- Underwear, recommend sports bras for women
- Swimsuit, or running shorts for men

Gear should be packed in soft canvas bags, as suitcases are difficult to store aboard.

West Marine: 800-538-0775
Patagonia: 800-638-6464
Hally Hansen: 800-943-5594
REI: 800-426-4840

APPENDIX 2

PREPARATIONS FOR OFFSHORE SAILING AND CRUISING

TOOL KIT

Recommendations for a seagoing tool-box might look like the following:

- Complete supply of fasteners including screws, nuts, and washers.
- Duct tape, of course
- Assortment of screwdrivers, both flat head and Phillips head, including tiny screwdrivers for repair of eyeglasses.
- Pliers
- Needle nose pliers
- Wire cutters
- Wire strippers
- Soldering kit
- Grommet making kit
- Rivet gun
- Sturdy set of Vise grips
- Crescent wrenches
- Adjustable wrenches
- Monkey wrenches
- Allen wrench kit
- Grips to remove oil filters
- Hand brace and bits
- Hand drill and bits, rechargeable drill with inverter on board

- Socket set including metric sockets
- Hacksaw with spare blades
- Box cutters with spare blades
- Ruler
- Small wood saw with spare blades
- Clamps and/or a vise
- Sandpaper
- Tin snips
- Hammer
- Chisels
- Clamp-tite tool

SPARES FOR THE OFFSHORE YACHT

Spares for the fiberglass hull:

- Resin
- Resin catalyst
- Fiberglass cloth
- Roving
- Tape
- Winch repair kits

A rigging spare parts list should include the following:

- Sail slides
- Hanks if appropriate

- Grommet kit
- Turnbuckles
- Toggles
- Cotter pins
- Clevis pins
- Shackles
- Chain or straps to lengthen standing rigging
- Cable clamps, Nicropress unit, Sta-Lock or other system for fabricating terminal eyes.
- One strand of rigging wire equal in length to the longest stay on board.
- Wire cutters heavy enough to cut all rigging on board.

A spare parts list for the steering system:

- Rudderhead fitting
- Replacement parts kit for electronic autopilot
- Replacement parts kit for wind vane
- Pre prepared plan for rudder replacement, with portions of the rig fabricated and ready for use.

A list of recommended spares for the engine and transmission:

- Replacements for all belts
- Replacements for all hoses
- Hose clamps
- Engine oil, at least two gallons
- Transmission fluid
- Water pump
- Water pump impellers
- Starter solenoid
- Starter motor, except if a crank mechanism is available.
- Alternator

- Fuel pump
- Fuel filters, primary and secondary
- Antifreeze if in colder climates
- Injector lines

A list of recommended spares for the electrical system:

- Spare batteries for all sizes in use on board
- Bulbs to replace all sizes in use on board.
- Fuses
- Electrical tape
- Copper wire of various sizes to repair anything on board
- Wire strippers
- Ring and captive-fork wire terminals
- Crimper tool
- Soldering kit.
- Rip-Free or other stuffing box repair material
- Penetrating oil
- Gasket paper
- Engine gasket kit
- Gearbox oil seal
- Gasket compound
- Gas engine spare parts: points, condenser, rotor, impeller and pin, diaphragm, ignition spray, spark plugs, coil.
- Electrician's fish tape

A list of suggested spares for the tankage, piping, and heads:

- Head repair kit including all necessary replacement parts.
- Sanitary hose replacements
- Hose clamps

- Hose connectors
- Silicone
- A siphon hose
- Wood bungs

Recommendations for a seagoing toolbox:

- Duct tape, of course
- Assortment of screwdrivers, both flat head and Phillips head, including tiny screwdrivers for repair of eyeglasses.
- Pliers
- Needle nose pliers
- Wire cutters
- Wire strippers
- Soldering kit
- Grommet making kit
- Rivet gun

- Sturdy set of Vise grips
- Crescent wrenches
- Adjustable wrenches
- Monkey wrenches
- Allen wrench kit
- Grips to remove oil filters
- Hand brace and bits
- Complete supply of fasteners including screws, nuts, and washers
- Hand drill and bits, rechargeable drill with inverter on board
- Socket set including metric sockets
- Hacksaw with spare blades
- Box cutters with spare blades
- Ruler
- Small wood saw with spare blades
- Clamps and/or a vise
- Sandpaper

APPENDIX 3

INSPECTION CHECKLISTS

BASIC INFORMATION

Make of Vessel _____   LOA _____

Year _____   LWL _____

Hull Type _____   Displacement _____

Construction Material _____   Draft _____

Port of Registry _____   Beam _____

Owner's Manual		Navigation instruments	
Documentation papers		Safety gear	
Legal registration		Liferaft	
Bill of Sale (Copy)		EPIRB	
Insurance documents		Flares	
Maintenance history		Communications equipment	
Recent work done		Condition of hull	
Sail inventory		Condition of deck	
Engine(s)		Condition of engine(s)	
Fuel capacity		Standard of maintenance	
Water capacity		Overall vessel condition	
Deck layout		Overall first impressions	

THE HULL AND ADJOINING STRUCTURES

Hull condition		Running lights	
Gelcoat blemishes		Stern light	
Rub rail		Compass	
Toe rail		Compass light	
Cap rail		Ports	
Cleats		Hatches	
Stanchions		Bulkheads	
Lifelines		IGU	
Pelican hooks		Bilges	
Bow pulpit		Bilge pumps	
Stern pushpit		Manual	
Deck leaking		Electronic	
Fuel fittings		Keel bolts	
Water fittings		Keel	
Waste fittings		Centerboard	
Vents		Daggerboard	
Tank fittings		Delamination	
Cheek blocks		Depth sounder	
Sheaves		Sonar	
Line stoppers		Knot meter	
Lead blocks		Through hulls	
Line stoppers		Skeg	
Deck organizers		Rudder	
Lead tracks		Rudder post	
Handrails		Rudder bearings	
Liferaft fittings		Propeller	
Winches		Propeller shaft	
Teak decking		Sacrificial zinc	
Davits		Cutless bearing	
Dinghy		Other	

SPARS, RIGGING, SAILS AND CANVAS

Sheets		Turnbuckles	
Downhauls		Shroud eyes	
Topping lifts		Stay eyes	
Shackles		Main reefing	
Feeder line		Boom	
Cheek blocks		Boom vang	
Turning blocks		Outhaul	
Fairleads		Bails	
Main traveler		Mast bolts	
Mizzen traveler		Mast boot	
Line stoppers		Wiring	
Winches		Partners	
Mainsail		Mast position	
Jibs		Spreaders	
Mizzen		Steaming light	
Staysails		Deck light	
Spinnakers		Spreader lights	
Other sails		Anchor light	
Telltales		Strobe light	
Battens		Tricolor light	
Reef lines		Baby stay	
Forestay slide		Spinnaker track	
Foil		Mast tangs	
Roller reefing drum		Mast head	
Head swivel		Mast head sheaves	
Shrouds		Antennae	
Forestay		Wind instruments	
Backstay		Windex	
Running backstays		Notes:	
Chain plates			

GROUND TACKLE

Anchors		Bitter ends	
Thimbles		Snubber	
Shackles		Anchor rollers	
Swivels		Windlass	
Rodes		Other	

STEERING SYSTEMS

Rudder		Wind vane	
Rudderpost		Wind vane linkage	
Lower rudder bearing		Auxiliary rudder	
Upper rudder bearing		Trim tabs	
Tiller arm		Autopilot control unit	
Rudderhead fitting		Wire connections	
Steering wheel		Autopilot compass	
Steering linkage		CPU	
Quadrant/Radial drive unit		Drive unit	
Hydraulic lines		Drive linkage	
Hydraulic drive unit		Other	
Emergency tiller			

PROPULSION MACHINERY

Engine room light		Engine mounts	
Engine room vent		Fuel tank	
Bilge		Fuel clean	
Primary fuel filter		Fuel lines	
Secondary fuel filter		Fuel gauge	
Oil filter		Engine gauges	
Oil level		Throttle control	
Oil cleanliness		Throttle linkage	
Air filter		Solenoid	
Turbocharger		Starter	
Supercharger		Starter drive belt	
Raw water seacock		Alternator	
Raw water strainer		Fuel tank	
Raw water hoses		Fuel lines	
Raw water pump		Fuel valves	
Pump drive belt		Observation port	
Impeller		Transmission oil	
Heat exchanger		Oil pump	
Closed system pump		Oil filter	
Pump drive belt		Water cooling	
Thermostat		Hydraulic lines	
Expansion tank		Gearshift cables	
Coolant level		Drive-Propeller coupling	
Exhaust elbow		Prop shaft alignment	
Exhaust hose		Stuffing box	

THE ELECTRICAL SYSTEM

Batteries		Stereo	
Battery isolation switch		Instrument lights	
Grounding system		Navigation instruments	
Electrical panel		Fresh water pump	
Panel breakers		Bilge pump	
Running lights		Shower pump	
Stern light		Gas solenoid	
Anchor light		Windlass	
Steaming light		AC Main	
Deck light		Outlets	
Cabin lights		Battery charger	
Cabin fans		Water heater	
Saloon lights		Air conditioning	
VHF		Others	
Refrigeration			

TANKAGE, PIPING AND HEADS

Water fill deck fitting		Toilets	
Water tanks		Sanitation hoses	
Water tank vents		Y-valves	
Tank fittings		Anti-siphon valves	
Hoses and connections		Holding tanks	
Pipes		Holding tank vents	
Water pumps		Waste empty hoses	
Tank valves		Macerator	
Faucets			

SHIPBOARD AMENITIES

Galley stove		Passageways	
CNG		Handholds	
LPG		Navigation station	
Galley storage		Chart table	
Seawater pump		Charts	
Refrigeration		SSB	
Compressor		Satellite phone	
Condenser		VHF	
Cold plate		CD system	
Refrigerant		Stereo	
Gauge manifold set		Navigation equipment	
RDF		GPS	
Sight glass		Computer	
Gas locker		Bunks	
Sniffer		Storage	
Gimbals		Lee cloths	
Teflon tape		Others	
Locking mechanisms			
Saloon			
Saloon table			

SAFETY

PFD's		Latches on drawers, cupboards, etc.	
Fire extinguishers		Hull diagram showing seacocks,	
Whistle		Handholds below	
Bell		VHF, SSB, Satellite phone tested.	
Flare kit		Cockpit Chat	
Other visual distress signals		ship's rules, procedures	
Medical kit		night watch	
Special medical considerations		MOB discussion	
Liferaft		fire discussion	
Abandon ship bag		abandon ship discussion	
EPIRBs		seasickness discussion	
Crew identifications		Spotlight with cockpit outlet	
Jack lines		Emergency knife	
Harnesses/tethers		Binoculars	
Preventer		Flashlights	
Radar reflector		Others	
Man overboard pole			
Lifesling			
Sea anchor			
Reefing lines			
Storm sails			
Bow shroud			
Stove operation			

VESSEL PREPARATIONS FOR SEA

Inspection completed		Instruments	
Repairs completed		Logbook	
Gear supplemented and updated		Batteries charged, filled	
Engine monitoring		Anchors stowed	
Oil and filter changed		Hatches secured against leaking	
Fuel filters changed		Provisions stored	
Fuel is certified clean		Routing	
Engine running, gauges OK		Waypoints plotted and logged	
Raw water filter		Float Plan	
Impeller changed		Weather	
Transmission fluid		Cockpit chat	
Coolant fluid		Watch schedule posted	
Cooking fuel		Hull diagram posted	
Jerry jugs secured		Holding tanks empty, flushed	
Water jugs secured		Y-valves	
Water tanks full		Final communications	
Bilges empty, pumps operational		Final land head trip	
Lights		Have fun	

CREWMEMBER RESPONSIBILITIES AND DUTIES

GENERAL

Each member of the crew should become familiar with the location and operation of the vessel's equipment.

- Operating fire extinguishers
- Operating marine heads
- Understand the electrical panel
- Understand the battery isolation switch
- Operating the seacocks
- Operating the manual and electronic bilge pumps
- Putting up and taking down sails
- Operating the windlass
- Deploy liferaft
- Trimming and reefing sails
- Reading GPS location
- Reading the compass, depth sounder, speed indicator, and log
- Steering the course
- Operation of the autopilot/wind vane
- Starting and stopping the engine
- Reading engine gauges
- Operating engine and gear shift controls
- Understand the MOB procedures

- Operating overboard poles, Lifesling, etc.
- Lighting stove and oven
- Donning life preserver and harness
- Operating EPIRBs
- Operating flares and flare gun
- Keeping yacht Bristol
- Operating electric panel
- Understand and comply with watch schedule

- Knowing the location of:
    Fire extinguishers
    Seacocks
    Medical kit
    Electrical/propane/fuel shut-off
      valves
    Emergency tools
    Liferaft
    EPIRBs and flares
    Flashlights
    Binoculars
    Search light
    Storm sails

It is important to recognize any medical conditions that may exist well prior to the sailing date, to make certain they are handled in advance. This includes musculoskeletal pain, toothaches, cardiac abnormalities, diabetes, skin ailments requiring medication, allergies, incontinence, and phobias, etc.

All medications prescribed at the time of sailing must be brought along, included on a list along with name and dosage frequency. Please be certain you have enough to last the entire passage, and a few extras.

APPENDIX 5

FLOAT PLAN

VESSEL NAME _____

SKIPPER NAME _____

VESSEL DESCRIPTION _____

REGISTRATION NUMBERS _____

DOCUMENTATION NUMBERS _____

VESSEL CONTACT NUMBERS _____

CREW NAMES   PASSPORT NUMBERS
_____

_____

_____

_____

_____

VOYAGE ITINERARY
DATE   PORT OF DEPARTURE   DAYS AT SEA   DESTINATION
_____

_____

_____

_____

GENERAL POWER OF ATTORNEY

NOTICE: THE POWERS GRANTED BY THIS DOCUMENT ARE BROAD AND SWEEPING. IF YOU HAVE ANY QUESTIONS ABOUT THESE POWERS, OBTAIN COMPETENT LEGAL ADVICE. THIS DOCUMENT DOES NOT AUTHORIZE ANYONE TO MAKE MEDICAL AND OTHER HEALTH-CARE DECISIONS FOR YOU. YOU MAY REVOKE THIS POWER OF ATTORNEY IF YOU LATER WISH TO DO SO.

I, _____ [YOUR FULL LEGAL NAME], residing at

_____

_____ [YOUR FULL ADDRESS], hereby appoint _____ of

_____, _____,

_____, as my Attorney-in-Fact ("Agent").

If my Agent is unable to serve for any reason, I designate

_____, of _____,

_____, _____ _____, as my successor

Agent.

I hereby revoke any and all general powers of attorney that previously have been signed by me. However, the preceding sentence shall not have the effect of revoking any powers of attorney that are directly related to my health care that previously have been signed by me.

My Agent shall have full power and authority to act on my behalf. This power and authority shall authorize my Agent to manage and conduct all of my affairs and to exercise all of my legal rights and powers, including all rights and powers that I may acquire in the future. My Agent's powers shall include, but not be limited to, the power to:

1. Open, maintain or close bank accounts (including, but not limited to, checking accounts, savings accounts, and certificates of deposit), brokerage accounts, and other similar accounts with financial institutions.

    a. Conduct any business with any banking or financial institution with respect to any of my accounts, including, but not limited to, making deposits and withdrawals, obtaining bank statements, passbooks, drafts, money orders, warrants, and certificates or vouchers payable to me by any person, firm, corporation or political entity.

b. Perform any act necessary to deposit, negotiate, sell or transfer any note, security, or draft of the United States of America, including U.S. Treasury Securities.

c. Have access to any safe deposit box that I might own, including its contents.

2. Sell, exchange, buy, invest, or reinvest any assets or property owned by me. Such assets or property may include income producing or non-income producing assets and property.

3. Purchase and/or maintain insurance, including life insurance upon my life or the life of any other appropriate person.

4. Take any and all legal steps necessary to collect any amount or debt owed to me, or to settle any claim, whether made against me or asserted on my behalf against any other person or entity.

5. Enter into binding contracts on my behalf.

6. Exercise all stock rights on my behalf as my proxy, including all rights with respect to stocks, bonds, debentures, or other investments.

7. Maintain and/or operate any business that I may own.

8. Employ professional and business assistance as may be appropriate, including attorneys, accountants, and real estate agents.

9. Sell, convey, lease, mortgage, manage, insure, improve, repair, or perform any other act with respect to any of my property (now owned or later acquired) including, but not limited to, real estate and real estate rights (including the right to remove tenants and to recover possession). This includes the right to sell or encumber any homestead that I now own or may own in the future.

10. Prepare, sign, and file documents with any governmental body or agency, including, but not limited to, authorization to:

a. Prepare, sign and file income and other tax returns with federal, state, local, and other governmental bodies.

b. Obtain information or documents from any government or its agencies, and negotiate, compromise, or settle any matter with such government or agency (including tax matters).

c. Prepare applications, provide information, and perform any other act reasonably requested by any government or its agencies in connection with governmental benefits (including military and social security benefits).

11. Make gifts from my assets to members of my family and to such other persons or charitable organizations with whom I have an established pattern of giving. However, my Agent may not make gifts of my property to the Agent. I appoint _____, of

_____, _____, _____

_____, as my substitute Agent for the sole purpose of making gifts of my property to my Agent, as appropriate.

12. Transfer any of my assets to the trustee of any revocable trust created by me, if such trust is in existence at the time of such transfer.

13. Disclaim any interest which might otherwise be transferred or distributed to me from any other person, estate, trust, or other entity, as may be appropriate.

This Power of Attorney shall be construed broadly as a General Power of Attorney. The listing of specific powers is not intended to limit or restrict the general powers granted in this Power of Attorney in any manner.

Any power or authority granted to my Agent under this document shall be limited to the extent necessary to prevent this Power of Attorney from causing: (i) my income to be taxable to my Agent, (ii) my assets to be subject to a general power of appointment by my Agent, and (iii) my Agent to have any incidents of ownership with respect to any life insurance policies that I may own on the life of my Agent.

My Agent shall not be liable for any loss that results from a judgment error that was made in good faith. However, my Agent shall be liable for willful misconduct or the failure to act in good faith while acting under the authority of this Power of Attorney.

I authorize my Agent to indemnify and hold harmless any third party who accepts and acts under this document.

My Agent shall be entitled to reasonable compensation for any services provided as my Agent. My Agent shall be entitled to reimbursement of all reasonable expenses incurred in connection with this Power of Attorney.

My Agent shall provide an accounting for all funds handled and all acts performed as my Agent, if I so request or if such a request is made by any authorized personal representative or fiduciary acting on my behalf.

This Power of Attorney shall become effective immediately and shall not be affected by my disability or lack of mental competence, except as may be provided otherwise by an applicable state statute. This is a Durable Power of Attorney. This Power of Attorney shall continue effective until my death. This Power of Attorney may be revoked by me at any time by providing written notice to my Agent.

Dated _____, 20_____ at _____, _____.

YOUR SIGNATURE:

_____

YOUR PRINTED FULL LEGAL NAME:

_____

WITNESS' SIGNATURE: WITNESS' SIGNATURE:

_____   _____

WITNESS' PRINTED FULL LEGAL NAME: WITNESS' PRINTED FULL LEGAL NAME:

_____   _____

Acknowledgement:

STATE OF _____

COUNTY OF _____

The foregoing instrument was acknowledged before me this _____ day of _____,
20_____ by _____ [YOUR FULL LEGAL NAME], who is personally known to
me or who has produced _____ as identification.

_____

Signature of person taking acknowledgment

_____

Name typed, printed, or stamped

_____

Title or rank

_____

Serial number (if applicable)

This document was prepared by:

Name: _____

Address: _____

_____

APPENDIX 7

COLREGS

The *Rules of the Road* or *Collision Avoidance Regulations* (COLREGS) were designed to give direction to vessels in order to set a standard that everyone could follow in order to prevent collisions of two or more vessels. The rules are numerous and cover almost every imaginable sequence of events that may lead to collision. You do not have to memorize them all but be aware of the basic rules which apply in order to operate safely on the water.

GOOD SEAMANSHIP

Good seamanship develops over time by acquiring knowledge and skills. You must keep safety foremost in your mind when operating your boat. Do what you can to stay out of the way of other boats.

You will be using terms when dealing with the rules of the road which may be unfamiliar to you. Because the rules are federal laws, the definitions of these terms are important. The following terms are found throughout the rules of the road. You should have a thorough understanding of their meaning.

Vessel: Every craft of any description used or capable of being used on the water.

Power Driven Vessel (Motorboat): Any vessel propelled by machinery.

Sailing Vessel: *under sail alone* with no mechanical means of propulsion. A **sailboat propelled by machinery** is a motorboat (including motorsailing).

Underway: Not at anchor, aground or attached to the dock or shore.

Danger Zone: An arc of 112.5 degrees measured from dead ahead to just aft of the starboard beam.

Right-of-way: The right and duty to maintain course and speed.

Stand-On Vessel: The vessel which has the right-of-way.

Give-Way Vessel: The vessel which must keep clear of the stand-on vessel.

Visible (when applied to lights): Visible on a dark, clear night.

Short Blast: A blast of one to two seconds duration.

Prolonged Blast: A blast of four to six seconds duration.

PROPER LOOKOUT

The rules are very specific about maintaining a proper lookout. We must keep eyes and ears open to observe or hear something that may endanger someone or affect their safety. You must look up for bridge clearances and power lines, down for floats, swimmers, logs and divers' flags and side to side for traffic prior to turning your boat. A proper lookout can avoid surprises.

A good rule to follow is to assign one or more people to have no other assigned responsibilities except the task of lookout. They can then rotate the lookout duty.

SOUND SIGNALS

If you were to operate in New York Harbor or the Chesapeake you would well understand the importance of being able to signal your intention. The number of times I have used whistles to indicate my intentions only to find that the other vessel did not understand my intentions prompts this page.

Vessels are required to sound signals any time that they are in close quarters and a risk of collision exists. The following signals are the only ones to be used to signal a vessel's intentions (inland rules only).

1. **One short blast—I intend to change course to starboard.**
2. **Two short blasts—I intend to change course to port.**
3. **Three short blasts—I am operating astern propulsion (backing up).**
4. **Five or more short and rapid blasts—Danger or doubt signal (I don't understand your intent).**

Note: Inland rules (Great Lakes) use sound signals to indicate intent to maneuver.

Under international rules the signals are given when the maneuver is being executed.

The Rules of the Road
International Regulations for Avoiding Collisions at Sea

Part A - General

Rule 1
Application

(a) These Rules shall apply to all vessels upon the high seas and in all waters connected therewith navigable by seagoing vessels.

(b) Nothing in these Rules shall interfere in the operation of special rules made by an appropriate authority for roadsteads, harbors, rivers, lakes or inland waterways connected with the high seas and navigable by seagoing vessels. Such special rules shall conform as closely as possible to these Rules.

(c) Nothing in these Rules shall interfere with the operation of any special rules made by the Government of any State with respect to additional station or signal lights or shapes or whistle signals for ships of war and vessels proceeding under convoy, or with respect to additional station or signal lights for fishing vessels fishing as a fleet. These additional station or signal lights or whistle signals shall, so far as possible, be such that they cannot be mistaken for any light, shape, or signal authorized elsewhere under these Rules.

(d) Traffic separation schemes may be adopted by the Organization for the purpose of these Rules.

(e) Whenever the Government concerned shall have determined that a vessel of special construction or purpose cannot comply fully with the provisions of any of these Rules with respect to number, position, range or arc of visibility of lights or shapes, as well as to the disposition and characteristics of sound-signaling appliances, such vessel shall comply with such other provisions in regard to number, position, range or arc of visibility of lights or shapes, as well as to the disposition and characteristics of sound-signaling appliances, as her Government shall have determined to be the closest possible compliance with these Rules in respect to that vessel.

Rule 2
Responsibility

(a) Nothing in these Rules shall exonerate any vessel, or the owner, master, or crew thereof, from the consequences of any neglect to comply with these Rules or of the neglect of any precaution which may be required by the ordinary practice of seamen, or by the special circumstances of the case.

(b) In construing and complying with these Rules due regard shall be had to all dangers of navigation and collision and to any special circumstances, including the limitations of the vessels involved, which may make a departure from these Rules necessary to avoid immediate danger.

Rule 3
General Definitions

For the purpose of these Rules, except where the context otherwise requires:

(a) The word "vessel" includes every description of watercraft, including non-displacement craft and seaplanes, used or capable of being used as a means of transportation on water.

(b) The term "power driven vessel" means any vessel propelled by machinery.

(c) The term "sailing vessel" means any vessel under sail provided that propelling machinery, if fitted, is not being used.

(d) The term "vessel engaged in fishing" means any vessel fishing with nets, lines, trawls, or other fishing apparatus which restrict maneuverability, but does not include a vessel fishing with trolling lines or other fishing apparatus which do not restrict manageability.

(e) The term "seaplane" includes any aircraft designed to maneuver on the water.

(f) The term "vessel not under command" means a vessel which through some exceptional circumstance is unable to maneuver as required by these Rules and is therefore unable to keep out of the way of another vessel.

(g) The term "vessel restricted in her ability to maneuver" means a vessel which from the nature of her work is restricted in her ability to maneuver as required by these Rules and is therefore unable to keep out of the way of another vessel.

The term "vessel restricted in her ability to maneuver" shall include but not be limited to:

(i) A vessel engaged in laying, servicing, or picking up a navigational mark, submarine cable or pipeline;

(ii) A vessel engaged in dredging, surveying or underwater operations;

(iii) A vessel engaged in replenishment or transferring persons, provisions or cargo while underway;

(iv) A vessel engaged in the launching or recovery of aircraft;

(v) A vessel engaged in mine clearance operations;

(vi) A vessel engaged in a towing operation such as severely restricts the towing vessel and her tow in their ability to deviate from their course.

(h) The term "vessel constrained by her draft" means a power driven vessel which because of her draft in relation to the available depth and width of navigable water is severely restricted in her ability to deviate from the course she is following.

(i) The word "underway" means a vessel is not at anchor, or made fast to the shore, or aground.

(j) The words "length" and "breadth" of a vessel mean her length overall and greatest breadth.

(k) Vessels shall be deemed to be in sight of one another only when one can be observed visually from the other.

(l) The term "restricted visibility" means any condition in which visibility is restricted by fog, mist, falling snow, heavy rainstorms, sandstorms and any other similar causes.

Part B - Steering and Sailing Rules
Section I - Conduct of Vessels in any Condition of Visibility

Rule 4
Application

Rules in this section apply to any condition of visibility.

Rule 5
Look-out

Every vessel shall at all times maintain a proper look-out by sight as well as by hearing as well as by all available means appropriate in the prevailing circumstances and conditions so as to make a full appraisal of the situation and of the risk of collision.

Rule 6
Safe Speed

Every vessel shall at all times proceed at a safe speed so that she can take proper and effective action to avoid collision and be stopped within a distance appropriate to the prevailing circumstances and conditions.

In determining a safe speed the following factors shall be among those taken into account:

(a) By all vessels:

(i) The state of visibility;

(ii) The traffic density including concentrations of fishing vessels or any other vessels;

(iii) The manageability of the vessel with special reference to stopping distance and turning ability in the prevailing conditions;

(iv) At night the presence of background light such as from shore lights or from back scatter from her own lights;

(v) The state of wind, sea and current, and the proximity of navigational hazards;

(vi) The draft in relation to the available depth of water.

(b) Additionally, by vessels with operational radar:

(i) The characteristics, efficiency and limitations of the radar equipment;

(ii) Any constrains imposed by the radar range scale in use;

(iii) The effect on radar detection of the sea state, weather and other sources of interference;

(iv) The possibility that small vessels, ice and other floating objects may not be detected by radar at an adequate range;

(v) The number location and movement of vessels detected by radar;

(vi) The more exact assessment of the visibility that may be possible when radar is used to determine the range of vessels or other objects in the vicinity.

Rule 7
Risk of Collision

(a) Every vessel shall use all available means appropriate to the prevailing circumstances and conditions to determine if risk of collision exists. If there is any doubt such risk shall be deemed to exist.

(b) Proper use shall be made of radar equipment if fitted and operational, including long-range scanning to obtain early warning of risk of collision and radar plotting or equivalent systematic observation of detected objects.

(c) Assumptions shall not be made on the basis of scanty information, especially scanty radar information.

(d) In determining if risk of collision exists the following considerations shall be among those taken into account:

(i) Such risk shall be deemed to exist if the compass bearing of an approaching vessel does not appreciably change;

(ii) Such risk may sometimes exist even when an appreciable bearing change is evident, particularly when approaching a very large vessel or a tow or when approaching a vessel at close range.

Rule 8
Action to Avoid Collision

(a)Any action taken to avoid collision shall, if the circumstances of the case admit, be positive, made in ample time and with due regard to the observance of good seamanship.

(b) Any alteration of course and/or speed to avoid collision shall, if the circumstances of the case admit be large enough to be readily apparent to another vessel observing visually or by radar;
a succession of small alterations of course and/or speed shall be avoided.

(c) If there is sufficient sea room, alteration of course alone may be the most effective action to avoid a close-quarters situation provided that it is made in good time, is substantial and does not result in another close-quarters situation.

(d) Action taken to avoid collision with another vessel shall be such as to result in passing at a safe distance. The effectiveness of the action shall be carefully checked until the other vessel is finally past and clear.

(e) If necessary to avoid collision or allow more time to asses the situation, a vessel may slacken her speed or take all way off by stopping or reversing her means of propulsion.

(f)

(i) A vessel which, by any of these rules, is required not to impede the passage or safe passage of another vessel shall when required by the circumstances of the case, take early action to allow sufficient sea room for the safe passage of the other vessel.

(ii) A vessel required not to impede the passage or safe passage of another vessel is not relieved of this obligation if approaching the other vessel so as to involve risk of collision and shall, when taking action, have full regard to the action which may be required by the rules of this part.

(iii) A vessel the passage of which is not to be impeded remains fully obliged to comply with the rules of this part when the two vessels are approaching one another so as to involve risk of collision.

Rule 9
Narrow Channels

(a) A vessel proceeding along the course of a narrow channel or fairway shall keep as near to the outer limit of the channel or fairway which lies on her starboard side as is safe and practicable.

(b) A vessel of less than 20 meters in length or a sailing vessel shall not impede the passage of a vessel which can safely navigate only within a narrow channel or fairway.

(c) A vessel engaged in fishing shall not impede the passage of any other vessel navigating within a narrow passage or fairway.

(d) A vessel shall not cross a narrow passage or fairway if such crossing impedes the passage of a vessel which can safely navigate only within such channel or fairway. The latter vessel may use the sound signal prescribed in Rule 34(d) if in doubt as to the intention of the crossing vessel.

(e)

(i) In a narrow channel or fairway when overtaking can take place only when the vessel to be overtaken has to take action to permit safe passing, the vessel intending to overtake shall indicate her intention by sounding the appropriate signal prescribed in Rule 34(c)(i). The vessel to be overtaken shall, if in agreement, sound the appropriate signal prescribed in Rule 34(c)(ii) and take steps to permit safe passing. If in doubt she may sound the signals prescribed in Rule 34(d).

(ii) This rule does not relieve the overtaking vessel of her obligation under Rule 13.

(f) A vessel nearing a bend or an area of a narrow channel or fairway where other vessels may be obscured by an intervening obstruction shall navigate with particular alertness and caution and shall sound the appropriate signal prescribed in Rule 34(e).

(g) Any vessel shall, if the circumstances of the case admit, avoid anchoring in a narrow channel.

Rule 10
Traffic Separation Schemes

(a) This rule applies to traffic separation schemes adopted by the Organization and does not relieve any vessel of her obligation under any other rule.

(b) A vessel using a traffic separation scheme shall:

(i) Proceed in the appropriate traffic lane in the general direction of traffic flow for that lane.

(ii) So far as is practicable keep clear of a traffic separation line or separation zone.

(iii) Normally join or leave a traffic lane at the termination of the lane, but when joining or leaving from either side shall do so at as small an angle to the general direction of traffic flow as practicable.

(c) A vessel shall so far as practicable avoid crossing traffic lanes, but if obliged to do so shall cross on a heading as nearly as practicable at right angles to the general direction of traffic flow.

(d)

(i) A vessel shall not use an inshore traffic zone when she can safely use the appropriate traffic lane within the adjacent traffic separation scheme. However, vessels of less than 20 meters in length, sailing vessels and vessels engaged in fishing may use the inshore traffic zone.

(ii) Notwithstanding subparagraph (d)(i), a vessel may use an inshore traffic Zone when en route to or from a port, offshore installation or structure, pilot station or any other place situated within the inshore traffic zone, or to avoid immediate danger.

(e) A vessel, other than a crossing vessel or a vessel joining or leaving a lane shall not normally enter a separation zone or cross a separation line except:

(i) in cases of emergency to avoid immediate danger;

(ii) to engage in fishing within a separation zone.

(f) A vessel navigating in areas near the terminations of traffic separation schemes shall do so with particular caution.

(g) A vessel shall so far as practicable avoid anchoring in a traffic separation scheme or in areas near its terminations.

(h) A vessel not using a traffic separating scheme shall avoid it by as wide a margin as is practicable.

(i) A vessel engaged in fishing shall not impede the passage of any vessel following a traffic lane.

(j) A vessel of less than 20 meters in length or a sailing vessel shall not impede the safe passage of a power driven vessel following a traffic lane.

(k) A vessel restricted in her ability to maneuver when engaged in an operation for the maintenance of safety of navigation in a traffic separating scheme is exempted from complying with this Rule to the extent necessary to carry out the operation.

(l) A vessel restricted in her ability to maneuver when engaged in an operation for the laying, servicing or picking up a submarine cable, within a traffic separating scheme, is exempted from complying with this Rule to the extent necessary to carry out the operation.

Section II - Conduct of Vessels in Sight of One Another

Rule 11
Application

Rules in this section apply to vessels in sight of one another.

Rule 12
Sailing Vessels

(a) when two sailing vessels are approaching one another, so as to involve risk of collision, one of them shall keep out of the way of the other as follows:

(i)when each of them has the wind on a different side, the vessel which has the wind on the port side shall keep out of the way of the other;

(ii) When both have the wind on the same side, the vessel which is to windward shall keep out of the way of the vessel which is to leeward;

(iii) if the vessel with the wind on the port side sees a vessel to windward and cannot determine with certainty whether the other vessel has the wind on the port or the starboard side, she shall keep out of the way of the other.

(b) For the purposes of this Rule the windward side shall be deemed to be the side opposite that on which the mainsail is carried or, in the case of a square rigged vessel, the side opposite to that on which the largest fore-and-aft sail is carried.

Rule 13
Overtaking

(a) Notwithstanding anything contained in the Rules of Part B, Sections I and II, any vessel overtaking any other shall keep out of the way of the vessel being overtaken.

(b) A vessel shall be deemed to be overtaking when coming up with a another vessel from a direction more than 22.5 degrees abaft her beam, that is, in such a position with reference to the vessel she is overtaking, that at night she would be able to see only the sternlight of that vessel but neither of her sidelights.

(c) When a vessel is in any doubt as to whether she is overtaking another, she shall assume that this is the case and act accordingly.

(d) Any subsequent alteration of the bearing between the two vessels shall not make the overtaking vessel a crossing vessel within the meaning of these Rules or relieve her of the duty of keeping clear of the overtaken vessel until she is finally past and clear.

Rule 14
Head-on Situation

(a) When two power driven vessels are meeting on reciprocal or nearly reciprocal courses so as to involve risk of collision each shall alter her course to starboard so that each shall pass on the port side of the other.

(b) Such a situation shall be deemed to exist when a vessel sees the other ahead or nearly ahead and by night she could see the masthead lights in line or nearly in line and/or both sidelights and by day she observes the corresponding aspect of the other vessel.

(c) When a vessel is in any doubt as to whether such a situation exists she shall assume that it does exist and act accordingly.

Rule 15
Crossing Situation

When two power driven vessels are crossing so as to involve risk of collision, the vessel which has the other on her own starboard side shall keep out of the way and shall, if the circumstances of the case admit, avoid crossing ahead of the other vessel.

Rule 16
Action by Give-way Vessel

Every vessel which is directed to keep out of the way of another vessel shall, so far as possible, take early and substantial action to keep well clear.

Rule 17
Action by Stand-on Vessel

(a)

(i) Where one of two vessels is to keep out of the way of the other shall keep her course and speed.

(ii) The latter vessel may however take action to avoid collision by her maneuver alone, as soon as it becomes apparent to her that the vessel required to keep out of the way is not taking appropriate action in accordance with these Rules.

(b) When, from any cause, the vessel required to keep her course and speed finds herself so close that collision cannot be avoided by the action of the give-way vessel alone, she shall take such action as will best aid to avoid collision.

(c) A power driven vessel which takes action in a crossing situation in accordance with subparagraph (a)(ii) of this Rule to avoid collision with another power driven vessel shall, if the circumstances of the case admit, not alter course to port for a vessel on her own port side.

(d) This Rule does not relieve the give-way vessel of her obligation to keep out of the way.

Rule 18
Responsibilities Between Vessels

Except where rule 9, 10, and 13 otherwise require:

(a)A power driven vessel underway shall keep out of the way of:

(i)a vessel not under command;

(ii)a vessel restricted in her ability to maneuver;

(iii)a vessel engaged in fishing;

(iv)a sailing vessel;

(b) A sailing vessel under way shall keep out of the way of:

(i)a vessel not under command;

(ii)a vessel restricted in her ability to maneuver;

(iii)a vessel engaged in fishing;

(c)A vessel engaged in fishing when underway shall, so far as possible, keep out of the way of:

(i)a vessel not under command;

(ii)a vessel restricted in her ability to maneuver.

(d)

(i)Any vessel other than a vessel not under command or a vessel restricted in her ability to maneuver shall, if the circumstances of the case admit, avoid impeding the safe passage of a vessel constrained by her draft, exhibiting the signals in Rule 28.

(ii) A vessel constrained by her draft shall navigate with particular caution having full regard to her special condition.

(e) A seaplane on the water shall, in general, keep well clear of all vessels and avoid impeding their navigation. In circumstances, however, where risk of collision exists, she shall comply with the Rules of this Part.

Section III - Conduct of Vessels in Restricted Visibility

Rule 19
Conduct of Vessels in Restricted Visibility

(a) This rule applies to vessels not in sight of one another when navigating in or near an area of restricted visibility.

(b) Every vessel shall proceed at a safe speed adapted to the prevailing circumstances and condition of restricted visibility. A power driven vessel shall have her engines ready for immediate maneuver.

(c) Every vessel shall have due regard to the prevailing circumstances and conditions of restricted visibility when complying with the Rules of Section I of this Part.

(d) A vessel which detects by radar alone the presence of another vessel shall determine if a close-quarters situation is developing and/or risk of collision exists. If so, she shall take avoiding action in ample time, provided that when such action consists of an alteration in course, so far as possible the following shall be avoided:

(i) An alteration of course to port for a vessel forward of the beam, other than for a vessel being overtaken;

(ii) An alteration of course toward a vessel abeam or abaft the beam.

(e) Except where it has been determined that a risk of collision does not exist, every vessel which hears apparently forward of her beam the fog signal of another vessel, or which cannot avoid a close-quarters situation with another vessel forward of her beam, shall reduce her speed to be the minimum at which she can be kept on her course. She shall if necessary take all her way off and in any event navigate with extreme caution until danger of collision is over.

Part C - Lights and Shapes

Rule 20
Application

(a)Rules in this part shall be complied with in all weathers.

(b) The Rules concerning lights shall be complied with from sunset to sunrise, and during such times no other lights shall be exhibited, except such lights which cannot be mistaken for the lights specified in these Rules or do not impair their visibility or distinctive character, or interfere with the keeping of a proper look-out.

(c) The lights prescribed by these rules shall, if carried, also be exhibited from sunrise to sunset in restricted visibility and may be exhibited in all other circumstances when it is deemed necessary.

(d) The Rules concerning shapes shall be complied with by day.

(e) The lights and shapes specified in these Rules shall comply with the provisions of Annex I to these Regulations.

Rule 21
Definitions

(a) "Masthead light" means a white light placed over the fore and aft centerline of the vessel showing an unbroken light over an arc of horizon of 225 degrees and so fixed as to show the light from right ahead to 22.5 degrees abaft the beam on either side of the vessel.

(b) "Sidelights" means a green light on the starboard side and a red light on the port side each showing an unbroken light over an arc of horizon of 112.5 degrees and so fixed as to show the light from right ahead to 22.5 degrees abaft the beam on the respective side. In a vessel of less than 20 meters in length the sidelights may be combined in one lantern carried on the fore and aft centerline of the vessel.

(c) "Sternlight", means a white light placed as nearly as practicable at the stern showing an unbroken light over an arc of horizon of 135 degrees and so fixed as to show the light 67.5 degrees from right aft on each side of the vessel.

(d) "Towing light" means a yellow light having the same characteristics as the "sternlight" defined in paragraph (c) of this Rule.

(e) "All round light" means a light showing an unbroken light over an arc of horizon of 360 degrees.

(f) "Flashing light" means a light flashing at regular intervals at a frequency of 120 flashes or more per minute.

Rule 22
Visibility of Lights

The lights prescribed in these Rules shall have an intensity as specified in Section 8 of Annex I to these Regulations so as to be visible at the following minimum ranges:

(a) In vessels of 50 meters or more in length:

a masthead light, 6 miles;

a sidelight, 3 miles;

a towing light, 3 miles;

a white red, green or yellow all-around light, 3 miles.

(b) In vessels of 12 meters or more in length but less than 50 meters in length;

a masthead light, 5 miles; except that where the length of the vessel is less than 20 meters, 3 miles;

a sidelight, 2 miles;

a sternlight, 2 miles, A towing light, 2 miles;

a white, red, green or yellow all-round light, 2 miles.

(c) In vessels of less than 12 meters in length:

a masthead light, 2 miles;

a sidelight, 1 miles;

a towing light, 2 miles;

a white red, green or yellow all-around light, 2 miles.

(d) In inconspicuous, partly submerged vessels or objects being towed;

a white all-round light; 3 miles.

Rule 23
power driven Vessels Underway

(a) A power driven vessel underway shall exhibit:

(i) a masthead light forward;

(ii) a second masthead light abaft of and higher than the forward one;

except that a vessel of less than 50 meters in length shall not be obliged to exhibit such a light but may do so;

(iii) sidelights: and

(iv) a sternlight.

(b) An air-cushion vessel when operating in non-displacement mode shall, in addition to the lights prescribed in paragraph (a) of this Rule, exhibit an all-round flashing yellow light.

(c)

(i) A power driven vessel of less than 12 meters in length may in lieu of the lights prescribed in paragraph (a) of this Rule exhibit an all-round white light and sidelights.

(ii) a power driven vessel of less than 7 meters in length whose maximum speed does not exceed 7 knots may in lieu of the lights prescribed in paragraph (a) of this Rule exhibit an all-round white light and shall, if practicable, also exhibit sidelights.

(iii) the masthead light or all-round white light on a power driven vessel of less than 12 meters in length may be displaced from the fore and aft centerline of the vessel if centerline fitting is not practicable, provided the sidelights are combined in one lantern which shall be carried on the fore and aft centerline of the vessel or located as nearly as practicable in the same fore and aft line as the masthead light or all-round white light.

Rule 24
Towing and Pushing

(a) A power driven vessel when towing shall exhibit:

(i) instead of the light prescribed in Rule 23(a)(i) or (a)(ii), two masthead lights in a vertical line. When the length of the tow measuring from the stern of the towing vessel to the after end of the tow exceeds 200 meters, three such lights in a vertical line;

(ii) sidelights;

(iii) a sternlight;

(iv) a towing light in a vertical line above the sternlight;

and

(v) when the length of the tow exceeds 200 meters, a diamond shape where it can best be seen.

(b) When a pushing vessel and a vessel being pushed ahead are rigidly connected in a composite unit they shall be regarded as a power driven vessel and exhibit the lights prescribed in Rule 23.

(c) A power driven vessel when pushing ahead or towing alongside, except in the case of a composite unit, shall exhibit:

(i) instead of the light prescribed in Rule 23(a)(i) or (a)(ii), two masthead lights in a vertical line. When the length of the tow measuring from the stern of the towing vessel to the after end of the tow exceeds 200 meters, three such lights in a vertical line;

(ii) sidelights;

(iii) a sternlight.

(d) A power driven vessel to which paragraph (a) or (c) of this Rule apply shall also comply with rule 23(a)(ii).

(e) A vessel or object being towed, other than those mentioned in paragraph (g) of this Rule, shall exhibit:

(i) sidelights;

(ii) a sternlight;

(iii) when the length of the tow exceeds 200 meters, a diamond shape where it can best be seen.

(f) Provided that any number of vessels being towed alongside or pushed in a group shall be lighted as one vessel,

(i) a vessel being pushed ahead, not being part of a composite unit, shall exhibit at the forward end, sidelights;

(ii) a vessel being towed alongside shall exhibit a sternlight and at the forward end, sidelights.

(g) An inconspicuous, partly submerged vessel or object, or combination of such vessels or objects being towed, shall exhibit:

(i) if it is less than 25 meters in breadth, one all-round white light at or near the front end and one at or near the after end except that dracones need not exhibit a light at or near the forward end;

(ii) if it is 25 meters or more in breadth, two or more additional all-round white lights at or near the extremities of its breadth;

(iii) if it exceeds 100 meters in length, additional all-round white lights between the lights prescribed in subparagraphs (i) and (ii) so that the distance between the lights shall not exceed 100 meters.;

(iv) a diamond shape at or near the aftermost extremity of the last vessel or object being towed and if the length of the tow exceeds 200 meters an additional diamond shape where it can best be seen and located as far forward as is practicable.

(h) When from any sufficient cause it is impracticable for a vessel or object being towed to exhibit the lights or shapes prescribed in paragraph (e) or (g) of this Rule, all possible measures shall be taken to light the vessel or object being towed or at least indicate the presence of such vessel or object.

(i) Where from any sufficient cause it is impracticable for a vessel not normally engaged in towing operations to display the lights prescribed in paragraph (a) or (c) of this Rule, such vessel shall not be required to exhibit those lights when engaged in towing another vessel in distress or otherwise in need of assistance. All possible measures shall be taken to indicate the nature of the relationship between the towing vessel and the vessel being towed as authorized by Rule 36, in particular by illuminating the towline.

Rule 25
Sailing Vessels Underway and Vessels Under Oars

(a) a sailing vessel underway shall exhibit:

(i) sidelights;

(ii) a sternlight.

(b) In a sailing vessel of less than 20 meters in length the lights prescribed in paragraph (a) of this Rule may be combined in one lantern carried at or near the top of the mast where it can best be seen.

(c) A sailing vessel underway may, in addition to the lights prescribed in paragraph (a) of this Rule, exhibit at or near the top of the mast, where they can best be seen, two all-round lights in a vertical line, the upper being red and the lower Green, but these lights shall not be exhibited in conjunction with the combined lantern permitted by paragraph (b) of this Rule.

(d)

(i) A sailing vessel of less than 7 meters in length shall, if practicable, exhibit the lights prescribed in paragraph (a) or (b) of this Rule, but if she does not, she shall have ready at hand an electric torch or lighted lantern showing a white light which shall be exhibited in sufficient time to prevent collision.

(ii) A vessel under oars may exhibit the lights prescribed in this rule for sailing vessels, but if she does not, she shall have ready at hand an electric torch or lighted lantern showing a white light which shall be exhibited in sufficient time to prevent collision.

(e) A vessel proceeding under sail when also being propelled by machinery shall exhibit forward where it can best be seen a conical shape, apex downwards.

Rule 26
Fishing Vessels

(a) A vessel engaged in fishing, whether underway or at anchor, shall exhibit only the lights and shapes prescribed by this rule.

(b) A vessel when engaged in trawling, by which is meant the dragging through the water of a dredge net or other apparatus used as a fishing appliance, shall exhibit;

(i) two all-round lights in a vertical line, the upper being green and the lower white, or a shape consisting of two cones with their apexes together in a vertical line one above the other; a vessel of less than 20 meters in length may instead of this shape exhibit a basket;

(ii) a masthead light abaft of and higher than the all-round green light; a vessel of less than 50 meters in length shall not be obliged to exhibit such a light but may do so;

(iii) when making way through the water, in addition to the lights prescribed in this paragraph, sidelights and a sternlight.

(c) A vessel engaged in fishing, other than trawling, shall exhibit:

(i) two all-round lights in a vertical line, the upper being red and the lower white, or a shape consisting of two cones with their apexes together in a vertical line one above the other; a vessel of less than 20 meters in length may instead of this shape exhibit a basket;

(ii)when there is outlying gear extending more than 150 meters horizontally from the vessel, an all-round white light or a cone apex upwards in the direction of the gear.

(iii) when making way through the water, in addition to the lights prescribed in this paragraph, sidelights and a sternlight.

(d) A vessel engaged in fishing in close proximity to other vessels engaged in fishing may exhibit the additional signals described in Annex II to these Regulations.

(e) A vessel when not engaged in fishing shall not exhibit the lights or shapes prescribed in this Rule, but only those prescribed for a vessel of her length.

Rule 27
Vessels Not Under Command or Restricted in Their Ability to Maneuver

(a) A vessel not under command shall exhibit:

(i) two all-round red lights in a vertical line where they can best be seen;

(ii) two balls or similar shapes in a vertical line where they can best be seen;

(iii)when making way through the water, in addition to the lights prescribed in this paragraph, sidelights and a sternlight.

(b) A vessel restricted in her ability to maneuver, except a vessel engaged in mine clearance operations, shall exhibit:

(i) three all-round lights in a vertical line where they can best be seen. The highest and lowest of these lights shall be red and the middle light shall be white;

(ii) three shapes in a vertical line where they can best be seen. The highest and lowest of these shapes shall be balls and the middle one a diamond.

(iii)when making way through the water, a masthead light, sidelights and a sternlight in addition to the lights prescribed in subparagraph (i);

(iv) when at anchor, in addition to the lights or shapes prescribed in subparagraphs(i) and (ii), the light, lights, or shape prescribed in Rule 30.

(c) A power driven vessel engaged in a towing operation such as severely restricts the towing vessel and her tow in their ability to deviate from their course shall, in addition to the lights or shapes prescribed in Rule 24(a), exhibit the lights or shapes prescribed in subparagraph (b)(i) and (ii) of this Rule.

(d) A vessel engaged in dredging or underwater operations, when restricted in her ability to maneuver, shall exhibit the lights and shapes prescribed in subparagraphs (b)(i),(ii) and (iii) of this Rule and shall in addition when an obstruction exists, exhibit:

(i) two all-round red lights or two balls in a vertical line to indicate the side on which the obstruction exists;

(ii) two all-round green lights or two diamonds in a vertical line to indicate the side on which another vessel may pass;

(iii) when at anchor, the lights or shapes prescribed in this paragraph instead of the lights or shapes prescribed in Rule 30.

(e) Whenever the size of a vessel engaged in diving operations makes it impracticable to exhibit all lights and shapes prescribed in paragraph (d) of this Rule, the following shall be exhibited:

(i) Three all-round lights in a vertical line where they can best be seen. The highest and lowest of these lights shall be red and the middle light shall be white;

(ii) a rigid replica of the code flag "A" not less than 1 meter in height. Measures shall be taken to ensure its all-round visibility.

(f) A vessel engaged in mine clearance operations shall in addition to the lights prescribed for a power driven vessel in Rule 23 or to the light or shape prescribed for a vessel at anchor in Rule 30 as appropriate, exhibit three all-round green lights or three balls. One of these lights or shapes shall be exhibited near the foremast head and one at each end of the fore yard. These lights or shapes indicate that it is dangerous for another vessel to approach within 1000 meters of the mine clearance vessel.

(g) Vessels of less than 12 meters in length, except those engaged in diving operations, shall not be required to exhibit the lights prescribed in this Rule.

(h) The signals prescribed in this Rule are not signals of vessels in distress and requiring assistance. Such signals are contained in Annex IV to these Regulations.

Rule 28
Vessels Constrained by their Draft

A vessel constrained by her draft may, in addition to the lights prescribed for power driven vessels in Rule 23, exhibit where they can best be seen three all-round red lights in a vertical line, or a cylinder.

Rule 29
Pilot Vessels

(a) A vessel engaged on pilotage duty shall exhibit:

(i) at or near the masthead, two all-round lights in a vertical line, the upper being white and the lower red;

(ii) when underway, in addition, sidelights and a sternlight;

(iii) when at anchor, in addition to the lights prescribed in subparagraph (i), the light, lights, or shape prescribed in Rule 30 for vessels at anchor.

(b) A pilot vessel when not engaged on pilotage duty shall exhibit the lights or shapes prescribed for a similar vessel of her length.

Rule 30
Anchored Vessels and Vessels Aground

(a) A vessel at anchor shall exhibit where it can best be seen:

(i) in the fore part, an all-round white light or one ball;

(ii) at or near the stern and at a lower level than the light prescribed in subparagraph (i), an all-round white light.

(b) A vessel of less than 50 meters in length may exhibit an all-round white light where it can best be seen instead of the lights prescribed in paragraph (a) of this Rule.

(c) A vessel at anchor may, and a vessel of 100 meters and more in length shall, also use the available working or equivalent lights to illuminate her decks.

(d) A vessel aground shall exhibit the lights prescribed in paragraph (a) or (b) of this Rule and in addition, where they can best be seen;

(i) two all-round red lights in a vertical line;

(ii) three balls in a vertical line.

(e) A vessel of less than 7 meters in length, when at anchor not in or near a narrow channel, fairway or where other vessels normally navigate, shall not be required to exhibit the shape prescribed in paragraphs (a) and (b) of this Rule.

(f) A vessel of less than 12 meters in length, when aground, shall not be required to exhibit the lights or shapes prescribed in subparagraphs (d)(i) and (ii) of this Rule.

Rule 31
Seaplanes

Where it is impracticable for a seaplane to exhibit lights or shapes of the characteristics or in the positions prescribed in the Rules of this Part she shall exhibit lights and shapes as closely similar in characteristics and position as is possible.

Part D - Sound and Light Signals

Rule 32
Definitions

(a) The word "whistle" means any sound signaling appliance capable of producing the prescribed blasts and which complies with the specifications in Annex III to these Regulations.

(b) The term "short blast" means a blast of about one second's duration.

(c) The term "prolonged blast" means a blast from four to six seconds' duration.

Rule 33
Equipment for Sound Signals

(a) A vessel of 12 meters or more in length shall be provided with a whistle and a bell and a vessel of 100 meters or more in length shall, in addition be provided with a gong, the tone and sound of which cannot be confused with that of the bell. The whistle, bell and gong shall comply with the specifications in Annex III to these Regulations. The bell or gong or both may be replaced by other equipment having the same respective sound characteristics, provided that manual sounding of the prescribed signals shall always be possible.

(b) A vessel of less than 12 meters in length shall not be obliged to carry the sound signaling appliances prescribed in paragraph (a) of this Rule but if she does not, she shall be provided with some other means of making an efficient signal.

Rule 34
Maneuvering and Warning Signals

(a) When vessels are in sight of one another, a power driven vessel under way, when maneuvering as authorized or required by these Rules, shall indicate that maneuver by the following signals on her whistle:

one short blast to mean "I am altering my course to starboard";

two short blasts to mean "I am altering my course to port";

three short blasts to mean "I am operating astern propulsion".

(b) Any vessel may supplement the whistle signals prescribed in paragraph (a) of this Rule by light signals, repeated as appropriate, whilst the maneuver is being carried out:

(i) these signals shall have the following significance:

one flash to mean "I am altering my course to starboard";

two flashes to mean "I am altering my course to port";

three flashes to mean "I am operating astern propulsion".

(ii) the duration of each flash shall be about one second, the interval between flashes shall be about one second, and the interval between successive signals shall not be less than ten seconds.

(iii) the light used for this signal shall, if fitted, be an all-round white light, visible at a minimum range of 5 miles, and shall comply with the provisions of Annex I to these Regulations.

(c) When in sight of one another in a narrow channel or fairway:

(i) a vessel intending to overtake another shall in compliance with Rule 9 (e)(i) indicate her intention by the following signals on her whistle.

two prolonged blasts followed by one short blast to mean "I intend to overtake you on your starboard side";

two prolonged blasts followed by two short blasts to mean "I intend to overtake you on your port side".

(ii) the vessel about to be overtaken when acting in accordance with 9(e)(i) shall indicate her agreement by the following signal on her whistle:

one prolonged, one short, one prolonged and one short blast, in that order.

(d) When vessels in sight of one another are approaching each other and from any cause either vessel fails to understand the intentions or actions of the other, or is in doubt whether sufficient action is being taken by the other to avoid collision, the vessel in doubt shall immediately indicate such doubt by giving at least five short and rapid blasts on the whistle. Such signal may be supplemented by at least five short and rapid flashes.

(e) A vessel nearing a bend or an area of a channel or fairway where other vessels may be obscured by an intervening obstruction shall sound one prolonged blast. Such signal shall be answered with a prolonged blast by any approaching vessel that may be within hearing around the bend or behind the intervening obstruction.

(f) If whistles are fitted on a vessel at a distance apart of more than 100 meters, one whistle only shall be used for giving maneuvering and warning signals.

Rule 35
Sound Signals in Restricted Visibility

In or near an area of restricted visibility, whether by day or night the signals prescribed in this Rule shall be used as follows:

(a) A power driven vessel making way through the water shall sound at intervals of not more than 2 minutes one prolonged blast.

(b) A power driven vessel underway but stopped and making no way through the water shall sound at intervals of no more than 2 minutes two prolonged blasts in succession with an interval of about 2 seconds between them.

(c) A vessel not under command, a vessel restricted in her ability to maneuver, a vessel constrained by her draft, a sailing vessel, a vessel engaged in fishing and a vessel engaged in towing or pushing another vessel shall, instead of the signals prescribed in paragraph (a) or (b) of this Rule, sound at intervals of not more than 2 minutes three blasts in succession, namely one prolonged followed by two short blasts.

(d) A vessel engaged in fishing, when at anchor, and a vessel restricted in her ability to maneuver when carrying out her work at anchor, shall instead of the signals prescribed in paragraph (g) of this Rule sound the signal prescribed in paragraph (c) of this Rule.

(e) A vessel towed or if more than one vessel is being towed the last vessel of the tow, if manned, shall at intervals of not more than 2 minutes sound four blasts in succession, namely one prolonged followed by three short blasts. When practicable, this signal shall be made immediately after the signal made by the towing vessel.

(f) When a pushing vessel and a vessel being pushed ahead are rigidly connected in a composite unit they shall be regarded as a power driven vessel and shall give the signals prescribed in paragraphs (a) or (b) of this Rule.

(g) A vessel at anchor shall at intervals of not more than 1 minute ring the bell rapidly for five seconds. In a vessel 100 meters or more in length the bell shall be sounded in the forepart of the vessel and immediately after the ringing of the bell the gong shall be sounded rapidly for about 5 seconds in the after part of the vessel. A vessel at anchor may in addition sound three blasts in succession, namely one short, one long and one short blast, to give warning of her position and of the possibility of collision to an approaching vessel.

(h) A vessel aground shall give the bell signal and if required the gong signal prescribed in paragraph (g) of this Rule and shall, in addition, give three separate and distinct strokes on the bell immediately before and after the rapid ringing of the bell. A vessel aground may in addition sound an appropriate whistle signal.

(i) A vessel of less than 12 meters in length shall not be obliged to give the above mentioned signals but, if she does not, shall make some other efficient sound signal at intervals of not more than 2 minutes.

(j) A pilotage vessel when engaged on pilotage duty may in addition to the signals prescribed in paragraph (a), (b) or (g) of this Rule sound an identity signal consisting of four short blasts.

Rule 36
Signals to Attract Attention

If necessary to attract the attention of another vessel, any vessel may make light or sound signals that cannot be mistaken for any signal authorized elsewhere in these Rules, or may direct the beam of her searchlight in the direction of the danger, in such a way as not to embarrass any vessel Any light to attract the attention of another vessel shall be such that it cannot be mistaken for any aid to navigation. For the purpose of this Rule the use of high intensity intermittent or revolving lights, such as strobe lights, shall be avoided.

Rule 37
Distress Signals

When a vessel is in distress and requires assistance she shall use or exhibit the signals described in Annex IV to these Regulations.

Part E - Exemptions

Rule 38
Exemptions

Any vessel (or class of vessel) provided that she complies with the requirements of the International Regulations for the Preventing of Collisions at Sea, 1960, the keel of which is laid or is at a corresponding stage of construction before the entry into force of these Regulations may be exempted from compliance therewith as follows:

(a) The installation of lights with ranges prescribed in Rule 22, until 4 years after the date of entry into force of these regulations.

(b) The installation of lights with color specifications as prescribed in Section 7 of Annex I to these Regulations, until 4 years after the entry into force of these Regulations.

(c) The repositioning of lights as a result of conversion from Imperial to metric units and rounding off measurement figures, permanent exemption.

(d)

(i) The repositioning of masthead lights on vessels of less than 150 meters in length, resulting from the prescriptions of Section 3 (a) of Annex I to these regulations, permanent exemption.

(ii). The repositioning of masthead lights on vessels of 150 meters or more in length, resulting from the prescriptions of Section 3 (a) of Annex I to these regulations, until 9 years after the date of entry into force of these Regulations.

(e) The repositioning of masthead lights resulting from the prescriptions of Section 2(b) of Annex I to these Regulations, until 9 years after the date of entry into force of these Regulations.

(f) The repositioning of sidelights resulting from the prescriptions of Section 2(g) and 3(b) of Annex I to these Regulations, until 9 years after the date of entry into force of these Regulations.

(g) The requirements for sound signal appliances prescribed in Annex II to these Regulations, until 9 years after the date of entry into force of these Regulations.

(h) The repositioning of all-round lights resulting from the prescription of Section 9(b) of Annex I to these Regulations, permanent exemption.

Annexes
The COLREGs include four annexes:

Annex I - Positioning and technical details of lights and shapes

Annex II - Additional signals for fishing vessels fishing in close proximity

Annex III - Technical details of sounds signal appliances

Annex IV - Distress signals, which lists the signals indicating distress and need of assistance.
Annexes I and IV were amended in 1987 to clarify the positioning of certain lights carried on smaller vessels and to add "approved signals transmitted by radio communications systems" (ie distress alerts transmitted in the GMDSS). A section on location signals from search and rescue radar transponders was added in 1993.

The Ocean boundary is defined as water seaward of the COLREGS Demarcation Lines as indicated on National Ocean Service navigation charts. And what does that mean? Take a close look at your charts and you will see this line - the COLREGS DEMARCATION LINE - defined. If you are sailing inshore of this line then you are in internal waters. If you are sailing to the ocean side of this line then you are in ocean water

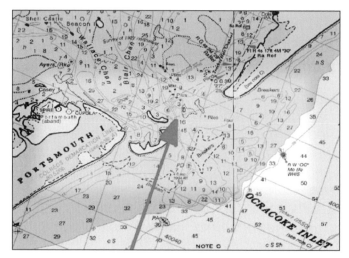

Note the arrow below, pointing to the COLREGS Demarcation Line.

MEDICAL PROBLEMS AND EMERGENCIES OFFSHORE

PATIENT ASSESSMENT AND TREATMENTS FOR OFFSHORE MEDICAL CONDITIONS

The human body requires a constant supply of oxygen, an adequate circulating blood volume, a constant core body temperature, with appropriate nutrient and water intake. Disruption of any of these factors can lead to malfunction or breakdown. We'll discuss the basics of first aid, along with how to diagnose and manage conditions most apt to be encountered at sea.

First aid is defined as the preliminary, rapid measures, involving relatively simple equipment and techniques, taken to reverse immediate, life-threatening situations. This may lead to resolution of the medical condition, or provide stability until definitive treatment can begin at advanced medical facilities.

When approaching a victim of accident or illness, an early assessment is made as to the situation. This assessment should consider the following:

- Is there any immediate further danger to the victim, or to the attendee?
- What injuries or illnesses are obvious
- What was the cause?
- Is the person responsive or unresponsive?
- Is the person breathing, conscious?
- Is there any obvious blood loss? If so, put on gloves to prevent exposure.

PRIMARY PATIENT SURVEY

Once this preliminary assessment is completed, proceed to the Primary Patient Survey, used to identify and treat immediate, possibly life-threatening conditions.

Unresponsive Patients: A method used to evaluate a patient's level of alertness is called the AVPU Scale.

Alert: The person appears to be conscious and fully aware of his/her surroundings.
Verbal stimulation evokes a response from the patient who is not alert.
Painful stimulation (pinching the fingertips gently) evokes a response, but not a verbal stimulation.
Unresponsive patients fail to respond to verbal or painful stimuli.

The situation is considered an emergency whenever a patient is deemed unresponsive. When this occurs, immediately alert the crew of the situation, and have someone make contact with designated emergency medical assistance numbers. Then quickly assess the patient's ABC's - airway, breathing, and circulation.

Airway

Check whether the person is breathing. If no breathing sounds are heard, immediately open the mouth to assess the airway for obstructions. The patient may have to be rolled on his/her back before this is possible. This must be very carefully done to avoid aggravating a spinal injury.

To turn the patient, kneel down near the shoulders. Cross his/her far ankle over the top of the near one. Cradle the back of the neck just below the head to support it, and with the other hand under the far upper arm, gently roll the person toward you. Take every precaution to avoid twisting the neck or spine.

Once this is done, make sure the airway is clear. Open the mouth, make sure the tongue has not fallen back to obstruct the throat, and look for blood, mucous, or other matter. Any movement that brings the lower jaw outward also brings the tongue away from the airway. Gently tilt the head back, and extend the jaw outward with digital pressure at the chin. If this fails to clear the airway, move behind the patient's head, place your hands behind the angle of the mandibles, and lift the jaw outward with both hands (jaw thrust maneuver).

Examination of the oral cavity may reveal visible foreign material or an object that obstructs the airway. With one finger, hold the mouth open by pushing down where the lower lip meets the gum line. Use the forefinger of the other hand to hook the object and attempt to sweep it out of the mouth.

Breathing

With the airway open, assess breathing by listening and watching for the chest rising and falling as normal. If breathing starts, monitor the airway to make sure it stays open. If there is inadequate, or no breathing discernable, begin rescue breathing without delay (see below).

A foreign object (meat, eg.) obstructing the airway necessitates rapid action for removal and restoration of breathing. The Heimlich maneuver is performed on the supine (lying on his/her back) patient by first kneeling down and straddling the person, facing the head. Place the heel of one hand midway between the bottom of the rib cage and the navel. Interlock the fingers of your other hand with the first, and apply quick, upward pressure against the person's abdomen. Your goal is to press against the diaphragm to force air upward through the trachea hard enough to dislodge the material into the mouth.

Repeat the maneuver several times as needed, and then open the mouth and pull the tongue and lower jaw outward. Insert the index finger into the mouth and deep into the throat, feeling for the object. Be very careful not to force anything backward into the throat.

Next, attempt rescue breathing again, repeating the Heimlich procedure if necessary.

When the Heimlich maneuver is necessary on a pregnant or obese person, compression is applied to the chest cavity instead of the abdomen. Apply pressure just above the bottom of the rib cage, in mid-thorax.

On a conscious person who is standing or seated, the Heimlich technique is performed from behind the patient. Make a fist with one hand, place it sideways against the person's abdomen or thorax, and place the other hand over the first to apply the sudden pressure necessary.

Circulation

Blood circulation is best determined by digitally feeling for a pulse in the carotid artery of the neck. This is a major artery located on either side of the Adam's apple, within a depression between the trachea and a large neck muscle, the sternomastoid. Apply two fingers to the area, not pressing too hard, and concentrate on feeling the pulse of this artery. The pulse may be weak in many patients, weak and rapid (shock victim for example) or weak and slow (hypothermia), so be careful to detect any pulse at all. You may also listen at the chest for a heartbeat.

If you detect a strong pulse, assume for the time being a normal circulatory system. A weak pulse of any type must be monitored continuously for any changes. *Do not perform chest compressions when there is a pulse present.*

Be aware that the assessments of airway, breathing, and circulation take precedence over bleeding. You may have someone apply pressure to a bleeding wound, but concentrate on the ABC's first. A loss of either air intake or blood circulation will be rapidly fatal, while bleeding takes longer to kill. Once breathing and circulation are assured, re-focus attention on bleeding and a more thorough examination for injury.

Blood spurting actively from an open wound, however, is indication that the circulatory system is functioning. If the arterial blood appears the normal red color, then the breathing functions are probably adequate as well. When blood spurts, apply immediate pressure and assess breathing. If breathing is interrupted, continue pressure on the wound and work to restore the airway and active breathing first.

Pressure to the wound site, ideally applied with sterile gauzes from the medical kit, will eventually stop most bleeding. A major artery will continue to bleed though, and other means will be necessary. Bleeding from either arm can be controlled by pressure on the brachial artery. This is located inside of the upper arm, where the triceps muscles meet the upper arm bone (humerus). The pulse can be found readily by application of finger pressure to this area.

To stop hemorrhage from the arm, forearm or hand, apply firm pressure to the brachial artery with your fingers, or use a tourniquet. While this pressure is applied, place a small stack of sterile gauze pads over the bleeding area, and wrap them tightly with gauze and tape to apply more pressure locally. *Prolonged stoppage of blood flow through a major artery will eventually be cause for limb amputation. A tourniquet is only used when bleeding is massive, life threatening, or the limb cannot be saved.*

Bleeding in the legs is ultimately controllable by pressure on the femoral artery, located within the groin area, between the pubis and upper thigh. Pressure here is best applied digitally.

Rescue Breathing

Use a mouth shield or pocket mask to protect against transmissible diseases such as AIDS and hepatitis. Begin the procedure by pinching the nostrils closed. A pocket mask covers the patient's nose, so pinching it off becomes unnecessary.

With the patient on his/her back, maintain the airway by either tilting the head back with gentle pressure of one hand on the forehead, or by using the jaw thrust technique at the back of the mandible with one hand.

Take a deep breath, and seal your lips around the patient's open mouth. Give a breath of about 1½ to 2 seconds in length, then repeat a second time. As you breathe into the mouth, observe the patient's chest, which should rise as the air enters the lungs. If the chest doesn't rise, the airway is probably still obstructed. In this case, perform the Heimlich maneuver as discussed above and then monitor for breathing and reassess the patient.

Chest Compressions

Lack of a discernable pulse indicates that the heart has stopped beating (cardiac arrest), and chest compressions must begin, along with rescue breathing (full CPR). The goal of chest compressions is to depress the heart enough to force blood out into the lungs and rest of the body to maintain at least minimal circulation of body tissues. Although the cardiac output of blood is only a quarter of normal, it can be enough to keep a person alive.

Place the patient in the supine position, on a firm surface, with the head lower than the body to promote blood flow to the brain. To locate the proper hand positioning, find the area where the lower ribs on either side of the body intersect in the middle. Place your index finger and middle finger in this position, and then place the heel of your other hand just ahead of that index finger. This is the place to apply compressions; on the left side of the chest, about two ribs up from the lower rib.

Now, staying in that location, interlace the fingers of both hands, with the lower hand facing downward, and the upper hand on top. Straighten both arms, locking the elbows, and lean forward so that your shoulders are directly over your arms. Lean forward at the waist to begin compressions. The heel of the lower hand depresses the chest 1½ to 2 inches (in an adult). Then rock back, keeping your hands in place, to release pressure on the chest. Compressions should be at about 80 to 100 per minute. Count "one and two and three . . .", compressing on each number. If you're alone, give 15 compressions and then two rescue breaths in succession, repeating the cycle four times before pausing to assess for breathing and pulse. If another rescuer is assisting, the ratio is five chest compressions to one breath.

The rescuer in charge of breathing should feel for the carotid pulse to assess effectiveness of chest compressions. Stop each minute to assess for pulse and breathing, continuing CPR if necessary.

Airway Obstruction in Infants and Children

An obstructed airway should always be suspected when there is sudden onset of breathing difficulty in a previously well child. The Heimlich maneuver is suitable for children, but is not used on infants because abdominal pressure can damage the liver.

Lay the infant over your arm, facing down with the head lower than the body. Support your arm on your thigh. Deliver four crisp blows to the back with your hand to dislodge the foreign object. Next, turn the infant over, and use two fingers to compress the chest in the same location as the chest compressions for CPR. Alternate rescue methods until breathing is restored, intermittently examining the oral cavity for the object.

Rescue Breathing in Infants and Children

The sequence of CPR for infants and children is the same used in adults, but the techniques are modified. A child's air-

ways are smaller and obstruct more readily with fluids like mucus or vomitus.

Use the jaw thrust technique in infants to open the airway. In a patient with respiratory arrest, clear the airway, and perform rescue breathing with your mouth covering their mouth and nose. Use less air than for adults, with less forceful breaths. Their chest should rise when you breathe in, just like in adults. Breaths should be at a rate of once every three seconds, and last about a second each.

Chest Compressions in Infants and Children

An infant's pulse is easiest to assess at the brachial artery, just inside the upper arm bone. Use the carotid artery in children older than about one year. Chest compressions in children are performed using only one hand, depressing the chest 1 to 1½ inches. Compressions are in the same location as in adults.

The site of compressions for infants is two inches below an imaginary line between the two nipples. Use only two fingers, and depress the sternum only ½ to 1 inch 80 to 100 times per minute. For both children and infants, the ration of compressions to breaths is 5:1.

SECONDARY SURVEY

Once the primary survey is completed, and first aid administered as required, the patient must be assessed more thoroughly. This is best done below decks with the patient lying more comfortably in a berth. However, in the unconscious patient, any twisting or bending of the neck or spine could make injuries worse. Stabilize the head to prevent movement, and take the unconscious patient below extremely carefully, and only after allowing time for him/her to regain consciousness, as conditions permit. The conscious person is easier to assess, and should only be moved after thorough examination and questioning are done.

Begin the secondary survey by assessing the vital signs: pulse, respiratory rate and character, body temperature, color of the mucous membranes, capillary refill time (below), and clamminess of the skin.

Pulses at the carotid or radial artery (on the inside of the wrist, just beneath the thumb) are counted for thirty seconds, and then multiplied by two. Normal pulse rate is 60 to 80 beats per minute. Breaths are counted per minute; 10 to 15 are considered normal. The character of respirations means whether the breaths appear normal, shallow and rapid, labored, producing fluids from the mouth or nose, painful, etc. 98.6 degrees F is considered normal body temperature. Take the temperature rectally with a low-reading thermometer if hypothermia is suspected.

Mucous membranes are the gums, and conjunctival areas of the eyes (pull the lower lid down to examine). The normal color is pink when blood is being oxygenated and flow to the tissues is normal. Pale pink indicates blood loss, while blue (cyanosis) indicates poor blood oxygenation. Capillary refill time is examined by pushing down on a per-

son's gum enough to get the tissue white. Count the number of seconds it requires to refill with capillary blood flow, turning it pink once again. Normal CRT is about two seconds; anything longer indicates poor tissue perfusion.

A clammy feel to the skin can indicate shock, a condition in which the body responds to abnormal blood flow to the tissues.

Blood pressure, normally 120 systolic, is an indication of the efficiency with which blood is pumped to the tissues. Lower pressures indicate conditions with decreases in normal circulation such as shock, blood loss, and reaction to trauma as the most likely causes. The blood pressure can be taken, just as in the doctor's office, with a blood pressure gauge (sphingomanometer) and stethoscope with little practice. However, the blood pressure can be estimated by finding pulses in various arteries:

> Radial pulse (palpated at the wrists): blood pressure at least 80 mm Hg (millimeters of mercury).
> Femoral pulse: at least 70 mm Hg
> Carotid pulse: at least 60 mm Hg

Further assessment in the conscious patient involves questioning as to what happened to cause the illness or injury. Review information about prior illnesses, pre-existing conditions, medications, and allergies for the unconscious person.

Beginning with the head, the patient's whole body is examined meticulously. Abnormalities in pulse rates, breathing, and mucous membranes that indicate impending shock make examination of the chest, abdomen, pelvis, and thighs for injuries that cause internal bleeding very important. Remember to use extreme caution in moving the unresponsive patient.

Observe closely for pain, abnormal swelling, angularity of bones, grinding of bone segments, or bones protruding through the skin with blood loss. Concentrate on an area indicated by the conscious person first, but don't neglect any other areas after that has been tended to. Provide splinting or bandaging to stabilize any suspected fractures, often enough to control fracture-associated bleeding.

Procedure for Examination

Starting with the *head*, examine the scalp, face, and jaw for blood, abnormal coloring, wounds, sweating, swelling and bruising. Inspect the eyes with a penlight or flashlight. The pupils should appear equal in size, and should both constrict when the light is shined into either eye. Unequal or unresponsive pupils indicate a skull fracture or brain swelling.

Listen to the breathing for abnormal gurgling or difficult respirations. Check the ears for blood or a straw-colored discharge that indicates spinal fluid leakage from a skull fracture.

Proceed to the *neck*, where you look for a Medic-Alert tag first. Inspect for abnormalities, including bleeding, engorged veins, swelling or lumps, abnormal skin color, bruising, or scars. Note the positioning of the trachea; it should be on the midline of the neck all the way down. Gently move the neck from side to side and forward and back in the conscious patient

Note the breathing rate and character of breaths as you proceed to examine the *chest*.

Opening the shirt, feel with your fingers (palpation) from the collarbones to the ribs, front and back. Look for wounds, bleeding, lumps, swelling, scars, and asymmetries. Push gently at the sternum with one hand, and the back with the other. If an area hurts with a sharp pain in the responsive patient, there's probably a broken rib. Breathing will also be painful.

The *upper extremities* are each examined by carefully observing for abnormal bone angles, swelling, bruises, color and moisture. Check the shoulder, upper arm, elbow, lower arm, wrist, and hands. Compare the length of the arms. Unequal lengths indicate a fracture or joint dislocation.

The *back* is examined from the base of the skull to the tailbone. If the person is found lying in the prone (face down) position originally, this exam should take place before moving him/her to the supine position. Use your fingers and eyes to detect misalignment in the tips of the vertebral bones. Tenderness in any area indicates spinal injury. The unresponsive patient is turned over using *the log roll technique*, with one person holding the head in alignment with the spine while another person crosses the patient's distant foot over the near foot. In one single, smooth motion to avoid any twisting, the person is rolled over.

The *abdomen and pelvis* are examined next. Look for wounds, bruising, lumps and swelling. Gently depress different segments of the abdominal wall, called quadrants, which should normally be quite soft. Begin at the upper left quadrant, proceeding clockwise. If the abdominal wall muscles are difficult to depress and hard, internal injuries are indicated.

Gently but firmly press the two sides of the pelvis together, toward the middle. Pain or a grating feeling (crepitus) signifies a fracture. If that's detected, examine carefully for swelling (bleeding), or abnormal smells like urine or feces (loss of continence with nerve damage).

The lower extremities can be sites of great blood loss due to femoral fractures that tear the femoral arteries. Palpate for swellings, protrusions, crepitus, angular deformities, and bruising from the groin area to the feet. Ask the conscious patient to move all digits and extremities. Pinch the extremities gently, asking if he/she can feel the stimuli.

The secondary survey should provide you with enough information to guide your next actions. A major plus is ruling out acute head injury if the person is conscious and responding well. Injuries are attended to according to severity and the limits of your experience and medical kit. Certainly serious injuries or illness beyond those capabilities warrant a call for advice regarding care you can give, and evacuation of the seriously affected patient.

SHIPBOARD ILLNESSES/INJURIES

Medical Emergencies

Heart disease is the primary cause of death in the middle-aged and seniors. Atherosclerosis, or plaque-like deposits that lead to blockage of coronary arteries and result in heart attack, is the most common heart disorder. Symptoms of moderate cardiac disease are often unnoticed in people used to sedentary life styles, but become evident when they are stressed or engage in unusual amounts of physical activity, both of which can occur at sea.

Angina pectoris is chest pain that occurs when the heart muscle is temporarily starved of blood flow. It is seen during physical activity, requiring greater cardiac output that the narrowed coronary arteries can't deliver. The pain may be thought by some to be indigestion. Relief from angina comes from rest and medications to either dilate the coronary arteries (nitroglycerine) or to reduce the heart rate and increase contraction strength (digitalis or beta-blockers).

Anyone who experiences even minor chest pains should have a thorough cardiac workup before venturing offshore, and should at least be armed with medications to control the disorder or treat it in the acute situation.

Myocardial Infarction, familiarly called "heart attack," is the term used for the death of a portion of the heart walls due to complete blockage of narrowed coronary arteries. Rhythm disturbances and various heart valve and muscle disorders lead to other forms of cardiac arrest. The heart may beat wildly and without rhythm primarily or secondary to the episode.

The signs of heart attack are sudden, severe chest pain that may radiate to the left arm, jaw, and neck. When panic sets in, the body's response becomes part of the signs, and includes terror, cold and clammy skin, breathing difficulty, weakness, low blood pressure and cyanosis.

Pain is not relieved by cessation of activity and rest. Effective treatment is best given by trained personnel with advanced life saving equipment at a hospital emergency room. Unless there is a doctor on board with iv fluids, the correct medications, intubation equipment with oxygen, and defibrillator paddles, cardiac arrest at sea will likely cause death. We can provide comfort, possibly intravenous fluids and certain medications at best, but defibrillation is usually needed to regenerate normal heart contractions.

Stroke, or a cerebrovascular accident (CVA), is the interruption of blood supply to a part of the brain that results in cell death of the affected region. It can be due to a clot within the blood vessel, or vessel rupture. It is seen most commonly in the elderly with histories of hypertension, diabetes, arterial and certain cardiac disorders, and family histories of stroke. The episodes range from very mild with intermittent cessation of blood flow, with function returning to normal when flow improves, to massive in nature.

Symptoms include:

Impairment of mental status, ranging from mild confusion to coma.
Weakness or paralysis of one side of the body.

Turning of the head and eyes to one side.
Inability to reply when spoken to.
Loss of control over the tongue and muscles of the throat.

Emergency care includes measures to ensure adequate airway and breathing. Monitor the vital signs including blood pressure, mental acuity, pupillary size and response to light, general mobility, and allowing only clear liquids to drink initially because swallowing may be impaired. Stroke patients need rapid evacuation to hospital facilities.

Diabetes results from a decreased pancreatic production of insulin, a hormone that promotes the entry of glucose into cells from the bloodstream. Certainly a diabetic on board would have been diagnosed well in advance of sailing, is fully aware of the condition and methods of control. The captain and crew should be aware that a mate has diabetes, with familiarity in the administration of insulin and signs of low (hypoglycemia) or excessively high blood glucose levels (hyperglycemia, or diabetic ketoacidosis). Insulin must be refrigerated, so the vessel must have those facilities for a diabetic crewmember.

Hypoglycemia is the condition of abnormally low blood glucose levels. This can occur after insulin administration begins to drive glucose into cells. Other factors include abnormal activity, stress, fever, other illnesses, and an array of other situations. Hypoglycemia is more likely to occur in a diabetic person, but a non-diabetic can also become hypoglycemic under certain circumstances. The patient suddenly becomes mentally confused, pale with moist skin and rapid pulse, may exhibit muscle tremors, hunger, headache and dizziness. Without receiving something containing glucose, the signs may eventually lead to convulsions, loss of consciousness, and eventually death.

These symptoms can ensue without a traumatic event or accident in a person known to be diabetic. Treatment is to administer sugar to anybody who has diabetes, even if you aren't sure if the episode is high or low blood glucose levels. This sugar can be in the form of candy, sugar, orange juice, or solutions of glucose or dextrose in bottled form. If the patient has difficulty taking it orally, you can rub sugar water on the gums and it will be absorbed directly into the blood stream. In the case of hypoglycemia, improvement begins when sugar is absorbed, and is quite dramatic. When the person regains normal responsiveness, give more food. The person should rest and allow the body to regain normal function before resuming activity. Administering glucose to a person with high glucose levels will afford no improvement, but won't be a factor in making the condition worse.

Diabetic ketoacidosis (DKA), or uncontrolled diabetes, is a condition in which the lack of insulin to drive glucose into cells causes them to be starved of glucose. As a response, the body breaks down fat to supply glucose to the bloodstream and those cells. The rapid fat breakdown causes ketone formation as a by-product, which is an acid and causes the blood to become too acidic. Ketoacidosis should never be seen in a conscientious diabetic person who monitors the glucose levels and maintains insulin via injections or an insulin pump. DKA can occur in a person taking insulin. This is a hormone that must be refrigerated outside of the body to retain its characteristics. If it becomes warmed, the insulin may become ineffective.

Early signs of DKA include weakness, confusion, vomiting, and an acetone smell on the breath. It leads to *diabetic coma* and death if blood glucose levels and acidosis are not controlled. Once the patient reaches this stage, there is little hope of survival at sea. Patients in the early stages must receive insulin injections, rest, and intravenous fluids to improve circulation and relieve acidosis.

Carbon Monoxide (C0) Poisoning

The biggest danger of carbon monoxide poisoning occurs in a boat during cold or heavy weather conditions when the vessel is closed against the elements and the engine is running. Carbon monoxide is a colorless, odorless gas emitted as a byproduct of petroleum combustion. There must always be a means to evacuate the engine room of exhaust, even during such conditions.

People become mentally dulled from a lack of oxygen in the bloodstream. CO causes oxygen to bind very tightly to the hemoglobin molecules of red blood cells. This causes the skin and mucous membranes to become a characteristic bright cherry red color. Symptoms vary in severity, depending on the amount of CO in the bloodstream.

When the condition is discovered, immediately remove the person from the exhaust-filled environment to fresh air. If scuba gear is on board, administer air by way of the regulator. CPR may be necessary if the brain has been affected and can no longer control breathing and heart rate.

ACCIDENTAL TRAUMA INJURIES

Head Injuries

The patient with a head injury must be closely monitored over at least 48 hours. In every case of head injury, monitor and record the vital signs, especially level of responsiveness, appearance of the pupils, ability to move, and reaction to touch and pain. This should continue at least every two hours the night following the incident. Prevent the person from sleeping for at least 12 hours.

Except in minor incidents of head injury, make contact with shore-based medical facilities for advice, describe the incident, results of the examination, and patient's condition exactly, and then follow the recommendations given. Head injuries may not seem serious at first, but because of bleeding or swelling inside of the cranium, pressure can increase slowly, causing symptoms hours or even days later. Closed-head injuries may occur with minor outward evidence. Symptoms of brain injury signal the need for rapid evacuation to medical facilities. The following signs are indications of a worsening condition:

Patient becomes mentally dulled, confused, exhibits personality changes, or is difficult to awaken
Nausea and vomiting
Persistent, severe headache
Weakness, loss of sensation, paralysis on one or both sides of the body
Seizure activity begins.

Types of Head Injury

Lacerations of the head or face often cause dramatic bleeding because of the generous blood supplies to these areas. Control the bleeding by applying direct pressure with sterile gauze pads. Perform an examination to assess mental impairment and any other injuries. Butterfly strips or sutures can be placed to close the wound after the patient is stable.

Concussions are said to occur any time a head injury causes even momentary loss of consciousness or other brain dysfunction. Symptoms can include confusion, memory loss, dizziness, double vision or other visual impairment, nausea, and headache. Very close monitoring is warranted because these symptoms are similar to those of a closed-head injury with increasing intracranial pressure. Patients recover from uncomplicated concussion, and do not exhibit signs of a more severe intracranial injury. Crewmembers should prevent the victim from sleeping, because if intracranial pressure increases from a slow bleed, the patient's condition could worsen dramatically with nobody monitoring the situation.

Brain contusions are similar to concussions, except that they involve bruising

307

of the brain tissue, present more risk of closed-head injury, and the symptoms are more severe right after the incident. These could include unresponsiveness for five minutes or more, pupillary abnormalities (especially unequal sizes, or anisocoria), weakness or paralysis on one side of the body, and convulsions.

Skull fractures are a risk with any significant head trauma. Always assess thoroughly after head trauma, looking for depressions in the skull, and exposed bone or brain matter. Depressions in the skull indicate a skull fracture, and identify the injury as serious. Apply only gentle pressure *around* the area to control bleeding and avoid further depression of the skull segment, and notify ground-based medical contacts immediately. Take the patient below, place in a seated position, and follow medical advice.

Musculoskeletal Injuries

It can be difficult, especially right after such injury, to distinguish one form from another. When an accident occurs, perform the primary surveys and move the victim below as soon as possible. You may first have to apply bandages to the area for immobilization, even bandaging one leg to the other as a form of early splinting. Next perform the secondary survey to evaluate the specific injury, cutting off clothing if necessary. Immobilization by bandaging or splinting, elevation, application of ice, and rest are generally early treatment protocols for this group of injuries. Administer Tylenol # 3 at one tablet every four hours to control pain and help with anxiety. Re-evaluation after

a period of hours is often necessary to make a distinction of the particular injury. Any obvious dislocation of a joint, other than the fingers, or fracture warrants rapid communication with a medical facility for consultation.

Types of Musculoskeletal Injuries

Sprains occur when an accident causes undue pressure or torque of a joint capsule or ligaments that hold bones together. There is no bony abnormality, so this is called a "soft tissue" injury. Symptoms will include soreness, swelling with bruising of the area, pain when the joint is moved, and some degree of functional loss.

This may be difficult to distinguish from a non-displaced fracture, so treatment includes splinting, elevation, anti-inflammatory medication, and rest. The sprain will slowly improve over a period of days, which distinguishes it from a more serious injury.

Dislocation of joints occurs with forces similar in directionality to sprains, except that the forces are more powerful. The most common joints involved in dislocations are the shoulder, digits, and elbow. The joint capsule and ligaments are stretched and/or torn, allowing bones in the joint to move out of their normal alignment. The dislocated bones are typically locked into abnormal positions.

Symptoms include severe pain, some degree of deformity, loss of joint motion, and rapid swelling. Fingers can be replaced by pulling the segments apart, and twisting into normal alignment.

Other dislocations are best replaced by medical professionals, so use contact numbers immediately for consultation, advice, and to arrange evacuation.

Fracture is the term used in reference to any disruption in the normal continuity of a bone. Fractures are classified according to displacement of the bone fragments, the way in which the break separates bone segments, number of bone fragments, and whether there is protrusion of bone through the skin. Suspect a fractured bone when a traumatic incident causes:

- A wound with bony protrusion through the skin
- Deformity
- The victim hearing the bone snap
- Crepitus (grinding of bone segments)
- Abnormal movement of bone segments
- Persistent pain, even after immobilization and rest
- Loss of function
- Persistent swelling

Amputation

Massive limb injury resulting in mangled, devitalized tissue without blood supply must sometimes be removed to prevent infection from spreading to the lymph nodes and blood circulation, threatening the patient's life. With the communications available to offshore sailors today, the traumatic surgery of limb amputation shouldn't have to be performed at sea by unqualified persons.

Victims of this severe type of wound must be assessed, their airway, breathing, and circulation assured, and emergency first aid administered to control infection, pain, and blood loss. Rapid contact of shore side medical help will afford advice on how to maintain and monitor the patient while emergency evacuation is arranged. Please refer to *Advanced First Aid Afloat* for detailed instructions of the limb amputation procedure carried out at sea.

The most commonly injured extremities are the fingers, subject to damage from shearing, lacerating, and crushing injuries. Fingers can be caught in sheets under strain on winches, slammed in hatch covers, mangled by fish, and suffer severe damage countless other ways. Amputation or near amputation can be the unfortunate result. We should be able to care for this class of traumatic injury.

After the primary and secondary surveys have been performed, our goal is to save the digit. If the event causes massive tissue damage, it is often obvious whether preservation of the digit is possible. Any tissue that bleeds, though, may be salvageable, so assess carefully.

Administer Demerol by injection to control pain, and begin broad spectrum antibiotics, such as ampicillin 500 mg(make sure the patient is not allergic to penicillin) four times daily, to counteract infection. After the patient has been stabilized, carefully inject the area with local anesthetic to prepare for wound cleansing. The most effective cleansing is done using pressure flushing. This can be done with bagged, sterile saline or we can prepare our own lavage fluid. Boil water for at least 20 minutes. Add one teaspoon of salt to each quart of fluid. Aspirate the fluid into a large, sterile syringe. Open the wound flaps using sterile instruments from the medical kit, and squirt a stream of fluid into and through the wound, directing the flow away from the victim and yourself.

After several minutes, place the hand in a bowl of iodine solution mixed 50:50 with water. Allow the wound to soak in the solution for several minutes, and then gently swab away visible contaminants with iodine-soaked gauze.

Dry the area with sterile gauze pads, place the damaged finger segment in its approximate position with the finger stub, and either suture or apply strips of tape to hold the segments in place. Apply Furacin antibiotic cream over the entire wound area, and bandage with sterile gauze and elastic outer bandaging.

Continue the antibiotics four times daily, and pain medication as needed. Eventually cease the Demerol injections and administer Tylenol #3. Keep the injured area elevated, ensure food and water intake, and keep the patient comfortable. Bandaging must be removed and the wound inspected at least three times daily. The wound area will be reddened from inflammation, with only small amounts of pus in the best-case scenario. If the injured digit segment turns dark and then black, cell death is occurring, and gangrene may ensue. Maintain frequent contact with medical advisors, following their instructions, because gangrene cannot be allowed to spread. If the segment was not totally amputated, preservation is much more likely because some blood supply should remain.

ENVIRONMENTAL INJURIES

Near-Drowning (Submersion Injury)

Near-drowning occurs when the victim is removed from submersion in water before death occurs. Drowning results in a lack of oxygen (hypoxia) available to body tissues, causing irreversible brain damage. CPR should be attempted in all victims of submersion injury, because hypoxia can be delayed in some individuals. Submersion in cold water can cause physiological reactions in the body to decrease the need for oxygen and blood supply, keeping organs alive, even if submersion lasted for up to an hour.

The *mammalian diving reflex* is another mechanism the body uses to protect itself. Immediately after the body is immersed in cold water, the reflex slows the pulse and shunts blood to the core organs away from the skin, and causes breath holding. I experienced this once, while racing in the fall series in Lake St. Clair, Michigan. A crewmember went overboard when the lifeline snapped, and was instantly in trouble in the 50° waters. Attempts to throw cushions to him were unsuccessful because the wind blew them away in mid-air. When he began pleading with us to hurry back, I jumped into the water intending to swim toward a fender we'd thrown and take it to the victim. When I hit the water, it took my breath away, and I instinctively began panting for air. Swimming at that point in a rescue attempt was almost beside the point, because I was becoming a victim needing rescue myself. We both treaded water, staying above the waves, for several minutes until another boat, larger than ours, came alongside and hauled us aboard. The diving reflex is powerful, and actually makes survival more difficult because maneuvering is nearly impossible. The moral of this story is *never* jump in after someone unless you're tethered to the boat and wearing a life jacket. Whenever a victim is found in water, a true emergency situation exists. Remember to follow safety protocols of water rescue:

- Anyone entering the water must be wearing a life preserver, and should be tethered to the boat.
- Remove clothing that absorbs water and decreases buoyancy.
- Personnel on board must monitor the rescue efforts.
- The boat must be controlled and kept as stable as possible, with the propeller in neutral.

The American Red Cross has adopted recommendations for one-person rescue of a victim in the water. This procedure incorporates the tasks of turning the victim face-up, rapid assessment, and quick initiation of CPR in the unresponsive patient without breathing and/or pulse. This can only be attempted when conditions of visibility, wind, waves, and safety permit. In most circumstances, the person should be brought aboard the boat before life-saving measures are begun.

A procedure for rescue of the submersion victim, adapted from the Red Cross recommendations, follows:

- If the victim's head is face down, upon reaching the site the rescuer is positioned at the victim's side. Extend the arms over the head, grasp the arms and bring the person to the horizontal position.
- As soon as the body is horizontal, rotate the victim by pushing down the arm closest to you and pulling the other arm toward you.
- Cradle the victim's head with your arm to keep it above water and to support the neck.
- Ask "Are you okay?" in a loud voice. If there's no response, open the airway with the head-tilt/chin-lift technique. If there is no breathing, give two breaths and monitor for breathing. If two rescuers are available, one can support the patient while the other continues rescue breathing.
- Assess for a carotid pulse and observe the color of mucous membranes. Lack of pulse and cyanosis are signs that indicate the need for CPR.
- The crew on board should be pulling the party toward the boat with tethers attached to rescuers.
- Extricate the victim from the water as fast as possible, drain water from the oral cavity and trachea, resume rescue breathing and initiate full CPR if there is no carotid pulse.
- Vomiting is to be expected because of water ingestion into the stomach. Turn the victim sideways to prevent

aspiration. If this occurs, it signals possible regaining of responsiveness.

- Take the patient's temperature rectally to assess for hypothermia.
- If breathing resumes, stop CPR and begin to dry and warm the patient according to the guidelines for hypothermia below.

Any near-drowning patient, even if they appear normal upon regaining consciousness, should be monitored closely for temperature, breathing, and mental state for signs of possible complications. These can include hypoxic brain injury, pulmonary edema, hypothermia, and pneumonia. Always communicate with a medical facility for advice and possible evacuation of the near-drowning victim as soon as possible.

Hypothermia

Hypothermia ensues when the body temperature falls below 95°F. It can occur without freezing temperatures, because a combination of cold, wind, and water can work synergistically to reduce body temperatures. An initial drop of only one or two degrees triggers the shivering response, followed by clumsiness, stumbling, slow reactions, confusion, and difficulty in speaking. The patient may be unaware that this is happening.

When the temperature reaches 90°F, shivering will cease, and the muscles become rigid in an attempt to produce heat. Breathing and pulse rate decrease, and mental abilities diminish further, leading to coma, ventricular fibrillation,

and death when the temperature approaches 80°F.

Hypothermia can be categorized according to duration of exposure. This provides guidelines in differentiating the skin versus core body temperatures. The longer the exposure, the more the core is chilled, with a poorer prognosis. Subacute and chronic hypothermia patients also have decreased blood sugar levels, and blood acidosis increases due to lactic acid buildup.

Guidelines for categorization of the hypothermic patient:

- Acute – less than one hour.
- Subacute – one to 24 hours.
- Chronic – more than one day.

Hypothermia occurs most often to mariners who become wet from rain or spray with cold, windy conditions for extended periods of time. These are usually acute cases, and relatively easy to treat. *Submersion hypothermia*, occurring in near-drowning victims, is far more serious because the person is not only hypoxic from lack of oxygen, but is subjected to the complications of lowered body temperature as well.

Symptoms of Hypothermia

Body temperature	Symptoms
96 °F	Intense shivering with impaired ability to perform complex tasks
95-91°F	Violent shivering, difficulty speaking, mental dullness, amnesia

90-86 °F   Shivering ceases, muscles become rigid. Exposed skin is blue and puffy.
Movements are jerky. Patient can maintain posture, and is aware of surroundings

85-81°F   Coma, lack of reflexes, atrial fibrillation

78°F   Respiratory and cardiac failure, pulmonary edema, ventricular fibrillation and death

Assessment of Hypothermia

Hypothermia can be deduced by a consideration of the conditions and the patient's exposure. Assessing the degree of hypothermia is necessary as a guide to treatment, so knowing the core body temperature is important. This is best taken by rectal thermometer.

When hypothermia is suspected, based on history of exposure and symptoms, assess the patient's level of responsiveness, airway, breathing, circulation, and any obvious injuries or bleeding. Be very attentive to breathing and pulse, both of which will likely be slowed and more difficult to detect. Do not initiate CPR until you're certain it's necessary by lack of breathing and carotid pulse.

Primary Care of a Hypothermia Patient

Emergency care has three primary goals:

1. Prevent further heat loss
2. Take the rectal temperature, and begin re-warming the patient safely

3. Be very gentle to avoid causing ventricular fibrillation.

Mild hypothermia is defined as a core body temperature of 90°F. and above.

A healthy individual who is shivering can be warmed relatively quickly with little risk. Remove wet clothing and dry the person. Wrap in multiple warm blankets and cover the head, or use a hot shower to bring the temperature up. Administer hot, sweet liquids when swallowing is assured to elevate temperature and alleviate hypoglycemia.

Profound hypothermia or body temperature below 90°F causes metabolic acidosis, metabolic and electrolyte abnormalities, and ventricular fibrillation. These result in a high mortality rate, especially in the absence of immediate medical attention in an intensive care unit. These consequences occur in spite of warming efforts, and in some cases, are caused partly by the patient getting warmer. Our efforts must be to extricate from the cold, wet environment, prevent further heat loss, and allow warming to occur *slowly*. The best method of re-warming in these cases is wrapping in a sleeping bag and covering the head. Contact medical facilities immediately for advice and recommendations.

Breathing and heart rates are often difficult to detect in these patients. CPR should only be attempted after observing and assessing for several minutes, without signs of life, because CPR done when the heart is beating can cause ventricular fibrillation.

The exception to this rule is with a

victim of submersion hypothermia who is not breathing/has no heartbeat. *Since drowning may be involved, CPR is indicated immediately.*

HEAT-RELATED ILLNESSES

Elevated temperatures cause illness when the body's heat loss abilities can't cope with the ambient heat combined with internal heat generation. High ambient temperatures, elevated humidity levels, and prolonged physical activity, along with certain drug influences, can all contribute to elevated body core temperatures. Persons taking medications that lower blood pressure or diuretics, for example, are more predisposed to heat related illnesses.

Minor forms of heat-related illness are heat cramps and heat syncope. More severe illnesses are heat stroke and heat exhaustion. Fortunately, the relative cool of the marine environment, and the fact that vigorous activity is not usually prolonged, make hyperthermic illnesses relatively rare at sea.

Assessment of Heat Illness

Heat illness should be suspected based on the environmental conditions, a person's exposure to them, excessive physical activity in those conditions, lack of adequate hydrating liquids, and medications being taken (diuretics, blood pressure medications). Conduct the normal primary survey to assess level of responsiveness, airway, breathing, and circulation. Attend to any immediate problems.

The secondary survey assesses the pulse, respiratory rate, blood pressure, state of the pupils, and skin color, temperature, and moisture of the skin.

The following stages of heat illness are merely waypoints on the route to the most severe form. Unchecked, the progression can be quite rapid, and a person can get into serious trouble before realizing what's taking place. I experienced this while living in Texas, where I remodeled homes during all seasons for several years. The temperatures in the summer hover around 95 to 100+° daily, and outdoor workers must take extra precautions. The onset of illness for me began with profound sweating (almost upon leaving the house in the morning). This continues until a general feeling of fatigue begins, followed by aching in the neck muscles. If fluids aren't able to compensate, and you continue to work, light-headedness ensues followed by intense vomiting and generalized weakness. I never went further than heat exhaustion, ceasing to work for the day, but the progression would be rapid and dire if unchecked.

Heat Cramps

People who perspire heavily in hot, humid weather lose electrolytes at a rapid rate. This loss of sodium, potassium, and chloride will eventually cause muscles of the abdomen, back, and legs to cramp. Prevention is by drinking electrolyte-containing beverages like Gatorade. Emergency care is to remove the person from the hot environment, stop exercise, administer fluids, and massage cramping muscles.

Heat Syncope

This is a form of fainting caused by long periods of exposure to heat, especially when the person doesn't move very much. Skin capillaries open, increasing vascular volume, and blood return to the heart is diminished by the lack of muscular contractions. Decreased blood pressure affects flow to the brain, resulting in a fainting episode.

Care consists of removing the patient from the heated environment, and lying him down with the feet above head level.

Heat Exhaustion

Hypovolemia is a term that describes lowered blood volume that can cause shock as the body reacts. This is actually a progression of symptoms seen with heat cramps that has gone untreated. The signs of heat exhaustion are those seen when a person begins to experience low fluid volumes, and can proceed in severity:

- The patient becomes uncomfortably warm, with heavy perspiration, and feels thirsty. Then, weakness, vomiting, confusion, clammy skin, rapid and weak pulse, anxiety can occur.
- Blood pressure drops when the person stands up, due to low volume.
- Normal, or usually slightly elevated body temperature.

Care:
- Remove the patient from the warm environment.
- Take the body temperature.

- Remove heavy clothing.
- Administer electrolyte fluids, like Gatorade, if the person is alert and able to control swallowing. A solution of ½ teaspoon of table salt in 1 quart of water can be substituted.
- If the person cannot swallow safely, begin cooling by any means available. Examples include the following:
  a) Remove heavy clothing
  b) Apply ice to the skin, especially between the legs and under the arms
  c) Pour cold water over the patient (including head and neck) and fan
  d) Administer cold water enema.

Monitor vital signs while taking measures to cool the patient. These should be written in the medical logbook. Uncomplicated cases of heat exhaustion usually respond well, and should continue to be kept cool and re-hydrate. If there is not a rapid recovery, contact medical facilities, continue to monitor vital signs, continue cooling efforts, and follow instructions.

Heat Stroke

There are two categories of heat stroke; *classic* and *exertional*, either of which can be seen on a vessel at sea. Classic heat stroke occurs to those in a heated environment with decreased abilities to dissipate heat. Causes can be illness, age, infirmity, or combinations of drugs that decrease blood pressure or blood volume. Exertional heat stroke occurs when vigorous physical activity causes internal heat production that, in a warm environment, exceeds the body's ability to dissipate the heat.

Heat stroke results when the body becomes far too warm. Symptoms include:

- Hot, reddened, pale, or blue skin
- Sweating or not sweating
- Rapid pulse that may be strong (early) or weak (later)
- Variable blood pressure
- Possible mental confusion, dizziness, headache, weakness
- Temperature usually above 105°F.
- Progression of the disorder can result in:
  a) Central nervous system signs such as agitation, delirium, stupor, coma, seizures
  b) Vomiting, diarrhea, bloody stool
  c) Signs of shock (rapid, weak pulse, pale appearance, weakness)
  d) Bleeding.

Heat stroke is the more serious progression of heat exhaustion, and constitutes a true medical emergency. Continued untreated, it can lead to dehydration, electrolyte imbalances, organ damage, coma, and death. Observation of the symptoms above along with elevated body temperature is diagnostic.

Treatment is aimed at removing the patient from the heated environment, instituting cooling measures, monitor the vital signs, and contacting medical personnel.

- Remove the patient from the heat, have someone contact emergency medical personnel. Follow their instructions
- Institute cooling measures as for heat exhaustion

- Take the temperature initially, and every few minutes after cooling measures begin
- Monitor vital signs, paying special attention to the airway
- Position with the feet above the head to counteract shock
- Evacuation to a hospital will be recommended.

Lightning

A lightning strike is one danger over which we have no control at sea. Preparations are done primarily at dock side, grounding the boat to decrease chances of catastrophic damage. We either get struck or we don't.

Lightning injures the body just like any other electrical current, except that the duration of the bolt is extremely short. Burns are less severe than electrocution by exposure to a bare wire. A person struck by lightning usually incurs a characteristic superficial skin burn with a pattern resembling a fern leaf. It begins at the strike point, branching out from there, typically following the pathways of blood vessels. The clothes of strike victims are often exploded off the body, because any perspiration or wetness is instantly converted to steam. See the discussion below, Electrical Burns, for advice on the assessment and treatment.

Burn Injuries

Burns are injuries to the skin and mucous membranes caused by overexposure to radiant, thermal, or chemical energy. The most common burns are thermal, from hot water, fire, explosions, etc. Thermal burns are classed according to severity in the following manner:

First Degree or superficial burns involve only the outer layers of skin (epidermis). The skin appears reddened, is painful, but without blistering.

Second Degree burns extend through the epidermis, into the second skin layer (dermis). This layer contains more blood vessels, nerves, hair follicles, sweat glands, etc. than the epidermis. The pain and inflammation is therefore more intense, with blister formation.

Third Degree, or full thickness burns penetrate all layers of skin, and extend to the tissues beneath, the subcutaneous layers. The skin is charred, appearing blackened, thick, and dry, like meat burned at a barbecue. Blood and nerve tissue are destroyed; therefore there is no sensation of pain and no blisters form. A person with third degree burns likely has areas comprising all three burn categories. The size and degree of the burned areas is critical in treatment modes and prognosis. Size is universally estimated according to the *Rule of Nines*:

In adults, the head and neck account for 9% of the body surface area, the front and back of the trunk represent 18%, each arm is 9%, each leg 18%, and the genitalia are 1%. Children are configured differently, with the head accounting for 18%, front and back of the torso 18% each, arms 9% each, and each leg accounts for 13.5%, with genitalia as 1%.

Thermal Burns: Assessment and Emergency Care

- Flames on the person's clothing must be extinguished immediately. Tell the victim to drop to the deck or floor and roll. Move away from the area.
- Cut away burned clothing, and immerse the burned area in cool water for ten minutes. This stops additional thermal damage, and provides some relief. If more than 20% of the surface area is burned, apply cool water only briefly due to the risk of inducing hypothermia.
- Perform the primary survey (ABC's and level of responsiveness). Assess the extent of burned area, and categorize according to severity. Contact emergency medical help if the burns are at all significant.
- Protect the burned skin from contamination by applying sterile, moist compress pads, without salves or ointments.
- Assess and tend to other injuries.
- Continue to monitor vital signs, especially breathing and airway.
- You can administer 100 mg Demerol by intramuscular injection to control pain.
- Cleansing of burned tissue proceeds as follows. Begin by boiling water, allowing it to cool, and washing your hands with iodine solution *very thoroughly*. Put on sterile latex gloves, and wash the burns with sterile gauze pads and iodine solution.
- Re-apply cold compresses.
- Remove the compresses and apply

triple antibiotic, cover with more sterile gauze wrappings, and hold in place with Ace bandages.

- All second and third degree burns warrant contacting a medical facility. Only burns considered as minor should be treated without medical advice.

Loss of fluids, the anti-inflammatory reaction, and trauma can induce shock minutes to hours after a burn incident. Have the patient continue to drink as much as possible.

Monitor the urinary output carefully; decreased amounts or a lack of output indicate the onset of shock. Have the patient urinate as soon as possible, administer fluids, and record the amount produced in each hour's time. Record all events and findings in the medical logbook. Normal urine output is one ounce per pound of body weight per 24 hours. We expect production to increase over that, with the fluid administration. Less urine production than normal is a definite sign of impending shock. In this situation, the patient needs to be evacuated from the boat. You may be directed to begin subcutaneous or intravenous fluid administration in the meantime. Please refer to the section, Medical Procedures, for instructions.

Chemical Burns

Chemical burns cause damage to the skin by contact with strong acids or alkalis. Initial emergency care aims to remove the offending substance from the skin by prolonged (at least 15 minutes)

flushing with water, in a shower or by a deck hose. If the material is not dissolved in water, use cooking oil or olive oil sponged on gently, and then flush with water.

Dry material such as lime should be brushed off before flushing. After removing the chemical, remove the patient's clothing, and then cover the burned areas with sterile dressings. Contact medical personnel for instructions of specific measures.

Electrical Burns

Electrical current causes injury to many body tissues, depending mostly on the voltage involved and the duration of contact. Electricity affects the skin and local tissues, spreads readily through the body via blood vessels, and can directly damage any organ or tissue it reaches.

The skin will be burned at the strike site as second or third degree in most cases. The burns can reach deep tissues beyond the skin. The current can cause powerful muscle contractions bringing a loss of balance and falls, leading to further traumatic injuries. Direct affects on the musculoskeletal and nervous systems cause pain, paralysis, blindness, numbness, loss of hearing and speech, etc.

A loss of respiratory control indicates that the brain has been affected. This could become a life threatening situation because the lack of brain control causes cardiac arrest. Assessment begins with a site survey to assure that the electrical current is no longer threatening. The primary considerations are to assure that a patent airway, breathing and pulse are present, and to assess level of responsiveness. The following steps are recommended:

- Give basic life support, including CPR if necessary
- Perform a secondary survey as soon as possible, examining for possible secondary injuries from falling
- Treat as a closed head wound in cases of altered responsiveness
- Maintain a record of vital signs
- Communicate with your medical emergency contacts as soon as possible.

Sunburn

Ultraviolet exposure often exceeds expected levels at sea, with rays from above and reflected upward from the boat and water surface. Sunburn is a first or second-degree skin burn. Care of sunburned skin involves removing the patient from exposure and applying cool compresses to affected areas. Aspirin and/or Ibuprofen help to decrease the inflammatory reaction and severity of symptoms. Cooling ointments can be applied afterward.

"Rope Burn"

Whenever a line zips through one's bare hands, it abrades the upper skin layers, inducing rope burn, a misnomer but descriptive term. Treatment is to cleanse the affected hands to prevent infection, and allow healing to take place over the next few days. Triple antibiotic ointment can be applied, and covered with loose bandages to prevent infection to abraded skin. Anti-inflammatories (Ibuprofen, Aspirin) can help with discomfort.

Harmful Insects and Animals

Insects

Insects can bite, sting, or combinations of both. They have a small, tube-like structure used for stinging; it's attached to a venom sac. Following the bite, a local reaction takes place with redness, swelling, itchiness, and pain. In uncomplicated cases, apply meat tenderizer or a compress with moistened baking soda to relieve pain.

Those individuals allergic to insect venom may develop an exaggerated immune reaction known as anaphylaxis, a potentially dangerous condition that can lead to airway obstruction and shock. These patients should be identified by their history of such events, and should have epinephrine injection kits for such emergencies. Administer this injection and monitor vital signs while contacting medical facilities.

General principles of emergency care for stinging and biting animal and insect lesions include removal of any jewelry before swelling begins. Place a cold pack on the injection site to reduce absorption of venom. Monitor the airway, breathing, circulation, and level of consciousness until the patient is assuredly healthy, recording readings in the medical logbook. Itching can be controlled locally by hydrocortisone cream, or with oral prednisone at 10 mg twice daily for 5 days.

Injury by marine animals

Most injuries from marine animals are from bite wounds, stinging organs, or the spines of sea urchins, stingrays, stonefish, and catfish. We who sail offshore and in distant coastal regions should be aware of the animals that pose a risk to us.

Bite wounds from sharks, barracuda, etc. can include terrific tissue damage with severe blood loss. Measures in these emergencies include:

- Contact emergency medical personnel immediately, or as soon as practicable.
- Extricate the victim from the water as rapidly as possible.
- Apply direct pressure to control hemorrhage. This may include pressure to the brachial or femoral arteries or using a tourniquet with arterial bleeding.
- Assess A, B, and C with level of responsiveness, and begin basic life support measures if indicated. Contact emergency medical facilities.
- Administer 100mg Demerol intramuscularly to control pain and reduce anxiety.
- Begin therapy for shock as outlined in the Shock section.
- Remove any jewelry, apply sterile, moist compresses, and dress the wound.
- Splint an extremity.
- Continue to monitor vital signs and record in medical logbook.

Marine animal stings from stingrays, jellyfish, sea anemones, coral, and hydras cause painful wounds and reaction to injected venom. The venom can be potent, and causes muscle pain, itching, and burning sensation. A nematocyst is the part of a tentacle that contains venom. These can be left in or around the wound, and inject venom after the sting itself.

Immediate treatment is to rid the wound of remaining nematocysts. Methods include dousing with alcohol to neutralize toxin already discharged, flushing with vinegar, and flushing with seawater (not fresh water). Dry the area with alcohol, clean cloths, and remove the nematocysts with tweezers. Caution: wear rubber gloves when handling the affected area. Subsequent measures include applying a seawater/baking soda paste or a soothing hydrocortisone lotion and dressing. Monitor the vital signs closely for several hours, since anaphylaxis is a possibility with any injected venom.

Marine animal punctures, which can also introduce venom, are caused by stingrays, sea urchins, catfish, stonefish, scorpion fish, and the spines of the sea anemone. The aim of treatment is to reduce pain by inactivating the toxin with hot water. Remove any visible spines with a forceps and soak the affected area with the hottest water the victim can stand for up to 30 minutes. Deeply imbedded spines may require surgical removal. Monitor the vital signs and observe for symptoms of shock. Contact medical personnel if complications present themselves.

Food Poisoning

There are two ways that ingestion of fish can cause illness in people, allergic reactions and ingestion of toxins within the fish. Eating improperly cooked scombroid fish (tuna, mackerel) can cause an allergic reaction displaying itching, hives, nausea, diarrhea, and asthma from a histaminic reaction. These symptoms are effectively treated with antihistamines (diphenhydramine) from the medical kit.

Ciguatera fish poisoning occurs after eating fish that inhabit reef areas, where they ingest poisonous microorganisms as part of their regular diet. Beware of eating barracuda, grouper, parrotfish, kingfish, snapper, etc. from these areas.

Symptoms are acute abdominal pain, nausea, vomiting and diarrhea, along with weakness. The pulse becomes rapid with increased blood pressure, which drops two days later. Neurological signs include headache, numbness, dizziness, and a reversal in the perception of hot versus cold. The toxin is rarely fatal, but remains within the body, producing signs for weeks or even months. There is no specific treatment for ciguatera, but inducing vomiting may reduce the severity. Symptomatic treatments include rest and fluids.

Consuming shellfish that have themselves eaten poisonous microorganisms causes *shellfish poisoning*. The symptoms are distinguishable from ciguatera, however, and include numbness, tingling of the extremities, disorientation, and weakness. Signs involving the respiratory system such as drooling, difficulty in swallowing, and labored breathing may follow the others. Eventually, the patient can become paralyzed. Whenever these symptoms occur following

such a meal, induce vomiting immediately and contact emergency medical assistance. Monitor the vital signs, observe for the onset of paralysis, treat symptomatically as with ciguatera and follow the advice of a physician.

Miscellaneous Illnesses and Concerns

Shock

The term shock is used to describe a rapid circulatory collapse secondary to traumatic injury, blood loss, or severe illness/injury. The symptoms of shock reflect the body's reaction to inadequate flow of oxygenated blood to its tissues.

The circulatory system must have an adequately pumping heart, enough blood volume to fill the vessels, and blood vessels that respond correctly (dilating and constricting) to given circumstances to maintain adequate circulating blood pressure. When any external factor causes an imbalance in these mechanisms, the system can fail and shock ensues.

Hypovolemic shock occurs when the blood and fluid volumes are reduced, usually rapidly from bleeding or massive fluid loss. *Cardiogenic* shock reflects inadequate pumping of blood by the heart. This can be due to diseased heart muscle or efficiency (heart attack or cardiomyosis), blockage of arteries, or rhythm disturbances that prevent adequate blood volume in each heart beat (atrial fibrillation, ventricular fibrillation).

Vasogenic shock is a neurological malfunction in which the sympathetic nervous system fails to control tone in the blood vessel walls. The blood vessels become flaccid and dilated, making the normal blood volume inadequate to fill the greater vascular volume. This can occur in illness, anaphylactic shock, spinal injury, brain injury, etc.

All forms of shock are potentially lethal. The most common forms of shock seen in the marine environment are secondary to trauma with severe bleeding, dehydration, and cardiac failure.

The symptoms of shock are similar, regardless of the inciting cause. The signs we see are a reflection of the body's natural efforts to compensate for reduced blood flow. It attempts to maintain circulation to vital organs by shunting it away from the peripheral tissues, maintain blood flow, and increase breathing to oxygenate blood more efficiently. These measures produce the following initial signs:

- Increased heart rate
- Cold, clammy skin
- Pale, ashen appearance
- Pulse becomes weak and thready
- Cyanotic (blue) mucous membranes
- Elevated breathing rate

If the compensatory mechanisms fail to halt the progression, the symptoms proceed to:

- Restlessness and anxiety
- Nausea, vomiting
- Weakness
- Cyanosis deepens
- Dull, dry eyes, as fluid is taken away from the periphery

- Blood pressure decreasing
- Profuse sweating early
- Thirst
- Rapid breathing at first, then weakening, and then gasping
- Progressing mental dullness that can lead to stupor and coma.

If there was injury to the spine or central nervous system, shock may proceed without the signs relating to the nervous input. The pulse can be slow rather than rapid, there is no sweating, the skin feels warm and dry, and the color appears normal.

Assessment and Emergency Treatment of Shock

- Consider shock, or the development of shock, based on a consideration of the circumstances of injury or illness.
- Assess the airway, breathing, circulatory system, and level of consciousness. Begin rescue breathing or cardiac massage as warranted.
- Control bleeding that may contribute to shock.
- Communicate with contact medical facilities.
- Perform a more thorough survey, searching for neurological and hypovolemic causes of shock.
- Splint fractures and dislocations.
- Maintain body temperature.
- Keep the patient in the supine position.
- Monitor and log vital signs every 15 minutes.
- Instilling subcutaneous or

intravenous fluid therapy is usually beneficial in the management of shock. Do so under the advice of a physician.

Anaphylactic Shock

This is a form of shock caused by an exaggerated immune reaction to an allergen. Anaphylaxis can constitute a life-threatening situation in susceptible individuals. An insect sting or reactions to food or drugs usually cause the allergic reactions.

The body overreacts to a given allergen with a massive release of histamine, causing blood vessels to leak fluid, lowered blood pressure, walls of the bronchi to swell, and smooth muscle tissue to constrict. Symptoms include hives, respiratory distress, massive facial or neck swelling, nausea, intestinal cramps and diarrhea. The antidote is epinephrine given by intramuscular injection. Most people with known reactions to certain substances carry injectable epinephrine in kits with syringes full and ready to inject. A second injection may be called for in ten minutes if the response is not satisfactory.

Miscellaneous Items

Dehydration

People sailing offshore are particularly prone to dehydration because of queasiness, exposure to the outdoors, perspiration, and a lack of sufficient water intake. Children and the elderly are especially vulnerable. Persons taking diuretics or

medications to lower blood pressure may be more prone to become affected.

The dehydrated person may complain of weakness, headache, experience reduced urine production, and appear lethargic or drowsy. The skin becomes dry; it retracts slowly after pinching (more than 1-2 seconds), there is a lack of tear production, and the eyes appear dull and sunken. The pulse becomes rapid, the skin becomes cold and damp, and respirations become rapid. Exterior blood vessels are more difficult to see.

Treatment consists of fluid replacement, preferentially by mouth if there is no vomiting. Replace fluids along with electrolytes in the form of Gatorade, or salty drinks made by adding one teaspoon of salt to a quart of flavored water. Other forms of fluid administration are discussed below.

Headache

Headaches can be seen along with many illnesses and injuries, as well as being a primary disorder. Common causes are emotional stress, excessive glare, eyestrain, hypoglycemia, respiratory infection, and hangover. Head injury must also be ruled out. Migraine headaches appear as throbbing, very painful aches located on one side of the head, possibly causing nausea, and may be associated with blurred vision.

Persistent headaches may be associated with central nervous system disorders such as meningitis, a brain tumor, and high blood pressure, along with other diseases and disorders. Headaches are most commonly mild and benign, and are treatable with Aspirin, Ibuprofen, or

Acetaminophen. Anyone on board with severe, persistent headaches, associated with other symptoms such as increased thirst, drowsiness, personality changes, etc. should consult with a physician.

Constipation

This is a disorder to which people at sea are especially prone. Dehydration, lack of physical activity, fatigue, and disturbed sleep cycles, etc. are all factors. Anyone complaining of a sore tummy should be questioned about his/her latest bowel movement.

Laxatives are generally curative, although enemas may be required in stubborn cases. Sailors should be aware of their susceptibility at sea, and maintain hydration, eat meals containing fiber, and monitor their frequency of bowel movements. Jiffy Pop popcorn is a handy source of fiber. I usually surprise the crew with a batch around the third afternoon at sea, in time to avert constipation.

Diarrhea

Loose bowel movements lasting longer than a few hours are usually caused by a specific organism. The usual suspects are viruses and the organism giardia lamblia. If the patient is not systemically affected, administer Lomotil, remove from a harsh environment, and provide rest until symptoms abate. Make sure to maintain hydration, especially with electrolyte-containing drinks like Gatorade.

If diarrhea is associated with abdominal pain, fever, and nausea or vomiting,

further investigation is necessary. Take the temperature, blood pressure if possible, and question about the onset, duration and character of the diarrhea and vomitus. Dark, coffee-ground vomitus indicates stomach or intestinal bleeding. Consider these disorders in this case:

- Viral gastroenteritis
- Heartburn
- Appendicitis
- Gallbladder
- Chronic constipation or colitis

Take the patient's vital signs, along with information about the duration, character, specific location of pain, etc. and begin consultations with shoreside medical facilities for advice.

Acute Abdomen

This terminology is used to describe the symptom of a painful abdomen. This encompasses a number of disorders. The signs reflect either an inflammation of the abdominal wall (peritoneum), or of an intestinal abnormality.

The pain gradually spreads from the inciting area to involve the abdomen in general. The patient will experience fever, abdominal discomfort, and tenderness of the body wall, rigidity of abdominal muscles, a distended abdomen, nausea and diarrhea. As it progresses, signs of shock may begin.

Assessment and treatment begin by taking a thorough history of the onset and progression of the complaint. Search for anything ingested, any activity, prior history, or trauma that may be related.

Localize the site of discomfort, where it began, and how it has progressed.

Write down all of the symptoms. Begin a flow chart in the medical log-book of symptoms, their progression, and vital signs. Begin consulting with a physician.

Keep the patient in the prone position, on whatever side is most comfortable. Give no food or water until instructed to do so. Continue to monitor vital signs and symptoms. If shock develops, elevate the patient's legs and consider fluid administration. Many cases of acute abdomen require surgical intervention, so evacuation will likely be necessary.

Fishhook Removal

Fishhooks can become embedded while bringing a fish aboard or from careless handling of a fishing line. If the barb is through the skin, cut it off with wire cutters, and then pull the shank back and out of the skin. If the barb is embedded in the skin, you can push it out through the skin, cut the barb off, and pull the shank out. Alternatively, the hook can be pulled out by:

  placing a sturdy loop of fish line
      around the barb
  pushing the shank end down against
      the skin
  gently pulling the hook out with the
      fish line.

Swimmer's Ear

Don't discount the pain experienced with this seemingly benign condition. Caused by water—fresh or seawater—obstructing airflow in the external ear canal, bacteria that normally inhabit the area are allowed to proliferate in the anaerobic environment resulting in a nasty infection. The most common organism is *pseudomonas aeruginosa*, which is fortunately easy to treat.

Instill hydrogen peroxide into the canal, and allow it to bubble as it sanitizes the tissues. Flush with water to remove debris and clear the canal. Use Cortisporin Otic drops twice daily for several days until pain disappears.

Dressings and Bandages

Dressings are sterile materials placed over a wound. A bandage is actually the material used to hold a dressing in place. Sterile dressings are necessary on all open wounds to help control hemorrhage, prevent infection, and for wound protection. The bandage should be applied snugly to assure proper placement of the dressing.

Dressings are primary components of all medical kits. They may be in the form of non-adhesive pads with a semi-permeable plastic on one side (the so-called Telfa pads), square gauze pads in various sizes, Universal dressings made of thick, absorbable material in 9-inch by 36-inch pads for large wounds, Vaseline gauze for wound packing or bloody noses, or Band-Aids.

Bandage material also varies. Steri-Strips and butterflies are prepackaged bandages used to bring wound edges together. Roll gauze is applied over dressings, usually wrapping around a limb or body part to supply padding and security. Self-adhering roller bandage material is invaluable as the final layer of bandaging, or can be used in place of roll bandages to pad and secure dressings in place. I went through loads of this during my years of veterinary practice. Elastic bandages (Ace bandages) are used to apply pressure, or as supports for sprained ankles, wrists, or knees. Adhesive tape is available in several widths, with 1 and 2-inches being used most commonly. Waterproof tape is preferred on board. Tape is most valuable in taping blisters, splinting sprained ankles or fractured ribs, or securing dressings to flat surfaces.

It's advisable to shave haired areas before applying adhesive tape, which sticks more strongly than self-adhering roll bandages. Also, when applied around a limb, never totally encircle the extremity with a single strip of adhesive bandage, because it does not stretch, and can constrict blood flow very easily. Rather, cut strips several inches long, and apply them successively to extend around the limb. Monitor the tension of all encircling bandages when applied, and always leave the toes or fingers exposed to check for decreased blood flow. The digits would appear swollen with a bluish hue with inadequate circulation. The patient would also complain of the area becoming increasingly uncomfortable.

Bandages on moving parts like joints tend to move and loosen. The best bandage material to use is the self-adhesive roller bandages. Apply the bandage in a figure-8 pattern, beginning above the joint, and making several circles around the limb. Then bring the bandage diagonally across the dressing and make several turns around the limb below the joint. Next bring the bandage diagonally upward over the joint and dressing, making several turns above once again. Repeat this process until the dressing is covered and secure. Fix the bandage in place with adhesive tape strips.

To hold a dressing on the head, begin by encircling the head with roll gauze, and then apply self-adhesive bandage material wrapped around the head, over the dressing and gauze. Secure in place with strips of adhesive bandage. A hat often holds the bandaging in place the best.

A roll of gauze placed over a gauze pad is the best dressing for the inner fingers or palm of the hand. The roll gauze is secured by wrapping around the hand with self-adhesive roller bandaging. In some instances, strips of self-adhering bandage material are cut long enough to stretch from the wrist, to and around the fingers, and back to the wrist on the other side. Then self-adhesive bandaging encircles those strips to secure them in position.

Injection Technique

Most injections will be given within muscle tissue, or intramuscularly (IM). The best areas for IM injections are the fleshy part of the buttocks, within the triceps muscle at the back of the upper arm, and the muscles at the back of the thighs.

The technique is similar for all locations: Using a cotton ball soaked with isopropyl alcohol, clean the top of the medication container. Insert the needle into the bottle, and withdraw the syringe plunger slowly to withdraw more medication than will be needed. Holding the medication container upside down, squirt medication back into the bottle until the correct amount is left in the syringe. Remove clothing from the site of injection. Swab the area with alcohol-soaked cotton. Aim the syringe at a 45-degree angle to the muscle. If using the arm or thigh areas, be conscious of where bones are situated, and be sure not to point at the bones. Insert the needle gently but firmly. If you do it too slowly, it will hurt more. Pull back on the syringe plunger a bit, watching the syringe base for the appearance of blood. If blood appears, the needle is in a blood vessel. Withdraw the needle ¼ inch, and aspirate again, looking for blood. When no blood appears in the syringe, gently but firmly depress the plunger to administer the medication. Withdraw the needle when the syringe is empty, and hold a dry cotton ball over the needle hold to prevent bleeding and loss of medication through the opening.

Administering Subcutaneous (Sub-Q) Fluids

The word subcutaneous refers to the space below the skin layers. This is an open area just above the muscle layer. Fluids may be injected into this space, and will be absorbed by the body into the bloodstream to supplement losses in fluid volumes. This technique is both easier and safer than the intravenous route, although the fluids reach the bloodstream a bit more slowly. The best sites for sub-Q fluid administration are the upper chest and upper thigh regions, in the front of the body.

Begin by inserting an intravenous line into a bottle or bag of fluids. Suspend the fluids above the patient. A sterile needle is put into place on the other end of the line. Note a flow control device present somewhere along the length of the line. This device operates by moving a circular component upward or downward within a housing. When moved in one direction, the line is constricted; moving in the other direction opens the line.

Place the flow control in the constricting position to begin. Take a hold of the skin and pull it up so that you form a tent of skin. Direct the needle into the tented area, through the skin, but not into the underlying muscle tissue. Keep the needle virtually parallel with the skin. Open the fluid line and allow fluid to run. It will cause a swelling of the area, and eventually flow will stop.

At that point, remove the needle and prepare to use the next site. Monitor the fluid that is given, writing the amounts in the medical logbook. Continue administration until the prescribed amount of fluid is given. This could be several quarts of fluid over a 24- hour period, depending on the level of dehydration.

Wound Care

While all wounds are disruptions of the skin surface, they vary in their presentations and degrees of severity. Wounds are categorized to define the approach to effective management.

Shearing forces that scrape away layers of the dermis, but don't usually extend to the subcutaneous tissues cause abrasions. Pain is related to damaged nerve endings over the extent of the wound. Bleeding is usually limited to capillary oozing, rather than arterial flow.

Lacerations are irregular tears of the skin, sometimes leaving ragged tags of skin remaining. Lacerations can involve the skin only, or extend deeply into subcutaneous structures. Bleeding depends on the blood vessels torn, ranging from slight to profuse. Blood vessels that are torn, rather than cut cleanly, tend to constrict more effectively to curtail blood loss.

Very sharp objects such as knives or razor blades cause *incision* wounds. The wound is precise, with no ragged edges. The slicing of vessels results in more hemorrhage than those torn by laceration.

Avulsions often occur in association with lacerations. The skin is torn away from the underlying tissue, with a skin flap remaining. These are often in a V-shape.

Puncture wounds are caused by sharp, thin objects thrust into the skin and underlying tissues. They can be superficial, or extend into body cavities as life-threatening lesions. They may appear as small skin lesions with minor bleeding, but present great danger, with damage to internal organs or vessels. Impaling is the term that describes a puncture wound with the object remaining, extending through the skin into deeper tissues.

Amputations occur when an extremity or limb is torn or sliced away from the body.

Despite the variations in lesions, assessment and treatment is the same no matter the location, size, or severity of a wound.

Begin with an early assessment of the situation. Be mindful to take "universal precautions" against disease by contact with blood by using latex gloves. Your primary survey of the patient assesses A, B, C and level of responsiveness. Assess the wound by removing overlying clothing as needed.

Bleeding is controlled first by applying direct pressure, elevation, and pressure point control (brachial and femoral arteries). A tourniquet is only used to control spurting arterial bleeding when pressure point control is insufficient, or to control hemorrhage associated with amputation.

Control of further contamination. All wounds are considered contaminated when they occur. Our task is to eliminate further exposure to microorganisms and to fight infection by those already introduced. Remove obvious contaminants such as shards of wood or fiberglass.

Cleansing of wounds that will be seen by a physician within a few hours is less vital than when assistance may be a few days off when we're at sea. The most effective cleansing is done using pressure flushing. This can be done with bagged, sterile saline, or we can prepare our own lavage fluid. Boil water for at least 20 minutes. Add one teaspoon of salt to each quart of fluid. Aspirate the fluid into a large, sterile syringe. Open the wound flaps using sterile instruments from the medical kit, and squirt a stream of fluid into and through the wound, directing the flow away from the victim and yourself.

Small wounds are closed with butter-fly bandages or Steri-Strips. Apply a bead of triple antibiotic ointment, and dress accordingly. Dressings are checked twice daily for signs of infection. Lacerations and avulsions are treated in a similar fashion. Avulsion flaps are replaced and protected with dressings and bandaging.

Puncture wounds should not be closed. Those that don't penetrate the body cavity are flushed very thoroughly with an iodine solution (Betadine) added to the saline. Use antibiotic ointment, and dress only to prevent further contamination and to protect the wound. These wounds must heal by "second intention healing", meaning from the inside out to prevent deep infections and to allow for drainage.

Impaling wounds, with the object in place, are generally cleaned from the outside, with the object bandaged in place until care by a physician is available. In this unfortunate circumstance, without help available at sea, seek instructions via communication with a contact physician.

Amputations of limbs should be a rarity at sea. These must be treated as massive lacerations, with control of hemorrhage, pain medication, very thorough flushing, and bandaging done according to the advice of a doctor, with arrangements for evacuation begun immediately. Amputated digits can actually be replaced into position, after cleansing, by suturing the skin together. Medicated dressings are then applied and checked routinely, and systemic antibiotics administered to prevent infection.

Suturing Wounds

Suturing is used on somewhat larger wounds with edges that tend to pull apart if not held in position. Cleansing is done as usual. Your medical kit should contain:

Packaged 3-0 silk or nylon sutures swaged onto a cutting needle. That is, the suture material is attached to the needle used for suturing the skin.

Needle holder, used to manipulate the needle, in a sterile package. The needle holder may also be able to cut the suture material. If not, you'll need scissors.

Sterile skin forceps, used to hold the skin while placing the needle through it.

Sterile gauze pads.

Ampoules of Xylocaine for local anesthesia of the skin, along with sterile syringes and 22-gauge needles.

Very fresh wounds, on a hearty sailor, often don't require local anesthesia. Wounds several hours old become more sensitive after the initial natural local numbness wears off. The suturing procedure is as follows:

Wash your hands very thoroughly in sterile water, scrubbing with iodine solution. Don sterile latex gloves, and avoid touching anything but sterile objects until the job is done. You'll likely need an assistant to help from this point on.

Fill the syringe with Xylocaine, put the needle on the sterile syringe, and inject the wound edges to form small blebs around it.

Allow several minutes to elapse and anesthesia to take hold, meanwhile covering the wound with sterile dressing material.

Open the suture packet, and remove the suture needle with the needle holders. Begin suturing about 3mm from one end. Grasp the skin with the forceps, exposing it to the needle.

Insert the needle straight into the wound edge, perpendicular to it. The curved needle will keep the suture from going too deeply. It will appear in the lesion gap.

Grasp the needle with the forceps, and take hold of it with the needle holders. Now direct the next placement from the inside of the wound edge, outward and upward through the skin on the opposite side.

Grasp the needle with your fingers, pulling the suture through the wound until only a few inches remain on the other side. Now tie the suture, using a reef, or square knot. Be careful to just bring the skin edges together. Place the first "throw" or portion of the square knot and then bring the second throw down upon the first without tightening the suture

material. Place three square knots in the suture, then cut both ends of suture, leaving about ½ inch tag.

Continue this procedure, placing sutures about 3mm apart, until the wound is closed. Apply triple antibiotic ointment to the wound, dress and bandage.

Most sutured lesions heal within 7-10 days. Monitor the dressing in the meantime, watching for swelling, drainage of pus or excess pink-tinged fluid. Other signs of infection are pain, fever, swelling of lymph nodes in the vicinity, redness and heat at the wound site.

If these signs occur, the wound is infected. Remove the dressing, remove all sutures— whatever type—and open the wound to promote drainage. Flush with sterile water/salt/ iodine solution to fight infection. Apply antibiotic ointment, dress the open wound, begin systemic antibiotics, and consult with a physician.

Tetanus

Tetanus is caused by *clostridium tetani*, a bacterium that takes hold and thrives in damaged, dying tissue without proper aeration. The organism is most prevalent in soil; however, and therefore exposure is less likely at sea. Puncture wounds that extend deeply are most at risk of tetanus infection. The organism produces a toxin that causes serious muscle spasms that can impair breathing. Tetanus is prevented by inoculations at infancy, with boosters given at least every ten years. Anyone going to sea should ensure that their tetanus booster status is current.

Antibiotics

Wounds at sea are at risk of infection because of the presence of seawater and the lack of physician care. Infected wounds, even small ones, can lead to serious infections such as gangrene.

Everyone on board should bring with them a list of whatever substances to which they are allergic, including antibiotics. Never administer antibiotics to a crewperson without checking their allergy status. Administering antibiotics is not a substitute for proper wound cleansing and maintaining the wound with clean, medicated dressings.

All wounds are considered contaminated, and have the possibility of infection. Antibiotics are warranted in wounds obviously contaminated, especially those exposed to septic substances such as bilge water, sewerage, seawater, etc. These cases deserve antibiotic therapy of:

Ampicillin, 1.2 million units by intramuscular injection, followed by 500 mg capsules orally four times daily for five days.
Doxycycline, 100 mg capsules, one capsule twice daily for five days.

Stop antibiotics after the initial five days, monitoring the body temperature twice daily for the next three days. If signs of infection appear, begin administering one antibiotic at double the dose and monitor condition closely. If the condition does not improve, add the second

antibiotic to the regimen and monitor closely. By this time, you should certainly be in contact with a physician.

Antibiotics are used for treatment of infections other than wounds. They are only effective against bacterial infections, not those caused by viruses and other organisms. In general, if symptoms are not improved within three days of antibiotic therapy, they should be stopped. There are general guidelines for their usage that should always be followed:

Check the patient for drug sensitivities before giving any antibiotic.

Use antibiotics only for more serious infections, not for minor annoyances.
Antibiotics are effective against different organisms. Choose the appropriate antibiotic.
Use antibiotics at the prescribed dosage schedule. A standard course of antibiotics is five days. Within that time, there should be a definite improvement of the clinical symptoms and signs. Continue the antibiotic one day after the remission of signs and symptoms.
Observe closely for three days after discontinuing antibiotics. If symptoms of infection recur, begin another regimen of the antibiotic, extending it to 7 days. Make contact with a physician whenever antibiotics do not bring an infection or illness under control.

APPENDIX 9

TABLES

FAHRENHEIT TO CELSIUS CONVERSION

Degrees Fahrenheit to Degrees Celsius:			
32.0	0.0	67.0	19.4
33.0	0.6	68.0	20.0
34.0	1.1	69.0	20.6
35.0	1.7	70.0	21.1
36.0	2.2	71.0	21.7
37.0	2.8	72.0	22.2
38.0	3.3	73.0	22.8
39.0	3.9	74.0	23.3
40.0	4.4	75.0	23.9
41.0	5.0	76.0	24.4
42.0	5.6	77.0	25.0
43.0	6.1	78.0	25.6
44.0	6.7	79.0	26.1
45.0	7.2	80.0	26.7
46.0	7.8	81.0	27.2
47.0	8.3	82.0	27.8
48.0	8.9	83.0	28.3
49.0	9.4	84.0	28.9
50.0	10.0	85.0	29.4
51.0	10.6	86.0	30.0
52.0	11.1	87.0	30.6
53.0	11.7	88.0	31.1
54.0	12.2	89.0	31.7
55.0	12.8	90.0	32.2
56.0	13.3	91.0	32.8
57.0	13.9	92.0	33.3
58.0	14.4	93.0	33.9
59.0	15.0	94.0	34.4
60.0	15.6	95.0	35.0
61.0	16.1	96.0	35.6
62.0	16.7	97.0	36.1
63.0	17.2	98.0	36.7
64.0	17.8	99.0	37.2
65.0	18.3	100.0	37.8
66.0	18.9		

BEAUFORT SCALE OF WINDS AND SEAS

The **Beaufort scale** is an empirical measure for the intensity of the wind based mainly on sea-state or wave conditions. Its full name is the **Beaufort wind force scale**. It should be noted that the wave heights given pertain to the conditions found at open sea.

The Beaufort wind scale is used for estimating wind speed when there is no standard instrumentation available.

Beaufort number	Wind Speed [knots]	Wind Speed [mph]	Wind Speed [m/s]	Sea Wave Height [feet]	Sea Wave Height [meters]	WMO Description	Effects observed on sea	Effects observed on land
0	under 1	under 1	0.0 - 0.2	~0	~0	Calm	Sea like mirror.	Calm; smoke rises vertically.
1	1 - 3	1 - 3	0.3 - 1.5	0.25	0.1	Light air	Ripples with appearance of scales; no foam crests.	Direction of wind shown by smoke drift but not by wind vanes.
2	4 - 6	4 - 7	1.6 - 3.3	0.5 - 1.0	0.2 - 0.3	Light breeze	Small wavelets; crests of glassy appearance, not breaking.	Wind felt on face; leaves rustle; vanes moved by wind.
3	7 - 10	8 - 12	3.4 - 5.4	2.0 - 3.0	0.6 - 1.0	Gentle breeze	Large wavelets; crests begin to break; scattered whitecaps.	Leaves and small twigs in constant motion; wind extends light flag.
4	11 - 16	13 - 18	5.5 - 7.9	3.5 - 5.0	1.0 - 1.5	Moderate breeze	Small waves, becoming longer; numerous whitecaps.	Raises dust and loose paper; small branches are moved.
5	17 - 21	19 - 24	8.0 - 10.7	6.0 - 8.0	2 - 2.5	Fresh breeze	Moderate waves, taking longer form; many whitecaps; some spray.	Small trees in leaf begin to sway; crested wavelets form on inland waters.
6	22 - 27	25 - 31	10.8 - 13.8	9.5 - 13.0	3.0 - 4.0	Strong breeze	Larger waves forming; whitecaps everywhere; more spray.	Large branches in motion; whistling heard in telegraph wires; umbrellas used with difficulty.
7	28 - 33	32 - 38	13.9 - 17.1	13.5 - 19.0	4.0 - 5.5	Near gale	Sea heaps up; white foam from breaking waves begin to be blown in streaks.	Whole trees in motion; inconvenience felt when walking against the wind.
8	34 - 40	39 - 46	17.2 - 20.7	18.0 - 25.0	5.5 - 7.5	Gale	Moderately high waves of greater length; edges of crests begin to break into spindrift; foam is blown in well-marked streaks.	Breaks twigs off trees; generally impedes progress.
9	41 - 47	47 - 54	20.8 - 24.4	23.0 - 32.0	7.0 - 10.0	Strong gale	High waves; sea begins to roll; dense streaks of foam; spray may reduce visibility.	Slight structural damage occurs.
10	48 - 55	55 - 63	24.5 - 28.4	29.0 - 41.0	9.0 - 12.5	Storm	Very high waves with overhanging crests; sea takes white appearance as foam is blown in very dense streaks; rolling is heavy and visibility reduced.	Trees uprooted; considerable structural damage occurs.
11	56 - 63	64 - 72	28.5 - 32.6	37.0 - 52.0	11.5 - 16.0	Violent storm	Exceptionally high waves; sea covered with white foam patches; visibility still more reduced.	Accompanied by widespread damage.
12	64 and over	73 and over	32.7 and over	45 and over	14 and over	Hurricane	Air filled with foam; sea completely white with driving spray; visibility greatly reduced.	Accompanied by widespread damage.

SOURCES
Guide to Sea State, Wind, and Clouds. U.S. Department of Commerce, National Oceanic and Atmospheric Administration, National Weather Service.
Air Force Manual 15-111: Surface Weather Observations. Department of the Air Force, 1 November 1998.

DEW POINT CONVERSION

Table 1 - Dew Point Temperature - °F
Difference Between Dry Bulb and Wet Bulb - °F

Dry Bulb °F	0	1	2	3	4	5	6	7	8	9	10	12	14	16	18	20
40	40	38	35	33	—	—	—	—	—	—	—	—	—	—	—	—
41	41	39	36	34	—	—	—	—	—	—	—	—	—	—	—	—
42	42	40	38	35	33	—	—	—	—	—	—	—	—	—	—	—
43	43	41	39	36	34	—	—	—	—	—	—	—	—	—	—	—
44	44	42	40	37	35	—	—	—	—	—	—	—	—	—	—	—
45	45	43	41	38	36	34	—	—	—	—	—	—	—	—	—	—
46	46	44	42	40	37	35	—	—	—	—	—	—	—	—	—	—
47	47	45	43	41	38	36	33	—	—	—	—	—	—	—	—	—
48	48	46	44	42	40	38	35	—	—	—	—	—	—	—	—	—
49	49	47	45	43	41	38	36	33	—	—	—	—	—	—	—	—
50	50	48	46	44	42	40	37	34	—	—	—	—	—	—	—	—
51	51	49	47	45	43	41	38	36	33	—	—	—	—	—	—	—
52	52	50	48	46	44	42	40	37	34	—	—	—	—	—	—	—
53	53	51	49	47	45	43	41	38	36	33	—	—	—	—	—	—
54	54	52	50	48	46	44	42	40	37	34	—	—	—	—	—	—
55	55	53	51	50	48	45	43	41	38	36	33	—	—	—	—	—
56	56	54	53	51	49	47	44	42	40	37	34	—	—	—	—	—
57	57	55	54	52	50	48	46	43	41	39	36	—	—	—	—	—
58	58	56	55	53	51	49	47	45	42	40	37	—	—	—	—	—
59	59	57	56	54	52	50	48	46	44	41	39	33	—	—	—	—
60	60	58	57	55	53	51	49	47	45	43	40	35	—	—	—	—
61	61	59	58	56	54	52	50	48	46	44	42	36	—	—	—	—
62	62	60	59	57	55	53	52	50	47	45	43	38	—	—	—	—
63	63	61	60	58	56	55	53	51	49	47	44	39	34	—	—	—
64	64	62	61	59	57	56	54	52	51	48	46	41	35	—	—	—
65	65	63	62	60	59	57	55	53	51	49	47	42	37	—	—	—
66	66	64	63	61	60	58	56	54	52	50	48	44	38	—	—	—
67	67	65	64	62	61	59	57	55	53	52	49	45	40	34	—	—
68	68	67	65	63	62	60	58	57	55	53	51	46	42	36	—	—
69	69	68	66	64	63	61	59	58	56	54	52	48	43	37	—	—
70	70	69	67	65	64	62	61	59	57	55	53	49	44	39	33	—
71	71	70	68	67	65	63	62	60	58	56	54	50	46	41	35	—
72	72	71	69	68	66	64	63	61	59	58	56	52	47	42	37	—
73	73	72	70	69	67	66	64	62	60	59	57	53	49	44	38	—
74	74	73	71	70	68	67	65	63	62	60	58	54	50	45	40	34
75	75	74	72	71	69	68	66	64	63	61	59	55	51	47	42	36
76	76	75	73	72	70	69	67	66	64	62	60	56	53	48	43	38
77	77	76	74	73	71	70	68	67	65	63	62	57	54	50	45	39
78	78	77	75	74	72	71	69	68	66	64	63	58	55	51	46	41

Table 1 - Dew Point Temperature - °F (cont.)
Difference Between Dry Bulb and Wet Bulb - °F

Dry Bulb °F	0	1	2	3	4	5	6	7	8	9	10	12	14	16	18	20
79	79	78	76	75	73	72	70	69	67	66	64	59	57	53	48	43
80	80	79	77	76	74	73	72	70	68	67	65	61	58	54	50	44
81	81	80	78	77	75	74	73	71	70	68	66	63	59	55	51	49
82	82	81	79	78	77	75	74	72	71	69	67	64	60	57	52	50
83	83	82	80	79	78	76	75	73	72	70	69	65	62	58	54	52
84	84	83	81	80	79	77	76	74	73	71	70	66	63	59	55	53
85	85	84	82	81	80	78	77	75	74	72	71	68	64	61	57	54
86	86	85	83	82	81	79	78	76	75	73	72	69	65	62	58	56
87	87	86	84	83	82	80	79	78	76	75	73	70	67	63	59	57
88	88	87	85	84	83	81	80	79	77	76	74	71	68	64	61	59
89	89	88	86	85	84	82	81	80	78	77	75	72	69	66	62	60
90	90	89	87	86	85	83	82	81	79	78	76	73	70	67	63	61
91	91	90	88	87	86	85	83	82	80	79	78	75	71	68	65	63
92	92	91	89	88	87	86	84	83	81	80	79	76	73	69	66	64
93	93	92	90	89	88	87	85	84	83	81	80	77	74	71	67	65
94	94	93	92	90	89	88	86	85	84	82	81	78	75	72	68	67
95	95	94	93	91	90	89	87	86	85	83	82	79	76	73	70	68
96	96	95	94	92	91	90	88	87	86	84	83	80	77	74	71	69
97	97	96	95	93	92	91	89	88	87	85	84	81	78	75	72	70
98	98	97	96	94	93	92	90	89	88	87	85	82	79	76	73	72
99	99	98	97	95	94	93	92	90	89	88	86	83	81	78	74	73
100	100	99	98	96	95	94	93	91	90	89	87	85	82	79	76	74
101	101	100	99	97	96	95	94	92	91	90	88	86	83	80	77	75
102	102	101	100	98	97	96	95	93	92	91	89	87	84	81	78	76
103	103	102	101	99	98	97	96	94	93	92	91	88	85	82	79	78
104	104	103	102	100	99	98	97	95	94	93	92	89	86	83	80	79
105	105	104	103	101	100	99	98	96	95	94	93	90	87	84	82	80
106	106	105	104	102	101	100	99	98	96	95	94	91	88	86	83	81
107	107	106	105	103	102	101	100	99	97	96	95	92	90	87	84	82
108	108	107	106	104	103	102	101	100	98	97	96	93	91	88	85	84
109	109	108	107	105	104	103	102	101	99	98	97	94	92	89	86	85
110	110	109	108	106	105	104	103	102	100	99	98	95	93	90	87	86

APPENDIX 10

SCHEMATIC VIEW OF VOYAGER

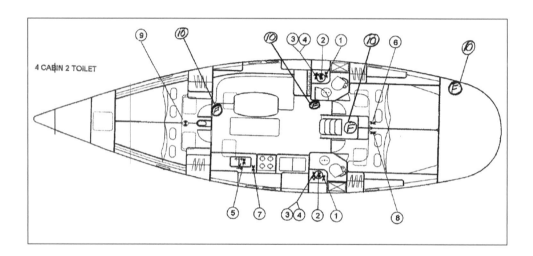

SEACOCKS, THROUGH HULLS, AND FIRE EXTINGUISHERS

1) Head discharge
2) Head intake
3) Washbasin discharge
4) Shower discharge
5) Sink discharge
6) Engine cooling water intake
7) Ice box drainage
8) Stern tube cooling intake valve
9) Speed/log, depth sounder through hulls
10) Fire extinguishers

RECOMMENDED READING

Allen, Philip. *The Atlantic Crossing Guide*. W W Norton & Co Inc, New York, NY. 1983

Bauer, Bruce A. *The Sextant Handbook*. International Marine/Ragged Mountain Press, Camden, ME. 1995

Bergin, Edward J. *A Star to Cross Her By*, Seaworthy Publications Inc., Port Washington, WI. 1983

Bruce, Peter. *Adlard Coles' Heavy Weather Sailing*. Adlard Coles Nautical, London, UK. 2004

Mapes, Captain Edward. *Ready to Sail*. Sheridan House, Dobbs Ferry, NY. 2008

Burch, David. *The Star Finder Book*. Paradise Cay Publications, Arcata, CA. 1995

Calder, Nigel. *Boatowner's Mechanical & Electrical Manual*. International Marine/ Ragged Mountain Press, Camden, ME. 2005

Cornell, Jimmy. *World Cruising Routes*. International Marine Publishing, Camden, ME. 1998

Dashew, Steve & Linda. *Mariner's Weather Handbook*. Beowulf, Inc., 1998

Dumas, Vito; Guzzwell, John & Slocum, Joshua. *Great Voyages in Small Boats*. John de Graff, Tuckahoe, NY. 1976

Eastman, Dr. Peter. *First Aid Afloat*. Cornell Maritime Press, Centreville, ME. 2000

Gray, Leonard. *100 Problems in Celestial Navigation*. Paradise Cay Publications, Arcata, CA. 1999

Hahne, Peter. *Sail Trim: Theory and Practice*. Sheridan House, Dobbs Ferry, NY. 2005

Hiscock, Eric. *Beyond the West Horizon*. Sheridan House, Dobbs Ferry NY. 1987

Hiscock, Eric. *Cruising Under Sail*. International Marine, Camden, ME. 1986

Hiscock, Eric. *Voyaging Under Sail*. Oxford University Press, New York, NY. 1970

Henderson, Richard. *Sea Sense*. International Marine Publishing, Camden, ME. 1979

Howard, Jim & Doane, Charles J. *Handbook of Offshore Cruising*. Sheridan House, Dobbs Ferry, NY. 2000

Louttit, James R. *The New Skipper's Bowditch*. W W Norton & Co Inc, New York, NY. 1984

Maloney, Elbert S. *Chapman Piloting and Seamanship*. Hearst Books, New York, NY. 2006

Markell, Jeff. *The Sailor's Weather Guide*. 2nd edition, Sheridan House, Dobbs Ferry, NY. 2003

Munns, Harry. *Cruising Fundamentals*. International Marine Publishing/McGraw-Hill, Camden, ME. 1992

Nielsen, Peter. *Sailpower*. Sheridan House, Dobbs Ferry, NY. 2004

Noel, John V. *Knight's Modern Seamanship*. Van Nostrand Reinhold/co Wiley, New York, NY. 1989

Pallas, Jean-Luc. *Marine Diesel Engines: Maintenance and Repair Manual*. Sheridan House, Dobbs Ferry, NY. 2006

Pallas, Jean-Luc. *Outboard Motors: Maintenance and Repair Manual.* Sheridan House, Dobbs Ferry, NY. 2006

Pardey, Lin and Larry. *Storm Tactics Handbook.* Paradise Cay Publications, Arcata, CA. 1999

Payne, John C. *Marine Electrical and Electronics Bible, 3rd edition.* Sheridan House, Dobbs Ferry, NY. 2007

Pyzel, Mike. *Coastal Navigation.* American Sailing Association, Marina del Rey, CA. 1987

Weatheritt, Les. *Atlantic Crossings: A Sailor's Guide to Europe and Beyond*, Sheridan House, Dobbs Ferry, NY. 2006

Rousmaniere, John. *The Annapolis Book of Seamanship.* Simon & Schuster, New York, NY. 1999

Sala, Enrico. *Rigging.* W.W. Norton & Co. Inc., New York, NY. 1988

Shlereth, Hewitt. *Celestial Navigation in a Nutshell.* Sheridan House, Dobbs Ferry, NY. 2000

Street, Donald Jr. *The Ocean Sailing Yacht.* W.W. Norton & Co. Ltd., New York, NY. 1980

Turner, Ted and Jobson, Gary. *The Racing Edge.* Simon and Schuster, New York, NY. 1979

Vaitses, Allan H. *The Fiberglass Boat Repair Manual.* International Marine/Ragged Mountain Press, Camden, ME. 1988

VanDorn, Richard G. *Oceanography & Seamanship.* Cornell Maritime Press, Centreville, MD. 1993

Watts, Alan. *The Weather Handbook.* Sheridan House, Dobbs Ferry, NY. 1999

INDEX